JOHN RUSSELL

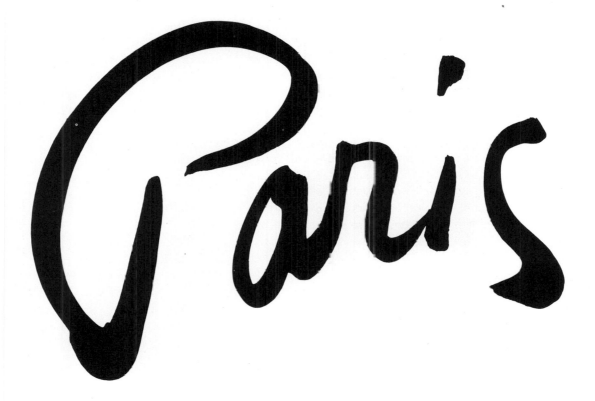

Paris

Foreword by Rosamond Bernier

HARRY N. ABRAMS, INC., PUBLISHERS, NEW YORK

For Rosamond

This book owes its new, enlarged, and updated existence to the galvanic activity of my wife, Rosamond Bernier. Not only did she convince me that it was a good idea, but she persuaded our friend and neighbor Robert Morton, Director of Special Projects at Harry N. Abrams, Inc., that it was the kind of book that Abrams could foster without disgrace. Within Abrams itself I had the delight of working above all with Eric Himmel, who turned out to know Paris better than I do, although he has never yet been there.

The multifarious documentation of the book owes a great deal not only to Rosamond Bernier but to our friend Claude Nabokoff, who undertook many a difficult task for us in Paris and proved herself a scholar, a diplomat, and something of a saint.

We also think with gratitude and affection of our friends at the Metropolitan Museum of Art, the New York Public Library, the Cooper-Hewitt Museum, and the Musée Carnavalet who took so much trouble on our behalf.

J.R.
Valentine's Day, 1983

Designer: Dirk Luykx

Endpapers: *Nouveau Paris Monumental, A Visitor's Practical Itinerary in Paris.* Garnier Frères, 1900

Page 1: The gardens of the Palais Royal, 1960. Henri Cartier-Bresson photograph

Page 2–3: *Place Vintimille.* Edouard Vuillard
Just off the Boulevard de Clichy, the Place Vintimille has been renamed Place Adolphe-Max since Vuillard lived there.

Page 4–5: On the boulevards, c. 1860. Ferrier and Solier photograph

Page 6: *The Evening Party.* Jean Béraud, c. 1890s

Page 10: The grand staircase of the Opéra

Library of Congress Cataloging in Publication Data
Russell, John, 1919–
Paris.
Includes index.
1. Paris (France)—Description—1975–
I. Title.
DC707.R87   1983   914.4'3604838   83–2589
ISBN 0-8109-1457-3
ISBN 0-8109-2308-4 (pbk.)

Text © 1983 John Russell
Illustrations © 1983 Harry N. Abrams, Inc.

Printed and bound in Japan

Quality Paperback Book Club® offers a wide range of opera, classical and jazz recordings. For information and catalog write to QPB Recordings, Camp Hill, PA 17012.

Contents

Foreword

By Rosamond Bernier

When I first read John Russell's *Paris*, I remembered particularly a very small room halfway to the sky in what was then my favorite Left Bank hotel. The rooms on the top floor of the Pont-Royal are not as large as the ones lower down, but after trying some of the others I decided to perch above, where each room had a small balcony and you could step out through the French windows, and there in front of you was a clear view across Paris.

You could look down to the right and follow the Rue du Bac on its straight reach for the Seine. Eighteenth-century town houses with flat stone façades—not yet sluiced clean on André Malraux's orders—and elegant doorways lined one side of the street, rising to steep, humped roofs (gray tile, usually) bitten into by Mansard windows with projecting triangular hoods. Across the river was the cluttered mount of Montmartre topped by the ridiculous but endearing white fantasy of the Sacré-Coeur. To the left was the Eiffel Tower and, still further, the gold-ribbed dome of the Invalides. Paris in my pocket.

This is where I came to live in the late 1940s when an American magazine sent me to Paris to report on the arts. The Pont-Royal was cheap in those days, and it was near to everything that I wanted.

I was extraordinarily lucky to be starting a career at that time, when Paris was still a great center of intellectual and artistic energy. Art and life were beginning again after the long dark night of the German occupation. As Cyril Connolly once wrote about French writers, "intelligence flows through them like a fast river." The river was indeed flowing fast. The great figures of twentieth-century art were still in full activity. There were new magazines, new books, new art galleries, new plays, new hopes. Even new music was beginning to make its way.

Writers, publishers, art dealers from all over stayed at the Pont-Royal or met there. Fred, the Swiss concierge, knew them all and kept a fatherly eye out for me. When I came home from work he might tell me, "Monsieur Skira left this morning to visit Monsieur Matisse in Vence. Monsieur Matisse didn't sound a bit pleased when he telephoned." (The Swiss publisher Albert Skira was chronically late and never answered letters, which infuriated the supermethodical Matisse.) Or he might say, "Monsieur and Madame Miró are arriving tomorrow from Barcelona for a week. Monsieur Curt Valentin is expected from New York Tuesday." (Curt Valentin was the most imaginative New York art dealer of the day.) "Monsieur Stephen Spender came in from London and was looking for you."

My room with its turkey-red carpet, brass bed, and nubbly white coverlet offered few amenities: one chair; an old-fashioned stand-up wardrobe; watery lights. The telephone was cradled uneasily on two metal prongs. Its function was mainly symbolic. Even the most exasperated jiggling rarely caught the attention of the *standardiste*. Often it was quicker to go out, buy *jetons*, and call from a café. Once, in a rage of frustration, I stormed down to confront the telephone operator face to face, only to find her standing in her cubicle, tape measure in hand, intently fitting a friend for a dress while her switchboard flashed futile appeals.

The bar, downstairs from the lobby, was conspiratorially dark, and filled with deep and overstuffed brown leather armchairs and sofas. This was my club, a quintessentially Parisian listening post where you went to find out who's in, who's out, and who's gone away and will never come back. Publishers and authors negotiated over the new fashionable drink in France: "le Scotch." The painter Balthus, more Byronic than Byron himself, would drop by and give me news of Picasso. Jean-Paul Sartre and Simone de Beauvoir were regulars. At that time their fame and the provocative aura that surrounded the word "Existentialist" (practically nobody knew what it meant) had made them objects of universal curiosity, and they had abandoned their previous headquarters at the Café Flore for the less exposed Pont-Royal.

Later, when I had an apartment, I continued to see Jean-Paul Sartre and Simone de Beauvoir, though neither of them cared much for Americans in general. Once when Sartre came to lunch he gave an offhand demonstration of mental agility: without stopping the general conversation he deciphered, one after another, the formidably difficult word-and-picture puzzles on my dessert plates.

Although I moved from the Pont-Royal I never left the quarter. It was, and is, a neighborhood of bookstores and publishing houses. The grandest, Gallimard, is a few steps from the Pont-Royal. I used to go to its Thursday afternoon garden parties every June; they were long on petits fours and short on liquor. Alice B. Toklas lived around the corner from my office and was always ready to receive the favored visitor with enormous teas. She was exquisitely polite, and even when very old she would insist on serving the guest herself. When I did her some small favor, she sent a charming note of thanks in such minute handwriting that I had to take out a magnifying glass to read it. Although her dress was monastic, she loved elaborately flowered hats, and would appear at my apartment, a diminutive figure under a herbaceous border that not even Russell Page himself would have imagined. She bought one such hat every year, she told me.

In Paris, you are on easy terms with the past. I would nod to Apollinaire, a favorite poet, as I went by 202, Boulevard Saint-Germain, where he lived after coming back wounded from the front in World War I. I liked going by the Jesuit-style Église de Saint-Thomas-d'Aquin, set back from the boulevard, where Apollinaire was married, with Picasso as witness. On my way to Nancy Mitford's I would go by 120, Rue du Bac, a handsome house from which Chateaubriand set off every afternoon to visit Madame Récamier. Ingres, Delacroix, Corot, George Sand, Madame de Staël, Voltaire, Wagner (he finished *Die Meistersinger* in Paris) were among the friendly neighborhood ghosts.

It is often said, and with some reason, that Parisians are not hospitable to the foreigner. But what an abundance of generosity and hospitality came my way! I remember Picasso rummaging through the indescribable chaos of his vast studio on the Rue des Grands-Augustins to try and dig up some drawings I wanted to publish. (He found them, I gave them back, and he never could find them again.) Fernand Léger lined up his recent work for me and asked which canvases I liked best. Pleased with my choice he whacked me jovially across the back: "You're a good girl, you have a good strong stomach." Matisse received me with all the books he had illustrated meticulously opened out so that he could explain in each case what problems he had solved, and how. The admirable, austere Nadia Boulanger (who taught so many American composers, beginning with Aaron Copland) invited me to her icy apartment on the Rue Ballu to hear her latest protégé. The composer, Francis Poulenc, a bulky pear-shaped figure, was droll beyond words and yet indescribably poignant as he accompanied himself on a small upright piano and sang the soprano solo—that of a woman desperately trying to hold on to her lover—from his *La Voix Humaine*. President Vincent Auriol took me on a tour of the Palais de l'Elysée after a press conference to point out the famous Gobelin tapestry. And I remember the ultimate Parisian accolade: a great French chef, the late René Viaux of the restaurant in the Gare de l'Est, named a dish after me.

A few years after my Pont-Royal days I was starting my own art magazine, *L'Oeil*, in a minute office at the back of a cobbled courtyard on the Rue des Saints-Pères. It was sparsely furnished—no pictures yet. The wall behind me was painted a shade of blue I like particularly, the color of a package of Gauloise cigarettes. When Alberto Giacometti came by for a chat, I said a bit apologetically that it must seem odd—an art magazine office with no art around. "Not at all," he answered, looking at me across my desk. "You are a *personnage sur fond bleu*, that's all you need." (Giacometti characteristically tried to discourage us from running an article on him in the first issue. "It will ruin the chances of your magazine. No one will buy it if it shows my work." Naturally, we paid no attention.)

For the magazine, we needed good writers and got in touch with a young English art critic whose weekly column in the London *Sunday Times* was indispensable reading if you wanted to know not only what was going on in England but on the Continent as well. It was clear that, unlike many critics, he loved art; he wrote about it with informed enthusiasm, and he wrote in crystalline prose. There was not a dull phrase to be weeded out in translation (French translation did wonders for some of our German, Dutch, Italian, and English-language contributors) and, what is more, he knew France and the French language very well.

We corresponded. He sent in his articles—on time. We met. Our conversations centered on ideas for features and deadlines. I had the intense seriousness of the young and the harassed, and I was producing a monthly publication on a shoestring as thin as the one Man Ray wore in lieu of a tie. In private life both of us were programmed, to use computer language, in other directions. Unlikely as it seems, I had no idea that while I was discovering Paris and the Parisians he was working on a book about Paris.

Some twenty years later, Reader, I married him. Only then did I discover John Russell's book, *Paris* (originally published in 1960). Here was sustained delight. No one else could combine the feel and the look, the heart and the mind, the stones and the trees, the past and the present, the wits, the eccentrics, and the geniuses of my favorite city with such easy grace.

Reading this book, for me, was like sauntering through the city where I had lived so long. By my side was a most civilized companion who casually brought all the strands together and made them gleam—not forgetting to stop for an aperitif and a delicious meal en route. The book was long out of print, and I felt it unfair to keep this to myself. I showed it to a publisher friend. He immediately agreed that others would enjoy John Russell's *Paris* as much as we did. He suggested it be brought up to date, in an illustrated edition.

The author and I went to Paris to gather the illustrations. There was some confusion about our hotel reservation, and the receptionist at the Pont-Royal apologized for giving us a small room on the top floor. Here the circle closes in the most satisfactory of ways: it was the identical room, no. 125, in which I had lived when I first came to Paris. The turkey-red carpet was now royal blue, the furniture was spruced-up modern, there was— is this possible?—a mini-bar. And there was a pushbutton telephone that clicked all of Europe and America into the streamlined receiver.

We stepped out onto the little balcony. Deyrolle the naturalist's, where I used to buy crystals and butterflies, was still across the street. There were some new chic boutiques, but the noble eighteenth-century façades still stood guard over the past. We looked around happily: there they were, our cherished landmarks—the Invalides, the Eglise de Sainte-Clotilde, and the Eiffel Tower on the left, and on the right the former Gare d'Orsay, soon to be a museum of late-nineteenth-century art, the Sacré-Coeur, and the Grand Palais.

The huge open sky overhead had drifted in from the Ile de France. The bottle-green bus bumbled down the Rue du Bac. The tricolor flew the way it flies in Delacroix's *Liberty Guiding the People*. I was back again, this time in John Russell's Paris.

The Pont-Neuf. Pierre-Auguste Renoir, 1872

Opposite: *The Vert Galant.* Raoul Dufy, 1926

Le Vert Galant—The Gay Blade—was France's nickname for Henri IV, who was on the throne when the Pont-Neuf was completed between 1598 and 1606. The bronze equestrian statue of the King stands at the western tip of the Ile de la Cité, where the bridge crosses the island.

I

Introduction

It is fifty years almost to the day since I first set foot in Paris. My ambition was to merge
unnoticed into the Parisian scene. To that end, I had mastered the street map, pored over
the Métro system, checked out the landing stages of the water-bus (since then long dis-
continued), and memorized the classic Parisian promenades. I already knew Paris—or so
it seemed to me—by sight, by sound, and by smell. I had read all that there was to read
and heard all that there was to hear. By the end of the short Easter vacation the cool-
hearted Queen of the West would have no secrets from me.

It didn't quite work out, of course. There is no way to pass as a born Parisian when
you have to sport not only the peaked cap and the emblemed blazer that were the mark
of my school in London, but the knee-length gray flannel trousers that went with them.
Given these accouterments, there could be no mistaking the ethnic group from which I
sprang.

A Windy Day on the Pont des Arts. Jean Béraud, c. 1880–81

I also underestimated the difficulty of getting to know Paris. Paris is the most volatile of cities. It is also—in ways that reveal themselves slowly—one of the most reclusive. To anyone who has been reared on the steady, consistent, and virtually unbounded openness of many North American societies, it must sometimes seem that in Paris every door is marked "Private," every notice means "Keep Out" (even if it doesn't actually say it), and all information is classified.

Even so, I made a good start. I went to the middle of the Pont des Arts and looked upstream toward the equestrian statue of Henri IV, the many-colored brickwork of the Place Dauphine, and the towers of Notre-Dame. I wandered in bemusement through the Oxonian courtyards of the Institut de France. And I made sure to be on hand for the moment ("the hour," as the French call it, "between dog and wolf") when the gas lamps light up along the Rue de Rivoli and the glass roof of the Grand Palais hovers like a great green crinoline above the chestnuts of the Champs-Elysées.

Encouraged by all this, I rode the open rear platform of the omnibus, I put my nose inside the irresistible shops of the pastrycooks, I paced the quayside on which a great poet had walked a lobster on a leash, and I made my way past countrified courtyards to the airfield where Lindbergh had landed not so long before. I walked through the lobbies of the best hotel, I listened for the first time to the threefold thump that gives the signal for a French play to begin, and I sat in a famous café in Montparnasse and called for pen, ink, and paper. (They came, by the way.) I knew no one in Paris, and I was royally happy.

I did not, however, delude myself. I sensed already that it would take forever to know Paris. Not only did Parisians not particularly care to be intruded upon, but there was about Paris an element of changeability that resisted analysis. Its very name, when spoken by Parisians, had a fugitive lightness, as if it had been waiting for centuries for Francis Poulenc to set it to music. A true Parisian brought out the first syllable with a quick sudden tap, leaving the rest to make an arrowy flight upward. How solid and stolid was the sound of "London" by comparison!

It is absolutely right, that flyaway music in the name. Parisians are in no doubt that they live in the most fascinating city that ever was; why should they stoop to argue the case? The history of Paris has a luster more continuous than that of any other European city—so much so, in fact, that no Parisian feels bound to hold on to the past in the way that the Athenian holds on to Plato and Pericles, the Venetian cleaves to Titian, the Viennese remembers Schubert, and the Florentine can hardly shave himself without thinking how Leonardo da Vinci would have designed a better razor.

Gifted people have never been rare in Paris, and Paris has often taken them for granted. Racine touched perfection in his tragedies, but Madame de Sévigné didn't think that they would last. When Bossuet, Bishop of Meaux—one of the great preachers of all time—climbed into a Parisian pulpit, he often looked down upon a half-empty church. Paris has had great architects—men who did as much for Paris as Sir Christopher Wren did for London—but not one Parisian in ten thousand can tell you who they were. Hector Berlioz bears one of the greatest names in French music, but Paris to this day has not heard a proper performance of his greatest work. Insofar as there is a specifically Parisian turn of mind, it is fundamentally dismissive. You will never hear from a Parisian taxi driver the equivalent of the cry of "Ecco Roma!" with which his Roman colleagues point to some hallowed sight. Even less will you hear from anyone at all in Paris the full-hearted enthusiasm with which the resident of Los Angeles or of San Francisco will carry on about those two very different cities. It is bred into the Parisian that the superiority of Paris, like the goodness of God, is self-evident.

There is something of arrogance in this, but it has its basis in qualities of which the Parisians often see themselves as having a monopoly. Reason is one; logic, another. Paris

The Place de la Concorde in 1829. Giuseppe Canella, 1829

for centuries has had what it claims to have: a self-renewing energy to which there is no end. There has never been any reason to sit back and give in to the past. The next new thing has genuinely been quite different from the last new thing. When great men die, Parisians give themselves over to grief with an almost Neapolitan fullness of feeling. Nowhere are funeral processions larger or more spontaneous. People tear their clothes, fling themselves upon the coffin, howl aloud when called upon to speak. Hamlet at the grave of Ophelia was hardly more distracted than many of those who follow the great Parisians to the cemeteries of Père-Lachaise or Montparnasse.

But on the way home they remind themselves that for every great Parisian who lies in a vault there is another great Parisian on the way up. It has always been so: why should it ever not be so? Paris is not a mummified *ville d'art,* like Venice or Florence. It has not been castrated, like Berlin. History has not moved away from it. Nor does it live in an artificial isolation and cultural sterility, like Moscow, Leningrad, and Prague. People do not walk through Paris as they walk through Bruges, or through the Alhambra in Granada, in wonder that so much of the past should remain intact. It is as natural for Paris to have old streets and old houses as it is for an English duke to wear old clothes in the country. Such things are never paraded in Paris, a city in which there is no dead ground—nowhere from which life has drained away, leaving only a heap of stones and a drowsing guardian. Even the Roman Arènes de Lutèce were long the scene, every summer Sunday, of a bowls tournament that was patronized by some of the more enduring contributors to French twentieth-century literature.

Saint-Germain-l'Auxerrois. Claude Monet, 1867

The conjunction of old and new is fundamental to Paris. Life as Henri IV planned it has withdrawn from the Marais, but the modish animation that has replaced it is nonetheless infectious for being backed by the façades of Libéral Bruant and the reliefs of Regnaudin. Even the secret gardens of the 7th *arrondissement* have nothing forlorn about them, and the student of the Rue Saint-Denis (the subject of a History hardly shorter than the *Decline and Fall of Ancient Rome*) will find it full of people whose business it is to bring him back to the present.

Perhaps it is this refusal to give in to the past that dissuades so many visitors from the orthodox routine of the sightseer. Only in the museums, in Notre-Dame, in the Invalides, and possibly in the Ile Saint-Louis may we count on meeting the vague tread and upturned gaze of the seeker for knowledge. Visitors do not get up early to see Saint-Germain-l'Auxerrois, as they would for Santa Maria Miracoli in Venice; they do not press for admission to the room in which Chateaubriand died, or rise promptly from the luncheon table in order to appraise the layout of the Hôpital Saint-Louis; and whether they bowl through the Bois de Boulogne by daytime, or flee in terror from the satyrs and satyresses who lurk in its coverts by night, they do not view the artificial landscape with the attention that they would accord to it if it were in England and had been laid out by Humphrey Repton. They are stunned by the present. Today has them fast by the throat, and the person to release them is not the cicerone who so blandly conducts them through Florence or Toledo.

Yet if this be so, it is not for lack of trying. A glance at the General Catalogue of the British Library will show that the Parisian guidebook has a history almost as long as that of Paris itself. The orthodox guide is nonetheless an unsatisfactory companion in Paris. Parisian values are unstable—so much so that one senses in those harassed pages a nostalgia for cities in which Titian is Titian till the end of time and the edition of 1875 needs to be reprinted rather than recast. Sentiment plays a great part in the appreciation of Paris. The Sacré-Coeur is ridiculous; the steeples of Sainte-Clotilde look like German jewelry, and the towers of Saint-Sulpice like municipal inkwells; but it is with a start of pleasure that we return after long absence to those churches. Even the Grands Boulevards, whose "huge blank pompous featureless sameness" was deplored by Henry James and decried by every nineteenth-century commentator—even these have been domesticated by the genius of the Impressionists, so that we see their implacable straightness as a virtue and take pleasure in the mechanical ornamentation of balcony and cornice.

The Place de l'Europe on a Rainy Day. Gustave Caillebotte, 1877

In retreat, therefore, from the vagaries of Parisian taste, the aspiring guide may prefer to turn to first causes. He may think of Paris in terms of the primitive settlements of Villejuif and Grenelle, and take his tone from the *Misopogon* of the Emperor Julien; but alas! the Paris of prehistory has been studied as closely as the Paris of Louis XIV, the Paris of Baron Haussmann, and the Paris of Marcel Carné and René Clair. If he renounces the general view altogether, and picks on some diminutive aspect of the capital—there again, I am afraid, the verdict of that redoubtable catalogue (each volume cuffed with brass and reinforced with hide) must exclude any hope of novelty. Even the migrations of dukes have their historian; and as for the department stores, the vanished fairs, the triumphal arches and standing columns, the gas brackets, and the surviving great trees—all are old stuff to the infantrymen of Parisian history.

In the way of archival scholarship, wonderful things have lately been done by an English historian, Richard Cobb. A great many books about Paris, however, are not scholarly at all. They are the work of professional rememberers. There are hundreds of Parisian memoirs, and some of them are indispensable guides to the general tone of Parisian life. In the volumes of Horace de Viel-Castel the corruption of the Second Empire is revealed in sentences that freeze at a touch; the reporting of Alphonse Daudet, Théophile Gautier, and Victor Hugo can never be bettered; and the two volumes of *An Englishman in Paris,* though not by an Englishman, are delightful reading. But many a more recent book has prompted its readers to try to relive the immediate past. Nowhere is this so futile as in Paris, where fashion is cruelly abrupt, and success, when once cut off, is cut off forever. The rememberers bring great disappointment in their train, for Paris is hard on those who try to live other people's lives. It is a city in which to act on impulse is one of the secrets of happiness, and Occasio, the bald goddess of Opportunity, should at all times be propitiated.

For this reason it seems to me that, to make the most of what Paris has to offer, the visitor should not draw up too stringent a program for himself. For the general temper of his visit, Apollinaire's "Voyage à Paris" has set the proper note:

> Ah! la charmante chose
> Quitter un pays morose
>   Pour Paris
>   Paris joli
>   Qu'un jour
> Dut créer l'Amour
> Ah! la charmante chose
> Quitter un pays morose
>   Pour Paris.

But life does not always live up to Apollinaire's jingle; and in any case the point of Paris is not the gloss of good living, which any visitor can enjoy, if he has the money. Nor is it the sharpened edge that the city gives to personal relationships of every kind. It is the quality of animation that Paris gives to every detail of existence. Paris is the antithesis of those ancient cities in which the sanctified monuments are separated from one another by street after street in which no one could wish to linger, let alone to live. Paris is in itself a work of art—and greater, in this respect, than any of its individual buildings. It so happens that Notre-Dame has been painted as often as any building in the world; but in the gross matter of Paris, in the mere look and substance of a blind wall or a half-effaced advertisement, there can be found the materials not only of art but of a lifetime of rewarded curiosity. And what is true of the eye is true also of the nose and the ear.

Parisians are inquisitive by nature, although they are rarely so naive as to fall back on the direct questions current elsewhere. They like to get at the facts, nonetheless. Moreover, the Bottin, or all-purpose telephone directory, is in itself, and quite apart from the millions of facts that it has to offer, one of the most revealing of Parisian institutions. Indispensable to the serious explorer, it can be consulted in all hotels, cafés, restaurants, post offices, and railroad and air terminals. Most private subscribers to the telephone also have it, though the ponderous volumes do not always accord with current fashions in interior decoration and not everyone has the complete set.

The Eglise de Notre-Dame-de-Lorette, with the Sacré-Coeur in the distance. Pierre Jahan photograph

The Bottin in its pure form (I except, that is to say, the Bottin Mondain and other variants) is a combination of telephone book, *Kelly's Directory*, and *Metropolitan Pilot*, with elements also of a cut-down and less selective *Who's Who*. Under "Alphabétique" you will usually find a note, not always either accurate or comprehensive, of the subscriber's occupation; and under "Rues" you will find, if not "who's who," then "who's next to who"; and this, in Paris, can be of great interest. The proportion of persons in Paris who have a house all to themselves is not large; and although in certain quarters the juxtapositions are all on the same social level, so that you will find Radziwill next to Faucigny-Lucinge, and Cabot Lodge across the landing from Cantacuzène, this is not a truly Parisian arrangement. A classic instance of Parisian lodging would rather unite in the same house a field officer in retirement, a custom shoemaker, two stenographers from the United States Embassy, a locomotive engineer on the Bordeaux run, and a professor of the harp. All such matters are made clear by the Bottin, which, to those who have learned to read it, is as beguiling as anything by Simenon.

I recommend in particular the volume entitled "Professions" to those who like to

Beginning in 1909, the French banker Albert Kahn commissioned a team of photographers to travel around the world making colored lantern slides, called autochromes, for a collection he named "The Archives of the Planet." Here, from among the many taken in Paris, are the Rue de Mogador, 26 July 1914, by Georges Chevalier (upper left), the Rue des Chartres, 23 July 1914, and the Rue Edouard-Colonne, 29 July 1914, both by Stéphane Passet (lower left and above).

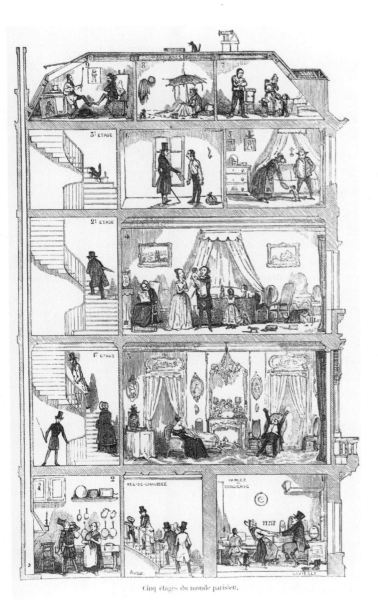

Cinq étages du monde parisien.

know how, and by what, other people exist. Photographs would be a welcome addition, at certain points, but I cannot approve of the new practice of truffling the Bottin's laconic pages with cultural information. We do not go to the Bottin to learn that Voltaire was a well-known writer or that Joan of Arc was put to the stake in 1431. Such things can be left to Larousse. Nor am I sure that, in a decomposing society, the Bottin Mondain can be taken at its face value. But it, too, has its amusement, in particular for the student of that discreet form of boasting, the auxiliary address.

It is, however, not really to my interest that readers should cleave too closely to the Bottin, for I cannot pretend to have treated my subject with anything approaching that authority's encyclopedic and impartial turn of mind. Nor can shortage of time or space be my excuse; this is a fat book, and it has been a very long time in the hatching. The reasons lie elsewhere, and are of more than one sort. I have not, for instance, said much about Montmartre. This is not because I cannot see the ancient beauty of the Rue Cortot, or the charm and discretion of the little Place Dancourt in which the Théâtre de l'Atelier is to be found, but because so much of those steep slopes is given over to a form of night life that is particularly dismal and spurious. Nor have I ventured much into Passy or Auteuil; both have their points of curiosity and are delightful to live in, but I do not think that they have many rewards for the casual visitor. (Brassaï in a classic photograph made the monumental statuary in the dogs' cemetery look as beautiful as the lions on Delos; but that is, after all, a poet's license.)

And then there are subjects too great to be handled here at the length they deserve. I have not, for instance, said much about the enormous wealth of works of art on offer in the public collections of Paris. To put in a page or two on the Musée du Louvre, for instance, would seem to me derisory. Besides, in many cases the collections in question are in full ebullition. More has happened in the Paris museum world these last ten years than can possibly be encapsulated. Old museums have been reinstalled and reembellished. New ones—very controversial, some of them—have come into being. It may well be that more bad feeling was aroused by the arrival of the Centre National d'Art Contemporain Georges Pompidou—generally known as "Beaubourg"—than by any other single event in the world of the arts in Paris since the end of World War II. It was almost as it had been at the time of the Dreyfus case: father was sundered from son, brother from brother, and betrothed from betrothed. These are not matters that can be summed up in a sentence.

To come upon Beaubourg unexpectedly is a shock, even for those who love it. When we begin to feel our way about Paris, it is rather in terms of those monuments that give us a sense of orientation. August or absurd, cherished or merely convenient, they have it in common that we cannot imagine Paris without them. The Sacré-Coeur is one such. Irremediably conspicuous, it turns up even when we think we have got well clear of it— when we are strolling in the Luxembourg Gardens, for instance. Notre-Dame is another. It may change color—russet brown in the little painting that Jean Fouquet made a little more than five hundred years ago, soot black in the 1940s, today an elegant steely gray. It has been much added to and much taken away from in the course of its long life. But we cannot imagine it elsewhere than where it is, so subtly adjusted to the line of the great river and the two islands. And we are convinced that no matter what else changes in Paris, people would always align themselves in relation to Notre-Dame, and to the Sacré-Coeur, and to the Eiffel Tower, and to the Louvre.

Faced with those buildings, we fall in with the notion—not everywhere defensible, by any means—of an unchanging Paris. It has a great appeal. When George Moore tells in his *Memoirs of My Dead Life* of how once, one distant April, "I loitered in the Luxembourg Gardens to watch the birds and the sunlight . . . and began to wonder if there was anything better in the world worth doing than to sit in an alley of clipped limes smoking, thinking of Paris and myself"—when he says that, we recognize the place, and the feeling, as identical with those still available to us. But then George Moore, now so little regarded, is the godfather of all those of us who love Paris. No one will ever describe better than he the journey through Paris by water—"the white architecture, the pillars, the balustraded steps, the domes in the blue airs, the monumented swards"—and when it comes to a French interior, the salon or the bedroom of an agreeable woman of the world, not Colette herself is more exact or more evocative, nor Vuillard subtler in touch and tone. None of all this has dated, though his views on what he called the "upper lower classes" may now read strangely. "Paris," he concludes somewhere, "has been my life, for did I not come hither in my youth like a lover, relinquishing myself to Paris, never extending once my adventure beyond Bas Meudon, Ville d'Avray, Fontainebleau, thereby acquiring a fatherland more true, because deliberately chosen, than the one birth impertinently imposed? *Un pays ami* is a truly delicate delight—a country where we may go when daily life is becoming too daily, sure of finding there all the sensations of home, plus those of irresponsible caprice."

George Moore was, of course, a natural romancer and sometimes his blossomy, handmade Paris is what dull persons would call "a little too good to be true." But his instinctive sensuality was too strong for him to give a picture false in any vital particular, and for that reason his books, like those of Daudet, Gautier, and Maupassant, are in spite of everything a better guide to Parisian life than much that has been written since. The notion of "unchanging Paris" can, all the same, be overdone. The historic center has been preserved, but only just. The outskirts of Paris are all but indecipherable to anyone who last saw them twenty years ago. The quarter of La Défense has heroic energy, whatever may be said against it, but the tower of Maine-Montparnasse is an unmitigated disaster. As for the high-rise satellite cities, they could be anywhere. What Denys Chevalier called "the assassination of Paris" has been carried out here and there with a thoroughness that reminds us that assassination is one of the historical specialties of Paris.

What we are discussing here is not the destruction of "old Paris." It is the destruction of Paris as an architectural continuum. Reading *Architectures Paris 1848–1914* by Paul

The Sacré-Coeur, with Notre-Dame in the foreground. Pierre Jahan photograph

The Luxembourg Gardens at Twilight. John Singer Sargent, c. 1879

Chemetov and Bernard Marrey, we learn that in the 1970s more than one in ten of the iron-framed buildings that made Paris "the capital of the nineteenth century" were pulled down, and that many more can be accounted as doomed.

I doubt, all the same, if anything short of wholesale destruction will ever affect the fundamental character of Paris. The *fond d'égoisme* is too intense, too positive in its effect; too many people want too much out of Paris. Even the inconstancy of Parisian taste is a safeguard, in this respect; and there is the fact that, whereas in English-speaking countries most people who can do so keep the best of themselves for the country, in France the reverse is the case. For nine months of the year, almost everything that is of consequence in France is to be found in Paris: this there is no denying. And although many of the changes of the past ten years or so are regretted by those whose experience goes back even a quarter of a century, there is one respect in which I see an improvement—a return, even, to the great traditions of two or three hundred years ago.

Even half a century ago, size was a generally accepted unit of judgment: the great house, the two-score servants, the dinner of eight courses and forty covers; the Blue Train with its twenty-six coaches and its toiling steam locomotive; the country house two hundred yards long—these were the things that impressed people. Today this is no longer the case; even to have a very big automobile is an error of taste. The admired thing is to have a manageable apartment with the best cook in the world and a *cottage coquet* on which someone spent a fortune. When you take the train, it is with two suitcases. The coach

Above: Barricade in the Rue de Flandre, 18 March 1871
Below: The Orgues de Flandres, apartment buildings by Martin van Treeck in the Rue de Flandre today

that you board is one of six. The train has a Diesel engine, takes a cross-country route, and averages over a hundred miles an hour. You can telephone from it, give dictation to a real live secretary, and in general treat it as home. In these lightweight trains, there is an echo of that now-lost American specialty, the club car—and very welcome it is.

If you eat out in Paris, it may be at a restaurant that was there before you were born, but it may equally well be at one quite new, where there are seven tables and no menu and the personnel look as if they were too young to stay up so late. Paris for a long time was a city in which seniority was all-important. With seniority came houses, collections, friends, enemies, toadies. The diary of the Goncourt brothers (1851–96) is as eloquent on this subject as is the diary of Saint-Simon (1692–1752). But then suddenly, and not so long ago, seniority and all that went with it seemed to be not so important after all.

All this I have fancied a little, but it is broadly true, and what is true of fashion's leaders will leak through, in time, to people who formerly would have ruined themselves to carry through life more ballast than they could really afford. It amounts to a blow for individualism and, as such, is in the true Parisian line. Paris exists in order that we should become more, and not less, like ourselves; and if we are to make the most of it, it is important not to go, as it were, against one's particular grain—in the choice of an hotel, for instance.

Hotels, like restaurants, are a subject upon which advice is usually fatal. The choice of an hotel is as private a matter as the choice of a wife. But there are at any rate various categories among which it is useful to distinguish. With hotels, as with many other things, the most expensive are the best. Nothing can top the great hotel, with its enormous and splendidly wasteful corridors, its tasteful if sometimes shabby apartments, its high windows open on to the Place Vendôme or the Place de la Concorde, and its cat-footed unsurprisable servants. Even the *chambres de courrier* or personal servants' rooms on the carpetless topmost floor have a style of their own; those who secure them are like beggars at the gates of a great city. The misshapen byrelike rooms may not have any noticeable charm; one must cleave to the incomparable view—the far-flying roofscape crowned by the gold-wreathed dome of the Invalides or the wedge-shaped roof of the Comédie-Française—and to the long walk down through floor after floor and the places where, among the high, clear, spoiled laughter of the American young, there are enclaves of traditional French activity, where the seamstress bends over the needle in the golden circle of the gas lamp. It is not for the pointless bustle of the ground floor, but for these Vuillard-like interiors, and for the costly silence, the padded quiet of the upper rooms, that the great hotel is irreplaceable.

The station hotel is a special taste, but those who have formed it will remember the Gare d'Orsay, where the posters peeled on the wall and the phantom goods-train never left; they will also remember lunching at the Gare des Invalides, when cries of "Les passagers pour Saigon, en voiture!" or "Arrivée des passagers de Buenos Aires!" gave a sense of fugacity to the painstaking regional meal. The station restaurant at the Gare de l'Est is one of the finest in Europe, and the mural paintings in the Gare de Lyon are not at all to be despised. Enthusiasts take comfort, also, from the fact that their taste chimes with that of one of the most fastidious of recorded natures. Max Beerbohm—known also for his patronage of the Great Western Hotel—was a connoisseur of the station hotel, and in his essay "Fenestralia" he evoked an aspect of Hittorf's edifice with which few of his readers will be familiar:

"You know," he says, "the huge grey façade of the Gare du Nord, and may have noted that it is adorned (or at any rate weighted) with rows of proportionately huge statues, one on each side of every window, symbolising the Continents, and the principal French provinces and cities, and Liberty, I think, and Justice, and many other things of national or universal import. But you may not be aware that all the windows on the first floor are those of an hotel, an hotel that occupies this one floor only, and consists of twelve vast bedrooms (each with a small anteroom and bathroom) and nothing else. Behind the bedrooms runs a corridor whose opposite side has windows through which you see, far down, the many platforms of the station and the steam of arriving and departing trains. The windows are of thick double glass. The corridor is a quiet one. Little locomotives are seen and not heard. But the bedrooms are the great point. They seem to have been built for

The garden restaurant at the Hôtel Ritz, 15, Place Vendôme, 1900s. Harry Ellis photograph

giants and giantesses, so vast are their ancient wardrobes, dressing-tables and beds; and each of their two windows is in proportion to the stone figure that stands on either side of it, planting a colossal foot on the sill. If I remember rightly," Sir Max continues, "it was from between the ankle of a masculine Africa and a feminine Marseilles that I looked forth early on my first morning. . . ."

Not every visitor, however, is an enthusiast of the Railway Quarter. The clifflike tenements, the Alsatian restaurants, the disquieting glass-roofed passages, and the submarine smells that drift from the shellfish stalls along the Rue Saint-Lazare—these are not for every taste, when it comes to choosing an hotel. The tapering cabins of the 6th *arrondissement* are more generally in favor. ("Streets round the Rue de l'Université," we read in Cyril Connolly's *The Unquiet Grave*, "Rue Jacob, Rue de Bourgogne, and Rue de Beaune, with their hotel signs and entrances and their concierges walled in by steamer-trunks. Stuffy salons, full of novels by Edith Wharton, purple wall-paper which later we

Hôtel du Nord

grow to hate as we lie in bed with grippe, chintz screens round the bidets, high grey panelling with cupboards four inches deep. . . .")

Every seasoned visitor has a list of that kind: hotels in the silver formality of the Place du Palais Bourbon; hotels near the Rue Monge, where the deep-frying never stops beneath the window and Arabs fall unconscious in the street; hotels on the Rue Saint-Honoré, where English actor-managers bicker quietly in the winter garden and Americans play the phonograph all night; hotels that seem to be run without human intervention, and hotels where, to start the elevator, or to dislodge your key from its rack, you need the wiles of Old Diplomacy; hotels where people stay for thirty years, and hotels where an hour is the usual term; hotels on the Ile de la Cité, where the green water of the Seine is reflected on the ceiling; suburban hotels where the frame comes away with the door and the toy heaters pop and purr; hotels that have outgrown their strength and lie—huge, filthy, three-quarters empty—on the slopes of Montmartre; hotels where every move is watched and the visitor sweats out the life of a Kafka hero, and hotels where even the arrival of an orangutan could not disturb the fairy-tale slumber, the lace-curtained indifference of the personnel. Hotels deep in the Faubourg Saint-Germain, where the wind in the trees can be heard at a hundred yards and a locomotive could turn on its axis in the courtyard; hotels on the Quai Voltaire, where the view has not changed since Thomas Girtin drew it and Wagner stayed on to finish *Die Meistersinger;* hotels near the Carrefour de Buci, where the tap water runs red and the market opens up at four in the morning; the hotel in the Place Saint-Sulpice where Djuna Barnes wrote *Nightwood* and the late breakfaster eavesdropped on the improvisations of Marcel Dupré; hotels that could be in small French country towns, and hotels that could be in Fez; hotels that give one silicosis, and hotels that face the acacia-scented culverts of the Boulevard Péreire. The hotel in which the night porter acted with Duse, and the hotel that belonged to Proust's Céleste. The hotel that was once the British Embassy, and the hotel in which Oscar Wilde died.

The choice of an hotel has always been a controversial matter; since Buckingham and the future King Charles I of England put up at the Pomme du Pin under the names of Tom Smith and John Brown, eyebrows have been raised, and graying heads wagged, at the insecurity of Anglo-Saxon judgment in this context. The English novice used to aim at a reasoned conservatism. Based behind the Madeleine, on shelving ground north of the Champs-Elysées, or in that hothouse of the intelligence, the 6th *arrondissement,* he at first did not dare to set out without map, compass, telescope, and brandy flask. Timid by nature, he spent a lot of time in his room.

That room was much the same, no matter where he was, unless he had a great deal of money. The bedstead was of burnished brass. The counterpane was heavy, white, and adorned in high relief. Beside the bed was a telephone receiver on a gibbet of archaic design. The windows were eight feet high and opened inward, though it took a professor of jujitsu to bring this about. The wallpaper, though flowered, owed nothing to the examples preserved in the Conservatoire des Arts et Métiers. The lighting was poor, and adapted to no known human activity. The bath was down the hall and the lavatory, secreted in a circular stairwell, was preempted as often as not.

Labor was cheap in those days, and automation unheard-of. Hotel life was based therefore on a chain of human contacts, male and female. Personal service was on a scale that had changed hardly at all since the days of Molière and Beaumarchais. Words like "valet," "porter," "chambermaid," and "bootboy" were in continual use. Everything had to be negotiated, but when that had been done we might have been in a great English

Hôtel de la Toison d'Or,
Rue des Mauvais-
Garçons, 1966

country house, rather than in a second-rate French hotel. Hot water was brought, shoes were cleaned, errands were run, every last stitch of clothing was cleaned and pressed, newspapers were fetched, bow ties were knotted. We were spoiled, and at minimal cost.

Still, we had to go out sometime. At that point it became clear that locomotion, or How To Get About, is a problem of great importance in Paris, where distances can be disconcertingly great. A taxi solves everything, of course—but always to take a taxi is as dull as it is ruinous. Never to take one, on the other hand, is to miss an important element in Parisian life. Much of the mythology of the Paris taxi and its driver is now obsolete. The last of the barrel-bodied sedans vanished a while ago, together with the last of the White Russian colonels who drove them. The typical Paris taxi of the 1980s is an agile, beetle-like affair, none too comfortable for those long in the leg, and its driver may well be in his twenties. (Legend is also contradicted by the fact that you are safer, in most taxis, than you are when driven by your friends.) As a face-saver when you would otherwise be late, the taxi is indispensable in Paris. But as there are always times when you simply cannot get one it is a good plan to memorize, if you can, the outline of the four or five routes on the subway which will get you out of almost any such difficulty.

The Métro was always the instrument of liberty for those who have mastered the network. First mooted in the 1870s, it was begun in October 1898 and inaugurated—though only part of the network was ready—in July 1900. Though not without its troubles at the outset, it soon became a favorite with Parisians, and by 1914 it was carrying four hundred million passengers a year.

It was not a treat, however. Though fast, clean, prompt, and safe by the standards of today in New York, it was dreary. It had a distinctive smell—identified by one historian as a mixture of tar, sweat, carbonic acid, and metallic dust—and as one barely distinguishable station followed another, an enveloping cheerlessness swept through the train. As Roger H. Guerrand says in his "Mémoires du Métro," the Métro became "the true Museum of Man: the museum of living man, man naked . . . Empty-eyed, every man sinks into himself and becomes a statue of himself—or, to be more precise, his own mirror."

Add to this the fact that to change trains could mean up to five minutes' fast walking along dimly lit corridors lined with mutilated beggars, and it will be clear that the Métro had its penitential side. It had its unexpected rewards—as it does to this day when the train takes to the air, sweeps across the Seine on the Pont Bir-Hakeim, and trundles, a last survivor of the great metropolitan elevated railways of the late nineteenth century, along the Boulevard de Grenelle at third-floor level. But in general it was a dismal business. It is a grim notion that many thousands of Parisians in the first half of this century spent in all at least two full years of their lives in the Métro.

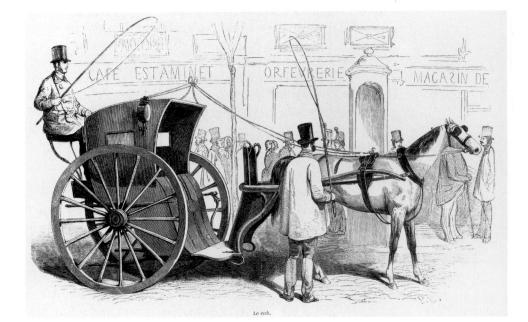

Le cab.

So it is a pleasure to be able to say that the Métro has lately been much regenerated. Not everywhere, perhaps: but to a degree that would astonish those whose last rides were in the 1950s. The Métro of the 1980s looks better, rides better, and smells better. Some of its stations are even amusing. Its layout—basically unchanged in eighty years—is still convenient. The new express lines make it possible to get in and out of Paris in record time in any one of four directions. Altogether—and given the state of road traffic above ground—the new-model Métro is a blessing.

But one Métro tunnel, one platform, one clacking turnstile—each is much like all the others; and even if there were surprises on the way you could not stop the train to take advantage of them. What most of us enjoy is to potter about at surface level, free to stop, and look, and linger, as we please. It is for this reason that in any alphabet of Parisian worthies, O would surely stand for Omnes. Not, as you might think, the beginnings of a Latin tag, but the surname of a man of affairs from Nantes who, in 1828, endowed Paris with one of the simplest and most economical of its instruments of pleasure: the omnibus.

Where Cardigan, Mackintosh, Spencer, and even John Collins got their names intact into everyday usage, poor Monsieur Omnes is now remembered only by one or two social historians. His mistake was to compound his name with that of the thing he invented, for the result has a ring of such rightness that we take it rather for some rough-and-ready classical derivation than for a corruption of "Omnes' bus."

The buses of today do not have the individualistic names adopted by the companies who took up Monsieur Omnes's idea. We cannot speak, for instance, of taking an Ecossaise, an Algérienne, a Dame Blanche, an Hirondelle, or a Béarnaise. Nor have we the

The Place de la Concorde. Robert Doisneau photograph

choice of colors that gave the painter such varied opportunities. Where he could have a red, a yellow, and a chocolate-brown bus on one and the same canvas, we have the never-changing bottle-green single-decker. Here too, progress has eaten away at the traditional design. That open platform at the rear, for instance, which gave a headlong air to even the most perfunctory advance, was always the best place from which to get a first general view of Paris. Even horseback or a high-backed Rolls-Royce of 1925 could not afford a better view. But in buses of today's design all this is done away with; and the customer, boxed in from the start, loses all intimacy with his surroundings. Even the emergency departure is denied us, and the practiced manipulation of the chain in its slot, and the head and shoulders so recklessly outboard as the bus charges down our favorite alley. In bad weather the interior may have its points; but, even then, the platform was the refuge of the free spirit, and I grieve to see it gone.

With a *carnet* of bus tickets and a preliminary look at the map, the visitor can see more of Paris in one day than he would achieve in a week by any other means. Not only is his point of vantage superior, but his route will be diverse, well chosen, and logical. His pace will be ideal, neither too fast for observation nor so slow as to suggest that he may be wasting time. He will be in continual contact, too, with the people of Paris; and

Omnibus on the Boulevard Saint-Martin, 1855. Adolphe Braun photograph

Building the Hôtel de Salm. Anonymous, 1786

from their gait, dress, and demeanor he will learn much about the differences between one quarter and another. With the *petite ceinture* he can patrol the circumference of Paris, as if marking out the limits of a croquet lawn; and with any one of fifty or more inner routes boredom can be sent packing for the day. Altogether Monsieur Omnes deserves a statue—or perhaps we could all be given a free ride on his birthday?

The layout of Paris is not difficult to grasp, but the level ground, the general sameness of the late-nineteenth-century streets, and the immense length of certain dismal but inescapable arteries—all combine to confuse the beginner. The Rue de Vaugirard, for instance, is as long as life itself; beginning just south of the Odéon, it cuts a swathe right across the city and would probably have gone on to Le Mans if Paris were not rigid in the matter of its boundaries. For there is never any doubt as to where Paris ends or begins. Paris begins at the gates of Paris, and nowhere else: not in the ocean-rolling forests of the Ile de France; not on the royal belvedere of Saint-Germain-en-Laye; not among the lunatic villas that border the electric railway lines that lead into the Gare Saint-Lazare; not at Joinville-le-Pont, that sad little, sooty little town on the Marne; not on the sturdy hillock of the Mont Valérien; not in the ill-named village of Plaisir; not on the hippodromes of Saint-Cloud and Maisons-Laffitte, or the airfields of Orly and Roissy. Nor should we give geography its head; the *bassin Parisien* covers more than a quarter of France. No, Paris begins where it always began: at the gates of Paris, where the huge apartment houses have been left out like pretentious toys and in wintertime the furred and leathery couples stamp up and down the omnibus terminal like Eskimos waiting for the next floe.

By this triumph of persistence the boundaries of Paris have been kept roughly as they were in the reign of Louis-Philippe. The outline of the city has been unchanged for very much longer. It is the same rather casually minted coin that was flung down on the map of France more than four hundred years ago and has lain there ever since. The Enceinte de Thiers, laid out between 1841 and 1845, is very much larger in area than the Enceinte of Philippe-Auguste (1190–1213); in fact, the dimensions of Paris had increased

Louis XVI and Benjamin Franklin. Niderviller Manufactory, c. 1780 Louis XVI is here seen handing to Benjamin Franklin the treaty of alliance between France and the United States of America in 1778.

considerably ever since the Mur des Fermiers-Généraux was completed in 1797. But the basic outline was the same, and across all three coins there ran, like a silver flaw, the hoop-shaped line of the Seine. For any real change in the layout of Paris we should have to go back to prehistory, when the Seine was three and a half miles wide, and a hundred and twenty feet deep; all that survived above the flood were the four high points that are now the Butte Montmartre, the Colline de Chaillot, the Montagne Sainte-Geneviève, and the heights of Belleville. Those really were different days, for, in the words of one recent historian, "a tropical vegetation lay thick over all, and strange creatures propelled themselves hither and thither with wing and fin."

Since the parting of these great waters, neither wing nor fin has played any role in the history of the city. Human beings are what matter in Paris, and here also there has been no real change in the last few hundred years. Parisians are what they always were. Their newspapers were formed, once and for all, by the first Parisian newssheet—that of Théophraste Renaudot; their gossip is still recognizably that of the *historiettes* of Tallemant des Réaux. In the *Tableau de Paris,* compiled by Sébastien Mercier on the eve of the Revolution, there is a complete portrait of the Parisian as he is today: brisk, ironical, self-regarding, invalidish, mischievous, fickle, and dry. The Parisian is violent; the blood of the barricades is still hot in his veins. There is a great continuity of human types in Paris—and none, certainly, of those revolutions in conduct that make the manners of

Elizabethan or Georgian England seem those of a race quite removed from the English of today. The wit, the intelligence, the enlightened materialism, and the spry, darting physique of the Parisian have not altered since the Renaissance.

The great advantage of the Parisian studies, therefore, is that they are never merely archaic. Knowledge is never wasted where Paris is concerned. Even the great novelists will still ring perfectly true; the boardinghouse in *Le Père Goriot*, the Parliamentary intrigues in *Lucien Leuwen*, and the big dinner parties in *L'Education Sentimentale* could be transposed almost word for word into contemporary life, and it is easier to catch the tone of Parisian conversation from Mérimée's *La Vase Etrusque* than from even the most conscientious of academic studies. In more recent years, such books as André Breton's *Nadja* and Aragon's *Paysan de Paris* invest familiar Parisian themes with a high degree of poetic imagination; and there are parts of Paris to which Proust is an incomparable guide. For those who, like one of the main characters in *The Tragic Muse*, "think the Théâtre Français a greater institution than the House of Commons," there is still great instruction in that marvelous novel; for Henry James is quite up-to-date in his assessment of the English in Paris, just as Hazlitt is up-to-date, on the whole, in his assessment of the Louvre.

Parisians in general do not, in point of fact, care much what the rest of us think of Paris. Politenesses apart, they feel that Paris belongs to them and that they alone can master its every nuance. If foreigners don't like it, they are welcome to go elsewhere. For this reason there grew up over the years a small but eminent group of anti-Parisians. We cannot imagine, for instance, that Bernini left Paris with any feelings of regret or affection at the end of the six months that he spent there at the invitation of Louis XIV. (His French colleagues weren't sorry to see him go, either.) Mozart thought of Paris as a place where he was kept waiting for hours in an ice-cold room before being made to play on an instrument that sounded like nothing on earth. Lesser people, and perhaps even we ourselves, have been out of humor with Paris from time to time.

But when that is said, how much must be put on the opposite side! How many minds opened, how many hearts brought to maturity, how many powerful natures fulfilled! There could never be an end of it. No matter where we look, Paris turns out to have been the decisive element. Without Paris, Jefferson would not be Jefferson, Franklin would not be Franklin, Chopin would not be Chopin, Turgenev would not be Turgenev, Strindberg would not be Strindberg, Freud would not be Freud, Diaghilev would not be Diaghilev, Gertrude Stein would not be Gertrude Stein, Picasso would not be Picasso. That list could be remade a hundred times over, and in almost every domain of human activity.

The role of Paris in all this is active, not passive. The people I have named did not "have a good time" in Paris. Paris drove them to give of their best and defied them to fall short of it. In the winter of 1920–21, James Joyce put that point once and for all when he wrote to a friend, "There is an atmosphere of spiritual effort here. No other city is quite like it. It is a racecourse tension. I wake early, often at five o'clock, and start writing at once." *That* is what Paris has to give.

Thomas Jefferson knew that, when he went every day to monitor the building of the Hôtel de Salm until finally he got a bad crick in the neck for his pains. Henry James knew it, when he took Ralph Waldo Emerson through the painting galleries in the Louvre and was disconcerted by Emerson's lack of response. ("Certain chords were wholly absent," he noted. "The tune was played—the tune of life and literature—altogether on those that remained.") That Hemingway and Scott Fitzgerald knew it hardly needs saying. That George Gershwin knew it we can judge from the specific character of his "An American in Paris," so distinct from that of his other works. But then no sensitive American, from John Adams to John Ashbery and Elizabeth Bishop, has ever failed to know it.

Likewise, the English visitor to Paris can feel that he is fulfilling the historical destiny of his race. The English have always loved Paris. The philosopher can call upon the shades of Duns Scotus and William of Ockham as he goes to lectures at the Sorbonne; the diplomat can call to mind the Duke of Suffolk's negotiations for the marriage of Louis XII to Henry VIII's sister Mary; the dramatist remembers Wycherley's apprenticeship in wit at the Hôtel de Rambouillet; the chemist, the watchmaker, and the Scots Guardsman all have their illustrious forerunners; the fatigued barrister can measure himself against

Sutton Sharpe, the friend of Stendhal and Mérimée and their peer in conversation and debauch; the politician can dream of becoming the poor man's Burke; the collector has Lord Hertford's example before him, as he leafs through the print shops of the Rue de Seine; the idler can point to the inspired eavesdropping of George Moore; and the watercolorist can point to Thomas Shotter Boys. An indestructible attraction to Paris has been the mark of the eminent Englishman in every age: Coryat, Evelyn, Garrick, Macaulay, Kipling—the names could not be more oddly assorted, but the central passion is the same. Perhaps there is little to show for this unchanging adherence—little, indeed, but the Jardin Anglais, the Fontaine Wallace, and the raincoat; but the lesson of Paris does not reside primarily in things seen, or heard, or individually learned. It is the lesson of civilization as Sainte-Beuve defined it. "Civilization," he said, "*life*, as we know it, is something that is learned and invented. This we must never forget:

Inventas aut qui vitam excoluere per artes

(*The Aeneid*, Book VI)

A few years of peace, and we lose sight of this truth, and we come to believe that our cultivation is innate; we come to confuse it, in fact, with nature."

Of all such inventions, Paris is the greatest.

Paris, Looking Toward Montmartre. Raymond Mason, 1976

II

Parisian and Parisienne

Dinner at the Ambassadeurs. Jean Béraud, c. 1890
The Café-Concert des Ambassadeurs was in the gardens of the Champs-Elysées. It was pulled down in 1929.

Paris would be great, some people say, if it weren't for the Parisians. Parisians—so they say—are abrupt, edgy, rapacious, egoistic, and smug. They will feign to speak no English, even if they know it perfectly. If the foreign visitor asks them a question in French, they correct his grammar, laugh at his accent, and go on their way. (I owe to my friend Richard Eder, sometime chief of the *New York Times* bureau in Paris, the insight that: "It is not our mistakes that the French particularly object to, though they will correct them out of pedagogical compulsion. What they cannot abide is the lack of assurance, the hesitation, the low water pressure with which Americans or Englishmen get their words out.") What a change, people say, from the soft obliging speech of the Londoner, the warmth of the Florentine, and the ponderous good will of the Berliner.

All this is both true and not true. It is true that some Parisians are disagreeable. A Parisian post office, for instance, is not a place of pleasure. There are Parisians who delight in telling you that your hotel room is not ready, that the play you most want to see is sold out, and that they wouldn't dream of cashing your traveler's check. To meet Parisians of this sort is daunting. But the thing to remember is that although they are disagreeable to you, they are quite as disagreeable to one another. There is nothing personal about it. It is a fact of acclimatization, like the huge toes of the sloth.

In private, Parisians are not necessarily cold and inhospitable, as is often supposed. They love to be amused, and will go to great lengths to bring that about. Nowhere is friendship more enduring, or hospitality more subtly resourceful, than in Paris. But Parisians are by nature both wary and impatient. They have a very low tolerance of boredom. Foreign visitors as such are not fascinating to them. They have a dread of ties that may turn out badly. It has been bred into them that "stranger" rhymes with "danger."

In their relations (or lack of relations) with one another, they are terrifyingly and everlastingly observant. Neutrality plays no part in Parisian life. Knives are never sheathed, nor curtains fully drawn. The Parisian *concierge* has an eye like a coast guard, an ear like a piano tuner, and a tongue like that of a lizard on the run. Parisians have very long memories and the gift of immediate recall. Watching them button their coats right up to their chins, watching the quick step that gets them from place to place, and watching the way they look over a room and decide what, if anything, is in it for them, we recognize them as heirs to a civilization that is as unforgiving as it is ancient.

Parisians take nothing for granted. Faced with the general, they break it down not merely into the particular, but into every known subdivision of the particular. They can never have too much detail. Marcel Proust—in some ways the ultimate Parisian—was a

Avenue Ledru-Rollin.
Robert Doisneau
photograph

Carton Vendor. Carle Vernet, 1820s

Vinegar Seller. Abraham Bosse, 17th century

prime example of this. "Précisez!" he would say when someone told him something that caught his fancy. "Mais précisez, cher Monsieur, précisez!" Every Parisian is a precisionist, to whom vagueness is abhorrent.

It was always so. If we look at the *Cris de Paris*—the engravings, colored or black-and-white, that list the ways in which people could set up in business in the streets of Paris—we see at once that they are not at all like their English equivalent, the *Cries of London,* or indeed the cries of any other city. The traditional *Cries of London* are pretty, if you like that sort of thing, but we don't believe in them. In the *Cris de Paris,* the people concerned get a thorough going-over. Inspector Maigret himself could not do a better job. We know that the shoeshiner would give value for money, that the lanterns would hold up in bad weather, that the goose quills for the pens are properly cut, and that the coffee is fresh, the lettuce free from grubs, and the *vielle* in tune. Moreover, these people are not "types." They are individuals, and we recognize them as such.

That instantaneity of recognition is the true note of Parisian life. "It takes one to know one," and nowhere more so than in Paris. Parisians watch people the way birders watch birds, and they are never deceived. You can live half your life in Paris; you can love Paris, marry a Parisian, raise Parisian children. But none of that will make you a Parisian. This is irksome, if you are by nature a joiner rather than a looker-on, but it gives Parisian life a tautness, an inner coherence, and a ferocious continuity. Paris in this sense is a secret society.

That this should be so does not make the Parisian any less excited to see a new and celebrated foreigner. When William Faulkner went to a cocktail party given by his publisher in Paris, not long after World War II, people crowded round to stare at him. ("But he drinks like an Englishman!" they said to one another as the great man accepted yet another straight whiskey.) Anyone who can think on his feet and has some kind of reputation will be kindly received in Paris. But if you are awkward in speech, look like nothing much, and have not had your way prepared for you, then the traditional hazards of Paris are likely to open before you, one by one, and you will feel yourself both a victim and a butt.

It follows from this that no two people have the same experience of Paris. If you don't know anyone there, you may well judge the population by its hall porters, chambermaids, waiters, policemen, cab drivers, and salespeople. In each of these categories

there are to be found the very crown jewels of humanity. Crown jewels are, by definition, rare. But they exist. One of the most haunting portraits of a Parisian is that of an unnamed waiter who looks out at us from an establishment called A L'Homme Armé in a photograph by Eugène Atget. Whether Atget willed it or not, there is a singular irony in the juxtaposition of the name of the restaurant with the image of a man armed only with his clean white napkin.

Even today, when personal service is often confused with slavery, Paris is full of

A l'Homme Armé, 25, Rue des Blancs-Manteaux, 1900. Eugène Atget photograph

people who ask nothing more than to make life easy and agreeable for us by the performance of acts that are miscalled "menial." The waiter, the hall porter, the chambermaid, the policeman (yes, even the policeman), the cab driver, and the small shopkeeper in Paris know perfectly well that the right thing well done can turn life around for the visitor. And some of them enjoy doing it, just as Dorine in Molière's *Tartuffe* and Françoise in Proust's *Remembrance of Things Past* enjoy making life more pleasant for people they respect. It so happens that Marcel Proust in life was able to give very large tips, and that the people to whom he gave them were mostly employed at the Ritz Hotel, but we don't have to go to the Ritz, or give ten times the normal tip, to experience the ancient free-spoken tradition of Parisian service.

In this matter, the *Cris de Paris* of Edme Bouchardon are still valid. No longer, it is true, do the one-person stores stalk the streets with their wares on their backs. They find it pleasanter and more comfortable to wait indoors, knowing very well that Parisians have an instinct for high quality and will seek them out. That confidence is well founded, after all. The house of Antoine, now at 10, Avenue de l'Opéra, has been selling umbrellas since 1740. (Initially it also rented umbrellas. In wet weather, you could pick one up at either end of the Pont-Neuf and turn it back when you got to the other side.) La Civette, at 157, Rue Saint-Honoré, has been the no. 1 shop for cigars in Paris since the eighteenth century. Caro the billiard-table maker at 252, Boulevard Voltaire has been in business since 1789. Schilz the saddle-maker was founded in the year of the battle of Waterloo and has been at 30, Rue de Caumartin since 1860.

If you need a gunsmith of the highest class, Faure-Le Page at 8, Rue de Richelieu has been open since the year 1718. If a visiting card and an engraved letterhead are more to your taste, then a terrible choice awaits you. Are you to go to Maquet, 45, Rue Pierre-Charron, which was founded in 1841 by Maquet, the inventor of the envelope, or to Stern, 47, Passage des Panoramas, which was founded a year earlier and had the patronage of Emperor Napoleon III? If your silver and your silver gilt are showing signs of wear, Camus-Rigal at 24, Rue des Gravilliers has been dealing with problems of that sort since 1883. If you think that the hand-held fan went out when air conditioning came in, a visit to Duvelleroy, 37, Boulevard Malesherbes, will show you your mistake. Duvelleroy was founded in 1827 and still has all the business it can handle.

That Parisians like to eat well is no secret. In that domain, also, they have their conservative side. But then who would not be tempted by the chocolates at Debauve & Gallais, 90, Rue des Saints-Pères, where the little shop bears the date of its foundation (1819) above the entrance and the interior has kept its decoration almost intact since that distant day? Emile Zola in his novel *Le Ventre de Paris* has a good word for the *charcuterie* on offer at Battendier (now at 8, Rue Coquillière and two subsidiary addresses). Among other houses of ancient repute, Baggi at 38, Rue d'Amsterdam has been known since 1850 for the quality of its nonindustrial ice creams, while A La Mère de Famille at 35, Rue du Faubourg-Montmartre has been selling cakes and candy in profusion since the year 1761.

Common to these establishments and to many of their juniors—as to which I recommend a careful search through the *Guide de Paris* of Gault and Millau—is a feeling for perfection, alike in the thing done and in the way it is presented. Perfection of that kind is nurtured almost as much by those who patronize it as by those who produce it, and the very high quality of individual service in Parisian specialty stores owes something to the bright and beady eye of the Parisian customer, male and female alike.

Another great Parisian institution is the theater. Parisians love to be amused, and they have remained remarkably consistent in their tastes. You may no longer be able to enjoy a *café chantant,* an evening of Grand Guignol, or a melodrama of the kind that had our great-grandparents hiding under their seats. Among entertainments best avoided by the English-speaking visitor, Parisian musicals rank very high. But if the Parisian theater in general is no longer what it was in the nineteenth century—the locus of feeling and imagination in which people of every age and class were united—it has held up remarkably well against both movies and television.

This is in part because Paris has a tradition, now three centuries old, of literate theater. There are more great plays in the French language than in any other. The modalities of the theater—tragedy, high comedy, farce—have been explored more thoroughly and to greater effect in France than anywhere else. French manners, French habits of speech, and French perspectives on the ups and downs of life were formed in the theater for many generations. This is true of Paris above all. A city that nurtured the tragedies of Racine, the comedies of Molière, Marivaux, and Beaumarchais, the farces of Feydeau and Courteline, and the operettas of Offenbach was a city in which dull people were out of place.

Of course many Parisians have had, and have more than ever today, a fondness for the most terrible trash. But there is still a Parisian minority that thinks of the theater as fundamental to life. For that reason, the major writer is rare in France who does not try his hand at it. What will Samuel Beckett be best remembered for, if not for plays first performed in Paris? With what did Jean-Paul Sartre first make a worldwide name, if not

Four pages from *Studies of the Lower Orders* or *Les Cris de Paris*. Bouchardon, 1746. "Coffee" (upper left), "Rat Traps" (upper right), "Rabbit Skins" (lower left), "Kindling" (lower right)

Antiquités, 21, Rue du Faubourg Saint-Honoré, 1902–1903. Eugène Atget photograph

with *No Exit*? Where did Jean Genêt, Eugène Ionesco, and many another leave their brand upon our century, if not on the Parisian stage? Where could Peter Brook have based his experimental theater, if not in Paris?

This feeling for great theater is owed in part to the Parisians' fondness for the word in all its more exalted manifestations (and in some of its more rudimentary ones, too). But it is also owed to the fact that before movies, before radio, and before television it was the theater above all things that set the tone of life for a huge public. Paris has had great actors and actresses since the days when Molière first formed his troupe. Individual players have been carrying all before them since Mademoiselle Clairon was the rage of Paris in the 1740s, and Talma was Napoleon's favorite actor, and Frédérick Lemaître was the Romantic Movement incarnate, and Sarah Bernhardt made her debut at the Comédie-Française in 1862. Nor is the line quite extinct, though it would be invidious to say who best upholds it today.

The Parisian public remains loyal to the theater, by and large. It has to be loyal if it is to survive the discomfort of most Parisian theaters, the bother of going through one ordeal after another to get to one's seat, and the poor quality of much that is on view. We cannot wonder that so much of the Parisian appetite for drama should now be slaked by the movies. Parisians have movie fever, the way Spaniards have bull fever. There is no hour of the day and night at which you cannot catch a good movie in Paris. The Cinémathèque, founded in Paris by the late Henri Langlois, was the first and will always be the best thing of its kind. Movies that in other parts of the world are a discardable distraction are often a matter of life and death to young people in Paris. They fight over them as their ancestors fought over Victor Hugo's *Hernani* in the 1830s. Parisians *believe,* and they love to fight over what they believe.

They have never quite lost—movies and television notwithstanding—the feeling for live entertainment. That one man or one woman should pit his skills, his courage, and his imagination before the huge indifference of the mob still fascinates them. The acrobat, the mime, and the one-man band can still find a public in the streets of Paris, even if that public often drifts away, just as it did in Daumier's day. The Parisian is also loyal to the circus, year-round. There may no longer be the private circus that we know from a painting by James Tissot, in which gentlemen of high degree could perform feats of skill and daring before an audience of their peers, but we can still find the small professional circus that Fernand Léger memorialized in the 1950s, with its preliminary parade, its acrobats, its tumblers, its clowns, and its well-endowed equestrienne.

Paris in this has the character of a southern city, even if for much of the year it has an unmistakably northern climate. The Parisian street is a place where passions can be acted out and fatal decisions made. They may be mimicked, as in street theater, but they may also be for real, as they often have been throughout Parisian history. Anyone who has seen Marcel Carné's *Les Enfants du Paradis*—and no greater film about Paris will ever be made—will remember how the sense of fun that runs through the street scenes is

Amateur Circus. James-Jacques-Joseph Tissot, c. 1882

Procession of the League in the Place de Grève.
Anonymous, 1590

The Place de Grève is now the Place de l'Hôtel-de-Ville.

darkened by a sense of criminality. Thousands of people are having a good time, in those tumultuous scenes, but in the midst of it all man is matched against man in a struggle that can have only one outcome.

The compulsion to quarrel—or to push differences of opinion just as far as they will go—is endemic to Paris. When Parisians come to blows over the newest (or the oldest) movie, the true point of comparison is not the state of current opinion in London or New York. It is the metropolitan civil war that has wracked Paris in one form or another for hundreds of years and is still present as an energizing element in Parisian life. This war may take many different forms, but it has not gone away. And when Parisian rises in wrath against Parisian, the rest of us would do well to stand aside.

In the sixteenth century, as everyone knows, it was religion that set man against man. Catholics gave Protestants a very hard time in Paris, and those not directly involved treated the consequences as street theater, much as the inhabitants of Pamplona in northern Spain treat the annual stampede of young bulls through the streets of the town. When Anne du Bourg, an eminent parliamentarian, spoke up for the Protestants in 1559 he was sentenced to be both hanged and burned in the Place de Grève. A huge crowd—many of them women—gathered to look on, and did so with every appearance of satisfaction.

As for the massacre of Saint Bartholomew's Day, it was the very archetype of the collective savagery that from time to time runs like poison through the veins of a great city. We must imagine to ourselves one of those stifling days toward the end of August when the air of Paris is heavy and still. In the belfry of Saint-Germain-l'Auxerrois, just across the way from the Louvre, the bells give the signal. Other bells, all over town, take up the Catholic message. All over town, killers go to work. It is hot work, on a hot day. By nightfall, thirty thousand Protestants have been done to death. People have been killed in their beds, killed on the staircase, killed in the street. The river Seine runs red.

It settled nothing, of course. But it set a style of savagery that has never been completely laid aside. Paris is for instance a great place for processions. Processions in London or New York are on the whole pacific affairs that owe more to the tradition of the kermesse than to anything else. Who ever felt intimidated when a parade marched down Fifth Avenue? The Lord Mayor's Procession in London is a sedate, untroublesome affair. But in Paris there is often the feeling that—to quote a favorite saying of the painter Georges Rouault, himself born in Paris during a bombardment in 1871—"man is a wolf to man." That feeling is epitomized in a painting by an unnamed artist in the Musée Carnavalet. Dated toward the end of the sixteenth century, it shows the so-called Holy League in procession across the Place de Grève. (The Holy League was a Catholic association, with King Henri III as its patron and leader, that has the distinction of having driven the people of Paris to take to the barricades, in 1588, in a way that was often to be repeated over the next four hundred years.)

Like most bodies of its kind, the League thrived on provocation. Our unknown painter filled in the scene with a Brueghelesque profusion. We see the armed men and the armed children. We see the dukes and the learned doctors, the priests and the casual killers. We also see the everyday life that went on as usual: the patient horse with his empty cart, the boys larking in a corner, the water carrier, the horsemeat butcher, and the peddler of a very thin soup. In the rearground is the cathedral of Notre-Dame, and to the left the northern end of what later became the Ile Saint-Louis but in our painting is just a grassy knoll on which the lavender-sellers put out their linen to dry.

No one would call this a great work of art, but for anyone who wants to know Paris it is a key painting. What it has to tell us is that Paris is a place where things happen on the street, rather than behind closed doors. Social passions are acted out; faction faces faction; Parisian meets with Parisian and beats him over the head. Our painting dates from the 1590s, but the basic situation was the same during the troubled upheavals of 1789, or 1830, or 1848, or 1871. It was the same during the years before 1939, and during the war in Algeria in the 1950s, and during the student revolt in 1968. It will never go out of style.

This is not a political history, and I do not propose to take the reader day by day through all the tumultuous commotions that Paris has undergone. But I must point to one or two recurrent features of the long-running civil war between Parisian and Parisian. The first and most evident characteristic of the Parisian commotion is its vivacity. Parisians are like hand grenades that go off the moment the pin is pulled. Their commitment is total, moreover. I am thinking in particular of an engraving that dates from the popular rising of 1830. There is fighting in the street. In most other cities those who were safely indoors would have shot the bolt and hidden under the sofa. Not so in Paris: young and old alike climb out of the windows and join in with whatever is nearest to hand.

The second recurrent trait of the Parisian upheaval is that the rough work is done by young people. It was the students of the École Polytechnique, in 1830, who stood up to the Garde Royale. In doing so, they fulfilled the immemorial role of young people in Paris, which is to get themselves beaten up or killed for an idea. Walking around central Paris today, we find here and there a wall tablet in memory of someone who was killed by the Germans during the liberation of Paris. Rare is the tablet that commemorates

Opposite: *Act of Courage, 28 July 1830*

During the fighting between the Royal Guard and the revolutionaries, a young student from the Ecole Polytechnique risks his life to retrieve a cannon, and claims it for the people.

Right: *The Besieged*

"The upper floors of a house in the Faubourg Saint-Antoine. Even among the humble, Liberty found noble defenders. 20 July 1830."

Below: The execution of General Thomas and General Lecomte in the Rue des Rosiers in Montmartre, 18 March 1871

Construction of a barricade in Belleville (a quarter of Paris), 1944. Robert Doisneau photograph

anyone aged over twenty-five. There are people who for reasons of their own would like to wish that fact away, but the truth is that Eugène Delacroix, though himself no man of action, was not fantasizing when in his *Liberty Guiding the People* he personified Liberty as a beautiful young Parisienne and her immediate henchman as a boy not yet out of school.

Paris has also at all times had its full quota of scoundrels, young and old. The novels of Balzac are as good a guide as any in that matter. Faced with Balzac's arch-villain Vautrin, we recognize *homo Parisiensis* in majestic, Lucifer-like, and unforgettable form. But we also remember what General de Gaulle said when someone called Jean-Paul Sartre a public nuisance: "He, too, is France." And Vautrin, too, is Paris. Vautrin is Saint Louis in reverse, Pascal in reverse, Bossuet in reverse. He is grandiose in his lack of scruple, in his vast criminal ingenuity. He is the dark angel of Paris, and in the shadow of his broad wing a whole under-population lived.

Guidebooks do not as a rule linger over the prisons of Paris. Visitors are encouraged to visit the Conciergerie on the Ile de la Cité; but the Conciergerie, like the Tower of London and the Peter and Paul Fortress in Leningrad, is presented as a picturesque survival of bad times long past. We shudder to read Turgenev's account of a public execution that occurred in 1870 outside the prison of La Roquette. But we console ourselves with the thought that the prison of La Roquette no longer exists and has been replaced by new apartment buildings and a playground. Gone likewise is the prison of Sainte-Pélagie, which was a house of correction for prostitutes before harboring Madame Roland, Madame du Barry, and Joséphine de Beauharnais during the Revolution of 1789. (It was in Sainte-Pélagie that Gustave Courbet painted at least one of the finest of all French still lifes, when he was imprisoned there for his presumed part in the destruction of the Colonne Vendôme in 1871.) Gone, finally, is the prison of Saint-Lazare, which numbered the poet André Chenier and the painter Hubert Robert among its inmates during the Terror.

All these prisons are remembered primarily for inmates to whom the name of "criminal" would not now be given. But the huge and sinister Prison de la Santé on the Boulevard Arago still speaks for the unreconstructed and often unrepentant malefactor. At any given time, Paris has a large number of people of that sort. Some are in prison, some are just out of it, others will be back in when the police catch up with them. It would be a ridiculous book that did not count them as Parisians. Not only do they carry on a continuous guerrilla warfare against the society of which they are a part, but they are the subject of a huge literature.

The crime novels in question, though not much studied in centers of higher education, have much to teach us about Paris. We should not disdain the poor man's Vautrin. Nor should we forget that in the formative years of the French cinema—the 1930s, that is to say—crime was as often as not the hinge on which the story turned. It would have been difficult to grow up with those movies and not have to this day both a private geography of Right Bank Paris and a specific idea of how Parisian and Parisienne then behaved to one another.

Perhaps it is time to say that throughout history most Parisians have not died a hero's death, nor been to prison, nor indeed done anything in particular except look after themselves and live as well as they could. Parisians are very good at that, and so are Parisiennes. Not that they boast of it: just how well they live is none of our business, in their view. This is not the Garden District in New Orleans, where within living memory any presentable stranger who looked in admiration at a well-kept house would be asked to come inside and look around. When the French government tried to put into force, not so long ago, a tax on "external signs of wealth," they had a terrible job to find any. Only in the 1970s did the tyranny of *le design* spread to Paris and cause people to wonder if they shouldn't do their houses over.

Parisians in general are conservative, where their houses or apartments are concerned. Many of them have lived in the same place forever. No matter how many new shops offer the latest in furniture and design, Paris is still very largely an old-fashioned city in which people live much as they did fifty years ago. A Parisian bathtub may well look much as

The Bathtub. Alfred Stevens, 1867

it looked when Alfred Stevens painted it as the latest novelty in everyday living. An upright piano may be put to use exactly as it is put to use in Giovanni Boldini's painting (or Cézanne's, for that matter, or Matisse's) of mother and daughter, or sister and sister, working their way through a four-hand arrangement. The concept of the free-form salon has never quite gone out in Paris, even if people no longer have visiting cards that tell us on which day in the month they have open house.

Intergenerational friction has always been intense in Paris. Younger people today would rather spend their money on vacations, fast cars, amusing clothes, and a little house in the country than on the kind of somber unchanging interior that was mandatory a hundred years ago. Indoor Paris is in many ways a museum of taste, in which the clocks of decoration stopped quite some time ago and the present owners act, willingly or unwillingly, as custodians. It is as if the modalities of the agreeable life had been fixed once and for all and there was no reason to change them.

And everyday life in Paris can indeed be very agreeable in ways that were indeed laid down at least two hundred years ago. A supremely evocative painting in this context is Martin Drolling's *Interior of a Dining Room*. (Along with its pendant, *Interior of a Kitchen*, it was shown at the Salon of 1817.) The householders in question are neither rich nor poor. The husband is taking a late breakfast. In the far room his wife is practicing on what looks like a fortepiano. The housemaid is making order. The family dog stands in expectation of a little treat.

We see in the room two big ornamental urns, some eighteenth-century engravings, and the kind of chesty little stove that talks very big about getting the smoke out of the house. There is an antique head over the doorway, and the detail of that doorway—as of the paneling, and the dado—is elegant without being pretentious. The tiles in the floor have been lovingly set. The master of the house is clearly not in a hurry as he dips a crust of bread into the coffee that stands waiting in one of those portly, basin-style cups that Frenchmen like to see around at breakfast time. Neither his robe, his trousers, nor his heelless velvet slippers are quite new, but the green of the slippers rhymes nicely with

Music for Four Hands.
Giovanni Boldini,
c. 1890

The Apartment of the Comte de Mornay.
Eugène Delacroix, 1833

the Genoese cut velvet on his armchair. We sense at once that these people lead an orderly, rational, and contented existence. They live in a great city, but they are not oppressed by it. They have some pretty things, but they see no reason to insure them. They live at their own pace, with light and silence as their accomplices.

This painting does, of course, date from 1817—from a time, that is to say, at which the Industrial Revolution had not yet struck. People got on perfectly well in a handmade way without electricity, without gas, and without complication. A beautiful spareness was the measure of everyday life. To have too much of anything would have been a nuisance, whereas later it came to be a distinction. Nor was it a disgrace to do nothing, like the young man in Gavarni's *Far Niente*. Only later did it become a man's duty to produce, consume, and multiply. Gavarni in the 1830s thought it perfectly all right to dream the day away, just as Eugène Delacroix in 1833 did not think it affected or extravagant of the young Comte de Mornay to turn his sitting room in the Faubourg Saint-Germain into a Moorish tent. Mornay had been to Morocco in his capacity as a diplomatist. He had liked it there, and he wanted to prolong the experience. Why shouldn't he?

Interiors like the Comte de Mornay's had about them a perfect naturalness. They were not meant to impress, or to reassure. Housefronts like those built near the church

of Sainte-Clotilde in 1831 have that same easy naturalness. But in Paris, as in London and Berlin and Vienna, that state of affairs was too good to last. Before long, the almost lunatic profusion of the High Victorian style was to make its way under one name or another across every country in Europe.

Interior of a Dining Room. Martin Drolling, 1817

Parisian and Parisienne alike caught the contagion. Balzac, for instance, had always had a very sharp eye for an interior, though his erratic circumstances had usually prevented him from building a satisfactory one of his own. But in 1846 he bought himself a house in the street that now bears his name in the fashionable Beaujon quarter of Paris. This quarter had been built on what had once been the parkland of a banker called Nicolas Beaujon, and Balzac would certainly have noted the speed and assurance with which the construction had been pushed through.

Balzac did not live to enjoy his new house for long. (Nor did he finish paying for it.) But from what Théophile Gautier and others had to say about it we know that Balzac moved with the times in his choice of an interior. His dining room was all in dark oak, with hardly a surface that had not been carved and sculpted. His drawing room, hung with buttercup damask, had doors, cornices, plinths, and embrasures of ebony. His books

Interior of a Kitchen.
Martin Drolling, 1817

were in ponderous bookcases encrusted with bronze and tortoiseshell in the style of Boulle. The door to his library was covered with bookshelves, so that once inside, a stranger might never find his way out. His bathroom was of yellow stone, with bas-reliefs in stucco. There was a domed boudoir, with mural paintings all around, and a top-lit gallery that was to turn up in his novel *Le Cousin Pons*. How different is this weighty, eclectic, pseudo-luxurious installation from the ones that Balzac had put into his earlier novels!

In such matters, as in most others, Balzac missed nothing. When he looked back, it was with an eye that never forgot. He remembered how in 1819 or thereabouts a shopkeeper in the perfume business on the Rue Saint-Honoré would have his shop at street level, his living quarters on the floor above, his servants (of whom he was enormously proud) on the floor above that, and on yet another floor his kitchen, his cook, and his all-purpose apprentice. Higher still was a depository of bottles, porcelain jars, and other accessories. At attic level, the dull work was done. Nor did Balzac forget that in order to have a drawing room that would do credit to himself and his wife, the shopkeeper had taken a floor in the house next door and knocked down the intervening wall.

Balzac also remembered the rococo interiors that were in favor during the Restora-

Interior in the home of Mlle. Sorel of the Comédie-Française,
99, Avenue des Champs-Elysées, 1910. Eugène Atget
photograph

Sarah Bernhardt at home

tion. The walls of the salon were hung with yellow silk, offset by borders of the color favored by the Carmelite order for its nuns' habits. If the housewife (as in Balzac's *Les Employés*) was the daughter of an auctioneer, every folly was permitted to her at minimal cost. She could, for instance, have on the walls of her dining room some Turkish carpets of high quality that she had bought for nothing on a quiet day in the salesroom. And she could frame them in ebony.

We are also indebted to Balzac for an introduction to that perennial Parisian figure, the architect who does some decorating on the side. Grindot was the name that he gave him. Alike in *Illusions Perdues* and in *La Cousine Bette*, Grindot calls the tune. It is he who covered the walls in green linen held in place by nails headed with gold, bought up chandeliers by Thomire and resold them at ten times the price, had a brisk little business in Persian carpets, put a round table ornamented with *pietre dure* in the middle of the sitting room, and fell back when pressed for time on a drawing room all in white and gold, hung with crimson damask. Every generation has its Grindot, and in every generation he has his clients, but it was Balzac who fixed him once and for all.

We should also remember that Balzac was a man who had been haunted by creditors at a time when people were sent to prison for debt. For him and for many another Parisian, a solid interior was not simply a matter of vanity. It was a reassurance, a surety, an ark that would rise above no matter what flood. We must also remember that the very notion of a house that was clean, dry, and sweet was quite new in the Paris of the nineteenth century. Only in 1831, for instance, did it become mandatory that every roof have its gutter. The houses in which most people lived were dirty, damp, dark, and smelled bad. Poverty is relative, as we all know; but no matter how we look at the figures, Paris in the nineteenth century was primarily a city in which more than half of the inhabitants lived very badly.

Imagine, therefore, the effect of changes by which staircases no longer stank, gas cast its gentle glow, the garbage was collected, and it was possible, at a price, not to hear your neighbors through the wall. It cost money, of course, but the improvement somehow beat it into both Parisian and Parisienne that an agreeable interior is worth fighting for. And they have never forgotten it. As so often happens, what began as an almost unimaginable luxury gradually became the norm. Most older apartment houses, for instance, are wasteful of space. Corridors are endless, hallways palatial, ground plans full of serpentine recesses to which no one use can be assigned. Even the common staircase has its niches, and its statues in those niches. Such buildings went up until the late 1930s, and no one wondered at them.

In the largely nineteenth-century city of Paris, people who lived at all comfortably felt themselves part of a society that was expanding both sideways and upward. Whereas survival, in one form or another, had been the basic ambition of earlier Parisians, sights were set on accumulation in the second half of the nineteenth century. People lived behind double doors and quilted partitions. A visitor who stood at the bottom of the broad corkscrew staircase of the newer apartment houses was awed by the moneyed silence, the social uniformity, the discretion. What a change, he thought, from the promiscuous uproar, the convivial tumult, the enforced togetherness of older houses! It was then that the Parisians learned to hide from one another in ways that persist to this day.

Behind those wadded doors there could often be found the kind of apartment, and the kind of life, that Alphonse Daudet described in 1877 in his novel *Le Nabab*. "The apartment might have been in the Palais des Tuileries," he wrote. "The furniture was quite good enough, there was blue satin on every wall, a lot of objects in the Chinese taste, some very good paintings, a lot of little objects that were well worth looking at, in fact a real museum—and one that overflowed onto the landing outside. Excellent service, too: six servants, who wore chestnut livery in the winter and in summer were dressed Nankin-style. . . ." And all that, be it noted, in a second-floor apartment on the Boulevard Haussmann, a broad faceless street that had not even been dreamed of a generation before.

Glimpses of this sort tell us two things about Parisians and Parisiennes. They are quick to get on to the new thing when the new thing offers them a better look, a better life, and a bigger splash. Furthermore, they live as well as they can. Paris has its share of misers and savers, but they are outnumbered by the people who like to shut the door

The Goncourts' Dining Room in the Rue Saint-Georges. Jules de Goncourt, c. 1865

The Departure of the Dragoon. Michel Garnier, 1789

It was for many generations the accepted thing that young Frenchmen of good family leave home and join the army. In this particular parting the young man in question is going off to serve the cause of American independence, three thousand and some miles away.

on the world outside and celebrate their own well-being. If I linger in the second half of the nineteenth century, it is because certain attitudes were perfected at that time.

Since the 1950s, there have been radical changes in Paris. Whole quarters have lost their former petit-bourgeois identity and been pushed up the social scale, the way a chimney sweep was once pushed up a chimney. Prosperity is on the move, that is to say, much as it was in the age of Emile Zola's novels. This is reassuring, insofar as many people now live better than they used to, but it also means that in quarter after quarter a long-nurtured personality has been junked. The sense of neighborhood has gone, never to return. The one-person shop, the solitary craftsman, the frugal, secret, and yet dignified life—all have been lost. Paris was not meant to be a uniform city, but uniformity is being forced upon it in the interests of a standardized well-being.

Looking at the new-model streets and the new-model apartment houses, where every square millimeter is measured and charged for, we remember to what an extent the great Parisian achievements have been the work of people who vanished into the great city like mice in an old cheese. A privileged anonymity was what Paris offered to the poets and novelists, the painters and sculptors and composers whom we most honor. And they in their turn loved the individuality of the Parisian street, the corner café, the ripened oddities of the one-person shop.

Before the great tradition of Parisian individuality is threatened still further, let us take another look at it. The old-style Parisian knew that he was part of an ever-expanding city. (The population of Paris reached its first million in 1846, the year of Balzac's *Le Cousin Pons*. By 1877, the year after Zola published *L'Assommoir*, it was two million.) Zola knew that there were people around who craved what he called "a violent luxury," that there were housewives who wanted to be set up like kept women, and that there were househusbands who wanted to live as in a bank vault, with servants to match. But the old-style Parisian didn't go along with that. He knew that fashions in living come and go, and he treated them as theater: something to be looked at with a lingering amusement.

Edmond de Goncourt, the diarist, novelist, playwright, and critic of art, was a Parisian of that sort. Both in the short lifetime of his brother and coauthor, Jules, and during the years that followed Jules's death in 1870, Edmond de Goncourt was the archetypal Parisian: the man who missed nothing, savored everything, and had his own opinion as to what was worthwhile and what was not. We can read his diaries forever. They are a monument to the individuality of Paris and the Parisians. In them, we see Paris change, block by block. We hear the cleverest Parisians of the time as they talk, talk, talk their evenings away, and we notice that what Edmond de Goncourt most prizes, in the end, is the voyeur's instinct, the sense of tragic idiosyncrasy, and the terrible turn of phrase that were the mark of the elderly Parisian in his time. These were people who had pushed life to its extremest point, sometimes mistakenly, sometimes not, and were ready to tell all about it when the dishes had been cleared away, the last waiter had left the room, and Gustave Flaubert, Ivan Turgenev, and Alphonse Daudet had stayed behind to listen.

The conversations in the Goncourt diaries are archetypally Parisian in that the people concerned were beyond surprise. They knew that Paris was a very peculiar place, and that in matters of money, ambition, intrigue, and sexuality, there was no such thing as the impossible in Paris. And they talked it all out, without a word abated or a fact glossed over. They knew that Parisians and Parisiennes could be monsters even in their moderation, let alone in the excesses that so many had committed and to which so few would willingly confess. Nothing astonished them. After Victor Hugo was buried in 1885, for instance, there was a priapic free-for-all among the bushes and coverts of the Champs-Elysées, in which both men and women threw off their clothes and coupled like goats. Not by so much as a raised eyebrow did anyone in the Goncourt circle treat the news of this as anything unusual.

They were also archetypal old-style Parisians in that in the end, after the last good meal had been eaten and the last good-looking woman laid, what mattered most for them were three things: art, learning, and literature. (None of them was musical.) They were not infallible—who is?—but they cared. Any one of them would have put his hand in the fire for the right phrase, the right patch of color in the right place, or the right connection between this and that historical fact.

The Amateur. Honoré
Daumier, c. 1865

"My favorite daydream," Edmond de Goncourt wrote as a man of seventy-two in 1894, "my castle in Spain, would be to possess a hall, like the main hall of the Gare Saint-Lazare, with bookshelves all round the walls up to chest height, and, above them, glazed cabinets for ornaments and *bibelots*. A gallery running round the whole of the interior, with walls hung with drawings in three rows, would constitute the next floor. Above that would be another gallery, hung with brightly colored eighteenth-century tapestries that would reach as high as the roof. In this hall I should work, sleep, eat, and take exercise (on horseback). The ground floor—artificially heated—would be a winter garden planted with the finest known evergreen shrubs. In the center, their green leaves would frame Carpeaux's *Four Quarters of the Globe,* executed in best-quality white stone."

That is collecting on the scale of epic, if not of mania. But Daumier, for one, shows us the Parisian collector as he was and still is. Intent on the new print, the new drawing, or the new small sculpture, he takes his ease. If friends drop by, they can look over his shoulder if they like, but his collection comes first. For that matter, the Parisienne is also a collector, and a collector of artists as well as of art. Throughout Parisian history there have been houses where artists were made especially welcome, and this too is a tradition that has not died out. Madame Verdurin and her "little clan" are as fundamental to Paris as they are to Proust's great novel. Without them, and without the small friendly commotion that they set up, Sunday by Sunday at lunchtime, the day-to-day life of Paris would be greatly diminished. Rare is the novelist, the painter, or the sculptor who does not enjoy being fêted, just now and then, and rare the fellow guest, likewise, who does not feel more alive for having sat at the same table.

In point of fact, there are a great many Parisians who never open a book, care nothing for painting, and do not know what it is to be transformed by an idea. In the context of art, literature, and pure thought they are so much inert matter. Forever beyond galvanization, they are the deep mud at the bottom of a river that above them flows clear and swift. Yet in a mysterious way these same people give bulk and density to Paris. A great city cannot be all Bossuet, all Voltaire, all Lavoisier, all Littré, all Mallarmé. Not everyone in Paris can be dressed by the great *couturiers,* or eat at the great restaurants, or keep up with what has been done in music by Pierre Boulez, in anthropology by Claude Lévi-Strauss, in literary criticism by Roland Barthes, or in history by Fernand Braudel. They may never read the autobiography of Michel Leiris, hear Sylvain Cambreling give an easy eloquence to Schönberg's opera *Erwartung,* or guess at the amount of care, thought, and dedication that has gone into the presentation of French painting in the Louvre. They may go through life without ever hearing an original thing said or recognizing in a shopwindow the book that is going to change the way we look at the world.

Yet in their relationship to their city they, too, are Parisians. They have the impatience, the driven look, the will to get there first. Even in their pleasures there is often an element of getting as much as possible exactly right. Witness the *tiercé,* a form of playing the horses that is distinctly Parisian. Where in other cities the trick is to find the winner, in the *tiercé* the Parisian falls upon the race in a veritable frenzy of divination and backs himself to find not only the winner but the second- and third-placers as well.

Parisians by nature are not passive. They are doers, provokers, and pouncers. Nowhere does political infighting have a greater vivacity. Nowhere does political scandal move faster or have a more appreciative audience. In criminal matters, Parisians favor a summary judgment, carried out, if possible, in hot blood. The guillotine is a true Parisian invention: where other nations got stuck with the ax, the hangman's rope, and the electric chair, with their latitude for error and their unspeakable side effects, the Parisians perfected in 1790 a noiseless, instantaneous, unfailing alternative.

It is evident *a priori* that all these traits must find their way into everyday life, both private and public. Nowhere are family hatreds more intense than in Paris, nor divorces more savagely contested. In public and private alike, Parisians when provoked to rage are vindictive in the extreme. Parisians have in fact a capacity for tearing one another apart that has been the wonder of many a seasoned observer. To study the Commune of 1871, the Dreyfus Case between 1894 and 1906, or the years of the German occupation of Paris during World War II is to shudder at the Parisians' delight in detestation. Then, truly, was man a wolf to man.

But with that vivacity of response there goes from time to time a beautiful unanimity of feeling. Where elsewhere the public meeting has largely gone out, and people prefer to learn of great issues from a few stumbling sentences on television, Paris can still give the words "a live audience" their true meaning. It is a sacred platitude of social history that the broad straight streets of central Paris were built to make it easy for any popular rising to be put down by Authority; but anyone who has lived in Paris will remember occasions on which the Parisians turned out in the tens of thousands and walked down those same broad streets as if impelled by a collective sense of what was owed to them as free human beings.

Of the Parisienne, much could be said. Some of it, I hope, will be clear by the end of this book. Contrary to legend, the standard of looks among Parisiennes is not high. By the standards of Florence, Parisiennes as a race are not distinguished. By the standards of California, they are badly built and unhealthy in their general appearance. By the standards of Barcelona, they do not move well. There are many well-dressed women in Paris, but the visitor cannot count on seeing them in the streets. (Curiosity about the new

The Prodigal Son Among the Courtesans. Flemish school, 16th century

Prostitutes Passing Through the Porte Saint-Bernard on Their Way to the Salpêtrière. Etienne Jeaurat, 1757

Founded as a hospital for the poor in 1656, the Salpêtrière became, in effect, a prison where undesirables and outcasts were swept out of sight.

64

Gertrude Stein at Pierre
Balmain's. Horst P.
Horst photograph

season's fashions is almost universal in Paris. Even Gertrude Stein, herself no snappy
dresser, was sometimes seen at Pierre Balmain's. But for most women in Paris those
novelties often have a merely notional existence.)

Fundamentally it is with the Parisienne as it is with the Parisian. She is not open to
the foreign visitor. It is difficult for us even to look at her, as we can look at the women
of Rome or Milan. The Parisian *flâneur*—the person who walks through Paris at his ease
and waits to see what it will bring—is masculine in gender. The more rewarding the
Parisienne, the less likely it is that the foreign visitor will even glimpse her. How many
foreign visitors are mentioned in the letters of Madame de Sévigné? Except for the minority
that prides itself on being cosmopolitan, Parisian women are like Parisian men: they find
foreigners more trouble than they are worth. Thomas Jefferson and Benjamin Franklin
were made welcome, but did Ernest Hemingway, or did Scott Fitzgerald, ever get to be
at home in a Parisian house of any distinction? Never. Foreign visitors throughout the
ages have spent their evenings in Paris with one another. (Henry James said the last word
on that just a hundred years ago, when he spoke of "the same rather threadbare circle of
our sweet compatriots, who dine with each other in every possible combination of the
alphabet—though none of their combinations spells the word satisfaction.")

For this reason, the foreign visitor has often a terror of Parisian bad company. A
classic early instance of this is a Flemish painting of the sixteenth century in the Musée
Carnavalet. It suggests that even at the very gates of Paris the foreign visitor was waylaid
by the women of Paris. Wine flowed. Good food was there in abundance. Music did away
with inhibition. The apparatus of venal seduction was complete, with Notre-Dame, the

river Seine, and the still uninhabited Ile Saint-Louis as a backdrop. In this detailed, explicit, and rather brutish painting we see set out a view of the Parisienne that is still current—and not least in Paris itself. The Parisienne who sells her person to one degree or another is part of a perennial alternative society.

There has always been a total down-to-earthness about that alternative society. It is a fact of life in Paris that most men are out to get as many attractive women as they can and that most women who exert that kind of attraction are very well aware of it. Parisians do not see this as something to be covered up, but as an energizing, life-giving force. When the young Louis XV showed no particular interest in women his advisers did not congratulate him on his immunity to temptation. On the contrary: they packed him off to the country with seventeen more than presentable young women and told him to get on with it.

In this matter, both art and literature have much to teach us. Art can tell us not only what the *femmes galantes* of Paris looked like, at one time or another, but what they did. (It will also tell us of the vengeance that Authority wreaks from time to time upon women whose sole crime is to have given pleasure to men at an honest price.) Art is also very good on the salon—the thought-out interior in which men and women meet on an exploratory basis. Nor does it fail us as a dictionary of the women in Paris, though it is naturally strongest on those whom posterity has dragged clear of anonymity. Paris itself—contrary to rumor—has not been especially well served by painters, but the Parisienne has no cause for complaint.

As for literature, the French-language material on the Parisienne is inexhaustible, all

Parisienne. Robert
Doisneau photograph

the way from Brântome in the second half of the sixteenth century to Stendhal, Balzac, Mérimée, Proust, Colette, and their successors. Henri-Pierre Roché's *Jules et Jim* and Raymond Radiguet's *Le Bal du Comte d'Orgel* have a rightness and lightness of touch that are not at all out of date. Nor should we discount the French movie as a source of information. Arletty in *Les Enfants du Paradis* is the very paradigm of the Parisienne.

It would be useless to pretend that English-language writers in general do well with the women of Paris. But there is one great exception. Henry James in *The Ambassadors* shows us to perfection the effect upon an unschooled young American of an accomplished Parisian woman of the world. (The fact that Madame de Vionnet is half-English does not detract from the general rightness of the portrayal.) Nor are the discernment, the wit, the sense of style, the sense of pace, and the unvarying discretion of Madame de Vionnet merely historical qualities. They are still around, and lucky indeed is the young man from a far country who happens upon them.

So there it is: Paris is, and has always been, a very peculiar place. It is shut where we hope to find it open, and open where we fear to find it shut. Parisian and Parisienne resist pinning down, defy generalization, and are a continual source of wonder and surprise. It is through the ear, as much as through the eye, that we must court them. Talkers themselves, they demand talk of others. And what talk they give in return! It is as true today as it was in 1461, when François Villon first formed the phrase, "Il n'est bon bec que de Paris." Nowhere do women talk so well, and nowhere do men have a better time with them.

III

The Louvre

The arcades of the Louvre. Nicolas Sapieha photograph

The Louvre is the largest of Parisian monuments, and the most inscrutable. It is not, as many people suppose, a picture gallery. It is a palace, in part of which pictures happen to be shown. Haphazard in appearance, it has in fact been more pondered over, more planned and replanned and schemed-for than almost any other building in Europe. It has served as a prison, an arsenal, a mint, a granary, a country seat, a publishing house, a Ministry, a menagerie, an Institute for Advanced Studies, a telegraph station, a shopping arcade, an hotel for visiting heads of state, and a fort. Its manipulations went on for five hundred years, and its present stability—it has undergone no important change since 1884—must be accounted a freak of fortune.

The Louvre has been disaffected, during its long and complicated history, from every purpose for which it was intended. The country round it—for so one must describe the great park of the Tuileries, the vanished Jardin de l'Infante, and the confused wharfage that once lay below the Pont-Neuf—has also changed beyond recognition. The result is one of the most elaborate paradoxes in the world of architecture. Of the great planned effects of the sixteenth and seventeenth and eighteenth centuries, almost all have lost the environment for which Lescot and Le Vau and Lemercier designed them. Time and politics have pulled them this way and that until they are hardly decipherable. But it is to these same deleterious factors that we owe one of the most arresting of Parisian sensations—the moment at which the omnibus crashes through the *guichets du Carrousel.* The dark slit in the wall might almost, itself, seem an inspired piece of planning—so deftly does it discharge us into the enormous gravelly bay of the Place du Carrousel.

This bay, enclosed between two long forelands of elaborate masonry, is so imposing as to appear intentional. The little Arc de Triomphe by Percier and Fontaine sets off quite perfectly the larger Arch that glowers from its hillock, two miles away. Even the whirling, semicircular motion of the traffic has something ceremonious about it; and as for the buildings themselves, they have a self-confidence, a sort of assured conservatism, which has worn rather well. They are not in the finest taste; but neither are they paltry. We find them flamboyant and imitative, but recent experience has shown that it is often better to be these things than to be original and sour. Certainly we should not describe the architects who conceived them as "Asiatic confectioners," as some of their contemporaries did. No: the two great headlands, and the far-stretching foreshore of polite parterres, seem to us a happy instance of planning on the grandest scale.

Of course, they were nothing of the sort. The buildings in question date very largely from the time of Napoleon III, and the two great arms were designed as the northern and southern sides of a rectangle closed to the west by the Château des Tuileries. The central part of this château had been in position since 1564, and until it was burned down by the Communards in 1871, the buildings—which now have such an open, expansive air—were turned in upon themselves; engravings of the period show them wearing the enclosed and private look of an interior courtyard.

Maillol statue in the Tuileries. Pierre Jahan photograph

Closing Time at the Louvre. François-Auguste Biard, 1847

But buildings, like people, are often more adaptable than they appear; and these particular buildings—or the older elements among them—have ridden out a lot of odd weather in their time. Grilles and gravel divide them now from the common life of Paris, and their aspect is sober and municipal. But it is barely more than a century since their surroundings were vastly less reputable and the Place du Carrousel had none of its present neutrality. Print shops, a theater, a school of dancing, a carriers' terminus, a house of rendezvous, and a number of miscellaneous hovels came crowding up to the very walls of the Louvre, and there were none of the extended vistas in which we now take pleasure.

Paris at that time was designed for the Parisians, and not for the bemusement of foreign buyers. Ever since the year 1678, when Louis XIV abandoned Paris as a place of residence, the Louvre had gone quietly downhill. The two Empires did much to reinstate it, but no amount of careful appearances will affect the fact that the Louvre is not, and never again will be, the center of Paris as it was in the days of the Valois. The fortress has become a thoroughfare, the palace a museum, and the living, pullulating, conspiring township a municipal carcass in which the decorous proceedings close each evening with the cry of "On ferme!" The visitor's homage is paid not to the building, but to the works of art that it happens to house. Power has moved westward, and the Louvre without its paintings and sculptures would be as dead as the Palais Royal.

The Louvre has, in fact, been robbed of its humanity; and the innumerable excitements of its past are as remote from today as are the treasures of the seabed from the traveler on the channel packet. This is doubtless one reason why the history of the Louvre, when treated in straightforward chronological fashion, taxes both memory and imagination. It may be difficult for a man to "hold a fire in his hand by thinking on the frosty Caucasus"; but worse still is the situation of the visitor who stands at the entrance to the Ministère des Finances and tries to scent the lavender fields laid out by Charles V. Small wonder that many conscientious narratives bog down long before the Louvre as we know it begins to be built, and leave us fumbling in the age of crenellation and crossbow.

The great object in studying the Louvre, on the other hand, is to recover that sense of glory of which Henry James speaks in *A Small Boy and Others*. It was in 1856 or 1857, when James was thirteen or fourteen, that he and his brother William took their walks in the Louvre. What impressed them most was the Galerie d'Apollon, which "seemed to

Left: *View of the Tuileries.* Claude Monet, 1876

Above: *The Louvre and the Tuileries.* Henri Cartier-Bresson, 1978

form, with its supreme coved ceiling and inordinately shining parquet a prodigious tube or tunnel through which I inhaled little by little a general sense of *glory*. The glory meant ever so many things at once, not only beauty and art and supreme design, but history and fame and power, the world in fine raised to the richest and noblest expression."

It is by seeing the Louvre with eyes such as these that we can reinvest it with its old authority as the first building of France and feel for the whole of it as James felt for the Grande Galerie—"that interminable and incomparable Seine-side front of the Palace, against which young sensibility felt itself almost rub, for endearment and consecration, as a cat invokes the friction of a protective piece of furniture."

Of the Louvres that have foundered without a trace, that of Philippe-Auguste will be the least regretted. The great round tower, begun at the end of the twelfth century and for many years the admired model in such matters, would cut a strange figure in the Louvre as we know it—an affair, after all, of unyielding rectangles, from which even Bernini's projected curves were indignantly excluded. Antiquarians treasure the round tower as a survival of the praetorian towers of Roman custom and the precursor of those donjons that impress, upon even the most phlegmatic visitor, an absolute idea of Girth. It was in the thirteenth century, too, that the Louvre—this same squat tower, that is to say—was first known as a treasure house; and from that period we can date the beginnings of the quadrangle, now quadrupled in size, that remains as the Cour du Louvre. Those who may wish from piety to inspect another of Philippe-Auguste's towers have only to go to the 3rd *arrondissement* where, at 57, Rue des Francs-Bourgeois, they will find an imposing fragment of one of the watchtowers erected by Philippe-Auguste before he left for the Crusades. Others may prefer to press on to the reign of Charles V (1364–80), for it is with this delicate monarch that several important traditions of the Louvre may be said to originate.

Himself a tall, pale, indoor man, he was the first to conceive of the Louvre as the daydreamer's paradise. It is, moreover, in the reign of Charles V that the iconography of the Louvre really begins. The spruce little castle with its towers and spires and needling turrets comes up as bright as enamel in the pictures of the time. It was no longer the bastion of Paris, but an ornamental mansion within that bastion. It gleamed, where once it had glowered. Charles V, like several of his successors, had his own ideas about architecture. There was time to gild the *flèches*, and the peasant on the opposite side of the Seine who looked up from his hoe could blink at the whiteness of the stone and the sharp blue of the tiled roofs. It was safe to have windows. There were frescoes of hunting scenes on the inner walls, a good deal of sculpture, and an amount of gold and crystal and alabaster that astonished those privileged to examine it.

The approach by water—now so sadly laid aside—was greatly to the taste of Charles V; it was by this means that, in 1377, he brought the Emperor Charles IV to the Louvre. It was there, too, that he set up the beginnings of the Bibliothèque Nationale. Cypress wood, fatal to insects, was used for the shelves on which reposed the texts of Ovid and Livy, the works of magic and scripture, the bestiaries and astronomies and the Catalan atlas on which he followed the travels of Marco Polo. The first of the Renaissance princes, Charles V practiced a universal curiosity. Hyssop and chess, artillery and the *Policraticus* of John of Salisbury—all interested him equally; and it is thanks to him that the Louvre has been for nearly six hundred years the first storehouse of France.

Not that there have not been deserts of dead time during which the Louvre has gone discreetly to pot. From 1380 to 1527, for instance: with the death of Charles V, the Louvre ceased to be the first preoccupation of the Kings of France and became a sort of national gun room. The fastidious gardens of Charles V declined into farmyards, political prisoners moldered in the tower, and the monarchs themselves preferred Touraine and the Berry to Paris. It was only with François I that the Louvre began to revive. His first action in 1527 was to pull down the big tower. Conservative opinion was greatly distressed by this; but to François I, who had himself been imprisoned in his time, the tower was an obsolete and a disagreeable encumbrance. To us, its demolition marks the beginning of the Louvre as we know it, and the onset of a hundred and fifty years of inspired activity.

The Louvre, which began as a fortress, and has ended as a center of administration, was neither of these things during the age that best embellished it. It was a residence.

There were elements of display for display's sake, and there was always a residuary garrison; but in principle the enormous building was built to be lived in. There was no committee work about the great age of the Louvre; individual taste sufficed, and in the case of François I, "individual" was the only proper word.

For his main alterations he called not on Sebastiano Serlio, who had already worked for him and might well have expected the commission, nor on the brothers Le Breton, who had worked for him at Fontainebleau and Villers-Cotteret, but on Pierre Lescot, a Frenchman, a friend of Ronsard, and a gifted painter as well as a practicing architect. Lescot was in charge of the Louvre from 1546 to 1578, and he brought with him Trebatti, a Florentine sculptor who had worked with Michelangelo, and Jean Goujon, the "French Pheidias," whose wraithlike figures add a last sovereign distinction to the top story of Lescot's Louvre.

Distinction was the mark of all that Lescot did, and in the last four hundred years the rest of the palace has fallen more or less into step with him. It stands for a coarser cosmopolitanism than Lescot would himself have admired, but it has something of the princely carriage and harmonious grandeur that he introduced. (Visconti, indeed, made it a point of honor to retain—as he thought—Lescot's general style.) When Lescot took over, on the other hand, he had to build side by side with the rude constructions of the Gothic era.

We ourselves, who are used to seeing Lescot's contribution as the southwestern section of the Cour du Louvre (immediately to the left when we walk in through the Pavillon des Arts), must remember that originally it formed not a sixth of the quadrangle, as it does now, but a good half. What is now weathered and discreet, a sympathetic survival in a vast courtyard of later design, was then a novelty, visible only at close quarters, and almost grotesquely out of accord with its surroundings.

There is nothing demonstrative about Lescot's designs. He was thirty-six at the time he was commissioned by the King, and he was not, by any reckoning, the first architect of France. He had nothing in particular to show for himself—except perhaps the *jubé* at Saint-Germain-l'Auxerrois, the beginnings of what is now the Hôtel Carnavalet, the allegiance of Jean Goujon, and—what may have been decisive—the patronage of Jacques de Ligneris, for whom François I had a particular respect.

A monarch who had employed Domenico di Cortona at the Hôtel de Ville, Philibert de l'Orme at Villers-Cotteret, Serlio at Fontainebleau, and Pierre Chambiges at Saint-Germain-en-Laye was no novice in architectural matters; nor was the patron of Titian, Cellini, Leonardo, and Primaticcio a beginner in the fine arts. The combination of Lescot and Goujon may nonetheless be considered his greatest triumph in patronage. It is one thing to hire an acknowledged master, and quite another to single out the man who will later assume that master's position. It was François I who set the tone for the Louvre, and that tone was followed, though with many concessions to enfeebled temporary taste, for the next three hundred years.

It was not, however, under François I, but under his successor Henri II that Lescot's Louvre really got under way. Its progress was always erratic; rooms were commissioned, completed, and then at once countermanded; there was no one consecutive intention behind the builders' activities, but rather a series of whims and spurts and fantasies, with which Lescot fell in as best he could. He himself died in 1578, after having survived into his fourth reign as architect of the Louvre. He had seen it change from a serviceable fortress into something very different. The evolution of the Louvre is, in fact, an allegory of the evolution of that elusive concept: *l'esprit français*.

Allusive, harmonious, and unemphatic, the reliefs and caryatids of Jean Goujon display the French genius for adaptation at its best and most luminous. The Louvre borrows continuously from Italy and Greece, but its borrowings are ground fine and small by the application of a sovereign intelligence. The Italian influences were not merely "in the air"—Renaissance particles blown northward from the golden Loire—they had as their champion the Italian princess, Catherine de Medici, who was the wife of Henri II, the mother of three kings who succeeded him, and the originator of the Petite Galerie and the Château des Tuileries. She and people like her—fastidious individuals who knew just what they wanted—were to count for much in the re-creation of the Louvre. Diane de

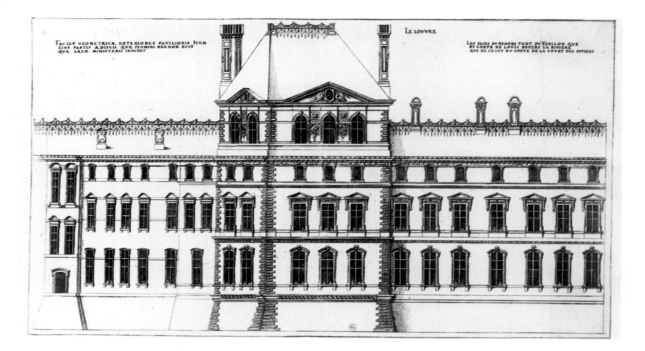

FACIES GEOMETRICA EXTERIORES PAVILIONIS ITEM EIVS PARTIS ADITVS QVA FLVMINI NECNON EIVS QVA AREA MINISTERIIS IMMINET

LE LOVVRE

LES FACES DV DEHORS TANT DV PAVILON QVE DV CORPS DE LOGIS DEVERS LA RIVIERE QVE DE CELVY DV COSTE DE LA COVRT DES OFFICES

Poitiers, the owner of Anet, Anne de Montmorency, for whom Jean Bullant built Ecouen, and his son-in-law the Duc d'Aumale—these were dandies of the architrave and the *beaux esprits* of the *avant-corps*.

But although the connoisseurship of those years was enlightened and competitive, it was also impulsive and haphazard. There remained, moreover, the obstinate relics of a more primitive age. The turrets of the primordial Louvre sealed off the building to the east, so that any expansion could only be to the west. Expansion of some sort became indispensable toward the end of the sixteenth century, and it was the Queen Mother, Catherine de Medici, who gave the signal, in 1564, for the building of the Château des Tuileries, and in 1566 for the building of the Petite Galerie, in which the Galerie d'Apollon was later inserted. These two novelties are associated with the names respectively of Philibert de l'Orme and Pierre Chambiges—though it is probable that Chambiges worked under Lescot's direction.

Nothing now remains of the Tuileries, and the Petite Galerie was gutted by fire in 1660, but in general the Queen Mother's initiative may be said to have fixed the dimensions of the Louvre as we know it, and also to have defined the problem later architects would be required to solve—that of bringing the Louvre and the Tuileries into some sort of organic relationship. It is from the 1560s that we must date not only the necessity of the Grande Galerie along the Seine but also the opportunity for the innumerable possible-Louvres that have been preserved for us in architectural engravings.

The perfect Louvre is a metaphysical concept which has tormented the mind of many a great inventor. From Bernini downward, architects have struggled to reconcile the demands of the two asymmetrical lodgings and the enormous space that lay between them. And their task was the more arduous in that they were not dealing with the level, open terrain that we know, but with a congested metropolitan area—a hardly decipherable jumble, in fact, of churches and fortifications and bowling greens and medieval alleys. Even the meticulous Plan Turgot—where every building looks in perfect repair, every bush has a flawless mathematical relation to its neighbor, and never a human being disturbs the scene—even the Plan Turgot cannot hide the fact that in the 1760s the Grande Galerie was as out of place as a furled umbrella in a farmyard.

Lescot may have set the tone for the Louvre, but the Louvre did not at all set the tone for Paris. Nor did life within the Louvre always correspond to the delicate allegories of Goujon. (Goujon himself had to go into exile, as a Protestant, in 1562.) Mars and Bellona figured side by side with Euclid and Archimedes on the second floor of Lescot's façade; centaurs and sea horses were carved on the doors of the *chambres de parade;* heavy,

Design by Pierre Lescot for the south façade of the Louvre, c. 1546

The Louvre, from the *Plan Turgot,* 1738

detachable ceilings were encrusted with wreaths of golden laurel; and windows were remorselessly heraldic.

Manners had not kept pace with these refinements. It would be unfair to take the massacre of Saint Bartholomew's Day as typical of life in the Louvre under the Valois, but no visitor should cross the Cour du Louvre without remembering that it was there, where now a harmless white hoop has been chalked on the stones, that Protestant members of the court were driven, on 24 August 1572, and shot down with crossbow and harquebus. Those who escaped into the Louvre itself were cut down in such a way that the walls were purple with blood, one chronicler tells us, and the stairs ran red till nightfall. It was at this same sanguinary time that lions and bears were housed in the Louvre, and men and dogs were made to fight them in the Cour, while the Académie des Valois debated above as to the respective merits of the active and the contemplative life. It was then, too, that Henri III's catamites used to whip themselves to the point of unconsciousness in frenzies of penitence. Even that most polite of rooms, the Salle des Cariatides, had its darker hour—in December 1591, when four men were hung from its beams.

The period of the Valois was, in fact, one of transition, in which the progress of the Louvre was continually arrested. With the arrival of that most inspiriting of monarchs, Henri IV, things became altogether more brisk. Few characters in history are more appealing than Henri IV. He personified that spontaneity that in French is called *le naturel.* Even in the Louvre he retained many of the habits of the serving soldier. He was plainly, not to say badly, dressed; often his clothes were neither new nor clean. Memorialists make great play with his big sponge and ivory comb, but it would seem that in spite of these classic aids to hygiene he invariably smelled strongly and disagreeably; ambergris, musk, and essence of violets were powerless to combat this.

In personal relations he was direct, lively, quick-witted, easy, and humane. He was small of stature, and prematurely gray, but he had a ruddy complexion, a fine commanding nose, and a truly royal beard and chin. He ate and drank in great quantities, but had the campaigner's gift of doing so, or indeed of going without, whenever he felt so disposed. His spirits were normally high—so high, in fact, that he was often to be found dancing and singing to himself in his study. Indifferent to protocol, he had been known to adjust his own throne in the middle of an audience, and to receive his ministers while lying in bed with his queen. And yet, with all this, he had an absolute authority; his mind was rapid, sure, analytical; and his speeches and letters prove him a master of invective. There were moments at which he no longer cared to hide the settled melancholy that underlay his effervescence; but in general it was his ebullience that conquered in the end—and never more easily than when he gave himself over, as he very often did, to some ephemeral gallantry.

The reign of this delightful personage was remarkable for the efficiency and dispatch with which he set about the remodeling of Paris. Had he not been killed in 1610, the evolution of the capital might have been all that the most enlightened urbanist could wish. Even as it was, the results of his sixteen years' residence there were enough to show that, of all those who have ruled Paris, it was Henri IV who best loved and best understood the city. His passion for Paris showed itself in small things, as much as in great. He loved, for instance, to douse the Dauphin in the Seine; and when the Pont-Neuf was still not nearly complete, he insisted on jumping from pier to pier till he had traversed its whole length. (When warned that several of his citizens had been drowned while attempting this, he pressed on, saying only, "Ah, yes, but they weren't kings.") In his handling of Paris he was assisted by two great men: Sully, his *Grand Voyer*, and that supreme administrator, François Miron. Between them, the King and his assistants transformed not only the Louvre but the whole of Paris.

Their first achievement was the Pont-Neuf. This was more than a bridge: it was a promenade, and the citizen who lingered to watch the hawkers, dentists, and buffoons who swarmed upon it could see, by raising his eyes, that the old jumbled waterfront was giving place to something noble and new. And if he looked the other way, he saw the Place Dauphine—that pink-and-gray triangle of which the last valiant fragment would have been destroyed by Haussmann, had he remained in office a year or two longer. The triangular form was one of three geometrical shapes with which Henri IV intended to

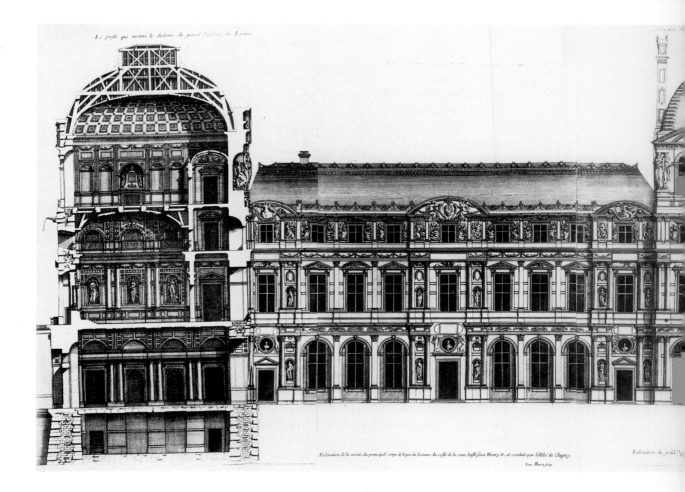

Explication de la moitié du principal corps de logis du Louvre du costé de la cour, basti sous Henry II. et conduit par l'Abbé de Clagny.

Jan Marot, fecit.

endow his capital. The second, the square, is still intact—in the Place des Vosges—but the third, the semicircle, which was to have been typified by the grandiose Place de France, was unluckily never begun.

These great schemes were not devised for geometry's sake; nor were they clamped on to the existing structure of the city without any concern as to whether or not they were suitable. Such blunders were left to the nineteenth century. The completion of the Hôtel de Ville (part of which was paid for by François Miron with his own money), the opening of the Savonnerie carpet factory, and the building of the Hôpital Saint-Louis in the 10th *arrondissement* are three characteristic achievements of this brief but munificent reign. The Hôpital, in fact, with its seignorial air, flowered courtyards, and espaliered trees, is typical of the King's intellectual magnanimity.

In the same way, the completed Grande Galerie was insinuated into the working life of Paris. Initially conceived as a permanent umbrella for use when walking from the Louvre to the Tuileries, it was occupied, under Henri IV, by the Mint, by a tapestry factory, and by a privileged company of painters, sculptors, goldsmiths, and clockmakers. It remained, nonetheless, royal ground. The Dauphin was especially fond of it, and could sometimes be seen exercising his pet camel along the whole of its immoderate length. The Louvre as a whole was particularly gay during the reign of Henri IV; for the King believed in continual festivity as a point of high policy. The only way to keep courtiers in their place, François I had once said, was to have them thoroughly amused at least twice in each week. And it is against a background of this sort that we should try to see the Louvre. Today's listless throng, with its heavy incidence of "museum foot," is not the public for which these buildings were intended. Nor do our seersucker suits and summer *imprimés* deputize for the blue and scarlet livery of the Bourbons.

The Louvre is, in fact, one of the rare cases in Paris in which historical reconstruction can alone give the true flavor of a place. The deserted Palais Royal has a twentieth-century poetry of its own; the Marais for centuries had a natural turbulence; but the Louvre has neither the special charm of the one nor the life-accepting tenacity of the other. As a building, it is sealed off from life. Nor is it one of those galleries, like the Mauritshuis at The Hague, that has a natural relation to the works of art inside it and can hardly be imagined apart from them. Its relations to the *Noces de Cana* and the *Winged Victory of*

Design for the southwest façade of the Cour Carrée of the Louvre. To the left is Pierre Lescot's original building of 1546. The central pavilion and the building on the right by Jacques Lemercier were added in 1625.

Samothrace are those of equal with equal. Neither is defeated; but nor is there that profound if illogical harmony that unites, for instance, the Mantegna cartoons with the palace at Hampton Court. No, there is nothing to be done with the interior of the public Louvre as it stands. Its life is the life of the works of art within it.

There is therefore no betrayal of the present in seeking to recapture the entertainments of three hundred and fifty years ago. The most splendid of these were, beyond question, the ballets. These ballets had little in common with those upon which our generation has been nurtured. They were not, indeed, ballets at all, in the sense that *Swan Lake* and *Petrouchka* are ballets. The music was unimportant, the scenario inane, and the performers not professional dancers but distinguished amateurs—headed, it might be, by the King himself. Henri IV was not as great a balletomane as Louis XIII, who went so far as to compose the music for one of those entertainments, but he put up with them, and we possess an eyewitness account, dated 1605, of one of the most lavish of recorded divertissements.

It began at midnight. The room on the first floor of the Louvre was crowded beyond endurance when the King walked in and began to exercise the prerogative, so often coveted by less privileged persons, of rearranging the seating. When this was done to his liking he gave the signal for the ballet to begin. Here again the word "ballet" would seem to us inappropriate alike to the spectacle and to the pleasure that it gave. We value the ballet as an elaborated form of the marvelous: the feats performed in it bear no relation to those of ordinary life, and even in the performers themselves we prize a certain strenuous remoteness.

Quite other was the ballet of 1605: it contained nothing that could not have been done by nearly everyone present, and the delights that it offered were those, first, of conspicuous expenditure, and second, of seeing one's friends dressed up in an arresting but not necessarily advantageous way. The thirty violinists in red silk, the silver-clad lutenists, and the famous Italian soprano may quite possibly have set up a most hideous row; the trumpets and drums played far too loudly, we are told, and we are probably lucky to have been spared their ferocious marches. What remained, then? Simply the pleasure of seeing the familiar faces of the court, from the Queen down to her monkey and the least of her dwarfs, in situations that heightened and diversified their personalities.

In the courtyard itself, other and more cumbrous spectacles were mounted; for these, also, midnight gave the signal, and torch and lantern light the inspiriting blaze. Here, too, there exists a witness to conjure for our bemusement the enormous tableaux representing Fire, Air, Earth, and Water, the impersonation of Neptune and Vulcan, the monkeys and the elephants, the wheeling horsemen, the drums and fifes, and the moment at which the whole cumbrous pageant was sent rumbling round the courtyard at a trot.

Henri IV loved a grand design in all things. (He even had his state papers filed in drawers lined with crimson satin.) He liked to think far ahead, whether in international politics or in the improvement and enlargement of the palace to which he brought such luster. Had he not been murdered in 1610, great plans would have been set in motion for the Louvre. As it was, his nine-year-old son came to the throne as Louis XIII. Meanwhile, the courtyard of the Louvre was hung with black velvet, and in the Salle des Cariatides Henri IV lay in effigy for eleven days. As if to defer his final departure from the Louvre for as long as possible, the wax Henri IV was served exactly as if he had been the Henri IV of flesh and blood. His meals came up on time; each dish was presented to him with due ceremony, though in silence; the life of the room went on as usual, except that those who would normally have been gossiping in the shadows were on their knees. When the boy-king came to pay his respects, five princes of the blood carried his train.

Louis XIII made himself quite at home in the Louvre. (For that matter, he had little choice, since his mother decided that he should spend forty-nine weeks of every year there.) He bore patiently with his formal studies, but what he really liked was to race up and down the Grande Galerie in a little carriage drawn by two mastiffs, or to amuse himself with the screech owl, the falcon, the lark, the hare, and the very small wild boar which made up his private menagerie.

When Louis XIII grew up, the Louvre took on a different cast. There were still the ballets; ambassadors were received with an identical pomp; and from the first-floor windows one could still hear, every so often, the music of those dances—the galliard, the branle, the canari, and the coranto—to which Stravinsky, in his *Agon*, gave new meaning and a sharpened point. The ballets were even longer, as a matter of fact, and the crowd even thicker. Four thousand invitations was the usual number, and the festivities began at eight in the evening and went on for twelve hours. The press was so great that on one occasion the King himself could not reach the scene of the ballets till half-past two in the morning. The chaos was vast, unchecked, convivial. People dared not sit down, for fear of being crushed to death; many contrived, while standing, to become most wantonly familiar with their neighbors.

There was, however, a more sober side to life in the Louvre under Louis XIII. The Grande Galerie, for instance, which now seems unsuited to any activity except roller skating and skittles, was regularly turned into an immense lazar-house; for Louis XIII, unlike his father and his son, made a point of observing the *cérémonie des écrouelles*. On such occasions the Grande Galerie was filled with a throng of scrofulous subjects; attested victims of the "king's evil," they knelt while the King and his advisers walked slowly along their ranks. The King paused before each of them, drew the sign of the cross on his face, and said, "Whom the King touches, God will cure!" This was, in fact, an early form of heliotherapy, since the King was believed to have the healing powers of the sun. The arrival and departure of these sad creatures must have accorded a final grimness to the main entrance of the Louvre, which at that time was narrow, dark, dirty, and encumbered.

Good works were not the only contribution of Louis XIII to the traditions of the Louvre. He had none of the easy mastery of human relations that distinguished his father, and his preferred companions were of quite a different stamp. The simplest of men, he was often known to lend a hand with the making of his bed; shy and unsupple in his handling of others, he had none of his father's telling informality; slow to make up his mind (he liked, when in council, to hear each subject debated to its farthest limits), he was the opposite of his father in all save his simplicity. His idea of hunting, for instance, was characteristic: where others made for open country, Louis XIII would mount one of the surviving gatehouses of Charles V's enceinte, and from this point of vantage he would loose off with harquebus at swallow and martlet. He was, nonetheless, a great bird man; the room that divided his apartments from the Galerie d'Apollon was equipped as an

aviary, and so devoted was he to its inhabitants that he would leave his bed in the middle of the night and go off to fondle them in their sleep.

The Louvre resounded not only to the delicate cries of these favorites, but also to homelier sounds such as are rare in royal apartments. Louis XIII had a passion for fine workmanship, and in his moments of leisure he was revealed as a fastidious craftsman: forge, gun room, printing press, and carpenter's shop—all knew his melancholy tread, and in each it was he himself who planed and sawed, set up the type, assembled and dismantled, blew the glass, and kept the barrels true. He was also a painter, a sculptor, and a pioneer cartographer. To all these activities, the ever-serviceable Louvre provided a grandiose and accommodating background, and it is of Louis XIII's pigeons and diminutive forge that we should think when stranded in the immensities of the Louvre of Napoleon III.

Perhaps, too, we might remember the most momentous of all the domestic events in the history of the Louvre—the evening, that is to say, of 5 December 1637, on which Louis XIII was constrained by a violent fall of rain to ask a night's lodging of his queen, Anne of Austria, who was then resident in the Louvre. (He himself was normally at Versailles.) This provoked a display of tenderness between the unloving pair; and nine months later to the day, on 5 September 1638, the Dauphin of France, the future Louis XIV, came into the world.

It was fortunate that Louis XIII cared so deeply about the Louvre, for the exuberant fancies of Marie de Medici had found outlet elsewhere—in the grandeurs of the Palais du Luxembourg, with its twenty-one canvases by Rubens and its Boboliesque parterres, and in that great novelty, the shady Cours-La-Reine. The Louvre itself got its due share of attention shortly after Richelieu's accession to power. It was in January 1624, in fact, that Louis XIII announced his intention of quadrupling the existing Cour, according to the plans laid under Henri II. His own tastes were not monumental, and are reflected rather in the intimacies of the Cour de Marbre at Versailles. Nor is it likely that Jacques Lemercier, who finally took charge of the new constructions, was himself a favorite of Louis XIII, since his nature is said to have been slow, heavy, and entirely practical. The improvements were a matter of policy rather than of passion, and it was barely two years before they were halted by a shortage of funds.

View of the Hôtel de Nevers and the Château du Louvre in 1637. Abraham de Verwer, 1637

Lemercier meanwhile had proceeded in an essentially conservative and amenable style. The surviving Tour de la Librairie and the famous spiral staircase, both dating from Charles V, had been pulled down, and the west front of the Cour was to comprise a central massif, the Pavillon de l'Horloge, and a northern section equivalent to that built by Lescot. There was no great departure of style, and the central pavilion had just that additional weight which would preserve the harmony of the whole. This pavilion is, of course, important to us because its lofty, flattened dome created the official "Louvre style" that was followed, in large degree, by the architects of the nineteenth century. It accounts, in fact, for the tone of bourgeois compromise that makes it discouraging to examine the later Louvre in close detail. In general, however, Lemercier worked with exemplary tact, and it was not his fault that the work was done in spurts, the great beams were brought to no purpose from the Forêt de Courcy, the courtyard itself sank into an encumbered bog, and even the foundations were liable to come up short against the walls of an hotel that nobody had remembered to appropriate.

In 1638 a more vigorous policy was initiated by the new Surintendant des Bâtiments, Sublet des Noyers. Noyers is one of the gallant failures of Parisian history. His term of office lasted only five years, and at the end of it he was summarily disgraced by Mazarin, but during that time he all but secured something that would have dignified the Louvre beyond measure—a series of ceiling-paintings by Nicolas Poussin for the Grande Galerie. Initially everything seemed to favor this project. Poussin was delighted to be called back from Rome and be received, almost, on bended knee. The King could think of nothing better than to have Poussin transform the look of the Grande Galerie. ("That's one in the eye for Vouet!" he said, perhaps thinking that Simon Vouet—his Court Painter since 1627—had had things his own way too long.)

But there were difficulties. Poussin was altogether too open about the contempt that he felt for his colleagues, and they lost no time in intriguing against him. In the end, Poussin went back to Italy with little to show for his stay but a handful of cartoons and the frontispieces to the noble editions of Horace, Virgil, and the Bible that were designed and printed in the Louvre at that time. Poussin's Hercules never got off the drawing board; the projected series by Van Dyck never got even as far. Except, in fact, for Sarrazin's caryatids of the Pavillon de l'Horloge, the reign of Louis XIII has little to show in the way of decoration; it was not till 1806 that Goujon's reliefs were balanced, on Lemercier's half of the western side of the great courtyard, by the ambitious if turgid creations of Moitte, Rolland, and Chaudet.

With the reign of Louis XIV the history of the Louvre reaches its full complication. Patronage was no longer spasmodic, provincial, and underfinanced. It was on the scale of an expanding society, and a great many eminent people were invited to take part in this particular aspect of French expansion. In the event, the architects responsible for the Louvre of Louis XIV were not the great international names, Mansart and Bernini, but Claude Perrault, who was originally not an architect at all, and Louis Le Vau, the builder of Vaux-le-Vicomte, the Hôtel Lambert, the church of Saint-Louis-en-l'Ile, and the Institut de France.

During the King's minority, the works undertaken were all of a minor, decorative character. Both Mazarin and the Queen Mother had a passion for elaborate and gilded interiors, and in the Louvre the Salle des Saisons and the Salle des Antonins, with their stuccowork by Michel Anguier and their ceilings painted by Romanelli, are prize examples of this opulent style. They were not, however, details in a vast overhaul. They were essential renovations, undertaken for illustrious lodgers in search of a comfortable billet. Anne of Austria, the Queen Mother, had been put up in very decent style in the newly built Palais Royal; her bathroom, for instance, had been decorated especially for her by Simon Vouet and Philippe de Champaigne. Nothing less could be provided if she were to forsake this most civilized and up-to-date of palaces for the grumpy old Louvre.

Few rooms in the Louvre can show even a vestige of their original decoration. It is even unsafe to assume that an unmistakable Renaissance ceiling is the mark of a room that has not been changed since the time of the Valois: ceilings can be moved like everything else, and some of those in the Louvre were built in removable sections. If the Galerie d'Apollon and some of the grand rooms in the section built by Le Vau remain broadly

Ceiling design for the Galerie d'Apollon. Jean Berain, c. 1670

intact, innumerable finesses of detail have vanished forever. Anne of Austria's bathroom, for instance: contemporary observers discerned in it an element of luxurious abandon which even the *Venus de Milo* (now housed in it) has proved unable to restore.

"The bath-room," we read in Sauval's *Antiquités de la Ville de Paris,* "was built under the direction of Jacques Lemercier. Gold had been used, at Fontainebleau and in certain private houses, but it had been used almost with contempt. Here it was employed in profusion; the panelling was ornamented with baskets of fruits and reliefs, all heightened with gold, and enamel, and paint, in such a way that both the eye and the hand of the observer were deceived. The bath is surrounded by six columns of black and white marble: the bases and capitals of these are of gilded bronze. . . . As for the marble itself, nothing could be more varied than its blacks and its whites: delicately shaded here, veined and speckled there, it includes pieces of unbroken black or white so enormous that they seem to have been stuck on independently. The ceiling was embellished with octagonal paintings by Eustache Lesueur, who also designed the five *camaïeux* inset in the panelling: these represented the virtues most associated with the Queen—Simplicity, that is to say, Fidelity, Magnanimity, Strength, and Justice. Further flatteries were to be found on the doors, where the famous women of Antiquity jostled for precedence. The Queen loved portraits; and from her bath, a block of solid white marble, she could gaze upon a series of effigies of the Spanish royal family; her contemporaries took these to be by Velázquez. Visitors were stunned by this bathroom; the royal iconomane was thought to have vindicated her country, her rank, and her sex; and the only people not pleased were the carpenters, whose bills were left unpaid for forty years."

These improvements did not affect the general unsuitability of the Louvre as the home of an enormous court. This court was continually growing larger, and its members were more exacting than the boyars of two centuries before. Most of the essential services were not housed in the Louvre at all. Even the kitchens were on the far side of the moat. There was nothing for it: the Louvre would have to be enlarged—but how, and in what style? And who would pay for it? These problems were not easy to settle. Grand designs of one sort and another had been in the air for a century. Lemercier had prepared one; but Lemercier had died. Sublet de Noyers had longed to perpetuate his name by some massive enterprise; but Sublet de Noyers had been disgraced. Mazarin was the heaver and insinuator of the renewed project; but even Mazarin found it difficult to further his plans. There was never enough money: houses had to be expropriated, materials bought, architects kept sweet with big salaries—and all this in wartime.

Mazarin shrank from no economy that might advance the project. He even went so far as to abolish the ballet, and hoped by this to save 300,000 livres a year. There were also many minor exasperations—such as that the Queen Mother had allowed Madame de Beauvais (Squinting Kate, as she was called in the Louvre) to plunder certain building materials from the courtyard of the Louvre and use them for the embellishment of her own house. Madame de Beauvais was an important person in the Queen's life, since it was she who gave the Queen certain necessary injections at crucial times; she had also been privileged to relieve Louis XIV, in his seventeenth year, of the burden of virginity. Altogether, Anne of Austria thought that she deserved her old stones, and no more was heard of the Cardinal's threat to dismantle the Hôtel de Beauvais and restore them to their place on the heap.

In June 1659 the preliminaries of peace were signed, and the work at once began. The east wing of the old Louvre was pulled down, carpenters and stonecutters were hired in readiness, workshops were constructed, and Le Vau settled in to continue, as far as possible, in the tradition of Lescot and Lemercier. Certain medieval elements remained—the reeking moat, for instance, with its compost of human droppings—but in the southerly, Seine-side wing (now marked by Perrault's façade) there was seen for the first time that great instrument of classical architecture: the Corinthian column. For here Le Vau felt liberated from Lescot: there was no earlier, adjoining façade with which to keep in step, and the novelty did no violence to the Petite Galerie. The topmost part of this southern wing was in perfect accord with its neighbors, though the central dome was full of conceits and boasted at least one feature—the *parallelipipède*—that was easier to admire than to pronounce.

Design for the riverside entrance of the Louvre. Louis Le Vau, 1659–64

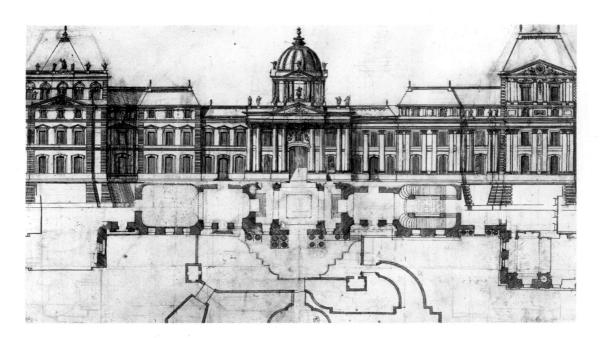

Le Vau was moving steadily ahead with his plans when, in January 1664, Colbert became Surintendant des Bâtiments—a post he held until his death in 1683. By 1664, Le Vau had continued the north wing of the quadrangle, completed the south wing, and had taken advantage of the fire of 1661 to remodel and enlarge the Petite Galerie. It is to this remodeling that we owe the Galerie d'Apollon. Le Vau also designed a large room that was, in effect, the first exhibition room of the Louvre: here it was that Charles Le Brun and Philippe de Champaigne lectured on Raphael and Titian to the assembled Académie.

At the time of Le Vau's disgrace, his plans for the eastern wing of the quadrangle were already in hand. The walls of the façade facing Saint-Germain-l'Auxerrois were nine feet high when Colbert took over and decided that Le Vau's design was not satisfactory. It had become traditional to ascribe this decision to personal animosity, but in recent years Fiske Kimball won support for his view that "a more fundamental cause, felt rather than analysed, lay in Le Vau's pronounced baroque trend. This was the deeper reason why Colbert subjected Le Vau to the humiliation of inviting designs from other architects."

Perhaps, too, Le Vau was not much of a courtier. Certainly he had not the "magical facility and promptitude of execution" that Kimball regarded as the great advantages of Charles Le Brun. Colbert treated him, in any case, in a way that cannot but have deeply offended the *Premier Architecte*. Not only were his plans put on view but his fellow architects were invited to criticize them and to submit alternative schemes. Some of them did not wait for this invitation, but had already submitted proposals of their own. Almost all of these displayed the recklessness common among those whose fantasies have never been put to the test of construction. Léonor Houdin, for instance, supplied a sort of *capriccio* which, if built, would have been about two miles in length, with a gigantic circus at each end. And as for the others, they came, and they prodded the wooden scale model of Le Vau's design, and most of them found fault with it and produced something or other of their own.

The grandest of them, François Mansart, produced no fewer than fifteen separate designs. The idea of an estimate of costs, however, was repugnant to him. It gave him, it was said, a terrible twinge. Nor could he decide upon any particular one of his fifteen designs. He preferred an open mandate, with liberty to discard all previous fancies in favor of another, a magical sixteenth, of which the elements could not as yet be consigned to the drawing board. It was at this point that the precise and actuarial mind of Colbert would seem to have snapped. Mansart, he thought, was taking too much upon himself. His dome-ridden designs, with their sculptural *décrochements* and their powerful lights and shades, their advances and their withdrawals, were consummately adapted to the site, the existing wings, and the fashion of a few years before. They displayed, if anything, an excess of accomplishment. Colbert's tastes lay elsewhere.

The other, lesser French architects were no more successful. Each was more frantic

Project for the east wing of the Cour Carrée of the Louvre. François Mansart, c. 1664

Project for the east wing of the Cour Carrée of the Louvre. Gian Lorenzo Bernini, c. 1664

than the other: their pyramidal chapels, histrionic statuary, and general demonstrativeness presented a rare blend of the unpractical and the effete. It was in these circumstances that Colbert fled from one fiasco in order to foment another, and issued an invitation to Bernini, Rainaldi, Candiani, and Pietro da Cortona. At one time this invitation was regarded as the high-water mark of Italian prestige in France, but we now recognize it as the dying thrust of a fashion which, inaugurated by François I, had given way slowly and progressively to the pure professionalism of France's native architects. In the end it was the mason, the practicing builder, who triumphed over the painters and sculptors who embraced architecture mainly as a department of fine arts. The visit of Bernini may be said, in fact, to mark rather the collapse of Italian influence than its apotheosis.

It was a collapse upon the grandest scale. Bernini was too great a swell to go quietly. He had been received with the honors normally accorded only to an Ambassador Extraordinary or a Prince of the blood. Turenne, Corneille, and Condé—a great soldier, a great playwright, and a great power in the land—had come as humble sightseers to his lodging. He had not even deigned to see Colbert to the door. And as for his French colleagues, he openly considered them "whoreson zeds and unnecessary letters." He despised everything that he was shown. He was disagreeable, grudging, self-infatuated, and mean. He even joked about the shape of Louis XIV's nose. Nothing was good enough for him. Even the stones of France, the hallowed quarries of Saint-Leu and Arcueil and Bicêtre and Saint-Cloud, were to be discarded in favor of Italian and Egyptian sources.

As for his designs, they were not so much buildings as fenestrated sculptures. To the claims of Lescot and Lemercier, as to the existence of Saint-Germain-l'Auxerrois and the distant prospect of the Collège des Quatre Nations, they were insolently irrelevant. Though ill-mannered, this was not otherwise remarkable. Our own self-doubts and antiquarian reverence for the past did not exist in 1665. There were plenty of old churches about, and a good new building was a perfectly fair exchange for a good old one. But Bernini would have sacrificed everything—comfort, usefulness, economy, even reason itself—to the ideal of display. Louis XIV had wanted the Louvre to comprise barrack rooms, a chapel, and an incomparable library. He wanted protection from the weather, and some reasonable regard for convenience. There was none of this in Bernini's plans, which might have been devised for Pantellaria instead of for Paris, and in which only ceremonial activities could possibly be carried on. Even his sample wall would not stand up to a Parisian winter. Altogether, when he returned to Rome there can hardly have been a human being in France who was not relieved to see him go.

Nothing remains, from his passage through Paris, but a Berninesque pastiche (the baldacchino in the Val-de-Grâce) and the memory of a misapprehension. But the fiasco is one that illuminates the whole history of French architecture. Bernini was a sculptor first and an architect afterward. In Italy, painter-architects and sculptor-architects were quite

common. In France, the architect was nearer to the engineer and the mason than to the visionaries of the Tiber and the Arno. The collocation of "Arts et Métiers" really means something in France, whereas its English equivalent, "Arts and Crafts," has still a cranky, ineffective ring. The collapse of the baroque was, in fact, one of the great triumphs of *l'esprit français,* and no one has analyzed it better than Louis Hautecoeur, the historian of French classical architecture.

"The baroque could never conquer France," he says. "The obstacles were too great. First, there was the practical sense of the French architect, which no theory, however classical, and no fantasy, however baroque, could subdue. These men were born to the game—cradled, one might say, in a mortar-trough. They were the sons and grandsons and great-grandsons of master masons, painters and sculptors. They had been brought up on architectural talk, and they had played with their fathers' instruments before ever they learned how to lay out a building and design its ornaments. The architect was indistinguishable, in those days, from the entrepreneur. Philibert de l'Orme used to boast that at the age of twenty he had been in charge of several hundred of his father's workmen. The Lemerciers, the Androuets Du Cerceaux, the Mansarts, the Gabriels, and innumerable others sprang from a long line of provincial masons; and when they became the King's architects they never denied their origins." These men were consummate realists, and they knew from the start that Bernini's narrow courtyards and Mediterranean marbles would never be accepted in France. His exuberance seemed to them vapid and ridiculous, his aims shallow and incompetent. They couldn't wait to see him go.

In the event, as everyone knows, the design adopted for the east wing of the Cour Carrée was as remote from the baroque ideal as Claude Perrault was remote, in character and experience, from Bernini. The precise degree of predominance achieved by Perrault in the councils that produced the design is still a matter of controversy—a controversy, moreover, that might surprise the joint authors of the scheme, who had none of our reverence for artistic copyright. Perrault, Le Vau, and Le Brun beat out the final plan in committee; and if we single out Perrault it is largely because he was the newcomer and they the long-established masters.

Perrault was a doctor, a mathematician, and a poet. His burlesque verses about the walls of Troy and his friendship with François Mansart alone foreshadow his interest in architecture. In fact, he only became predominant in the building of the Louvre in the year (1668) in which Louis XIV turned his attention from the Louvre to Versailles. With

Construction of Perrault's design for the east wing of the Cour Carrée of the Louvre, 1677

Le Vau employed mainly at Versailles, Perrault had a freer hand in the capital. That, rather than any outstanding architectural genius, is the secret of his success.

Today, Perrault's colonnade has lost whatever function it may once have had. It frames no triumphal entry, but an ordinary gateway through which disoriented sightseers occasionally pass. Since 1809, windows replace the niches that Claude Perrault had designed between each pair of columns. The height of the main entrance has been reduced by a lintel, above which is a souvenir of Napoleonic times: "La Victoire qui distribue les couronnes." The balustrade is quite bare, whereas Perrault had wished it to be topped by statues. The colonnade has become, in fact, the disregarded back door of the Louvre. As early as 1856, an observer remarked that: "This entrance, which should have been the most majestic in all the Louvre, has descended to the level of a way in-and-out for tradesmen—in so far, that is to say, as it is used at all."

As an accomplished engineer, Perrault took pleasure in devising the iron supports that everywhere reinforce the stone, and an elaborate scheme for the disposal of rainwater. Mutilated as it may be, the colonnade remains a revolutionary affair, and one that was to be greatly imitated. It represents the triumph of the horizontal over the vertical, of the mathematician over the poet, of antiquity over the Middle Ages, and of reason over inspired caprice.

It did not, however, add anything to the human history of the Louvre. The east façade is dead ground, in that respect, and so is the south front that Perrault stuck on top of Le Vau's design in the interests of symmetry. The rise of Versailles led automatically to the decline of the Louvre. Louis XIV feared and disliked his capital; he had never forgotten the terrors of his childhood—the winter days when he was imprisoned in the Palais Royal, the improvised beds in suburban châteaux, the continual half-focused anxiety of those who were near him. To hazardous Paris he preferred his own alembicated version of country life. The evolution of the Louvre was halted, both physically and

The Cour Carrée. D. F. Sodel and M. Brigaud photograph

morally, when Louis XIV removed to Versailles and put his trust in the accelerated methods of Jules Hardouin-Mansart. Once again, committee work had been a failure: Le Vau and Perrault had had visions of theaters, and amphitheaters, and naumachias, and borrowings from the palaces of Persia and Turkey, but in the end these went the way of the circuses and standing columns of ten years earlier. Even the colonnade was left for a hundred years without a roof; the ceremonious heyday of the Louvre was over.

There was much, however, to take its place. Crowned heads are not necessarily the most interesting of human beings, and the Louvre in the eighteenth century was as animated as ever. Admittedly, there was no Christina of Sweden to find fault with every-thing, and no Peter the Great to stamp through the Grande Galerie at six o'clock on a May morning: other tenants—painters, sculptors, and "sapient Sirs"—took over. They lost no time in doing so. Already in 1672 the Académie Francaise had staked out its claim, and it was soon followed by other learned bodies.

Then as now, the Académie Française had forty members. Initially, in 1629, they had met primarily to discuss problems of science. But when Richelieu raised the Académie to the rank of a national institution, the role of the Académie became partly ornamental, partly honorific, and partly representative. Its members, generally known as "the immor-tals," were not expected to teach, but rather to set a certain style. Such official tasks as they were given had no deadline attached to them. (Even the dictionary of the French language on which they have been involved for many generations has always lagged way behind the great unofficial enterprises of the same kind.) They did nothing, people said. But how weightily they did it!

The Académies that came to join the Académie Française in the Louvre were of many kinds. Some of them actually taught, as their name implies. Some of them thought long and deep about matters of exact science. They were the last court of appeal for anyone who was interested in painting, sculpture, architecture, medicine, ancient or ori-ental languages, mathematics, and the sciences. There was also, in the short-lived Aca-démie de Politique, the ancestor of the Ecole National d'Administration, which today forms so many of those whose business it will be to govern France.

All this meant that the arts and the sciences became more and more at home in the Louvre. Often they were in the service of officialdom. The more people knew about the medals of antiquity, for instance, the more stylish would be the productions of the Royal Mint. But officialdom also saw to it that the savants of France were very comfortably lodged in the Louvre and had all that they needed to carry on their work like people of

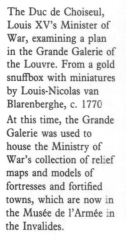

The Duc de Choiseul, Louis XV's Minister of War, examining a plan in the Grande Galerie of the Louvre. From a gold snuffbox with miniatures by Louis-Nicolas van Blarenberghe, c. 1770 At this time, the Grande Galerie was used to house the Ministry of War's collection of relief maps and models of fortresses and fortified towns, which are now in the Musée de l'Armée in the Invalides.

The Burning of the Pavilion de Flore.
Meunier, 1787
The Pavillon de Flore,
now part of the Musée
du Louvre, was
originally part of the
Palais des Tuileries.
Damaged by fire in the
late 18th century, it was
remodeled during the
Second Empire.

consequence. Crowned heads were invited to watch Lavoisier asphyxiate a bird, with Sage on hand to revive it with alkali. Others were invited to a formal session of the Académie Française, where Jean le Rond d'Alembert, its secretary in perpetuity, would pay them elaborate compliments in a tone of voice so screechy that they might as well have been insults for all that the visitors could make out of them.

Life of a variegated and unbiddable kind flowed back into the Louvre. There was an annual picture exhibition. This was not arranged according to the purest museographical principles. Six, seven, or eight tiers high, the frames overhung the visitor like a perpetual headache. Elsewhere the spectacle was less genteel: the royal apartments, where Henri III had danced and Henri IV had died, were given over to curiosities of science. A stuffed camel, the skeleton of an elephant dissected by Perrault himself—these were the cumbrous hors d'oeuvres to a feast of anatomical fragments that floated in tanks of alcohol. Model ships, model châteaux, models of machinery cluttered the rooms; Beaumarchais was there, masquerading as the Captain of the Royal Venery; Mazarin's apartments were destined for the royal library and its bookworms; the great palace was to become a hay loft, a Ministerial office, a pioneer telegraph station, an illimitable filing cabinet, and, above all, a free lodging house. It is this last aspect that introduces, into the history of the Louvre, the elements of picaresque comedy.

Some of these inhabitants were there by right. In 1671 Louis XIV had confirmed that certain distinguished artists and savants should have the privilege of free residence in the Louvre. The lower section of the Grande Galerie was put aside for this purpose, and the records of the 1680s establish that, among others, Théophraste Renaudot, the father of French journalism, Chastillon the engraver, Sanson the geographer, Bain the enameler, and Vigarani, Coypel, and Israel Silvestre were profiting by this hospitable arrangement.

As time went on, however, the favored ceased to be few, and many of them abused their advantages. They overflowed into other parts of the Louvre. Partitions and screens and supernumerary tapestries introduced the idea of "squatter's rights" into the enormous hangars for which quite different plans had been laid. Belongings were dumped all over the place. The sculptor François Girardon brought in a mummy. Tents were rigged up in rooms that had not yet been roofed. Amateur gardeners got down to work in the waterless moat, and the corridors reeked with the activities of amateur cooks. Widows moved in. Two monks built a laboratory in which they hoped to devise herbal remedies for gout, erysipelas, and stone.

The King's guests were never too nice in their acknowledgment of his bounties. Pictures vanished from the royal collection. When there were firework displays on the Seine, the distinguished lodgers set up a black market in seats, and occasionally devised erratic displays of their own that would have demolished a more fragile palace. Bad characters found shelter in the Louvre, and kept open house for their criminal associates. There was a lot of unauthorized overnight hospitality; sculptors, doubtless prized for professional strength of thew, were continually being rebuked on this account. As for the great courtyard and its narrow entrances, these were the scene of many a monstrous traffic; as early as 1701 the King's minister wrote to the Captain of the Louvre that: "His Majesty is informed that the courtyards of the Louvre have been given over to the most disgraceful excesses of prostitution and debauchery, and that the head porter of the Louvre has encouraged these practices by leaving the gates wide open. These gates are therefore to be closed for the future."

By 1773 the abuses had got completely out of hand. Even the paneling had been looted from the walls; dubious phalansteries had taken over room after room; there was continual danger of fire; ceilings had been pierced to give access to lofts and storerooms; stovepipes stuck out of dormer windows; even the rooftops were profaned by licentious young persons; and the flat roof of the colonnade was shaded for twenty years by a tenacious little grove of trees. A loud neighing disclosed that the Duc de Nevers had installed his horses in the south wing of the Cour Carrée. Alongside these disreputable characters were some names of quite another kind: Fragonard, Greuze, Hubert Robert, the Vernets (Horace Vernet was actually born in the Louvre) . . .

From time to time the condition of the Louvre made people uneasy. Architects like Boffrand and Chevotet and Titon du Tillet would have been delighted to have the opportunities that had been granted to Lescot and Lemercier. Jacques Ange Gabriel very nearly secured, in the enlargement of the Louvre, the opening that he was to exploit so well in the Place de la Concorde. The municipal authorities offered to pay for the completion of the palace in return for the use of one of its wings. When the Marquis de Marigny became Directeur-Général des Bâtiments in 1751, he summoned his friend Germain Soufflot from Lyons, and set him to work on the projected third floor of the Louvre. The colonnade, too, had begun to fall down before it had been completed, and the whole of the courtyard was encumbered with a boom town of sheds and shanties, in which were camped a large number of equivocal persons. In 1758 Louis XV decided to clear the ground between the colonnade and Saint-Germain-l'Auxerrois; but the distresses of the Seven Years' War soon combined to render these operations quite futile. Once again lemonade and old clothes were sold freely in the shadow of the Louvre; peddlers lurked everywhere; the scaffolding fell to pieces; and the grass seed rotted in its sacks.

When the war was over, the reconstruction of the Louvre became once again the preferred daydream of everyone who could tell a drawing board from the back of a dray. There was still, at this point, every chance of reintegrating the Louvre into the life of Paris. Soufflot, for instance, envisaged the colonnade as a kind of restful, roofed promenade for servants on their way to or from the Royal library. It was conceived that an equestrian statue of Louis XV would look well in the great courtyard. Bélanger aimed not only to join the Louvre to the Tuileries with a northerly Grande Galerie, but to build a circular opera house in the Place du Carrousel as well. There was a project that Fragonard should contribute a decoration to the Galerie d'Apollon. The vestigial Musée du Louvre was the subject of innumerable meetings, commissions, and memoranda. The momentum of all this was so considerable that the general idea of the Louvre as the center of France went lurching through the first years of the Revolution like a runaway stagecoach.

The Revolution tended, apart from anything else, toward the centralization of France. The daydream continued, therefore. The obnoxious marks of royalty could be concealed, could they not, with plaster? Even the idea of a circus was given its republican tinge, and the concept of the Musée du Louvre became daily more urgent, as wagonloads of paintings and sculpture came lumbering up from conquered Italy. (Engravings of these could be

The Salon of 1787. After Pietro Antonio Martini Jacques-Louis David's *The Death of Socrates* can be seen on the far wall, lower left center.

Exposition of Products of the Year 9 in the Courtyard of the Louvre In 1801 (the year 9 by the Revolutionary calendar), Napoleon decreed that the Cour Carrée of the Louvre should be given over to a mammoth exhibition of recent French achievements in furniture, textiles, ceramics, and the arts of the goldsmith and silversmith. In all, two hundred and twenty stands were made available to exhibitors from all over the country.

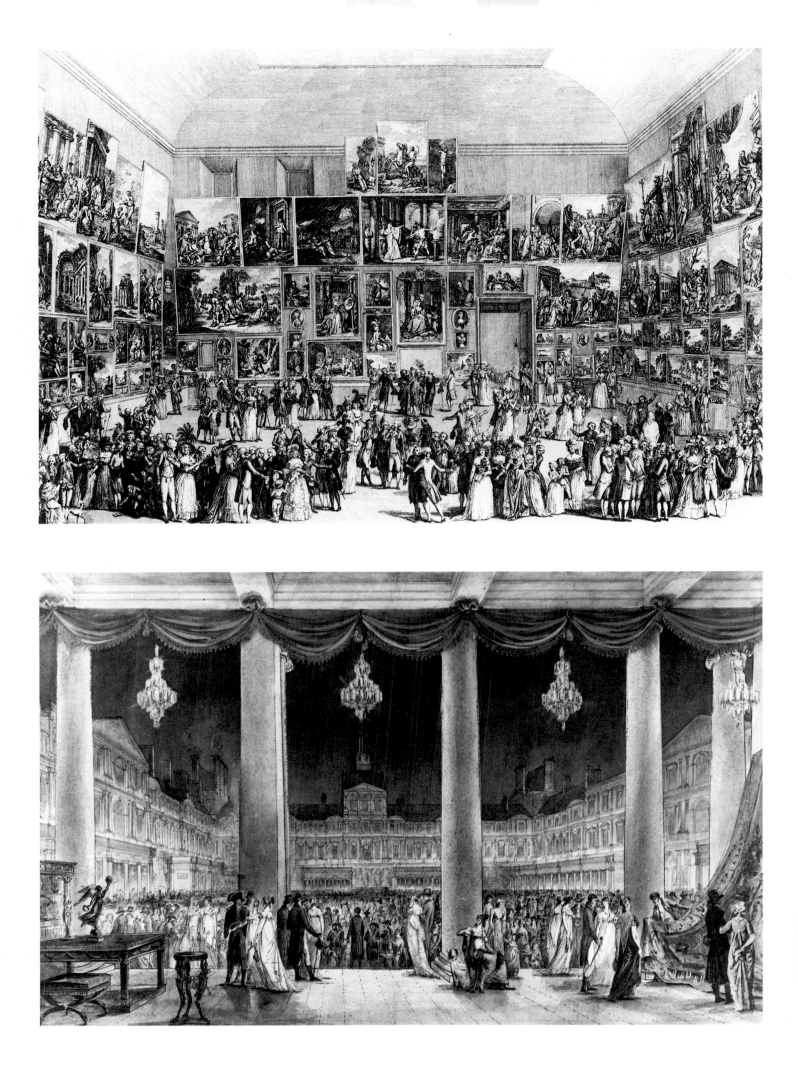

Napoleon and Joséphine Walk Through the Grande Galerie on Their Way to Their Marriage in the Louvre. Charles Percier and Pierre F. L. Fontaine, 1811

sold, it was thought, for the benefit of the republican treasury.) As always, however, individual vanity was more effective than generalized good intentions. The museum was in quite decent order by the end of the century; but it was only when Napoleon took the whole problem as a matter of his personal honor that the Louvre really awoke from its long slumber. Percier and Fontaine were the instruments of his will. Fontaine sat out forty-four years as chief architect to the Louvre, but the short period during which Napoleon was able to direct the operations was inestimably the most vigorous of all. It would, indeed, have reached its climax in the reestablishment of the Louvre as the residence of the sovereign, had not that sovereign been dispatched in 1815 to a less commodious apartment.

For Napoleon really loved the Louvre. It was in the Louvre—in the Salon Carré, made over as a chapel for the occasion—that he was married to Marie-Louise. It was along the Grande Galerie that he and his bride walked in solemn procession from the Tuileries. And it was in the Louvre that his henchman, Vivant Denon, set up the Musée Napoléon, which for just a few years comprised what was probably the most remarkable single collection of great works of art ever brought together.

It is difficult in our day to get anyone to say that the Musée Napoléon was anything but an outrage and a scandal. Vivant Denon was encouraged by Napoleon to search the

The Salle de la Vénus, Musée Napoléon. Charles Percier and Pierre F. L. Fontaine, 1811

length and breadth of conquered Europe for great works of art. What was the point of having conquered Europe if he couldn't do what he liked with it? Denon was not by nature either a vandal or a thief, and he prided himself on the moderation with which he had carried out his orders. But war was war, and it was taken for granted that the man who won the war won the art as well.

So neither Napoleon nor Vivant Denon saw anything outrageous in taking great works of art from Rome, from Florence, from Venice, from Bologna, from Parma, and from Milan. Denon went everywhere, saw everything, and took the best. Antwerp, Kassel, Vienna, The Hague, Ghent—all came under his scrutiny. He took the four bronze horses from Venice, and the Medici *Venus,* the *Laocoön* and the *Apollo Belvedere* from Rome. And Napoleon made all these things freely available to anyone who wanted to see them on Saturdays and Sundays. (Monday was given over to cleaning up.) There were astonishing new paintings, too, like the *Coronation of Napoleon* by Jacques-Louis David. Denon saw to it that the annual Salon of new painting was given due prominence, and many a visiting dignitary found in Denon the best and most eloquent of guides to the great museum.

By the standards of today it was all perfectly monstrous. Napoleon was greed personified. His actions were barbaric and indefensible. City after city had lost its proudest possessions. We are delighted that the Van Eycks' *Adoration of the Lamb* is back in Ghent, and the two Raphaels back in Madrid, and the Veroneses back in Venice, and the Ruysdaels back in Kassel. But when all that has been said, we can still reflect that these great works of art were shown in one of the few buildings north of the Alps that could house them worthily.

The completion of the Louvre was part of an immense plan by which Paris, hitherto one of the most intimate and closely knit of European cities, was to become an imperial capital. Architecture as a form of tyranny was something quite unknown in Paris. Buildings had never before been meant to domineer. In 1806, however, a different spirit was abroad. Hardly a week passed without an order for a triumphal arch, or a standing column, or a dozen new fountains on the Roman model, or an Athenian temple in honor of Napoleon and his marshals. Time has domesticated these erections. The Colonne Vendôme presides with graceful immodesty over Mansart's octagonal *place*, the Madeleine has redeemed itself with its flower market, and the Arc de Triomphe du Carrousel is a piece of superior garden furniture. There is nothing to be alarmed about in any of them, and the ideas that they promote are those of amenity and learned allusion, rather than of awe and subjection.

In the case of the Louvre, there was no question of any great revolution of taste. Not there, but in the new Place de la Bastille, was an enormous bronze elephant to spew water in perpetuity from its trunk. Percier and Fontaine were not innovators; a staircase here, a discreet stove there, a chimney piece with figures derived from Goujon—such was the initial scale of their efforts. Even Napoleon himself forbade any change in the outside of the old Louvre; and it was as much as they could do to embellish Lemercier's wing with the name of Napoleon and the effigies of certain unexceptionable figures from the histories of Egypt and Peru. They were famous improvisers, however, and their ephemeral decorations for the marriages of Napoleon and Marie-Louise had a great sense of ceremonial style. Their real test—the building of a new wing along the Rue de Rivoli—was yet to come. In fact, it might well never have come, for Percier and Fontaine had no fewer than forty-six rivals in the public competition of 1810. Eventually, however, they were chosen. It is to their sage conservatism that we owe the opportunity of examining, on the north side of the Place du Carrousel, the *ordre colossal* that Jacques Androuet Du Cerceau had employed in the Grande Galerie, and which was later most mistakenly removed.

The part built under Napoleon extends from the Pavillon de Marsan to the Pavillon de Rohan. The area immediately to the east of this was a shambles, and remained a shambles until the middle of the century. The Louvre, like its neighbor the Rue de Rivoli, pulled up short before this filthy and disquieting quarter. Geometrical reasons were advanced for the faintheartedness: it was impossible, people said, to get the new Louvre to harmonize with the old. Even Napoleon seems to have balked at the idea of razing the area, and to have been reconciled only after part of it had been blown open in an attack on his own life.

The disreputable old streets died hard; and the Rue du Doyenné, which for Gautier and Gavarni and Gérard de Nerval was an important part of Paris, is preserved for us in *La Cousine Bette*. This is how Balzac described the unsavory chaos that survived well into the 1830s. "Between the Rue du Musée and the guichet which leads through to the Pont du Carrousel, there are a dozen or so houses with ruined façades. Their owners have lost heart and no longer think of repairing them. They are the remains of a quarter which has been dismantled ever since Napoleon decided to finish the Louvre. . . . Half-burned already, since the level of the Place has been raised, these houses are enveloped in the perpetual shadow of the tall gallery of the Louvre. . . . The half-light, the silence, the icy air, and the cavernous deeps in the earth—all combine to turn these houses into crypts and living tombs. The traveler who drives in a cabriolet through this dead quarter and looks into the Rue du Doyenné feels a chill in his heart. Who can be living there, he wonders? And what can go on there at the end of the day, when the cut-throats are abroad and no matter what can be said beneath the mantle of the night?"

It was within a few yards of this cloaca that the approved artists of the Restauration settled down to their task. For the great mark of nineteenth-century patronage—its dread of unoccupied space—was already plain on the walls of the Louvre. Today, when official patronage is devoted to easel pictures rather than to large decorations, and a ceiling by Braque is matter for comment and surprise, we can hardly imagine the luxuriant patronage that was normal a hundred and sixty years ago. Both painters and sculptors were kept busy in the Louvre. Within smell and sound of the strange procedures in the Rue du Doyenné, Chardigny and Taunay and Gassies and Mauzaisse and Montoni and Bridan fils were toiling away, year after year, with chisel and brush. Tertiary names, you may think? Ephemeral reputations? But never did Géricault, Daumier, Manet, Courbet, Toulouse-Lautrec, Matisse, or Dufy receive such opportunities as they.

Nor were these contemporary masters the sole inspiration of Fontaine and his associates: they also employed the many-colored decorations of antiquity, which had just been revealed to the world by Jacques Ignace Hittorff, the future architect of the Gare du Nord. Suitably adapted, these appeased the craving for luxury that swept at this time through the sober old building. There were exceptions (Baron Gros's ceiling for instance, in the Salle des Colonnes), but in general this period was one of the most grievous in the history of the palace. It is the moment at which the long shadow of Respectability first falls upon the Louvre.

This shadow became a perpetual twilight after 1848, when Visconti was entrusted with the aggrandizement of the Louvre. It was, however, a penumbra in which there were points of light—glowworms and fireflies, which might have deluded an observer into thinking that the palace was about to enjoy a new maturity of taste and development. The new reign began, for instance, with the commission from Delacroix of new decorations for the Galerie d'Apollon. These were a very different matter from Baron Gérard's *Con-*

Examining the New Ceiling Painted by Delacroix in the Louvre. Honoré Daumier, 1852

The Entrance of the Louvre Museum. Etienne Bouhot, 1822

The Exhibition Gallery of the Louvre. Samuel F. B. Morse, 1831–32

The Salon Napoléon III in the Louvre, formerly used by the Ministère des Finances. Rozine Mazin photograph

stancy Leaning upon an Anchor. There were also some perfectly presentable attempts at restoration—notably, on the riverside façade of the Grande Galerie, and in the Petite Galerie, which was put back more or less to what it had been under Henri IV. But, of course, the new buildings were what mattered most, and for these Napoleon III chose Visconti, the designer, among other things, of Napoleon's tomb in the Invalides.

Louis Visconti and his successor Hector Lefuel were not so much artists as negotiators. They did not woo the muse of architecture; they parleyed with her. The results of their negotiations have a certain florid charm, a certain nobility of bearing; but the charm is one that quickly exhausts itself, and the nobility is of very recent creation. The new buildings have nonetheless an authority rare in the architecture of their period. There is nothing finicky or tentative about them. All challenges are met head-on. Visconti and Lefuel tackled their first great problem (that of the asymmetry of the Louvre and the Tuileries) by tucking it away out of sight in two oddly shaped interior courtyards. This done, they let fly with everything they could think of. Lescot and Le Vau seem correct and spinsterish beside them, and Goujon and Le Brun unworldly dreamers. The new wings of the Louvre are meant to impress, and impress they do—with the heavy, gun-metaled print of a mid-nineteenth-century thumb.

Napoleon III had wished to integrate the Louvre into the life of Paris. Not content to let it linger in honorable retirement as a museum, he wished it to become, once again, a council chamber, a Royal stable, a barracks, a Stationery Office, and a center of government. For most of these things, Visconti and Lefuel negotiated with the past. "The completion of the Louvre," as the Emperor said when he opened the new buildings, "has not been a momentary caprice, but the realization of a Grand Design which had been upheld for more than three centuries by the instincts of France."

The instincts of France cannot, however, be blamed for certain minor eccentricities. Lefuel had been forced, for instance, to add an extra story to Visconti's designs, and in doing so to sacrifice the *toits à la française* that Visconti had taken over in piety from Lescot. The Empress's delight in ornament had led him to plaster his façades with statues and columns and corbels and caryatids, where Visconti's purer taste would have omitted them. Within, the negotiations had even stronger results. Rooms were adorned with a lunatic profusion of marble trophies—boars, owls, donkeys, bucks, and stags. The staircase leading to the office of the Minister of Finance has Gothic vaulting, and the Escalier Mollien harks back to the ceilings of Romanelli and Anguier. There is a robustness about these borrowings that saves them from the stigma of pastiche. They exist, in fact, in a demented but vigorous dream world, outside of time and outside, perhaps, of any rational assessment.

The Château des Tuileries was noted during the Second Empire for a certain *Leutseligkeit*, or sociable well-being, which radiated from the person of the Emperor. It is now more than a century since the Château was burned down, and we have only documentary evidence as to what it looked like inside. But it so happens that the ceremonial rooms in what was till lately the Ministère des Finances have been restored to their original splendor. Nothing could better exemplify the superfine craftsmanship, the love of pleasure, and the weighty opulence of the Second Empire than this sequence of rooms. It is, in fact, one of the ironies of twentieth-century Paris that in the heavily ornamented ballroom where Waldteufel himself led the "Skaters' Waltz" there was for many years an august silence, permeated by thoughts of the forthcoming budget.

The Finance Minister of the day had until a year ago the right to live in the Louvre. So did, and does, the Directeur des Musées de France, under whose jurisdiction several hundred museums ultimately fall. The apartment in question is the exact opposite of the Finance Minister's. It is small and snug, with windows not much above street level, overlooking the Seine. With just one turn of the passkey the Director has the run of the Musée du Louvre, with all that that implies, but the apartment itself is the reverse of overbearing. Like the Director's House in the British Museum, it is designed for people who would not dream of showing off.

That being so, it would not have done at all for the best known (though not the most admired) of French museum officials in the second half of the nineteenth century. This was Count Alfred de Nieuwerkerke, Surintendant des Beaux-Arts during the Second Empire. He was the perfect counterpart of Lefuel's architectural style. He had florid, heavy good looks, was immensely ornamented, and could be mistaken for a gentleman at a hundred yards. The son of a poor captain in the cavalry who had married an heiress, he was fortunate enough, quite early in his career, to win the heart and the favors of Princess Mathilde. He was less discreet about this than is generally considered becoming. He never stood up for his subordinates, never troubled to inspect even the most important of the commissions for which he was nominally responsible, and was more interested in buying lapis lazuli buttons for his gaiters than in fostering the affairs of the Louvre. (The only good thing ever recorded of him in this connection is that when, in 1852, someone proposed that the Louvre should be sold for ready money, Nieuwerkerke so far bestirred himself as to oppose the idea.)

Even Ingres, never a satirical draftsman, could not but show Nieuwerkerke as the most pretentious of men, and there were few great painters of the period whose careers were not hindered by his appointment. (He said of Corot and Millet that their work was "the painting of democrats—men who don't change their linen, and want to put themselves over as men of the world.") Nor is there much to esteem in the literary sense of a man who, wishing to announce Flaubert's arrival at Saint-Gratien, said only, "There's a writer outside who smells of garlic."

Sainte-Beuve, from *Les Soirées du Louvre.* Eugène Giraud, c. 1860

Yet it was this same absurdity who restored to the Louvre its old status as the playground of *le tout Paris.* His Fridays were great occasions. Some went so far as to style them the last refuge of Parisian conversation. We must not, however, be so dazed by the names of Berlioz, Gautier, Delacroix, Sainte-Beuve, the Duc de Morny, and the Goncourts as to suppose that there was invariably a symposium that Plato would have wished to record. The preliminary entertainment was also undependable. It might consist of chamber music, a recital of operatic extracts, a succession of pieces for brass band, or even a lecture. Some of these lectures were penitential. Others took the form of humorous readings by well-known actors. The public was made up of writers, lawyers, artists, officials, priests, army officers, and persons from the great world.

A favored minority was invited at the end to join the host for tea and cigars in his private sitting room. Here they would be shown Nieuwerkerke's own collection of six-teenth-, seventeenth-, and eighteenth-century wax models, or told of the few paintings of which their host had any close knowledge: the erotic sequence that was given to Louis XV in order to put him in the right frame of mind on the occasion of his marriage. From this favored minority there was chosen a yet smaller group—those whose portraits were drawn on the spot by Eugène Giraud and preserved in one of the albums of the *Soirées du Louvre.* These albums present an incomparable review of the period. To figure in them was a mark of imperishable success. It was also something of an ordeal for those whose features had lost their first freshness; Sainte-Beuve, for example, told the Goncourts that he got ready for it by taking an enema to clear his complexion.

Nieuwerkerke's salon may not be the most delicate of subjects on which to take leave of the history of the Louvre, but it has its place in the evolution of French sensibility. It has also, as I have tried to indicate, a certain kinship with the architecture of the Second Empire—the massive, pretentious, and yet genuinely commanding Pavillons de Marsan et de Flore, the all-too-methodical alterations to the riverside façade of the Grande Galerie, the pinched little coppice that still surrounds the monument to Lafayette, and the general complacency of approach and detail that marks the whole grandiose construction.

After the revolution of 1830, those who had died in the cause of liberty were buried in a common grave beside the Louvre. One of them was followed to the graveside by his faithful dog, Médor, whose transports of grief earned him a place in Parisian history.

Nor is it, from a human point of view, too grossly unworthy of the traditions of the Louvre. Nieuwerkerke was a brute, but he knew that the Louvre had been for centuries the place to which all that was brightest and best in France would eventually find its way. André Malraux knew that, too, when he insisted that the state funeral of Braque should take place before the colonnade of the Louvre. "Braque is as much at home in the Louvre," he said, "as the angel of Rheims is at home in Rheims Cathedral." It is in that sense that the Louvre is fundamental to France.

IV

The Grands Boulevards

The Porte Saint-Martin. Maurice Utrillo, c. 1909

It is the law of life that all things wax and wane. Even so, our great-grandfathers would be amazed to know that in the last quarter of the twentieth century, people are not amused by the Grands Boulevards and regard time spent on them as a penance. "How is this possible?" they would say, for it was on the Grands Boulevards, a hundred years ago, that every visitor felt himself a Parisian by adoption. The Grands Boulevards were Cosmopolis itself, and there was not a city in Europe that did not envy them, copy them, and try to annex something of their animation. (To this day the Random House dictionary defines a *boulevardier* as "a sophisticated male *bon vivant*"; and the sound of the word "boulevard" is music, the world over, to the real-estate agent.)

"Boulevard theater" was fun theater, with no overtones of uplift or social awareness. Boulevard restaurants, boulevard cafés, and boulevard department stores set new standards of amenity. Boulevard people lived for appearances—both their own and other people's—

*The Faubourg and the
Porte Saint-Denis.*
Thomas Girtin, 1801

and were known to spend money freely in pursuit of their pleasures. Fine judges of horse and carriage alike, they treated the life of the boulevards as one long free entertainment to which each contributed as best he could. They would have been very surprised indeed to know that when our contemporaries are in search of a place to eat, a place to live, or a place to stay they disdain the Grands Boulevards and prefer the insidious side streets and secret squares that were there before the Boulevards were ever heard of.

The Grands Boulevards were not, of course, an invention of the Second Empire, though it was at that time that they were most popular. It was Louis XIV who invented them when he decided that there was no need for Paris to go on posing as a fortified city. To the north and the east of what was then quite a small city he had ramparts pulled down and ditches filled in. Before long, a broad sanded walk, shaded by four rows of trees, led from the Bastille to what is now the Place de la Madeleine. When the Porte Saint-Martin and the Porte Saint-Denis were built between 1672 and 1675, they became not so much gates, in any real sense, as landmarks on a very agreeable promenade.

Little by little, that promenade assumed its historic character. Wherever people come and go in search of distraction, other people are going to try to sell them something, and nowhere more so than on the Nouveau-Cours (as the future Grands Boulevards were then called). Street theater flourished. There was plenty to eat and drink. Shops of an amusing

sort were run up overnight in sheds and shacks and tents. All these things were stabilized when it became clear that the Grands Boulevards were there to stay. There was a lot of building, and much of it was of the implicitly festive sort that we find in places where people go to enjoy themselves. Before long there was very little that could not be had for the asking on the Grands Boulevards.

They had a long run, too. The first Baedeker that I bought, in 1931, said that for the visitor who wanted to see Paris at its best and most intense there was only one place to do it: the Grands Boulevards between 4 P.M. and nightfall. What one saw at that time was a scene of classic animation that had changed hardly at all in the previous fifty years. There was still a faint echo, that is to say, of the pride and joy with which the Parisians of the Second Empire had strolled up and down streets that were wide, clean, and safe. The roadway was macadamized, the air was comparatively fresh, the sidewalks were full of people who were having a good time, and there were a great many other people whose business it was to help them to do it. There were the theater, the cinema, and the music hall. The café was still a place of unhurried ritual, the restaurant still a sanctuary of nineteenth-century formalities. The Piazza San Marco in Venice might be "the finest drawing room in Europe," but the Café de la Paix on the Grands Boulevards came a pretty good second.

Boulevard des Italiens, Morning,
Sunlight. Camille Pissarro, 1897

All this had been taken for granted for a very long time. But anyone who thinks that it did not represent a colossal social change should read what William Hazlitt, best of all English essayists, had to say about the state of Paris in 1824. "Fancy yourself in London with the footpath taken away," he writes, "so that you are forced to walk along the middle of the streets with a dirty gutter running through them, fighting your way through coaches, wagons, and handcarts trundled along by huge mastiff-dogs, with the houses twice as high, greasy holes for shop-windows, and piles of wood, green-stalls, and wheelbarrows placed at the doors, and the contents of wash-hand basins pouring out of a dozen stories—fancy all this and worse, and, with a change of scene, you are in Paris." "Paris," he says a few sentences later, "is a vast pile of tall and dirty alleys, of slaughter-houses and barbers'-shops—an immense suburb huddled together within the walls so close that you cannot see the loftiness of the buildings for the narrowness of the streets." And even the Parisian's walk, that spry, darting little motion which we ascribe to an inbred rapidity of nervous response—even this, in Hazlitt's view, derived from quite a different source. "The very walk of the Parisians," he says, "that light, jerking, fidgeting trip on which they pride themselves . . . is the effect of the awkward construction of their streets, or of the round, flat, slippery stones, over which you are obliged to make your way on tiptoe, and where natural ease and steadiness are out of the question."

That is the Paris that we have exchanged for the subject of this chapter: the Paris of the Grands Boulevards. It is greatly abused, this nineteenth-century Paris. Nobody now claims to like it. Pissarro, among painters, tamed it; but the wandering aquarellist prefers the quays and the Luxembourg Gardens to the bristling and perilous activity of the Boulevard Haussmann. Life on the Grands Boulevards has none of the wayward, improvisatory quality that most visitors value in Paris. People do not linger there. The long, stiff, and largely uniform streets have not weathered; no interesting patina or evocative lichen varies their mechanical moldings; stifling in summer and inhospitable in winter, they greet the visitor with folded arms. They have the charm of a countinghouse and the distinction of a telegraph form. They are, in fact, the antithesis and rearward image of the old, free, shabby, conversational Paris; and when we read the melancholy predictions of Balzac, it is with the knowledge that his forecasts have been fulfilled a hundred times over.

Strolling on the Champs-Elysées. Anonymous, 1811

The Grands Boulevards constitute a sort of dictionary of metropolitan change. They answer, point by point, to Hazlitt's indictment; and their answers are decisive, even if they are not always welcome. The pavements, for instance: volcanic slabs were brought from the Auvergne under the Restauration by Chabrol, himself an Auvergnat; and although, as Balzac says, the result did not allow even three persons to assemble in comfort, the principle of pavements was established. These pavements, then as now, had each its own character. The stones may be the same; the trees may struggle up through the same iron grilles; but some stretches remain severe and unwelcoming ("On y passe," Balzac said, "On ne s'y promène pas") where others, identical in form, seem possessed of a potent though unaccountable gaiety. Some have remained bleak and formal—unassimilable, it would seem, irreducibly stiff—but elsewhere the same dismal forms have taken on an exhilarating, purely proletarian animation.

Now that the Grands Boulevards for much of their length have become somewhere to get out of as fast as we can, it is worth remembering that until the great railroad terminals came along they were—apart from everything else—the point at which Parisian met provincial and the foreign visitor took his first steps in the big city. If you arrived in Paris by public transport, there were only two ways to do it. You could come in by boat on the Seine, or you could come in by horse-drawn carriage. Most of the horse-drawn carriages set down their passengers in the area of the Boulevard des Italiens. Unlike the visitors of today, most of whom are put down in a field ten or twelve miles from Paris, the visitor in the 1830s and 1840s was brought to the very center of the city.

"In those days," the author of *An Englishman in Paris* wrote many years later, "most of our journeys in the interior of France had still to be made by the mails of Lafitte-Caillard, and the people these conveyances brought up from the provinces were almost as great objects of curiosity to us as we must have been to them." This section of the Grands Boulevards had therefore a built-in cosmopolitanism. Even its nicknames said as much: at one time it was called "Little Coblentz," after the amenable town on the Rhine where many French émigrés found it convenient to settle after the Revolution, and later

Terrace of a Café on the Boulevard. 1889

"May I have l'*Amusant* when you're finished with it, Madame—if it's still here!"

it was spoken of as Ghent Boulevard, or the Boulevard de Ghent, after the Belgian city that lay some two hundred miles to the north.

Once set down on what, not so long before, had been an archetypal wetland, the visitor could make himself very comfortable indeed. A metropolis in microcosm was his for the asking. As to what it was like, no one can better what Alfred de Musset wrote in 1840:

"The space in question is not large. A rifle shot would carry from one end of it to the other. It is muddy in winter and dusty in summer. The few chestnut trees that gave a little shade were cut down at the time of the barricades in 1830. By way of ornament, it has five or six skimpy saplings and a lantern or two. There is no reason in logic why

The Terrace of the Café de la Rotonde. Georg Emanuel Opitz, 1814

we should sit there, rather than anywhere else on the Boulevards, which are as long as Paris itself.

"Yet this dirty, dusty strip of street is one of the rare points on the surface of the globe where pleasure of every kind can be had for the asking. The foreign visitor remembers it as he remembers the Via Toledo in Naples and the Piazzatta in Venice. Restaurants, cafés, theaters, public baths, gambling dens—all are within a yard or two: the whole universe is there, and on the other side of the street is Kamchatka.

"Ghent Boulevard doesn't come alive before noon. (The waiters are on duty before then, but they will look down their noses if you try to order anything.) The dandys arrive soon after twelve, and they come into the Café Tortoni by the back door to avoid the stock market people who crowd in at the front The dandys—paragons, to a man, of hairdressing and close shaving—take luncheon till two o'clock. They make a lot of noise, and when they leave it is with an impenetrable air and in freshly varnished boots.

"At five o'clock, the Boulevard changes its character and empties completely until six o'clock, when the regular patrons of this restaurant or that go their separate ways. The well-to-do senior citizen, muffled from head to foot, heads for the Café Anglais. The man on the fringes of fashion goes to Chez Hardy. Rented carriages unload their cargo of English families at the Café de Paris, which they believe to be still all the rage. The private rooms of the Café Douix are open for parties of pleasure (ecstatic, but anonymous). The Club de l'Union is ablaze with light, and the dandys mince in and out of it on their way to the Jockey. By seven, the street is empty again. At 8:30, tumult: a hundred digestions work overtime, a hundred cigars glow in the dusk, there is a squeak of two hundred boots, hats are not quite on straight, walking sticks are brandished this way and that, waistcoat buttons burst. The dandys vanish once again, and the company becomes

Café, Avenue du Maine, 1932. Henri Cartier-Bresson photograph

frankly disreputable. The evening paper is hawked on the street. At 11:30 the theaters are over and people trample one another under foot to get an ice cream at Tortoni's before going to bed. At midnight a strayed dandy—worn out by his day—sinks into a chair, crosses his long legs, drinks a glass of lemonade between yawns, pats a shoulder here and there by way of saying good-night, and leaves. The lights go out. A last cigarette by moonlight, and everyone heads for home. All that remains on the street are two or three cabs, waiting patiently for the dawn run from the Café Anglais."

What Alfred de Musset set down, without knowing it, is a pattern of life that has been followed ever since in cities where people insist on enjoying themselves. The Grands Boulevards set the tone, and the timing, for that particular kind of enjoyment. If the life that Musset describes is now more common in resort towns than in capital cities, the fault does not lie with the example set by the Grands Boulevards between 1820 and 1900. It lies with the new, uneasy, alienated, and depressive character of big-city life in the last quarter of the twentieth century.

If the Grands Boulevards have gone out, it is in part because we no longer believe in the notion of having a relaxed good time in a great modern city. Yet there was a time when nothing seemed more natural. This is how Georges Courteline, playwright and novelist, describes the temptation of a café terrace on the Grands Boulevards in the year 1900:

"Once he sat down at a table, with his hat pulled down over his eyes, he felt wonderfully well. A huge quiescence came over his whole being. He longed to give in to life, carefree and thoughtless, with a convalescent's languor. The sun struck prisms from his full cup of coffee. His full glass of brandy threw sparks across the table that were the color of burnt topaz. He felt the way a lizard feels when it toasts itself in the sheltered corner of an old wall. He also felt like staying there till evening, over a pale glass or two of English beer, watching the first parasols of spring go by . . ." That is what we have lost, with the decline of the Grands Boulevards. It is a collective delight, not an intro-spective one, and we shall be hard put to find it again in our harassed capitals.

Meanwhile, what goes out of favor goes out of business. There is no café on the Grands Boulevards that has the prestige, or the originality, or the leisurely elegance of the Café Tortoni; nor is there, anywhere along their vast length, a restaurant of the top class. Uniformity is now the mark of the Boulevards. One café, one costly brasserie, is much like another, and nothing remains of the fantastic novelties of the nineteenth century—those strange, hospitable constructions that prompted Balzac to say that "if these buildings did not exist side by side with so many that are filthy, hideous, and ramshackle, the Boulevards could rival the Grand Canal in Venice for the fantasy of their architecture."

There were also, in these marvelous erections, a number of auxiliary services such as have now vanished from even the most cordial of cafés. At the Bains Chinois, for instance, the customer could take a bath, buy a pair of shoes, and read all the new books. There is none of that now. The mosques and the pagodas and the elaborate gilded balconies have gone. Even the ice creams are standardized. What remains are certain metropolitan habits which were first evolved in these streets: that of the "fork-luncheon," for instance— the informal snack devised in 1804 and popularized by the Café Hardy, at 20, Boulevard des Italiens.

Café, 1968. Henri Cartier-Bresson photograph

The Boulevards are, in fact, the original source of the fragmentary mode of life that makes the Parisian scurry to and fro like a nomad who has lost his tent. Their cafés were "home from home" in the strictest decorative sense; the gas lamps, the dominoes, the tall tarnished looking glass, the overcoats piled in the anteroom, the sense of security, the illusion, almost, of emancipated family life—all had a domestic air. Their exteriors, too, were marked either by an extreme fantasy or (as in the case of the Café de Paris) by the perfection of anonymous good breeding. The boulevard café today has none of these nuances. Its amenities are negative: one is not wet, not cold, not thirsty, and not on one's feet, and that is about all that can be said for them. The tone was that of a salon; it is now that of a waiting room. There was once, in every big café, some particular virtue in the food or drink supplied; today the greatest variation for which one can hope is the offer of some brackish local wine or a mouthful of bad whiskey at six dollars the glass.

Nor are there those distinctions of clientele that, during the heyday of the Boulevards, were known and accepted by all. Tortoni for the dandy, Minerve for the officer on half-pay, and the Estaminet Hollandais for the knowing foreigner: these were unalterable rules. And they were rules that could change by the hour, as the stockbroker gave place to the chess player, and the chess player to the Bonapartist and the clubman. The food could be excellent, but as the century wore on it turned more and more to those standard dishes that now make up nine-tenths of restaurant menus, and the fastidious eater was driven to smaller restaurants in narrower streets. I doubt, however, if even on the Boulevards themselves there was often to be encountered the meal recommended by one mischievous periodical to the really fashionable young person. "New-laid eggs, salad, pilaff, butter from Brittany, strawberries, tea, milk or cream, soda water, mufflings. The whole to be served at the same time, confusedly, with a certain graceful disorder. . . ."

The great hotels of Paris are now to be found to the south and to the west of the Grands Boulevards, but they can still boast a grand hotel that is worthy of the name. In fact they can claim to have the original Grand Hotel, which was built in 1857 at 12, Boulevard des Capucines, above the Café de la Paix, and now has its entrance at 2, Rue Scribe. Charles Garnier, architect of the nearby Opéra, worked on the Grand Hotel. It was designed to give the visitor a completely new idea of what an hotel could be. The

Cabaret. Edgar Degas, 1876

hotel designed from start to finish in the interests of the visitor was at that time a novelty; former travelers had put up in, and with, hotels that were really converted private houses. (The Balzacian will remember that when Lucien de Rubempré and Madame de Bergeton arrived in Paris they could find only "one of those ignoble rooms which are the disgrace of Paris, where—for all its pretensions to elegance—there is not one hotel where the wealthy traveler can feel at home. Lucien could not recognize his Louise in that cold room, where the sun never penetrated, the curtains were worn out, the polished floor stank of poverty and the furniture was dilapidated, in bad taste, and probably bought at second-hand.") Hotels like the Grand Hotel were part of Haussmann's foreign policy; and although our tastes have changed, and many people now prefer hotels that have been devised at gigantic expense in order not to feel like hotels at all, we have a lingering regard for those old pioneers, and a tenderness for their blending of fantasy and practicality.

The Grand Hotel (lately refurbished, by the way, like the Café de La Paix) is once again a very agreeable place in which to stay. It reminds us of the enormous change that the Boulevards brought about. Paris had always been a place in which people of power and privilege, energy and substance, had a wonderful time. But it had not been a place in which a wonderful time could be had for the asking. And now, quite suddenly in the second half of the nineteenth century, the general image of Paris became that of a city with clean wide streets, well lit and well frequented, where everything was done to amuse the visitor. You slept in great comfort, you patrolled public rooms that were infinitely more impressive than those you had at home, you had your choice of the best food and wine in the world, you could go to the theater and the opera, and you were yourself part of a continuous street entertainment that was the envy of every other city in the world.

But the real point of the Boulevards was that they were not primarily designed for the foreign visitor. The foreign visitor could eavesdrop, here and there, and the natives were happy to take his money. But the tone and the tempo of the Boulevards were set by Parisians. There were the newspapermen, in an age when the newspaper was still the single most important force for the formation of public opinion. There were the politicians,

Café, Place du Théâtre-Français. Edouard Manet, 1881

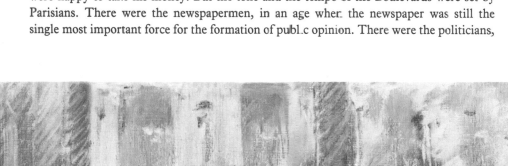

in an age when politicians still wrote their own speeches and could make themselves heard without microphones to an audience that was capable of following an argument. There were the actors and actresses, in an age when actors and actresses were outsize human beings. There were the composers, in an age when Rossini was the old master and Wagner the coming man. There were the writers, in an age when it was nothing unusual for Flaubert, Turgenev, and Henry James to be in town and in touch.

There were also the men and women of fashion, the bankers and the promoters and the real-estate men, the soldiers in retirement, and the landowner come up from the country. In fact, there were all the people who make the difference between a great city and a big provincial town, and every one of them felt better for being there. The Boulevards were not set in their ways, either. It was in the studio of the photographer and novelist Nadar, at 35, Boulevard des Capucines, that the first Impressionist exhibition was held in 1874, thereby inaugurating one of the most glorious periods in all European painting. It was across the street, at 14, Boulevard des Capucines, that on 28 December 1895 there was held what is said by some to have been the first-ever cinematic performance (in the so-called "Indian Room" at the Grand Café). If we consider that in the same short street both Offenbach and Mistinguett lived and died, it will be clear that the Grands Boulevards once deserved their name.

Nadar's studio, 35, Boulevard des Capucines, c. 1865. The signature across the façade was painted by
Antoine Lumière. The interior view (opposite) shows some of Nadar's own art collection, including
Daumier's *Washerwoman* and a Corot landscape. Nadar (Felix Tournachon) photographs

Nadar at the Place de l'Opéra. Snapshot taken by George Eastman with a Kodak box camera, 1890

Inauguration of the Opéra, Paris. After Edouard Detaille, 1878

To the general desuetude of the Grands Boulevards an occasional exception must be made in favor of the Paris Opéra. The Opéra, designed by Charles Garnier and opened in 1875, may well be the best-known single edifice in Paris after the Eiffel Tower. It holds the eye as firmly today as on the evening of its inauguration. It does, in fact, a great job of it. Unlike Covent Garden in London or La Scala in Milan, it stakes a claim for itself on sight as the grandest, the most ample, and the most conspicuous thing of its kind. The inside matches up, moreover. Never was a grand staircase more deserving of the name. Nowhere are promenades more spacious. (If you want to be sure that you are in a capital city, what better proof than the fact that the Grand Foyer of the Paris Opéra is 54 meters long, 13 meters wide, and 18 meters high?) Huge mirrors play their part. Painting and sculpture, likewise. There are marble columns three stories high, balustrades of Algerian onyx, caryatids in the likeness of Comedy and Tragedy.

The stage is enormous, too. (Up to five hundred persons can appear on it and not fall over one another.) The auditorium, though small in relation to the size of the building, has a considerable presence, much as one may regret the ceiling painting by Marc Chagall that dates from the year 1964. Everything about the Paris Opéra reminds us that in 1875 there was a large public for opera in Paris, and that it expected a great deal for its money. The first opera to be given in the new house was Halévy's *La Juive,* and the first new work to be mounted there was Mermet's *Jeanne d'Arc,* which to date has defied revival. It is the misfortune of the Paris Opéra, in its capacity as a house to rival London, Berlin, Vienna, Milan, or New York, that it was built at exactly the time when French grand opera petered out. It was in the Opéra-Comique, not the Opéra, that French opera was to reach one of its highest points with the first performance of Debussy's *Pelléas et Mélisande;* and although the Opéra continued, and to a certain extent continues still, to present performances of international standard there is no longer either continuity or coherence

OPÉRA (la fosse aux lions)

At the Opéra ("The Lions' Den"). Gustave Doré, 1850s

of repertory. How could it be otherwise, when the public is ignorant and vindictive, the singers and conductors are rarely French, and opera itself is no longer part of the Parisian bloodstream? There is no home team. The Paris Opéra seems to start from scratch every time the curtain goes up.

For an idea of what opera once meant to Paris, the informed visitor should address himself to the Musée de l'Opéra, one of the most touching things of its kind. It confirms what we know from memoirs beyond number—that the feeling for opera was very much alive in Paris from the year 1669, when Louis XIV founded the Académie de Musique from which the Opéra eventually derived, until the heyday of Rossini, Auber, and Meyerbeer. For two centuries it was fundamental to Paris. Today the Opéra is hardly more relevant to the Parisian than is the former Stock Exchange to the citizen of Leningrad or Moscow. It's there, and it still looks very handsome, but only on one or two evenings a year do we have the feeling that something of the highest quality is going forward inside.

So there is a certain sadness in the present state of the Grands Boulevards, and we catch ourselves turning more often than we might wish to the well-loved *colonnes Morriss*— onion-topped columns on which are posted announcements of the week's festivities in other parts of the city. These, the urinals, and the metropolitan trees alone vary the unbroken sweep of the boulevard, in which everything seems to have been built with somebody else's money and most people would rather be somewhere else. The stroller can, however, count on the shopwindows to keep him amused.

It used to be an article of faith with the Francophile that every Parisian restaurant was a good one and every Parisian shopwindow as pretty as a Dufy. Neither illusion can now survive. Restaurants and shopwindows alike have lost the aristocratic simplicity that was once the mark of French craftsmanship. Trash is trash, and no amount of presentation can make it anything else. Here too, the Boulevards had their contribution to make, above all, in the department stores which began under the Restoration and were apotheosized in the last decades of the century. Quite apart from considerations of technique (the soaring iron structure of the Printemps, for instance) and the economics of mass distribution, the big new shops represented a complete revolution in the conditions of ordinary life. In

1820, shops had plain wooden fronts, counters were half-lit by smoking oil lamps, and clients wore swallowtail coats and silver-buckled shoes; but by 1883, when Zola published his *Bonheur des Dames*, there were changes such as formerly would have taken four hundred years.

They began much earlier, of course. The Balzacian can site the pioneers in the emotional climate of their age—the Petite Jeannette, for instance, at 3, Boulevard des Italiens, where already in 1819 Madame Vauquer went to purchase a dress and a scarf. Such shops, Balzac tells us, were "poems of commerce," signaled to the far distance by painted signs and floating banners; illusions and optical effects completed the bemusement of the visitor, while the new practice of openly displaying the price of each object set a general tone of candor and probity. No longer were the silks, laces, and merino shawls half-hidden in the darkness of a fetid den: daylight shone in, clear and bright, upon the white and gold paint and red velvet of elegant mezzanines. The painted signs were of every sort, for the fashion was not confined to the *marchande de nouveautés*. There was the restaurant, with its clockface set forever at four o'clock (the hour, Balzac adds, at which a wedding breakfast is normally served); there were also the tobacconist, the lottery office, the learned hairdresser with his hexameters, the optician, the potter, and the umbrella man; the promenading Frenchman could glance up and choose, for his delectable irrelevances, between the Indian, the Persian, the Chinaman, and the many-wifed Turk. Even the English were represented by the mysterious novelty of Macassar oil.

In all these, however, there was the element of individual choice: objects were to be found in one shop, and not in any other, and the shopkeeper was known to his clients, just as they were known to him. Shopkeeping as Zola understood it was something as distinct from the Balzacian formula as a tank offensive from a leisurely morning in the butts. His Bonheur des Dames does not, I think, correspond to any one particular shop,

Interior of the Galeries
Lafayette, 1900s. Harry
Ellis photograph

The Rue d'Aboukir,
June or July, 1914.
Georges Chevalier
autochrome

and there is nothing prophetic about his description. Shops of the kind had been in existence for at least a quarter of a century before his book was written. There is nevertheless a great and authentic fascination in his analysis of the psychology of the department store.

Its owner's one passion, he tells us, "was to conquer the female race. He wished them to reign in his house. It was for them that he had built this temple, in which they were to be at his mercy. His strategy was to dazzle her with chivalrous attentions, to exploit her fevered senses, to traffic in her desires. And so he racked his brains, night and day, for new ideas. Already, in the hope of sparing the less vigorous among his clients, he had installed two lifts. Each was lined with velvet. Next, he had opened a buffet, where biscuits and restoring syrups were served free. There was also a reading room—an immense gallery, excessively luxurious in its decoration, where he even dared to hold exhibitions of paintings. But his greatest inspiration was this: those ladies who were impervious to coquetry he attacked by way of their children. There was no sentiment that he did not exploit. Soon he had special counters for little girls and boys; and mothers were brought up short by the offer of a pretty picture or a balloon for their children."

And Zola goes on to describe the new well-calculated devices of the great shopkeeper—the catalogues, each weighing two pounds and available in twenty-two languages, the engraved letterheads, the samples pinned at the side of the paper, the concept of the Bargain, the even more ingenious concept of Money Back If Not Satisfied. Even the distribution of the stock—gloves, scarves, and silks on the ground floor, linen and china above, and the more cumbrous merchandise, beds, carpets, and furniture, at the top—has not altered since Zola first examined it, nearly a hundred years ago. Penetrate the quarter immediately behind the Opéra, and you will find, not too much changed, the main doorway, "tall and deep as the porch of a cathedral," the interior like an immense palm tree of glass and iron, the buffets (no longer free), the elevators (where they have not been replaced by moving staircases), and on every floor a year-long bustle.

Such shops are strewn about Paris, much as obsolete dreadnoughts once cluttered the ocean—well-loved landmarks, but not quite as awesome, or as exciting, or as useful, or as up-to-the-minute as once they seemed to be. The dreadnought's guns have been spiked; her engines broken up for toothpicks; her hatches stick fast and her hawsers snap. Such immense constructions are not adaptable.

The dreadnought is vulnerable, as we know, to the one-man torpedo, and these nimble, irreverent craft have much in common with the Parisian, who prizes intelligence

Posters for the stores Au Moine St. Martin and Crespin & Dufayel

La Parade and *Weight Lifter (Hercules of the Fair)*. Honoré Daumier, c. 1865

above size and the individual above the mass. The great stores were primarily a phenomenon of investment. They exploited, moreover, the immense new market of the urban middle class, whereas the little shops of the 1830s were aimed at people who chose a necktie or a strip of ribbon with the deliberation of informed voluptuaries. The famous tailor Staub—who dressed not only Lucien de Rubempré but the most elegant of Lucien's real-life contemporaries—would never have been so coarse as to put his prices in writing. Nor would his tartan *gilets* and bronze-green greatcoats have been suited to the ready-to-wear department. The big stores stand for that moment of transition when a great part of society did not know how to choose for itself.

There comes a moment, however, when these leviathans close and only the watchman patrols their deserted spaces. Nightfall—"le soir charmant, ami du criminel," as Baudelaire called it—is in cities, as in people, the moment of transformation; and nightfall on the Boulevards is, or was, the moment at which the light turns blue as gentian and the street signs speak only of pleasure. It is the moment at which the routine of appraisal takes hold of the café-terrace, and there stirs in every breast the sense of private adventure. The near-German brasseries come heavily to life; the trees rustle like underskirts; in the newspaper kiosks, crone after crone switches on her lamp.

The night life of the Grands Boulevards is now almost entirely a domestic affair in which Frenchman meets with Frenchman; there is none of the internationalism that was the mark of the Boulevards a hundred years ago, when Charles Yriarte wrote of them as full of "tall bony Englishwomen, yellow Havanaises, bronzed Spaniards, rosy-pink Wallachs, sallow Italians, plump sentimental German fräuleins, and Russian women who dress well but have yet to learn how to walk properly. The Abayo merchant with his broad-brimmed hat and flashing rings walks side by side with the Hungarian in his Souvarow boots and the bearded engineer from New York who has a revolver in his armpit and the plans for a monster cannon in his inner pocket."

Perhaps it is the theater that has been least affected by the slow dilapidation of the Boulevards. Paris is not like London, where the theaters are so near to one another that one might suppose they were huddling together for warmth. There is no foretelling in which quarter of Paris a good play may not suddenly appear. But the Grands Boulevards, between the Madeleine and the Place de la République, can show several theaters that have held their place for nearly a hundred years; and if one were to add those that are within a hundred yards of the others, the number would be more than doubled. They are neither the largest nor the grandest of Parisian theaters; nor have they that particular smallness that once turned every evening at the Noctambules and the Vieux Colombier and the Oeuvre into an aesthetic conspiracy. They cater for that numerous body to which nobody will ever claim to belong: *le gros public*.

In this, as in other respects, the Grands Boulevards could once claim to lead opinion. It was to the comedies of the Boulevards that people looked for news and enlightenment: *that,* they thought, was how the Desirable Life was lived. That was how people dressed and ate and made love and received their friends. That was what they said, and—much more important—how they said it. People also looked to the Boulevard comedy for that precious thing that theatrical histories usually overlook: the element of perishable fun.

Because these comedies are now unreadable, and are presumed to be unactable, we attribute their success to contemporary aberration. This is unjust, not to the plays themselves, but to the great tacticians who once put them over. Because our own great actors, on the whole, do not appear in rubbish (or prefer, at any rate, rubbish that few people recognize as such), we find it demeaning that the giants of the past should have had no such scruple. For scruple they did not: and with their speed of wit, the unmatched mobility and expressiveness of their weathered old features, and the inherent, instinctive style that marked their every movement on the stage, they polished up the cynical stage carpentry of Victorien Sardou and Emile Augier until it might have been signed by Riesener or Œben.

Boulevard theater, then as now, was commercial theater. When people bought tickets they counted on seeing something that sailed steadily down the mainstream of entertainment. Men went into the theater business as they went into any other business. Theaters were not giddy adventures: they were *there*, like churches or banks, and their owners and

The Grands Boulevards in their heyday could not be better re-created than they were in that masterpiece of the French cinema, *Les Enfants du Paradis* (the "Paradis" of the title refers not to "paradise" but to the topmost and cheapest seats in the theater). Made in 1944 at a time of great national tribulation, this film mobilized all that was best in the French cinema of the day. It was as successful with the tumult of the so-called Boulevard du Crime as it was with the interiors of the theaters in which every performance was a life-and-death struggle between performers and the public.

Invitation to the Side-Show (La Parade).
Georges Seurat, 1887–88

managers were reliable citizens. They had in them nothing of the gypsy, the pirate, or the rebel. To find anything of that sort on the Boulevards you had to go farther east, to what was once called the Boulevard du Crime, and way back in time.

Anyone who has ever seen Marcel Carné's great movie *Les Enfants du Paradis* will remember the look of the Boulevard du Crime (the Boulevard du Temple, as it is today) in its heyday. On that long, broad, shelving street, theater and life were one. Actors and actresses did not wait behind locked doors for a middle-class audience to turn up on time, ticket in hand. They went out into the street and played their audience as an experienced fisherman plays his fish. The *parade*, or come-on, was fundamental to the Boulevard du Crime. Sometimes the players in question were homeless performers of the kind whom Daumier portrayed with an unsurpassed poignancy. But even if you had a theater of your own you had to go down into the street and get the customers to step right in. There was, and is, no better school of immediacy.

The Boulevard du Crime was not, by the way, predominantly the resort of bad characters, though we may be sure that there were pickpockets and confidence men and professional gamblers who worked the crowd. It got its name because the plays on offer there had to do with the red raw meat of popular theater. It was no place to go to for the wordy, dressed-up, middlebrow plays that people choose for "an evening out." The Parisian went there for melodrama, for farce, for the fascination of the Edith Piaf or the Lena Horne of the day—and for the animal excitement of a milieu that was part fairground, part cockfight, part courtroom. Performers were on trial, along that stretch of the Boulevards, and the preliminary hearings were carried on in the street. The public was quick to turn in their favor, when the public felt like it. But if they didn't feel like it, there was nothing for the performers to do but to go hungry away. At one extreme there was a charm that those present would remember for a lifetime. At the other, there was dehumanization of the kind that Georges Seurat set before us in his *Parade*.

This is only one of the senses in which the Grands Boulevards were once a metropolis in miniature and a working model of all that is best, and of all that is worst, in the notion of a capital city. That they should no longer be anything of the kind is a disappointment to those who would like life to stand still; but, in this context, instability is piped into the very air of Paris and will never go away.

V

Du Côté de Saint-Honoré

The Rue Saint-Honoré, 27 June 1914. Stéphane Passet autochrome

Most great streets have their backyard, and sometimes the backyard is more rewarding, in detail, than the frontage. This is the case, quite certainly, with the Rue de Rivoli, and it is also true of a great part of the Champs-Elysées. To the north of these two stupendous thoroughfares there lies a long and sinuous street, as old as Paris itself and for much of its length un-Haussmannized, which begins as the Rue Saint-Honoré and turns into the Rue du Faubourg-Saint-Honoré at the point where it intersects with the Rue Royale. Nowhere is it so arresting as the great ensembles that have made Paris a model for town planners, but in its detail it is one of the most distinguished of all Parisian streets. Remarkable above all for its adherence to the ideal of quality, it remains what it has been for many generations: a stronghold of the very good one-man and one-woman shop; and in this it contrasts particularly with its southerly neighbors.

The western end of the Rue de Rivoli, for instance, is one of the most beautiful of all metropolitan notions. If Napoleon I had done nothing else for Paris, he would still

The Rue de Rivoli, 1855. Adolphe Braun photograph

deserve our gratitude for having sponsored this majestic townscape, in which the idea of Regularity takes on a poetry all its own. All times, weathers, seasons suit it; and like the view from the Pont des Arts or a first sight of the Place de la Concorde by night, it gives Paris a flying start in the affections of every visitor.

The Rue de Rivoli is more than a fine piece of building; it is a gesture of confidence toward the whole human race. "This is what life can be," it says to us, "and now it's up to you to live it." The nineteenth century was to make, as we know, many such gestures; but none, I think, more acceptable in its form than this complex of buildings, which was begun in 1811. It was a great thing to be a Frenchman at that time; and when we look at the little shops that now flourish in the Rue de Rivoli we may remember how a noble name can peter out in a series of scandals, and a great victory stand for the name of an out-of-the-way railroad station. Not that the walk is wholly wasted at eye-level: one of the bookshops bears a name that Thackeray knew, and I myself have a great liking for the echoing saloons of the Hotel Inter-Continental. It's simply that fifth-rate "fancy goods" are not worthy of the Rue de Rivoli.

The visitor who turns inland up the Rue Cambon or the Rue d'Alger or the Rue du 29 Juillet will find himself in a region that has never quite sorted itself out since the convents were pulled down in the eighteenth century and the private gardens built over. Sometimes the walls are faceless, clifflike; and here and there at the rear entrance of a famous hotel we may glimpse one of the last unmistakable badges of great wealth: really beautiful luggage. There are hotels in this quarter where you may stay for a lifetime— superior lodging houses, in fact—and others in which you will be expected to bring no luggage and pay in advance.

The bars, too, are of many kinds. Some are Anglophile to the point of constituting an anthology of English prejudice. English beer is served from the wood, English prize-fighters and fox-hunting men stare down from the dark oak paneling. English checks are cashed (not always at their face value), letters from Vancouver and Melbourne and Johannesburg await their addressees, and the personnel affect a patois derived from cabin boy and Chantilly trainer's lad. These are, on the whole, masculine societies, but near at hand are the expense-account *bars-à-filles*, where the lights glow rose-to-amber, the windows are curtained with carpet, the drink chits wax colossal, a sad bargain can be driven at any hour of the day, and the atmosphere is inexpugnably *triste*. Both extremes bear the mark of the quarter in that they are both more or less single-handed concerns; for this is an area in which you can ask a shopkeeper for one of anything (cigar, collar stud, aspirin, tennis ball, peach) and not be snubbed.

English people tend to feel at home in the Rue Saint-Honoré, and it is no accident that two of its hotels, the France et Choiseul and the St. James et Albany, are particular favorites with them. (The St. James was at one time the British Embassy.) Both have kept an agreeable country-house flavor, but it would be a mistake to infer from their quilted welcome that Anglo-Parisian history has not its horrible side. It was in the Rue Saint-Honoré, not far from where the Hotel St. James now stands, that in the 1420s the English occupying forces armed four blind Frenchmen with clubs and sent them into a pen to kill a boar. And in general the English commanders did all they could to give the English a bad name in the quarter: "not for a single day," the historians tell us, "did the gibbets stand empty. People were hung, whipped, broken on the wheel, drawn and quartered, burnt alive, flayed, impaled: Paris was turned into a charnel-house and everywhere there were smells of burnt flesh and putrefaction. . . ."

But when the visitor turns out of the Place du Théâtre-Français and walks into the unpretentious beginnings of the Rue Saint-Honoré, it is not of these things that he is reminded. (Joan of Arc, as it happens, was wounded on just that spot in 1429.) Pleasanter forebears come to mind: Jean-Jacques Rousseau playing chess at the Café de la Régence in the Armenian costume in which he sat for Allan Ramsay; La Fontaine ornamenting his room with busts of Plato, Socrates, and Epicurus; Vauban living out his last years in the Rue Saint-Roch, and at 219, Rue Saint-Honoré *le Président* Hénault. For although the Rue Saint-Honoré has had the same shape on the map since the "plan d'Arnoullet" was engraved in the first quarter of the sixteenth century, it is to the seventeenth and eighteenth centuries that it owes its present complexion.

It opens quietly, like a street in a well-to-do market town, with a wholesale stationers and an all-purpose leather-goods shop to set the tone. Billboards are numerous at this point: chamber music, real estate, and lectures on exploration dispute the visitor's attention. Shops are narrow-fronted and dark inside; some have fine old lettering or pots and jars of noble design. Not until we near the Rue de Castiglione does the street take on any particular éclat, and before we get to that point the Rue du Marché-Saint-Honoré will have introduced its own likable commotions into the untroubled scene. The Eglise de Saint-Roch, likewise, has its organ note to contribute. Not many visitors put it on their list, but it is difficult to understand the Rue Saint-Honoré without going inside. Works of art it has in plenty; it is not easy, alas, to decipher Théodore Chassériau's frescoes, but for the amateur of French sculpture of the seventeenth and eighteenth centuries it is one of the richest churches in Paris.

Saint-Roch as we see it is not as it used to be. It grew by fits and starts, from the moment in 1653 when Louis XIV laid its first stone and work was begun on Lemercier's plans to the day, just a hundred and one years later, when Falconet's Chapelle du Calvaire completed the strange scheme. The church had benefited in 1701 by the proceeds of a public lottery on its behalf; and a generation later John Law, the bad angel of French finance, gave a thank offering of 100,000 francs on the occasion of his first communion. The lottery helped to pay for Jules Hardouin-Mansart's Chapelle de la Vierge which, with its ceiling-painting by J.-B. Pierre, is the most distinguished of Saint-Roch's many elements. What is lost to us is the façade as it stood in pre-Revolutionary times, with sculpture by Claude Francin and Louis de Montcan and a fine show of *trophées d'armes;* these were destroyed during the Revolution. (Saint-Roch has its place in military history, for it was from its ornamented façade that Napoleon repulsed a royalist attack in October 1795.)

But the relevance of Saint-Roch to our present purpose does not lie in the statues by Coustou, Coysevox, Le Moyne, Falconet, and the Anguiers, marvelous as many of them are, but rather in the burial rolls, which reveal how important a parish this was in the age of French classicism. Corneille, the dramatist, Le Nôtre, the garden designer, Diderot, the encyclopedist, Mignard, the portrait painter, Duguay-Trouin, greatest of sea-bears, d'Holbach, the *philosophe*—these are only a few who lie in what was for years their local church. Bossuet and Cherubini, Boucher and Molière likewise had close associations with Saint-Roch. Fashion has since moved elsewhere, and on most days you will have Saint-Roch to yourself; do not fail to press on the great doors.

Saint-Roch is a good example of the mania for building that Sébastien Mercier describes as typical of the eighteenth century; so great was it, he tells us, that even nightfall did not interrupt it, and "midnight in certain parts of Paris was more noisy than midday in a provincial town." There are many other buildings in the Rue Saint-Honoré that were run up at that time and still keep, in their proportions and texture, something of the *dix-huitième.* Indeed, the visitor who idles away an afternoon in the small shops that abound there may well imagine that the scale on which he is living is that of the eighteenth century, but with one great difference—that today's business is conducted indoors. Chestnut barrow and brandy man no longer stalk the streets; oysters and epaulettes are now bought over the counter, if at all; and from the gamut of open-air trading only the lottery ticket and the newspaper are still to be had out of doors.

The temper of life in the Rue Saint-Honoré is quite different from that lived two hundred yards away on the Grands Boulevards. The best shops are nearly all single-handed affairs; the custom shoemaker, the milliner whose stock of lace blouses goes back more than a hundred years, and even the great toy shop are tainted as little as possible by the wholesale distributor. (Where else, after all, can a stuffed tabby be had for the asking?) There are one or two duds, of course, but in most places the governing element is a passion to do one thing as well as possible. This was true, for instance, of Monsieur Camille Bloch, the bookseller whose shop was of the kind and size that Diderot would have enjoyed. Monsieur Bloch was not the easiest of men, and if you thought that he was there just to do your bidding you were much mistaken; but he was one of the last of the great private booksellers, and when you walked into his shop you trod where Guillaume Apollinaire and Paul Léautaud were glad, in their day, to tread.

The Rue Saint-Honoré is familiar and easygoing for nearly the whole of its length; the same could be said of the church, or chapel, of the Ladies of the Assumption, which has been dropped as if in a fit of absent-mindedness at No. 263. People are very unkind about this sturdy little building; Parisians go so far as to speak of it as *"le sot dôme"* because of the disproportion between that noble protuberance and the tiny structure beneath it. Physically, in fact, this is the Toulouse-Lautrec of churches, and it suggests that Errard, *peintre du roi*, who designed it in the 1670s, may have had his mind on an important canvas at the time. But it is not by any means as absurd as some critics have said, and inside it are meritorious paintings by Boulogne, Vien, and Vanloo.

Yet the fact is that any disproportion would seem monstrous to the visitor who has turned aside up the Rue de Castiglione and walked round the Place Vendôme. This is one of the finest pieces of metropolitan planning to be seen anywhere in the world. Mansart's original conception, in which he envisaged a central equestrian statue of about eighteen or twenty feet in height, has been falsified by the substitution of the mammoth Colonne Vendôme. But this is a case in which affection must be allowed to override aesthetics; most of us, I think, would be sorry to see the column pulled down.

It would be difficult to convey to a blind man the effect of the Place Vendôme; indeed, it is difficult enough to explain to oneself the precise blend of satisfactions that the great octagon can afford us. It is big, of course (213 meters by 224, or about 700 feet across), but not so big as to be out of scale with ourselves as we traverse it—more drawing room, in fact, than parade ground. It is purely metropolitan, and could not possibly be set down anywhere in the country; in this it differs from, let us say, the Josefsplatz in Vienna, where the great beauties of the ensemble do not exclude a certain rustic fullness in the forms. Nor is it in the least middle-class; it has too great a natural brilliance—and

Convent and Church of the Ladies of the Assumption, Rue Neuve. Henry Edridge, 1820

Cocoa vendor in the Rue de Castiglione with the Colonne Vendôme in the background, 1855. Adolphe Braun photograph

perhaps, also, too great a disregard for immediate usefulness. In a square like the Grand' Place in Brussels the immense vitality of the burghers comes out in exuberance of detail, but in the Place Vendôme the exuberance lies in the act of building at all.

For the great *place* looks exactly what it is: a design in which there is almost no gross matter, but one that makes promises that may not all be kept. It has a marvelous rhythm, a great swinging 6/8 like that which stands for the open sea in the first act of *Tristan,* but that rhythm does not work in depth, as do the very different reverberations of the *hôtels* of the Marais or the Noble Faubourg. Nor can we expect it to do so, for the Place Vendôme is, in literal fact, the skin of a great architectural invention rather than that invention itself.

There was a moment, that is to say, at which the façades were completed and nobody knew at all what was going to be put behind them. Originally Louis XIV had been persuaded that the area would suit perfectly for a grand ornamental design in which room would be found for the Académies Royales, the Bibliothèque Royale, the Monnaie, and certain foreign embassies. That idea was taken up in 1685, when the necessary expropriations were made and the future Place des Conquêtes (such was then its name) was traced out. But then the money ran out; and finally it was the City of Paris, with the help of five private speculators, that commissioned Jules Hardouin-Mansart and Germain Boffrand to complete the scheme and put it to other uses. When the façades were ready, the land behind them was sold at the highest possible price—to "financiers," for the most

The Toppling of the Colonne Vendôme

The Colonne Vendôme was pulled down by the Communards in 1871 and rebuilt in 1874.

part, and *fermiers-généraux*. It was not till 1720 that the *place* was complete; and even today there are some curious and inapposite warrens behind that dazzling frontage.

Sightseeing is hungry work, and it may be as well to say at once that the Saint-Honoré quarter is not a good one for eating: not good, that is to say, in proportion to the claims that it makes for itself. Only the convinced *table d'hôtard*, for instance, will choose to eat at one of the large hotels (the Ritz excepted, of course). Of the famous restaurants that abounded in the area only a generation ago, most have closed down, moved elsewhere, or somehow lost their cachet. Voisin, Larue, Montagné have disappeared, and the clients who relied upon them have taken their custom to other parts of Paris.

Yet it was in the Saint-Honoré quarter, and in the middle of the eighteenth century, that the name and notion of the restaurant first came into use. Boulanger was the pioneer's name, and his establishment was in the now-vanished Rue des Poulies. *Volailles au gros sel*, egg dishes, and soup were served on marble-topped tables to all who cared to ask for them. There was no lack of trade, either. Madame Boulanger was very pretty, and many people (Diderot among them—after a session, he tells us, of seven hours at the 1767 Salon) made a habit of dropping in for their meals. The name of *restaurateur* came into being because Boulanger hung outside his establishment a sign on which was inscribed a famous phrase from the New Testament: "Venite ad me omnes qui stomacho laboratis et ego vos restaurabo."

Restoratives of many sorts can still be got, of course, in the quarter. Money is well spent at the Ritz, or Maxim's, or Prunier's, or Drouant's, but there's no denying that it must be spent in great quantities. The good middle-price restaurant is rare hereabouts. The bistro of the first order, on the other hand, can be found, though with difficulty, and so can the kind of place in which an excellent luncheon of a modest sort is served on the first floor to office workers, most of whom eat there every day.

The Place du Marché-Saint-Honoré is as good a place as any other in which to consider the question of the bistro. The difference between a bistro and a restaurant is a simple one. Anywhere that closes between meals is, by that token, a restaurant and not a bistro. A bistro is a café-bar or *tabac* or *dépôt de vins* in which meals happen to be served, but where the business of providing those meals does not interrupt or discommode the day-long traffic at the bar itself. A bistro is perfectly democratic in tone, spends no money on display (linen tablecloths, decorators' looking glasses, leather *banquettes*, autonomous cloakroom), stands directly on the street, and is managed with amiable dispatch by an extremely small staff. It never advertises.

For a good bistro to keep its character gets more difficult every year; more and more French people, and young people especially, are content with a quick-lunch counter or an espresso bar, whereas the classical bistro cuisine takes time and trouble and love and is not, as things now go, very well rewarded. The temptation to carry on the same kind of business, a little less carefully, at restaurant level must always be great. All honor, then, to the remaining authentic *bistrotiers*—and all good luck to those readers who set out to find them.

Private hospitality has also its history on the Rue Saint-Honoré. A fact on which few have agreed is the exact number of the house in the Rue Saint-Honoré in which Madame

The Place Vendôme, 1950s. The diversity of building behind the uniform frontage can be clearly seen from above. The Place now has an underground parking lot. J. Behrard photograph

A Reading at Madame Geoffrin's Salon. Anicet-Charles-Gabriel Lemonnier after a drawing by François Boucher

The reader is the philosopher Jean le Rond d'Alembert.

Geoffrin came to live as a fourteen-year-old bride and remained until the day of her death, sixty-four years later, in 1777. I owe it to Georges de Lastic Saint-Jal that although the plaque adorns No. 374, the house was in fact No. 372. The visitor who presses boldly into the courtyard and looks up at the first floor will see the three tall windows behind which Hubert Robert brought out his sketchbook, Marmontel and d'Alembert read aloud, and David Hume, Edward Gibbon, and Horace Walpole—philosopher, historian, and exemplary correspondent—put their French to the most searching of tests.

Writers and painters do not go into the great world to see one another. When they dine out it is to meet their betters, and they are not always over-tender, among themselves, in speaking of those who offer them the opportunity of doing so. Many who now wax enthusiastic at the thought of Madame Geoffrin's Wednesdays (*philosophes,* above all) or Mondays (painters, mostly) would have had sharper words for her had they actually been there. Jean-François Marmontel, for instance, who benefited as much as anyone by Madame Geoffrin's hospitality, said afterward that she was an ignoramus who had never studied anything seriously, "had kindness, but very little sensibility, was beneficent, but without one of the charms of benevolence, and though eager to help the unfortunate did not see them for fear that the sight would upset her. . . ." Every age has its Geoffrin, and every age its Marmontel: that is why the intending visitor to Paris will find profit, as much as pleasure, in the study of the great hostesses of the *dix-huitième.*

Madame Geoffrin is, in more ways than one, a classic of her kind. She never lived elsewhere than in the parish of Saint-Roch, where she was born. She married a man thirty-five years older than herself, and it was as a comfortably off quasi-widow that she made her impact upon Paris. Her husband hated parties. So tremendous were the resulting quarrels, their daughter tells us, that: "I thought my mother would never survive them; but then everything was smoothed out; my father always gave battle, but in the end he always gave in." It was in her fifties and sixties that Madame Geoffrin's salon became one of the most famous in Europe: "a very good house," as Gibbon noted in his *Autobiography,* "regular dinners there every Wednesday, and the best company in men of letters and people of fashion."

Madame Geoffrin's hospitality, like her house, had a note of plain distinction which not all her successors have recaptured. She deliberately played down the decoration of her rooms, whereas today every attempt would be made to catch and surprise the eye. Her furniture was very good (Pierre Garnier, from whom she ordered much of it, was one of the finest ebenists of the day), but it was not at all showy. François Boucher and Hubert Robert made it quite clear that Madame Geoffrin liked her surroundings to be sober and unobtrusive—the better, no doubt, to set off the talk.

She enjoyed the company of those who were as free in tongue as they were in mind, and yet kept just the right side of the Church; her forthright "That's enough!" was sufficient to halt those—Boucher was a regular offender—who forgot that they were in a drawing room. She was a generous patron of the arts at a time when such patronage was something more than one of the elements of prestige; but, even there, events sometimes overtook her and gave her collection the ring of our own times. "It just proves," Grimm wrote of her in 1772, "that buying pictures and re-selling them later can be an excellent way of investing your money. That wasn't Madame Geoffrin's intention when she had Vanloo paint them: but now that she's enjoyed them for twelve or fifteen years the Empress of Russia has bought them off her—with her customary munificence, of course. . . ." Lucky, therefore, the painter or writer who finds his Madame Geoffrin.

It is when we cross the Rue Royale and get into the Rue du Faubourg-Saint-Honoré that the temper of the long street changes perceptibly. It is richer, of course, but it is also more grasping, more fickle, more intent on display: more Parisian, in fact. For this is, of all streets in the capital, the one that best comes up to the outsider's expectation of Paris as a center of luxury. Other rivals are coming up—Avenue Montaigne, Avenue Matignon—but the Rue du Faubourg-Saint-Honoré has the edge on them by reason first, of its ancient yet undimmed reputation, second, of its being still to some degree a street of palaces, and third, of its conspiratorial proportions. A wink will still tell from one side of the street to the other, traffic often slows to a walking pace, and enormous gateways and the glitter of distant uniforms remind us that this is still a ceremonious, as much as a commercial, quarter.

Salon of a Townhouse in the Faubourg Saint-Honoré. Edouard Texier, 1853

It has also a tradition of private eccentricity, which one or two apartment owners do their best not to let die. Wealth had, and has, a part to play in this; but wealth alone does not produce luxuriance of character, although it may make it easier for that luxuriance to find outlet. Balzac, for instance, was fascinated by money; but energy fascinated him still more, and it is energy—misdirected, perhaps, or turned in on itself, or even cut off at the source—that produced the strange mutations of human character that crop up all over the Faubourg Saint-Honoré at critical moments in its evolution. Anyone who goes there and buys an object which he cannot afford may be assured that he is the victim of an historical process that has been going on for a very long time. He may not be working on the scale of Arsène Houssaye—who at one time had seven houses in the quarter, and used to dodge from one to the other to such an extent that Alfred de Musset, Théophile Gautier, and his other guests never knew where to look for him—but he is in the same line of activity.

Long residence in the Faubourg brings out the freak in everyone; Jacques Hillairet tells us that the Marquis d'Aligre changed his will eighty times and never went out of the house, even to the theater, without taking his two doctors with him. The first Duc d'Albuféra trained his two parakeets to sing Vespers for the edification of all passers-by. In pre-Revolutionary times the home of Grimod de la Reynière at 1–5, Rue Boissy d'Anglas was the scene of many a famous dinner; Flemish rather than French in their abundance, these feasts were greatly sought after. (The host, a renowned gourmandizer, choked himself with foie gras and died with the napkin still round his neck.) Guests were sometimes invited to take a turn at the head of this hospitable table—on condition, that is, that they first swallowed twenty-two cups of coffee apiece, and eighteen cups of tea.

Like many who keep open house, the Grimods de la Reynière came to be taken for granted. When it was announced, at carnival time in 1783, that the master of the house had died, few of his friends took time off from their amusements to take formal leave of him. Bier, hearse, and funeral draperies were in place when those few arrived; but when they had sat out a charmless half-an-hour in an anteroom, the doors were thrown open and there, in the dining room, with the glittering table laid and good things beyond number upon it, was their host, amused beyond measure at the success of his joke and delighting, we may be sure, in the knowledge that these, at least, were true friends. He lived on to be eighty, and is remembered for having said: "The only time when you should mind being thirteen at table is when there's only food enough for twelve."

The Hôtel Grimod de la Reynière occupied what was then, and is still, one of the most coveted sites in Paris. Its owner could in fact be said to have the best view in the city. When the house passed out of private ownership it became successively the Turkish Embassy, the Russian Embassy, and the headquarters of a particularly brilliant and amusing club. It is on this same site that the United States Embassy was built in the 1930s, thereby continuing an official presence that even in the earliest days of the American republic was associated with great houses and well-chosen locations.

Proprietorship went to people's heads the last year of the Ancien Régime. Today there is no spare ground in the Faubourg, but in the 1770s and 1780s any amount could be had—and not for *hôtels* only, but for mazes, vineyards, ornamental waters, orangeries, and hothouses. No one took more advantage of this than Beaujon, the millionaire *receveur des finances*. Himself an invalid, confined to his wheelchair and a diet of boiled spinach, he commissioned Girardin in 1784 to build him the strange complex of buildings known as the Folie Beaujon.

This was grave enough when seen from outside, though perhaps the fat round tower at either end might be said to have given the alarm: within, there was no limit to the fantasy—rooms lined with mirrors and entered through revolving doors made of the same deceptive substance, beds made in the semblance of baskets of flowers and slung from the branches of artificial trees, and even the billiard room embellished by a favorite painter of the day. On this estate there followed, some thirty years later, the swings and slides and *montagnes russes* which survive so prettily in aquatint; but gradually, the quarter sobered down, and became built over, and then was cut to pieces again for the sake of an embassy here, or another six feet of roadway there.

Every visitor to Paris indulges from time to time in fantasies of proprietorship. Walking at nightfall through the streets he glimpses here the glister of moiré wallpaper, there the edge of a Bonnard, and he thinks, "*There* I could live forever and be happy!" or, "*That* would belong to me, if the world were properly arranged!" And the English visitor will not have walked far along the Rue du Faubourg-Saint-Honoré before he finds on his left a house that, in a sense, does indeed belong to him, rash as it would be to presume upon the fact. This is No. 39, which since 1814 has been the British Embassy.

The house, built by Mazin in 1723, was at first named after the Duc de Charost, tutor to Louis XV, whose family lived in it till 1803. It then passed to Napoleon's sister, Pauline Borghese. During her residence it acquired much of the distinction of detail that now makes it the envy of every Ambassador. Clocks, candelabra, *lustres,* and a particularly imposing gilt *surtout de table:* all came when the British Government paid over a paltry 870,000 francs for house, garden, stables, "furniture and fittings." And the house to which we may or may not be invited today is the house in which Dickens read aloud, Sydney Smith preached, Thackeray and Berlioz were married, and Somerset Maugham was born. Strange conjunctions! But not too strange for the house itself which, like every great Parisian mansion, adapts itself perfectly to all uses.

"The interior" (here I quote from an article in the London *Times* by Frank Giles) "is profoundly satisfying, striking exactly the right note between a stately official residence and a home to be lived in and loved. Downstairs are a series of inter-connecting salons, with the ballroom and state dining-room running out at right angles to the main block, in the form of low wings on the garden side. A noble staircase leads to the first floor and the library, the small dining room, the magnificent gold and white 'Ionic' salon, the *salon vert*—perhaps the least formal and most friendly room in the house—and Pauline Borghese's

The Galerie Dorée in the Hôtel de Toulouse, 39, Rue Croix-des-Petits-Champs. The Hôtel was built by François Mansart in the 1630s, but the Galerie Dorée is the work of Robert de Cotte, 1718–19. The Hôtel de Toulouse is now the Banque de France. Ionesco photograph

Above: The Passage Choiseul, 1825

Above right: Originally an open street, the Passage du Grand-Cerf was covered with a glass roof in 1825.

Right: The Galerie Vivienne, 1823

bedroom. Whether a thousand people are thronging the public rooms—as they did when the Queen invited them in the summer of 1957—or the Ambassador is giving a dinner for a handful of people whom he wishes especially to talk to and hear from, the atmosphere imparted by the house is always right: dignity without pretentiousness, comfort allied with proportion and space."

The British Embassy church in the Rue d'Aguesseau has a pronounced ethnic quality which will commend its services to the student of English manners. But on weekdays most visitors will look to the shops of the Rue du Faubourg-Saint-Honoré for the greater part of their amusement; and these have, for the most part, kept their traditional excellence. There have been encroachments, and some of the picture galleries are no great shakes,

One of the great metropolitan inventions is the covered walkway with shops on either side that is called in London an arcade, in Paris a *passage*, and in Italy a *galleria*. It has every advantage. The visitor is dry, warm, and safe. The light streams down from the glass roof overhead. The shops have the seduction of the alcove and are traditionally run by one or at most two people who are specialists in their field. London, Brussels, Milan, Naples, Leningrad—all had covered walkways of this sort. You could shop there, eat and drink there, meet your old friends there and make some new ones as well.

Paris from the 1820s onward had many *passages*. They were marvels of luxury, intimacy, and inventive good taste. They had floors of patterned marble, tall shopfronts that redoubled temptation, and a general atmosphere of silks and shadows, furs and flirtation. They were like stages on which everyone got to play a part and everyone looked their best.

When Haussmann began to remodel Paris and the big department store was all the rage, the *passages* went out of fashion. Some of them were torn down. Others slumbered, fell into decay and became dingy beyond redemption. But in recent years the *passage* has been brought back to life. The Passage Choiseul, the Galerie Véro-Dodat, the Galerie Vivienne, the Passage Verdeau, the Passage du Grand-Cerf—all these and many others repay investigation, and they are to be found mostly in the 2nd *arrondissement*, north of the Rue Saint-Honoré. Don't be put off if from outside they look like nothing.

Above: Monsieur Schwartz-Bart, Galerie Véro-Dodat

Above right: Monsieur Vittoz of J.-F. Vittoz, specializing in old recordings, 26, Passage Verdeau

Right: Madame Petit-Siroux, Librairie Petit-Siroux, 45, Galerie Vivienne

Robert Doisneau photographs

Three bisque dolls by
Pierre-François Jumeau,
1875–95

but in general the street is still one of the most teasing and tantalizing in all Paris. If there were a draftsman-observer today of the quality of Gabriel de Saint-Aubin, he could amble about, as Saint-Aubin did in the same street two hundred years ago, and pick out sight after sight that sets the fingers' ends atingle. His favorite was the famous doll in Mademoiselle de Saint-Quentin's boutique: the doll, dressed and redressed month by month in the height of fashion, was then sent off on its travels to show sheik and boyar what Paris was up to.

The Saint-Honoré quarter was known at the beginning of the eighteenth century for the quality of its contribution to the necessities of life: linen, cloth, silk, ribbons, laces, and feathers. Extravagance began when the glover brought gloves from Grenoble and Blois, the scent man scent from Genoa and Nice, and Mr. Marius perfected his collapsible umbrella. Before long Casanova was abducting the stocking woman from the corner of the Rue Saint-Honoré and the Rue des Prouvaires, and Labille the milliner for men had given the street its first big display windows. Dulac invented, and Madame du Barry made famous, the fashion of the face-patch or fragment of adhesive taffeta which came in the likeness of heart, moon, comet, crescent, or star and was called, according to its location, *la baiseuse, l'équivoque, l'assassine, la majestueuse, l'enjouée, la galante,* or *la friponne.* Le Brun made the street famous for fine furniture; and Voltaire did business with Hébert the ebenist on Madame du Châtelet's behalf. Intermittently the street has done a great trade in dolls: "The Parisians," Grimm once wrote, "are children who would gladly swap the Farnese Hercules or the Medici Venus for a doll from the Rue Saint-Honoré." Auctioneer, chemist, and makeup man completed a list which, even today, would need little amendment.

Toward its western end the Rue du Faubourg-Saint-Honoré becomes a street like any other, and as it shelves upward toward the Avenue de Wagram it loses entirely, I think, the special character of its earlier reaches. Washing machines and artificial leather sofas are useful things in their way, and it is from the Place Saint-Philippe du Roule that the connoisseur of place names may take an omnibus that stops at Mozart, George-Sand, and Paul-Valéry; but walking is not, from there onward, very much of a pleasure.

VI

The Marais

Crossroads of the Rues Bailleul and Jean-Tison. Thomas Shotter Boys, 1831

For many years the Marais was more often talked about than visited. Most people knew that it contained as many beautiful houses, yard for square yard, as could be found in any city in Europe. It also got about that many of these houses were in a deplorable condition. Often, therefore, a luncheon party of enlightened foreign visitors would get up from the table at a quarter to four with the object of "taking a look at the Marais."

How could they not be tempted, after all, by the Marais? The Marais is one of the most fascinating of all metropolitan quarters. It has everything—great architecture, close and authentic associations with all manner of people, a past heavy with history, a present as lively as it is disputable, a future that is being shaped before our eyes. Who would not want to see it?

It has the Hôtel de Montmar, in which Molière gave a reading of *Tartuffe* at a time when it was forbidden to perform *Tartuffe* in public. It has the Eglise Sainte-Elisabeth, of which Marie de Médicis laid the foundation stone in 1628. (It was consecrated by the Cardinal de Retz seventeen years later.) It has the Hôtel Guénégaud, which is by François Mansart and was not long ago turned with conspicuous success into a museum of the hunt.

It has whole streets—Temple, Francs-Bourgeois, Vieille-du-Temple, Thorigny, and many another—that have kept something of their original elegance despite two centuries of dilapidation. It has a novelty—at 40, Rue des Archives, a house that was identified in 1971 as having belonged to the son of Jacques Coeur, the sixteenth-century maritime adventurer who made it possible for France to trade with the Levant. It is therefore a small island of Renaissance architecture in what is primarily an eighteenth-century quarter.

It was in the Marais that the massacre of Saint Bartholomew's Day was organized, that Louis XVI and his family were imprisoned, and that Madame de Sévigné went regularly to listen to Bourdaloue, the finest preacher of his day. It was there that the child Mozart played, that François Couperin and his sons lived and worked, and that Marc-Antoine Charpentier was *maître de chapelle* at the Eglise Saint-Paul-Saint-Louis. Nowhere is the great classical age of French music more vividly present to us.

It was in the gateway of the Hôtel de Sully that Voltaire in 1725 was beaten up by

A sphinx in front of the Hôtel de Sully, 62, Rue Saint-Antoine. Built from designs by Jean Androuet Du Cerceau, 1624–30. Pierre Jahan photograph

The vestibule of the
Hôtel Hénault de
Cantorbe, 82, Rue
François-Miron. 1706

the servants of the Chevalier de Rohan in a way that he never forgot. It was in the then-modern church of Saint-Denis-du-Saint-Sacrement that Eugène Delacroix painted a Pietà in 1844. It was in the Hôtel de Sens that in 1913 Gabriele D'Annunzio wrote his repellent and all too characteristic *Martyrdom of Saint Sebastian,* and it was for 10, Rue Pavée that in 1913 Hector Guimard, famous for having designed the best-looking of all Métro station entrances, designed a particularly handsome synagogue.

Add to this the tumult of activity—some of it purely speculative, but some of it inventive in the highest degree—that has come about with the creation of the Quartier Beaubourg, and you have the kind of complexity that cannot be described, let alone disentangled, in a page or two. It should also be remembered that the Marais today is in full evolution, as much as at any time in its history. All statements about it are provisional.

Previously, this marvelous and contradictory quarter did not lend itself to improvisation. Foresight and a compass were essential if the visitor was not to get lost in the souks; some form of sociological sextant was also useful. For the Marais was not a life-size architectural museum in which people of low degree had contrived to camp out; it was a vigorous and unsubordinated quarter in which the tenement houses happened to be designed by some of the greatest of French architects. No one denied the beauty and singularity of the *hôtels* that were built in the Marais by Androuet Du Cerceau, Le Vau, Pierre Cottard, Mansart, Lepautre, Libéral Bruant, and others; often these great men left behind them a house in which, more than in many a larger commission, their particular genius could be studied at close hand. Nor were façades the whole of the Marais; within doors there could still be sought out decorations, often now merely vestigial, by Le Brun, Lesueur, Mignard, and Oudry.

But the Marais was a place in which Today had also its rights; the visitor who took the wrong turning could well walk out of an antiquarian's paradise and into a world unknown to the standard guides. Jean-Paul Clébert had much to say of this in his pioneering *Paris Insolite:* the quarter is one, he told us, in which "every street, every alley, every impasse, every cul-de-sac has a personality and a life all its own. Every group of houses, workshops, tenements and hovels is a closed world, with bistros, shops, ladies of easy virtue, habits, customs and manners quite distinct from those of any of its neighbors. The same is true of its architecture, its state of mind, its opinions, and its occupations."

Thus it was that in some streets the visitor came upon a scene unchanged since the days when the new novel was Daudet's *Fromont Jeune et Risler Aîné*—a street given up to piecework done to order for some nameless fashion house, where tiny pointless baubles are manufactured by the thousand: in fine weather the *ouvrière à domicile* brought her needle and her ancient chair out onto the pavement, there to converse with her colleagues as the ten-thousandth dragonfly was given the ten-thousandth pair of wings. Elsewhere, a wandering tourist felt himself far from home, unless he had Arabic enough to fend off hostile glances, or his fluency in Yiddish was such that he could penetrate to the full the rich and mysterious life of the Jewish quarter. In these small and overpopulated enclaves we saw the last of the truly cosmopolitan Paris—not the cosmopolis of the rich, but the older and more authentic society in which respect for the habits and personality of others was absolute. Those who have kept clear of poverty often believe it to be a great leveler, but you were more likely to find a standardized human being in the Hôtel Plaza-Athénée than in the Gorkyesque bistros of the Marais. Within it were concentrated elements from the life of the Baltic states, Central and Eastern Europe, the Mediterranean seaboard of Africa, the Sahara, Turkey, Lebanon . . . This was, in fact, the true Musée de l'Homme, with Chinese and Russian sectors within half an hour's walk and on every hand the craving for life in its residuary, rarely recorded form.

It was not a matter of picturesque detail: the Jewish bathhouse in the Rue des Rosiers, the sweetmeats that related to a particular town in Romania, the hammam-like café where the *copia verborum* of Arab conversation went into action all the twenty-four hours of the day. The point was that the Marais was the last sanctuary of certain ways of life. What you saw there in miniature was: Warsaw before the ghetto was razed, the oasis before the neon lights began to flare, Samarkand before the Soviet authorities brought it into line. In these diminutive colonies the old French tradition of liberty and hospitality was just, but only just, alive; so it is not surprising that the sightseer was not always welcome when he pushed open the door on which was chalked an inscription he could not decipher.

Already in the quarter of Saint-Paul demolitions were "cleaning up" a whole area that was given over to those who lived a nomadic, improvisatory life; elsewhere, the demands of public health, on the one hand, and bourgeois prejudice, on the other, were slowly getting the better of this unsubdued part of Paris. In the process there had already disappeared, near to the water's edge, a whole corner of medieval Paris, and there were many who wanted, from the highest motives, to see the work of disinfection carried northward, away from the Seine and into the heart of the Marais. Not that there would be much destruction: the buildings were too precious for that. But of rehabilitation there would be a great deal: façades cleared of improper additions, interiors rescued from degradation, gardens swept clean of the sheds and garages that infested them and reconstituted as *jardins à la française.* As to what would be done with the Marais when it had been put back to its beginnings, various views were held: a vast complex of museums, a Cité Universitaire, a cultural center on the lines of the Fondazione Cini in Venice—all could one day have their place. And it was tempting to imagine the Marais in pristine state, with restrictions on the automobile, a select population of enlightened people, and the Place des Vosges returfed with sods donated by the University of Cambridge. The sound of a harpsichord would be audible at a hundred paces, the secret gardens would flower as they flowered in pre-Revolutionary times, and the Marais, itself a work of art, would be the inspiration of art in others.

The idea was all right, of course, and if there could be added to it the projected Musée de la Demeure Française, with specimen interiors devoted to French achievement in the decorative arts, then the Marais would indeed have become a monument to one kind of civilized instinct. A few great houses were already examples of this—above all, the Hôtel Carnavalet, which is *par excellence* the Parisian's own museum, and the Hôtel de Rohan and the Hôtel de Soubise, which are now occupied by the Archives Nationales.

The Musée Carnavalet, 23, Rue de Sévigné. In the center can be seen the formal garden of the museum and the façade of the Pavillon de Choiseul, relocated to the museum from the Rue Saint-Augustin. Across the Rue des Francs-Bourgeois, toward the lower left of the photograph, can be seen the portal and courtyard of the Hôtel Lamoignon, 24, Rue Pavée, now the Bibliothèque de la Ville de Paris. D. F. Sodel and M. Brigaud photograph

A panel from the Cabinet des Singes in the Hôtel de Rohan, 87, Rue Vieille-du-Temple. Christophe Huet, 1745

The Carnavalet is a museum within a museum: the kernel of the building is, in fact, the little Renaissance *hôtel* that was designed by Pierre Lescot and Jean Goujon in 1544. (Jean Bullant completed it when Lescot and Goujon were summoned, in 1546, to prepare the "Vieux Louvre.") What the house lacked in height it gained in the elegance and distinction of the ornaments designed for it by Goujon; even today we can still glimpse, in these metaphorical carvings, the excitement of a world in which Authority went hand in hand with Abundance, and Genius could be summoned as easily as a favorite hound. And when the house was just over a century old, and its new owner called upon François Mansart to enlarge it to something approaching its present looks and size, it seemed natural that Strength and Vigilance should be personified above the front door. In 1677, when Madame de Sévigné became tenant of the house, she found the phrase that sums up, for ourselves as much as for her, the charm of the Marais in its heyday: she would never need to move, she said, for she had not only a beautiful house but also "bel air, une belle cour, un beau jardin, un beau quartier."

The Hôtel Carnavalet is still a very beautiful building, and in Madame de Sévigné's own apartments there are lingering intimations of a private existence. But the Carnavalet has inevitably taken on a municipal air. Additions have been made that, though sometimes admirable in themselves, are irrelevant to the *hôtel* itself: the "Arcade Nazareth" on the Rue des Francs-Bourgeois, for instance, which dates from the time of Henri II, the façade of the Maison des Marchands-Drapiers, which once stood in the Rue Sainte-Opportune, and the façade of the Pavillon de Choiseul, which was brought over, stone by stone, from the Rue Saint-Augustin. The student of François Anguier's sculpture will also find, in an inner courtyard, two statues of his which stood on the Porte Saint-Antoine until its destruction in 1778. To these things one might add the noble statue of Louis XIV by Coysevox, which now stands in the *cour l'honneur;* this could be called a particularly Parisian piece, in that it was erected to commemorate one of Louis XIV's rare visits to his capital and all the expenses were paid for by the Ville de Paris. There is, however, no denying that all these additions give the Carnavalet the air of a superior antique shop; this is not the Marais as its first inhabitants knew it.

The Carnavalet is one of the most delightful and amusing of all museums. To many visitors, on the other hand, the Archives Nationales may seem to have little to offer. Not everyone enjoys grubbing about among old papers; and even among those who do, there must be many who would not know what to ask for or how to exploit the enormous holdings of the Archives. A double reassurance, therefore: not only is there usually to be found at the Archives a special exhibition of great interest and manageable size, but the buildings themselves are among the most beautiful and arresting in all Paris.

Pierre-Alexis Delamair was, by all accounts, a little-known architect when he began the construction, in the first decade of the eighteenth century, of both the Hôtel de Rohan and its neighbor, the Hôtel de Soubise. The motto of the Rohan family is *Roi ne puys, Duc ne daigne, Rohan suys;* these two magnificent houses are, in a sense, the visible counterpart of that tremendous assertion. They have an aristocratic brilliance that disdains ingratiation. Likable they are not, but it is not their purpose to be liked. Their purpose is to impress, and impress they undoubtedly do, even if the Hôtel de Rohan has lost nearly all its original interior decoration and the great staircase of the Hôtel Soubise was redone under Louis-Philippe. Delamair's elevations ring out in the memory like a trumpet heard out of doors on a frosty morning; and inside the Hôtel de Rohan, where the decoration was debauched beyond repair by the hundred years' residence of the Imprimerie Nationale, you may still see one of the masterpieces of the *dix-huitième:* the Cabinet des Singes, with monkey motifs painted by Huet in 1745. Over the entrance to what was once the stables, there may be seen Robert le Lorrain's relief of the horses of Apollo—one of the most beautiful things of its sort since Hellenic times.

When we come to the Hôtel de Soubise there is, beyond question, a further heightening of tone. This is not, and can never have been, an ordinary private house. It was through the liberality of Louis XIV that Princess Anne de Rohan was able to buy up the Hôtel de Guise and erect the Hôtel de Soubise in its place. The horseshoe-shaped *cour d'honneur,* more than sixty yards long and more than forty yards wide, with its columns and its pilasters and its balustraded terrace, is the most imposing thing of its kind in Paris.

Robert le Lorrain was again called upon, to sculpt the four statues of the seasons (copies, now) that look down from the first floor of the great mansion. Seated figures of Prudence and Sagacity ornament the pediment, and at the foot of the *toit à la française* may be found those personifications on whom it was possible to call at will: *les Génies des Arts*. In the elevation itself, Delamair achieved a style yet more august than that of the Hôtel de Rohan, a style to which only a select few—*les grands*, as La Bruyère and Saint-Simon conceived them—could aspire.

If the Hôtel de Soubise has kept a great part of its interior decoration intact, the credit must go to the Archives, in whose care the house has been since 1808. But for the initial impetus of fine judgment we must go back to the splendidly named Hercule-Mériadec, Duc de Rohan-Rohan and later Prince de Rohan, who had possession of the house from 1709 until his death just forty years later. He it was who commissioned the rooms that, even today, give us an authentic idea of what a great town house was like in the reign of Louis XV. To those who cherish the work of Boucher and Carle Vanloo, or of Boffrand, Lambert-Sigismond Adam, Jean-Baptiste Le Moyne, Jean Restout, and Pierre-Charles Tremollières, the Hôtel de Soubise is a place of enchantment. To those who enjoy *la petite histoire*, I recommend the study of all that happened in these two great mansions in the eighteenth century. Not that much of it does not belong to History proper; it was Goethe, after all, who said of the trial of the Cardinal de Rohan in 1786 that it was "the first page in the preface to the French Revolution," and when the Cardinal was acquitted and a great crowd came to acclaim him it was at a window in the Hôtel de Rohan that he stood to return his thanks.

One or two private individuals have also shown what can be done to save the Marais. One of its most famous mansions is, for instance, the Hôtel des Ambassadeurs de Hollande at 47, Rue Vieille-du-Temple; "a house so beautiful," La Bruyère said, "that nobody could live in it." It is in very good hands and everything possible has been done to restore it to its original state—no small feat, in that after the Revolution the interior had been more or less entirely gutted and remodeled. But now the decorations by Cotelle and Jean-

The Horses of Apollo, frieze above the stables in the courtyard of the Hôtel de Rohan. Robert le Lorrain

The salon of Marie-Sophie de Courcillon, Princesse de Soubise, in the Hôtel de Soubise, 60, Rue des Francs-Bourgeois. Germain Boffrand, 1736–39. J. Guillot photograph

The main courtyard of the Hôtel des Ambassadeurs de Hollande. Built from plans by Pierre Cottard, 1650–60. The carving on the portals is by Thomas Regnaudin. R. Landin photograph

Baptiste Corneille are back in the *grande galerie,* as are Sarrazin's wooden reliefs in the *grand salon* and, in an adjoining room, the bas-reliefs and trophies of Regnaudin and the ceiling-painting of Michel Dorigny. The house is not normally open to the public, but even to see the two courtyards is an education in itself. Push gently, therefore, upon the great Medusa-masked street door (Regnaudin again—War and Peace are seated back to back above the lintel) and you will find yourself in the *cour d'honneur.* Cottard's mansion has the peculiarity that the pediment is supported by four figures of children—tiny stalwarts who nowhere betray, unless it be in their distended bellies, the strain of such a duty. The sidewalks, too, have their peculiarity: four huge sundials, the work of a Carmelite monk who was also a member of the Académie des Sciences. But it is in the inner courtyard that Pierre Cottard's ingenuity and sense of fantasy found fullest outlet—here it was that plays were acted, with pilasters and niched statues and a *trompe l'oeil* landscape to act as a permanent backdrop. Facing this is a terrace, at first-floor level, with an Ionic portico, and here and there may be seen those elegant inventions most neatly summarized as "the attributes of the arts and sciences."

Leopold Mozart and His Two Children.
Carmontelle, 1764

Such a house deserves great tenants, and two at least of those who lived in it in pre-Revolutionary times can be classed as such. Madame du Deffand was the earlier of the two; the other was Beaumarchais. It was in this house that Madame du Deffand conducted the salon so familiar to readers of Lytton Strachey and the Yale Edition of Horace Walpole. Here, too, Beaumarchais wrote *Le Mariage de Figaro*, and there was given to the world one of those archetypes of human impulse that each subsequent generation has to refashion for itself: Chérubin. For me to list all the great, and all the popular, and all the great *and* popular novelists who have had a shot at the Cherubinesque would be tedious. (Raymond Radiguet, in *Le Diable au Corps*, has a particularly Parisian variant.) In music the genre found late and sumptuous expression in the Octavian of Richard Strauss and Hugo von Hofmannsthal; but to most people, Chérubin in the opera house is Cherubino in the *Nozze di Figaro* of Mozart and Lorenzo da Ponte. And it is a curious fact that Mozart spent the winter of 1763–64, when he was eight years old, in the Marais.

That Mozart as a grown man was not happy in Paris is a fact only too comprehensible to those who have had anything to do with *le tout Paris* in its relation to music. We can call "Parisian," if we like, the extreme suavity and finesse of execution that marks the two works most often associated with his third visit to Paris: the concerto for flute and harp, K. 299, and the symphony in D major, K. 297. It is instructive, however, to contrast these pellucidities with the full truth, as it is revealed in Mozart's letters, of the boredom and exasperation that he endured in Paris.

But the Mozart that we can trace beyond question to the Marais is the indulged little boy whom we see in Carmontelle's famous family group. The Hôtel de Beauvais, at 68, Rue François-Miron, in which he stayed with his father and sister, is one of the most elegant and ingenious of Parisian *hôtels*.

The site did not allow of those august quadrilaterals—outer courtyard, *cour d'honneur*, garden—that had become normal, if not obligatory, in the Marais. We can still judge of the skill and originality with which Antoine Lepautre solved this problem: the rounded peristyle with the noble bareness of eight Doric columns gives on to the famous circular courtyard (two-storied, in Lepautre's time) with its wealth of delicate and allusive ornament. This is the kind of architectural feat that can only be appreciated *in situ*. No photograph can give the "feel" of Lepautre's achievement, and although we can reel off, item by item, the felicities that once amounted to a house of genius they were, after all, devised as part of an ensemble, and an ensemble that the visitor himself is privileged to complete. This is a masterpiece built to the human scale, and only when we are actually inside it does it yield itself entirely.

The Marais was, as I have said, aristocratic in its origins, and the Hôtel de Beauvais has the kind of distinction, the confident disregard for difficulty, that we may agree to call aristocratic. But it also had, from the start, one feature that looked quite the other way. For, whereas most of the great mansions of the Marais presented to the street a high blank face on which "I care nothing for trade" was written for all to see, the Hôtel de Beauvais let out its ground-floor front as shops.

Pierre de Beauvais was not in a position to look down on trade, since he had kept a ribbon shop at the time of his marriage to Catherine Bellier. His wife, lady-in-waiting to Anne of Austria, became in time the closest of her confidants. To her, in fact, fell the honor of relieving Louis XIV, then aged sixteen, of his virginity. When the news of this feat got about, a great wave of enthusiasm ran through the court, and not only Catherine herself but her husband and her father-in-law also were honored with many marks of favor. At that time the little ground-floor shops may not have seemed of much account to her; but later, when she was a widow and age had taken away such looks as she had ever had, they came in very conveniently and provided, it would seem, a great part of the money with which she bought herself lovers. So the practice of "living over the shop" in the Marais may be said to have begun even before the end of the seventeenth century.

It was, however, at the Revolution that the original owners of the Marais were turned out once and for all and the quarter was given over to commerce—much of it small in scale and individualistic in character. By 1825 fifty hatters, fifty-four gilders, and a horde of jewelers, founders, milliners, haberdashers, toy makers, and independent artisans were installed in the Marais, and it became a maze more fit for the Minotaur than for the uninstructed tourist. The Marais was one huge workshop, and those who dreamed of its reconstitution as a culture park had to reckon with municipal councilors like the one who protested not so long ago against the projected acquisition of the Hôtel de Juigné for use as a museum. "We've museums enough already," he said, "and, what's more, museums are bad for business."

The *commerçant* was often blamed for the look of the Marais, and of course, his activities were often pernicious from a purely architectural point of view. Anyone who tears the tripes out of a mansion by Mansart or Bruant must expect (and may be expected to ignore) our censure; and we can say the same of anyone who plasters the outside of

Above: The courtyard of the Hôtel de Beauvais, 1658. Deidi von Schaewen photograph. The plans below show how Lepautre utilized the awkward site, placing the *grande salle* on the second floor above the boutiques, and tucking the stables under a terrace garden. Opposite: It was from the central balcony of the Hôtel in 1660—on a day when the shops were closed—that Anne of Austria (the Queen Mother), the Queen of England, and Cardinal Mazarin awaited the triumphal entry into Paris of Louis XIV and Marie-Thérèse.

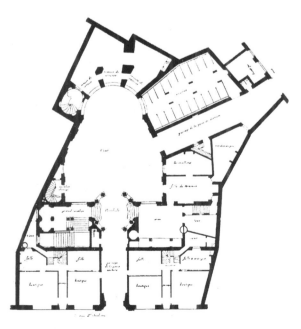

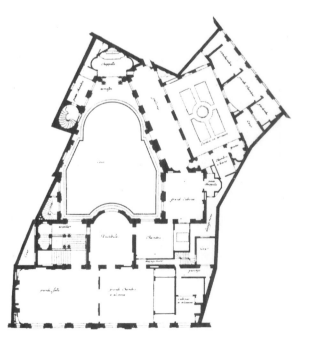

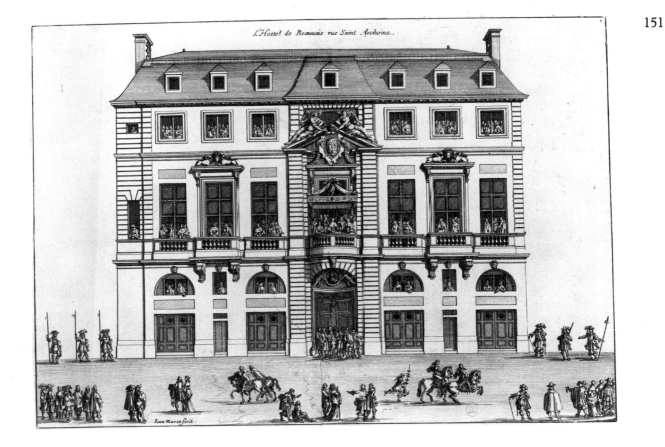

L'Hostel de Beauvais rue Saint Anthoine.

that house with embellishments drawn from the prehistory of advertising. Sometimes, I admit, these latter excesses acquire in time a full-bodied absurdity that has its likable side. Shotter Boys was not so nice, when he drew the Paris of the 1830s, as to leave out the advertisements that detailed across the whole height of a blank wall the merits of the Café Momus *(4 Billards: On Joue la Boule: Dejeuner à la Fourchette: Chocolat)* and those of M. Duclez, *tapissier*, who on occasion rented out *banquettes pour bals;* and it would be a poor stomach that turned at every billboard, failing to distinguish some fine freak of nomenclature here, a bold patch of nineteenth-century lettering there and, there once again, a turn of phrase that would have made the Goncourts reach for their notebooks.

Far worse than the exuberance of commerce was the behavior of those who bought up a great house and left it uncared for in the hope that, by degenerating beyond repair, it would allow them to replace it with some new and more lucrative construction. The Parisian takes a great pride in himself as a civilized being; but this won't wash with anyone who has made his way through knee-high grasses to where one of the highest products of French civilization lies rotting, with doors and windows wide open, rain coming through the roof, gutters stopped up, woodwork green with fungus, plaster tumbled all over the staircase . . . Such things were the true scandal of the Marais, and they resulted from a collapse of the will—an incapacity, that is to say, to carry through *any* policy, right or wrong, in respect of the Marais.

After an experience of this sort it is almost a comfort to retreat into a period when the Marais was frankly industrial, even if only *la petite industrie* was in question, and the aesthete had not even begun to say his say. Of this period *Fromont Jeune et Risler Aîné* is the classic portrayal; and it is worth noting that when Daudet came to describe the circumstances in which the book was written, it did not occur to him to say, whether by way of boasting or from a purely documentary motive, that the house in which he had lived, the Hôtel Lamoignon in the Rue des Francs-Bourgeois, was probably by one of the greatest of French architects, Jean-Baptiste Androuet Du Cerceau, and had been the home of Diane de France, daughter of Henri II, and the meeting place in the 1660s and 1670s of Racine, Boileau, La Rochefoucauld, and Madame de Sévigné. No: it was just a very old and rather comfortable house. "*Fromont* was written," he tells us, "in one of the oldest *hôtels* in the Marais. My study had very large light windows and looked out on to green leaves and the garden's blackened trellises. But immediately to the far side of this area of tranquillity and bird-song suburban working-class life took over. The smoke rose straight into the air from factory-chimneys, delivery wagons rumbled along the streets, and on the cobbles of a nearby yard we could hear, as Christmas approached, a sound that I can still call to mind: that of a hand-cart laden with toy-drums which rattled back and forth till seven in the evening. Nothing is healthier, nothing more stimulating than to write in the very place where one's characters have their being. My pages were traversed every day, at the appointed hour, by the inward and outward movement of employees, and by the bells that marked their coming and going. I never had to strain for 'local color': I had it all about me. The whole of the Marais was with me, working for me, bearing me aloft. . . .''

Now that the Hôtel Lamoignon has been remodeled in the interests of the Bibliothèque de la Ville de Paris we may once again consider it as one of the fiefs of literature. Its history in this respect has always been distinguished. Diane de France herself spoke Latin, Spanish, and Italian as well as she did French. When Madame de la Roche-Guyon rented the house in the 1650s, Benserade, one of the founding members of the Académie Française, was, as people say, "never out of the house." Lamoignon, her successor, entertained all the *beaux esprits* of the day. Madame de Sévigné has much to say of his hospitality—notably of an occasion on which Boileau was driven almost out of his senses by the suggestion that a Christian was not in duty bound to love God. (He left the room at a canter, sulked for the rest of the evening, and later, in the twelfth of his *Epîtres*, conjured before his astonished readers the image of the Deity rebuffing all those who had loved him and bidding welcome, instead, those who had come "to disabuse the angels of the necessity of loving Him.") But perhaps, to our taste, it was during Daudet's tenancy that a tape recorder would have been most useful at the Hôtel Lamoignon. Flaubert and Turgenev were frequent visitors, and we know from one or two tantalizing references that they both spoke with complete freedom there. Here is Edmond de Goncourt's first entry on the subject:

"Alphonse Daudet lives in the Hôtel Lamoignon, in the Marais. It's like a piece out of the Louvre with every corner lived in. In the immensities of what were once private apartments an immense number of tiny lodgings have been constructed—and workshops, too, each with its owner's name written up on the stone balustrade of the staircases. It was just the house that was needed to write *Fromont Jeune et Risler Aîné*. From the author's study you look out on to large gloomy glassed-in workshops and little gardens planted with black trees whose roots creep in and out of gas pipes. Little gardens where the pebbles are beginning to go green and boundaries are marked off with packing cases. Daudet has lived there for seven years. He told me that after a turbulent youth he had gradually 'settled down' in the peace and quiet of his steady and laborious surroundings and become, little by little, a different man."

Later entries are exasperatingly brief; but one in particular gives a real sense of occasion: "7th January, 1876. A gay and charming dinner at Daudet's, with a tureen of bouillabaisse and a roast of thrushes from Corsica. We were each of us next to people we liked, and things always taste better among people of talent who think well of one another. Flaubert's satisfaction burst out in an extreme violence of language, before which dear Mme. Daudet seemed to shrink into herself in terror. Zola took a perfectly natural delight in the way in which money and success transformed his way of life. Turgenev, who has the beginnings of gout, had come in his slippers. He had an original way of describing the experience. It was, he said, as if someone was trying to cut out his toe-nails with a round blunt knife."

We also have a child's-eye-view of these dinners. "We lived in an old house," Léon Daudet said in *Paris Vécu*, "which looked sumptuous but was divided into 'amusing' but inconvenient flats. Almost every Wednesday evening Flaubert, Zola, Turgenev, and Edmond de Goncourt would crowd into our modest dining room. I called them 'the giants' because Flaubert and Goncourt were so tall. ('Is it the giants' day today, Mama?') Flaubert and my father kept the table in a roar with their jokes. Flaubert's first words when he

The statue of Louis XIII in the Place des Vosges. Pierre Jahan photograph

arrived were invariably 'Good-evening, Alphonse, and how am I looking? Young as ever, don't you think?' The words 'Young as ever' always sent the 'giants' into fits of laughter. My mother had made me learn by heart the beginning of *Salammbo: C'était à Mégara, faubourg de Carthage, dans les jardins d'Hamilcar.* When I recited these beautiful lines to their author he would seize me in his powerful arms and lift me high in the air till I got a close view of his moustache *à la* Vercingetorix and his large and shining cheeks."

The Marais stayed as it was in Daudet's day for generations. The wholesale chemical manufacturers, the junk-jewelry makers, the "works of art" in bronze and zinc, the piece-work leather goods, the candelabra makers, the manufacturers of dental plates, pencil sharpeners, and abrasives, and the man who makes inkwells in the likeness of Notre-Dame—all were at home there, and they gave the Marais a favor very different from that of the great plain hideous Boulevard, two minutes' walk away, with which Beaumarchais's name has been disgraced. These were people independent in mind, if not in action, and it is as gross an error of judgment as of manners to treat them as regrettable adjuncts to the historic scene.

It was rare to hear of a foreign visitor lodging in the Marais. The quarter had, admittedly, certain disadvantages. Good restaurants were few. There was no theater, although once Beaumarchais had one of his own at 11, Rue de Sévigné. Hotels, though plentiful enough in the Bottin, turned out either to offer hospitality of a special sort or to be, in effect if not in name, apartment houses where a vacancy was rare. Dilapidation was often so far advanced as to scare away all but the most determined. The traveler might happen, as I said earlier, on a street so firmly given over to an exiled minority (Poles in the Rue de Jouy or the Rue des Nonnains-d'Hyères, Arabs in the Rue François-Miron) that he felt himself unwanted. There was also a great deal of prostitution in the western section of the Marais, though it was neither hectic nor ferocious: "tranquil" and "domesticated" were the first words that came to mind for the *bars à filles* of the Marais, where rough words were rare and it was rarer still to see a hand raised in anger. To provide such places was, as a matter of fact, one of the Marais' historic functions. Even the street names bear witness to it: Rue du Petit-Musc, for instance, is a corruption of the thirteenth-century Pute y Musse—"Whore-in-Hiding Street," that is to say. So these unpretending ladies should, by rights, have been ranked, façades and all, as historic monuments. But it was not everyone, all the same, whom it suited to live above them.

Visits to the Marais tended, therefore, to be of at most a day's duration. It was a mistake, as I suggested earlier, to set out without a specific itinerary in mind; and it was also a mistake to do as many people did and begin with the Place des Vosges. Ideal for the agoraphile, this majestic ensemble deserves, for one thing, a visit of its own. So much is it the contrary of everything else in the Marais—so much, in fact, the image of an enlightened uniformity—that a plenary session at the luncheon table may well be needed before we can respond fittingly to the irregular and secretive character of much that lies around it.

Several things are wrong with the Place des Vosges as it stands today; and one of them is the savorless *jardin public* that now stands where once the turf was smooth enough for croquet and the wrought-iron grille dated from 1682. The French genius for large enclosed spaces has decidedly not been exercised in the encumberment of the great *place* with degraded elements from a variety of inapposite periods. Yet there are openings here for genius of one sort or another: if ornamental waters were in fashion we could have an inland lake, a huge glittering quadrilateral that would turn the heart of the Marais into an Innen Alster, decorative beyond the dreams of Dufy and alive on fine Sundays with white sail and golden oar. But perhaps green is the color that would ideally complement the rosy brickwork, the white stone, and the razor-blade blue of the tiles. Grass, in fact, such as was laid out in the time of the founder of the *place*, Henri IV.

The Place des Vosges.
Alain Perceval
photograph

Henri IV loved the Place Royale, as it was then called. It was his idea, after all, to turn an enormous horse market into the largest and most elegant ensemble yet attempted in Paris. The entire southern side of the *place* was built at his own expense, and those who agreed to build on the other three sides in identical style were given their sites free. There was never a hint of fortification; no attempt was made to overbear; civilized intentions spoke out in the general design. And this design has survived almost entire: thirty-six out of thirty-seven pavilions still stand, each with its four-arched arcade at street level and its four tall windows on the first and the second floors. Within, much harm has been done; and although Le Brun's ceilings from No. 14 are now in the Musée Carnavalet, only the staircase in that once-famous ensemble had survived its adaptation as town hall (1795), primary school (1860), and synagogue (1866).

Persistence and a civil turn of phrase will, nonetheless, reveal much in the Place des Vosges that has come through in good state. Even to hear tell of the ceilings painted in 1660 at No. 5, the surviving Louis XVI boiseries in No. 9, which belonged to Rachel, the painted ceiling beams in No. 23, and the salon of the Hôtel de Breteuil, No. 4, was enough to make one dream of reconstituting the Place des Vosges as a kind of free city for the Francophile. To aim to reestablish it as the center of *le tout Paris* seemed pointless, however; the westward pull of fashion had had two hundred years' start. As a center of government, the Place des Vosges would be very awkwardly placed. What it could still provide in supreme degree is a residential center, with one or more hotels of a high class, a library, a chamber ensemble of Juilliard quality, and a select corps of Visiting Fellows who would be on hand, with no fixed obligations, for two or three months at a time. At the Abbaye de Pontigny in the days of Paul Desjardins it was possible to distill from the conversation of André Gide, André Malraux, Roger Martin du Gard, Léon Brunschvig, and many other less well known an image of French intelligence at its most luminous— and nothing can ever quite cloud that image. For there to be a place of that kind in the middle of Paris, in surroundings of extreme splendor, would be the wisest of official investments.

Meanwhile the Place des Vosges was neither one thing nor the other. It had none of the pauseless, antlike activity that marks the rest of the Marais. The texture of life was thin and dull. But the Musée Victor Hugo was not to be missed, and there was at any rate one point of interest that had to be sought out in classical Marais style: the pretty Petit-Hôtel de Sully, which is hidden away to the left of the inner courtyard of 9, Place des Vosges, and well repaid the trip.

Once away from the Place des Vosges, the basic character of the Marais reasserted itself. It became, that is to say, a place of secrets and surprises. (The Place des Vosges has, on the contrary, a sort of noble candor about it, a ruddy glow that seems to call rather for what Shakespeare called "daylight and champaign" than for the winding alleys, high blind walls and redoubtable doors of the Marais.) Every visitor will have his own hierarchy of sights in the Marais: the Gothic-fancier, for instance, will prize above many of the later monuments the pepper-pot towers of the *portail de Clisson*. These date from the 1370s and 80s, and when Delamair was building the Hôtel de Soubise he decreed, with an indulgence rare at that period, that the gateway, sole vestige of the Manoir de Clisson which had once stood on the site, should be left where it was. Those whose taste lies rather toward the immediately pre-classical era will probably prefer the Hôtel Fieubet on the Quai des Célestins; almost all of Mansart's work has been destroyed, but the so-called "Spanish Taste" ran splendidly riot in the ornament and decoration of the section that borders the Rue du Petit-Musc. For Louis XIII at its purest and most lyrical the Hôtel de Chalons-Luxembourg, 25, Rue Geoffroy l'Asnier, would be hard to equal; the garden front and the street doorway with its great sculpted cartouche are unforgettably fine. Those who take to the Hôtel de Rohan and the Hôtel de Soubise, on the other hand, will find similar qualities in the Hôtel d'Aumont, 7, Rue de Jouy, the Hôtel de Sagonne, 28, Rue des Tournelles, and the sumptuous Hôtel de Juigné (also called the Hôtel Salé) in the Rue de Thorigny. These are palaces and make no pretense to be anything else: the enormous stone panache on the *façade sur cour* of Jean Boullier's Hôtel Salé must, for instance, be one of the most grandiloquent things of its kind, and the staircase and vestibule inside that same *hôtel* are just this side of ostentation, with their wall motif of Corinthian

Hôtel Fieubet, 2, Quai des Célestins, now the Collège Massillon. Jules Hardouin-Mansart, 1678–81

pilasters, heavy-winged eagles, straining Atlases, and uxurious medallions. At the Hôtel d'Aumont no such dangers were run; Le Vau and François Mansart remained impeccably severe. This great house, with its garden (one of the largest in the Marais), has been the property of the Ville de Paris since 1938, and it does not speak well for the city's management.

The thunderers did not have it quite all their way in the Marais. Even in the sixteenth century, as we may judge from the tiny and distinguished *hôtel* in the courtyard at 20, Rue Ferdinand Duval, certain people were concerned to build beautifully on a restricted scale. The seventeenth-century façade of the Hôtel d'Albret, 31, Rue des Francs-Bourgeois, and the delicious little Hôtel de Delisle-Mansart, 22, Rue Saint-Gilles, are other examples of Style triumphant in the Marais. Best of all in this line is, to my taste, the house that Libéral Bruant, the architect of the Salpêtrière and the Invalides, built for himself in 1685. It stands in the Rue de la Perle, of which all the houses on the south side were built by Libéral Bruant in the 1680s. No. 1—and never did a house better deserve the number— is the least showy of buildings: door and windows stand in semicircular arcades, and between them are four circular niches, each with a bust of Roman inspiration. The pediment is triangular; two portly *génies* sit astride horns of plenty, and between them is an *oeil-de-boeuf* window. Anyone could draw this façade with a ruler and a pair of compasses, but in Bruant's hands it makes eye-music. (It is now, by the way, the Museum of the Lock, and more fun than that name might suggest.)

Hôtel Libéral Bruant

As I said earlier, the Marais is in full ebullition. Accounts of it are out of date before the ink is dry. Some of these changes are all to the good. Some of them are in fact the fulfillment of dreams long ranked as impractical. Some of them are horrible. As a result, the balance of the Marais is changing street by street and almost hour by hour.

The first and most obvious thing to be said is that money is coming into the Marais in quantities that have not been seen there since the eighteenth century. Public money is going into major projects like the enlargement of the Musée Carnavalet, the establishment of the Picasso Museum in the Hôtel Salé, and the rehabilitation, inch by inch, of houses great and small. Private money is going into the restoration of houses that can be made over into expensive apartments. It is also going into the shops and restaurants and services of many kinds that make life more agreeable for people who have a little money. If there is something of opportunism in all of this, and something quite often of fakery, there is also an imaginative energy that could turn out well.

It might be expected that the ancient life of the Marais—the life of the artisan, the *ouvrière à domicile,* the ethnic minority, the slippered savant, and the ambiguous bar—would be altogether driven out by these changes. But for one reason or another, the Marais cannot be made over in that way. Its inhabitants are too tenacious, for one thing. For another, the law for which André Malraux was responsible in 1962 rules out the kind of radical transformation that has happened in other parts of Paris. People who want to stay on in the Marais can usually manage to do so. There is a fundamental polarity, even

Flower market at Les
Halles, Rue Rambuteau.
The Halles Centrales,
the great market of the
Marais, built in cast-iron
by Victor Baltard and
Félix-Emmanuel Callet,
1851–54, was pulled
down in 1972–73.
Robert Doisneau
photograph

At Les Halles, a seafood-
restaurant owner buys fish
for bouillabaisse. Robert
Doisneau photograph

Centre National d'Art
Contemporain Georges
Pompidou. Renzo Piano
and Richard Rogers,
1971–77. Ken Windsor
photograph

so, between the Marais that is struggling to stay much as it always was and the Marais
that is becoming in effect a year-round resort town.

The Centre National d'Art Contemporain Georges Pompidou—more often known
simply as Beaubourg—has played a part in this. Though not opened until February 1977—
at a moment, therefore, at which the rehabilitation of the Marais was already well under
way—it brought to the area between the Boulevard de Sebastopol and the Marais an almost
frenetic animation. Not only that, but it changed both the look and the feel of Paris in a
completely new way. It took a piece of land that was both historic and largely derelict
and razed it, leaving only the Eglise Saint-Merri to speak for the charms of flamboyant
Gothic architecture.

On that piece of land it put down a building by Renzo Piano and Richard Rogers that was like nothing else in Paris. It was a building enormous in size, outrageous in color and design, and completely out of key with its surroundings. But it soon became clear that the Centre Pompidou was to the 1970s what the Eiffel Tower had been to the 1880s: an erection as indispensable as it was provocative. No sooner was it there than it was difficult to imagine Paris without it. In its first year of activity it drew more than six million visitors. Many of them swore never to go again, and among Parisians in particular there were many who took against it without ever having been near it. Yet it must have been doing something right, and now there is every sign that, so far from desecrating Paris, it has done Paris a great deal of good.

"What kind of good?" is the question. Beaubourg is not primarily a gallery of painting and sculpture, though it incorporates a museum of modern art whose collections have been very much improved and enlarged since Beaubourg was opened. It is not primarily a library, though it includes the first free-access public library that Paris has ever known. It is not an open university, since it neither gives out degrees nor holds formal courses. It is not a kindergarten, though children are encouraged to come and feel at home there. Nor is it a school of music, though it has an underground annex (eight thousand square meters in extent), directed by Pierre Boulez, that is the envy of many another capital city.

It is all of these things, and much else besides. Those who detest Beaubourg—and there are still plenty of them around—like to say that people ride the exterior moving staircase to the top, take a quick look around, and go back down again. But the truth is that these people see Paris from that moving staircase as no one has ever seen it before. The Pompidou Center is not a high building. The visitor can "see more" from the Eiffel Tower, or from the Sacré-Coeur. What he does not get from those higher points of vantage is the feeling of participation, the instantaneity, the sense of being way aloft and yet within hallooing distance of the ground, that he gets at Beaubourg. Beaubourg gives him in no time at all the texture of Paris, the inner life of Paris, the layered secrecies of Paris. It shows him how Paris has changed, and it also shows him how it has stayed the same.

And the visitor enjoys it all the more because almost everyone has by now experienced one of the great disappointments of the twentieth century—the fact that we really don't see anything much from an airplane. Doubtless we see the mysterious incisions on the landscape of Peru as no one ever saw them before. But for a close look, and an intelligent look, a balloon wins every time. And as we cannot go ballooning at will—and in Paris would have to get police permission for it—we'd better settle for Beaubourg.

If we turn aside from that moving staircase and walk into the museum proper, we may find ourselves disoriented. Beaubourg is not like any other museum in Paris. Its public is not the public of the Louvre, or of the Bibliothèque Nationale, or of the museums of modern art on the Avenue du President-Wilson. Its huge and eager public has an informal, unstructured, and faintly insubordinate mode of attention. It is the first generation of museum-goers to have been raised with a television set almost always at hand. And what it brings to a museum is not the traditional engrossment—often indistinguishable from mortal boredom—of the old-style visitor. It is an inquisitive, impatient, improvisatory turn of mind. People flick from room to room at Beaubourg the way they flick from channel to channel on a television set.

Neither the politics nor the poetics of Beaubourg lie within the scope of this book. Its outward appearance does, on the other hand. What differentiates Beaubourg from every other building in Paris is the total, the reckless, the unmitigated candor of its operation. In many aspects of their lives, Parisians are a secretive, devious, ungiving people. They mind their own business—so they would say—and they expect other people to do the same. Buildings are there to cover things up, not to leave them open to everyone who passes by in the street. Not only does Beaubourg display its every last secret in public, but it displays them *in color*. Nothing could be more abhorrent to the traditional Parisian. He would as soon show you his bank balance as let you see his plumbing, his ventilation system, or the material in his home computer. Beaubourg puts it all on view.

It is also held against Beaubourg that it works. This is not to say that it is a model of technical efficiency or inconspicuous hard wearing. Beaubourg was not built in expec-

Centre Pompidou. Ken
Windsor photograph

tation of anything like the degree of popular success that it has actually had, and it has
naturally had its problems on that account. But Beaubourg works, in as much as it makes
the arts accessible all the way across the board to a huge miscellaneous public. It also
makes thought and discussion accessible on a scale that was formerly the privilege of a
few.

Doubtless there is dilution: not everyone who goes to Beaubourg can take in all that
goes on there, any more than everything that goes on there reaches an ideal standard of
excellence. Sometimes the fairground takes over from the classroom. But Molière did not
despise the fairground, and neither should we. Beaubourg has broken the mold of Parisian
life in a way for which it will never be forgiven; but when we remember the tradition for
which we prize the Marais—the tradition of new plays, new books, new music, new
painting, new argument and new architecture—we may think that it is in Beaubourg, and
not in the boutiques, the reconstituted façades, and the million-dollar apartments of the
new Marais, that that tradition is still alive.

VII

The Paris of the First Empire

The Invalides. Alain Perceval photograph

Very few men have done as much for Paris as Napoleon I, and it is ironical that he, who wished to be buried "beside the Seine, among the people of France whom I have so dearly loved," should lie sunk in a well, with six coffins, a sarcophagus of porphyry, and twelve colossal figures of Victory between him and either the river or the people.

The company is good, certainly: Turenne, Vauban, and Foch, three of the greatest names in French military history, Napoleon's two brothers and his only son complete the little band; and, although the whole enterprise pulls Jules Hardouin-Mansart's church out of scale, Napoleon, no connoisseur in such matters, would probably not have cared. The Invalides is, if not the heart of France, at any rate the heart of *la Gloire;* and it is still easy to picture, in the magnificent setting that is Libéral Bruant's masterpiece, the occasions on which the Emperor passed his veterans in review. There are a great many relics of Napoleon in the Invalides museum, but their tenor is on the whole vespertinal—valedictory, one might say. Too many date from St. Helena, too few from his years of triumphant activity. Admittedly, few objects could be more evocative than his stick, bed, armchair, and dressing gown, and the garden seat from which one bar was removed to help him gaze in greater comfort to the South Atlantic. But neither there, nor in the stern beauties of the *hôtel* itself, is there any flavor of the Paris of 1811.

That is indeed the paradox of the Invalides. It is one of the noblest buildings that this earth has to show. The surroundings are just right, but they were laid out by Robert de Cotte in 1704. Even the recent elm disease could not destroy the nobility of the Esplanade, but that too owes nothing to Napoleon. Libéral Bruant was wonderfully seconded by Jules Hardouin-Mansart, who built the gaunt beautiful church and the stupendous dome. But it was Louis XIV, not Napoleon, who had the happiness of seeing those buildings go up. (He enjoyed it prodigiously, by the way.)

In no time at all, the number of soldiers who were looked after in the Invalides rose to five, six, and seven thousand. But that was long before Napoleon's time. Today we glimpse him merely here and there in the Invalides. If our fancy is caught by the eight bronze cannons that were cast in 1708 for Frederick I of Prussia, for instance, we may remember that they were brought back from Vienna by Napoleon in 1806. But in general, the Invalides as we know it is a monument to the age of Louis XIV. It was Louis XIV, not Napoleon, who formulated the notion of *la gloire* that is there enshrined.

If the Invalides in recent years has been brought back to concert pitch, the credit must go in large part to André Malraux. No mean adherent of *la gloire,* he set himself from 1962 onward to get the bureaucrats out of the Invalides and restore something of its original character, which was that of a magniloquent garrison with a hospital attached to it.

He did well, and many people think that the installation of the Musée de l'Armée within the Hôtel des Invalides is a great success, just as they are moved by the captured colors of this or that foreign regiment that hang in the church. These are delicate matters, into which a proper national pride enters. But I have to record a dissenting opinion. Despite the great beauty and peculiarity of many individual items of arms and armor that turn up in its display of early military equipment, the army museum is drab, regressive, and *triste.* Trailing from room to room, we do not hear the drumbeat or the trumpet call that made the French army in its great days the terror of Europe. We hear the cries of the wounded men who counted the long days in these same rooms, and we are entitled to remark that when we reach more recent times—the seventy-five-years' war, above all, that occupied France and Germany for much of the period between 1870 and 1945—the coverage lacks both substance and imagination.

These after all were colossal events. No Frenchman and no German born between 1850 and 1920 was left untouched by them. No European of any nation can fail to have been affected by them to one degree or another. They made inevitable the nature of American involvement in World War II. What we see in the Invalides in no way approaches a factual, much less an imaginative presentation of these matters. And this from a nation of great historians!

As for the captured colors in the Eglise Saint-Louis, they too must leave a somber impression upon an imaginative visitor. It is true that in May 1814 the officer in charge of the Invalides burned fourteen hundred flags that had been taken from the enemies of France, lest they fall into the hands of the victorious Allies. It is also true that something of the same kind was done in the summer of 1940 when the German armies were about to enter Paris. Admirable as all this was, it leaves the Eglise Saint-Louis with row upon row of tattered standards, most of which were captured during colonial wars in Africa and elsewhere. We no longer think those wars very grand, and I for one do not rejoice at the evidence of those paltry triumphs. There was much to be proud of in the French colonial record, but these particular butcheries do not come under that head.

For that matter, not everyone loves Napoleon, either. But what concerns us here is his influence upon the city of Paris, and upon the arts of decoration as they developed under his aegis. In particular, we remember his apotheosis in Notre-Dame—the day in 1804 on which the Pope looked on while Napoleon himself put the imperial crown on his head. He knew that thereafter it was for him to encourage the arts, to shape taste, and to leave his mark upon every department of decoration. He did not at first know how to

The Invalides seen from the Pont Alexandre III. Pierre Jahan photograph

do it—for a long time he slept in a bed that had been used by Louis XVI—but he knew that his people, his family, and he himself must somehow be validated in the arts. "His Majesty wishes to create what is new, not to buy what is old" was the standard reply to those who offered what we would call "antiques."

Gradually he found his way. Artisans who had flourished before 1789 were given new commissions. Factories were put back into use. Medals by the dozen were struck. The use of French silks was made mandatory both for wall hangings and for any lady who hoped to be seen at Court. Cabinetmakers and bronze founders got loans to get them on their feet again. Paris alone had more than nine hundred silversmiths during the Empire period, and Thomire the bronze founder could call upon up to nine hundred skilled men in times of high demand. Rarely have such beautiful guns, such seductive silverware, and such an allurement of bronze mounts been available as a matter of course.

As for the color, I owe to James Parker of the Metropolitan Museum of Art the observation that "the vibrant Empire colors have a symbolism all their own. There is the fiery poppy shade; it was worn because Napoleon brought back the seeds of Egyptian field-poppies in his boots, muddied by the Nile. There is the forest green of Napoleon's liveries. And there is the splendid amaranth, the deep cockscomb red beloved of the Bonapartes because it was the color of Immortality." It is not an everyday regime that sets itself that kind of criterion.

Meanwhile there is one great single monument to Napoleon himself: the center of Paris as we know it.

He himself had no doubts of this, though he wished that he had had longer to carry his projects through. The thought of Paris came back to him continually on St. Helena—more especially on those bad days when Lady Holland's ice-machine failed to work, the *Morning Post* was forbidden him, and he was reduced to asking his companions in exile for ready money. Egypt, for instance, had made an immense impression upon him; but nothing in Egypt, he felt, could compare with Paris and the Tuileries. There was a time, too, in 1816, when the English newspapers alleged that Napoleon, like other dictators, had salted away a vast fortune in some country other than his own. He retaliated, in the humid silences of Longwood, with a list of what he called his real treasure: the harbors, roads, canals, passes, factories, and farms with which he had embellished Europe, and in particular "the construction of the Louvre, the *greniers publics*, the Banque de France, the Canal de l'Ourcq; the Paris water supply; the drains, quays, and manifold improvements to that same great capital. . . ." And of his general policy in Paris he gave an interesting account, in August of the same year, while out on a country walk.

He had always dreamed, he said, of making Paris the true capital of Europe. "A city of two, three, even four million inhabitants, something fabulous, colossal, unknown in earlier times . . . with public buildings on an appropriate scale.

"If I had only had twenty years and a little leisure, people would have looked in vain for Paris as it used to be. I should have changed the whole face of France. I would have shown the world the difference between a constitutional Emperor and a King of France. The kings of France knew nothing of administration, had no civic sense, never showed themselves as anything but great gentlemen who ruined their bailiffs. And the people themselves . . . ephemeral whimsies were all they were fit for: nothing that would last. I never cared for those fêtes that the Ville de Paris wanted me to give—dinners, dances, firework displays that cost four, six, eight hundred thousand francs a time, brought Paris to a standstill for days on end, and were as expensive to dismantle as to prepare.

"When you've done as much as I have in life you'll understand how difficult it is to do anything properly. If it was a question of a private apartment in one of the imperial palaces, there was nothing that couldn't be done, and done quickly. But if I wanted to enlarge the Tuileries gardens, or unblock the drains, or clean up a few slums, or do anything at all for the general public, instead of for a privileged individual—why, it needed all my strength of will, and I had to write six or ten letters a day and work myself into a rage. I spent thirty millions on the drains of Paris, though nobody gives me credit for it now. . . . The houses that I pulled down to make room for the Carrousel and the Louvre cost another seventeen million. What I did was immense, but what I was planning to do! That was on a different scale altogether."

A pair of gilt bronze candelabra in the neo-classical style from the manufactory of Pierre-Philippe Thomire, c. 1810–15. Thomire was the foremost designer of bronzes in the early 19th century in France, and goldsmith to Napoleon.

Big talk, of course—but not boastful talk. Napoleon began, after all, from conditions of near-chaos. The *beaux quartiers* were abused or abandoned; craftsmen by the thousand had left the capital and gone abroad, or to the provinces. Light and water were available spasmodically, or not at all; fresh paint was unimaginable; churches did duty as arsenals or granaries; the very word "pavement" did not exist. Paris was still, in very large degree, a city of the late sixteenth century: Henri IV's "Grand-Ville," in fact. Those who doubt this have only to go and look at the Rue Visconti, which runs between the Rue Bonaparte and the Rue de Seine. This is the street in which Racine died, Delacroix painted Chopin's portrait, and Balzac set up his printing press. It is narrow, dark, and sad; one visit is usually enough. But in 1810 the Rue Visconti stood out as an exceptionally agreeable place in which to live.

When Napoleon began to reign, the Hôtel Biron was a dance hall, the Hôtel Conti a horse market, the Hôtel du Duc de Chabot a bathhouse, the Hôtel de Luynes a crèche. Feeling against the once-aristocratic Faubourg Saint-Germain was so intense that, even in 1815, when Napoleon on his return from Elba made a sally into the town, incognito, and was at once surrounded by an enthusiastic crowd, he had an anxious quarter of an hour when the way home led through the Faubourg. "A single stone," he said afterward, "an inflammatory word, or even an equivocal glance from me would have set off a riot. Not a house in the Faubourg would have survived." And although every draftsman was needed in the dilapidated capital, the Prefect of Police almost wished that they were fewer; for it was in the building trade, he said in his report of 30 May 1807, that disaffection spread fastest and was least easy to stamp out.

It was in these conditions that Napoleon built, or ordered to be built, in just over a decade, nearly everything that first strikes an attentive visitor to Paris. He was not a person of fine taste: *le grand,* not *le beau,* was his field. But wherever, in Paris, we are struck by the sheer amplitude of a conception; wherever an architectural motive stuns us into acceptance by bland repetition; wherever there stalk the specters of Greece and Rome, there Napoleon has been. And although everyone has, of course, his favorite corner of Paris, certain moments of revelation have an absolute quality and transcend the element of personal preference or discovery. One of these is—or was until the bridge was destroyed—our first sight of the view upstream from the Pont des Arts; another, the Madeleine in winter, with the flower sellers huddled in the blue twilight; the Arc de Triomphe at any season and from any angle, but especially when it overhangs us, silver and elephant-gray, at the summit of the streets that run north and south of the Etoile; the Rue de Rivoli late at night, with the gas globes receding almost, as it seems, to Vincennes; and the Colonne Vendôme at Christmas time, when it presides like a magisterial maypole over the beglamored windows of Cartier, Charvet, and the Ritz. The Bourse has, I know, no such popular appeal, but those who patronize the Trollopian chophouse that lies to the lee of it will remember with affection the look of its pinched white columns. And there is no surer mark of autumn's arrival than the moment at which the last brown leaf falls in the Tuileries gardens and across the twiggy vista there reappears the slant-faced façade of the Chambre des Députés.

In all these—the Bourse excepted—the common element is that of immediate effect. Usually, too, they impose from a distance; the unit of communication between them is not the conversational voice (as it is in the Marais) but the bugle call and the far glint of a helmet. A certain majestic regularity was the Emperor's first requirement in architecture; so far from regretting that his epoch was not one of individual genius in architecture, he was on the whole pleased and relieved. (When the projected Palais de Chaillot was under discussion he said, "It's to be in *my* honor—not in the architect's.") Such interest as he took was mainly technical; the Cenis and Simplon passes, for instance, seemed to him to be architectural feats, and there is no doubt that he would have been delighted if all his buildings could have been devised and carried out by engineer officers. Architecture he believed to be the sovereign's ruin; "Multiply by ten!" was his response to any architect's estimate of his cost.

A generation earlier, the title of *architecte du Roi* had carried with it many solid advantages; but the Emperor tended to bundle away such questions, as far as was possible, into the province of the Minister of the Interior. And the Minister, Montalivet, was so

much of his master's opinion that he openly declared that "architectural education has concentrated far too much on outward appearances and too little on the utility of the buildings in question and the most economical means of constructing them."

Two architects, at any rate, contrived to penetrate the Emperor's indifference. These were Percier and Fontaine. A more serviceable duo cannot be found in the history of the art; and although much of their work lies outside the scope of this chapter (they did especially well at Malmaison and Compiègne, in the vanished Tuileries, and in many ephemeral festive pieces), they deserve an affectionate salute from everyone who has enjoyed those greatest of all-weather, shopping streets, the Rue de Rivoli and the Rue de Castiglione. It is true that they were responsible also for much of the clifflike north wall of the Louvre; but the exhilaration of the Rue de Rivoli, the nice adjustment of levels between it and the graveled gardens of the Tuileries, and its way of making the visitor feel younger, richer, and about four inches taller—for these we must thank the sedulous pair.

Percier and Fontaine were, in a way, the first Victorians: for something approaching their energy, resource, assurance, allusiveness, and versatility we must jump two generations and cross the Channel. It was nothing for them to put a premonition of Euston Great Hall into a living room in Poland, Pompeii into Malmaison, the French Renaissance into the Tuileries and the Italian Renaissance into the Louvre, and, into the Royal Palace at Aranjuez, a frenzy of panels ornamented with landscape, townscape, and allegory. It was natural that Percier should have a special tenderness for the 1st *arrondissement:* his father had been a keeper in the Tuileries gardens. Fontaine, on the other hand, was the son and grandson of architects from Pontoise. Outstandingly gifted students who made

170

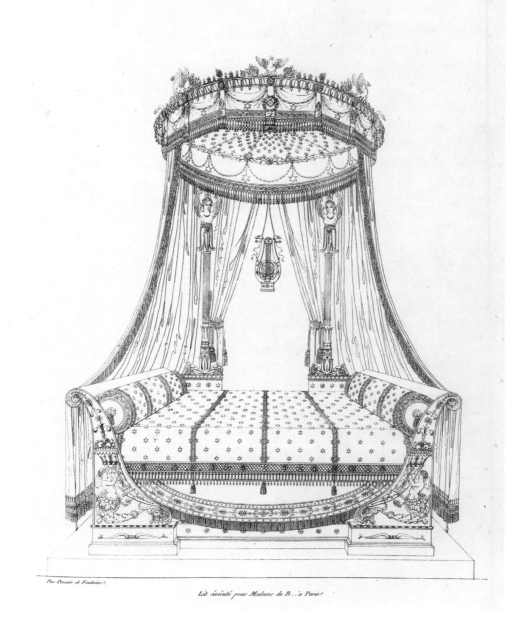

Par Percier et Fontaine.

Lit exécuté pour Madame de B....a Paris.

Design for a bed.
Charles Percier and
Pierre F. L. Fontaine,
1812

good use of their time in Rome (both were there at the outbreak of the Revolution), they were versatile enough to keep going with work of one kind and another until, in the early years of the nineteenth century, they made a name for themselves as decorators in the antique style. Percier was a very pretty draftsman, and Fontaine's preface (1797) to an edition of Rabelais reveals a nice judgment of the way society was going.

From the moment that they were invited to remodel Malmaison, their clock struck twelve at every hour of the day. There was nothing rigid about them: the great styles of the past were not, they said, "types to which we must conform, but subdivisions of one and the same activity. They are, in effect, like scientific discoveries which each of us may exploit in accordance with his particular needs." Mathematics were not enough for Percier and Fontaine: nor, in their view, could styles be transplanted at will. Even the craze for antiquity by which they themselves so greatly benefited was a matter, they admitted, rather of fashion than of innate fitness or necessity. *Classiques libéraux*, Louis Hautecoeur called them, and they had a liking, unknown to the pure *anticomane*, for the Quattrocento. The Rome of their inmost predilection was not that of the Caesars, but that pictured in their "Palais, maisons et autres édifices modernes dessinés à Rome" (1798): *modernes* is the word that counts.

One thing that is hidden from us as we pace the disgarnished acres of Napoleonic Paris is the exuberance of fancy that, for one reason or another, stayed on the drawing

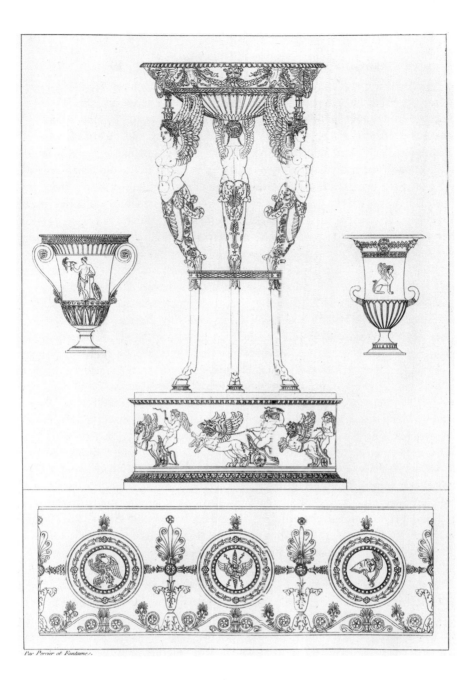

Design for a tripod,
vases, and frieze. Charles
Percier and Pierre F. L.
Fontaine, 1812

board. Even Percier and Fontaine never got going with their Palais de Chaillot—or with
the Palais des Archives which was to have dominated the Quai d'Orsay. These are great
mercies; but there are cases in which more flexible imaginations were curbed, one might
think, to excess. Ill-named Sobre, for instance, differs little in his completed work from
other able Empire designers, but his projected Temple of Immortality, in the form of the
upper half of a terrestrial globe, would have been a valuable addition to Paris. As it is,
Napoleonic Paris has little that will recommend itself in close detail to the promenader.
In the heyday of Napoleonic power the Arc de Triomphe du Carrousel, for instance, once
bore aloft the four bronze horses of Venice: now that they are back in Venice, the change
is not for the better. In intention a kind of lodge gate for the Château des Tuileries, this
little Arch now stands alone among municipal flower beds; but at least it has not been
done over. Bralle's palm-tree fountain in the Place du Châtelet, on the other hand, was
deformed in 1858. Napoleon regarded the fountain as one of the more immediately useful
forms of architecture and was prepared to go much further than usual, where one was
concerned, in the way of fancy. "Could we not," he once said, "make the fountain in the
Place de la Concorde in the form of a trireme, and keep the exact proportions employed
by the ancients?" "No" was the answer; but an attentive walker will notice other marks
of Napoleon's hydromania.

In the Rue de Sèvres, for example, a copy of the Capitol Antinous stands in a massive neo-Egyptian surround; the tell-tale eagle reveals that the architect (Bralle again) felt it necessary to bring his audience forward into the nineteenth century. The First Empire concerned itself almost entirely with public buildings and public amenities, and of most of these it demanded a shaven military face; but just occasionally a private citizen took over unwarrantedly some element of Napoleonic style, just as one may put a pheasant's feather in one's hat and yet never have touched a gun. In the Rue du Caire, for instance (long one of the most disreputable streets in Europe), the strange traffic of the *trottoir* is surveyed, from the first floor of No. 2, by three colossal Pharaonic heads. Elsewhere there are façades, like those of the Cité du Retiro, or of Lescot, the pharmacist in the Rue de Gramont, where the flat-patterned reliefs and serpentine figures seem to conjure, from the far end of the nineteenth century, the preoccupations of Art Nouveau.

But, of course, it was inside and not outside the houses of Paris that the "Empire style" really made itself felt. Where façades were, on the whole, monotonous and stiff, the interior decoration was varied and luxuriant. Not everyone can get into the Hôtel de Bourrienne or the Hôtel de Beauharnais, but a visit to Malmaison or Compiègne is indispensable to those who wish to see the First Empire at its best. Second-best will not do where this style is concerned, for one of its merits is perfection of workmanship.

Perfection is always expensive, and what passes for "Empire" in many antique shops is a mechanical reproduction of something that, in its original form, was of vastly greater finesse. (Even the new rooms in the Palais du Luxembourg contained a large proportion of imitated materials.) The society of the Empire was to a large extent a *parvenu* society. Insecurity made people strive to outshine their neighbors, and one way of doing this was to have a panoramic paper where they had *toile de Jouy*, a Turkish sitting room where they were still stuck in Pompeii, and a Gothic library where they had arabesques (white on royal blue), and a frieze dating from the Egyptian campaign. All this meant work for more men than could do it perfectly and, in consequence, erratic standards of execution. The Empire style is, for all that, the last of the great French historical styles. (To anyone who wishes for proof of this I recommend Room 38 in the north wing of the Cour Carrée in the Louvre. This includes the imperial throne from Saint-Cloud, the cradle of Napoleon's son, the King of Rome, and many other key pieces of the period.)

Many Napoleonic innovations now seem to us to have been ordained by nature. Street-numbering for instance; how could metropolitan life go forward without it? Beacons by night, firm ground beneath one's feet, water for the asking—Napoleon saw to it that these could be taken for granted. Of the other novelties of the period I should like to single out two only: a widespread taste for modern painting, and the habit of going to restaurants. The Salons were much visited in Diderot's day; but it was Napoleon who made it unthinkable not to be interested in painting. He did this in two ways—first, by inspired looting in the course of his foreign campaigns, and second, by making a point of going to exhibitions himself. (The last Salon of his reign included 1,359 new pictures.) Much the same thing happened where food was concerned. The age of Carême was an age of fine, but also of colossal eating; it saw the beginning of that Parisian institution, the tiny, ruinous, cosmopolitan food shop. Hamburg smoked beef and *mauviettes de Pithiviers* crossed the counter and reappeared in that new department of literature, the restaurant menu; and there began, in consequence, the habit of eating out, and likewise of entertaining out. Other elements of the Empire are now of mainly historic interest: the gambling rooms are closed, the circus is a dying art, the Scotch-and-soda has killed off the salon, and even the lecture by a member of the Académie Française takes place on television. But the restaurant holds firm. There *are*, of course, places where precooked food, horrible wine, and a radio in full cry combine to foul a great tradition; all who stand out against these things must count themselves First Imperialists at heart.

Meanwhile there is no one place in central Paris where Napoleon the human being is present to us. Napoleon the elemental force, Napoleon the master of men, Napoleon the personification of a Grand Design—all make themselves amply felt. But for Napoleon off duty we have to go to the Château de Malmaison, which stands about five miles to the west of Paris and is best reached by way of La Défense and the new town of Nanterre.

Long before the future Empress Joséphine bought it in 1799, Malmaison was a place where people enjoyed themselves very much indeed. It was not a big house, by the standards of the Ancien Régime. Nor was its ever-inviting park laid out by anyone in particular. It was an easy, informal, unpretentious property—one that lent itself to long amusing summer days and winter evenings by the fire. It never seems to have been in dull hands. The author of *Les Liaisons Dangereuses* was a frequent visitor in earlier days, and there was much in the life of Malmaison that might have amused him. It was a house in which Madame Vigée-Lebrun, the foremost portrait painter of her day, liked to spend time. When she went walking in the park, as she did every day, she went out alone and carried a branch from a flowering tree by way of indication that she did not want her reveries to be interrupted. "But when I saw someone I fancied," she tells us in her memoirs, "I made haste to throw the branch away."

Joséphine liked fun company as much as anyone else did, but what she wanted of Malmaison was that for once she would be alone with Napoleon. It was all very fine to be married to the most brilliant soldier in France, but she had had enough of being an army wife. She wanted a pretty house that would not be too large, a pretty garden with some unfamiliar flowers in it, and maybe a working farm a little way away. Napoleon would be seduced by all this to the point of putting away his campaign maps, hanging up his campaign boots, and turning into a country gentleman. "General of the Army, retired" sounded great to her.

So she went ahead, in her husband's absence, and like many another army wife in her situation she spent rather more on the house than Napoleon initially approved of. She was thirty-six at the time, ample and delicious in her person, with long days on her own to fill. She was right in thinking that once Napoleon got over the size of the bills he would take a lively and constructive interest in his new house. What she did not foresee was that in no time at all he would become, first, the effective head of the state and, second, a crowned and consecrated emperor.

As a result of this prodigious ascension Malmaison became two things in one. It was a beloved retreat, near Paris but not part of it, in which Napoleon could enjoy his rare moments of leisure in the midst of his family. It was also a place of business in which great decisions were taken and great deeds done. It was essential, for instance, to have a Salle du Conseil in which matters of state could be discussed in due form. Napoleon ordered that it should take the form of a campaign tent hung with the emblems of war. But it was also essential that he should sometimes be alone, and to that end he ordered the one-room pavilion that still stands not far from the house at the end of an *allée* of lime trees.

His favorite architects and decorators, Percier and Fontaine, were kept busy at Malmaison. Napoleon interfered all the time, gave them impossible deadlines, and in general drove them crazy. But he got what he wanted, plus some auxiliary inspirations on the part of Percier and Fontaine that have lately been brought back to something like their original state. We cannot see the wooden theater that they whipped up for him in a matter of weeks. But we can see the library, which in shape, scale, proportion, and detail is one of the great rooms of its period. And we can see the Salle du Conseil, in which among much else the Code Napoléon was decided upon. "That code of mine," Napoleon said later, "did more good for France than any and all of the laws that had been made for it. It put Justice—equal for all, and intelligible for all—at the service of every citizen of France."

There was of course no way for the house not to get bigger and more imposing. New wings were added to the right and left of the original nucleus. The silver-gilt table service by Henry Auguste—a gift from the city of Paris on the occasion of Napoleon's coronation as emperor—would have been way beyond both the means and the needs of a plain general, even if he were on full pay. But it was kept within bounds. Other, grander residences were not lacking. Malmaison was *home*, and at first he spent a great deal of time there.

For Joséphine likewise the years in question brought an unexpected expansion of her activity. From being an unspoiled country wife for whom every least flowering shrub was a delightful novelty, she became someone whom everybody in France was anxious to flatter, to cosset, and to appease. People brought her rare plants by the hundreds and rare animals in profusion. (A very young orangutan was trained to sit at table in formal dress and not to misbehave itself.) Nothing was too good for her. Even the working farm had

to be quite perfect. More and more land was added to the property, which eventually comprised five thousand acres. There were echoes of Marie-Antoinette in her plans for its embellishment, and visitors treated her as if she were Buffon, Cuvier, and Vivant Denon rolled into one.

Malmaison as it stands today is down from five thousand acres to fifteen, and even they are none too well kept. Unlike Versailles, and unlike Claude Monet's house at Giverny, Malmaison has never found an inspired fund raiser to bring it back to perfection. There is about the park something of the disconsolation that overcame Joséphine herself when Napoleon broke the news to her that for dynastic reasons he was going to leave her and marry somebody else. For her, as later for him, Malmaison became a place in which to remember a past gone beyond recapture. It was in Malmaison that Napoleon spent his last hours as a free man on French soil. Something of all this still pervades the house, just as the tokens of their initial happiness are offset by reminders of the time when everything began to go wrong—the berlin, for instance, in which Napoleon traveled to Moscow and back.

There is in all this a poignancy that brings us close to both Napoleon and Joséphine as human beings. But there is also—and at every point in the tour—evidence of the perfection of which the Empire style was capable. Better than anywhere else, Malmaison sets this off—in furniture, in decoration, in silver and gold, and in everyday things: satchels, letterheads, sewing sets. Malmaison is a museum, but it is also a lesson in living.

VIII

Revolutionary Paris:
The Faubourg Saint-Antoine

Certain great historical events, like the siege of Troy or the Battle of Waterloo, can be reconstructed *sur place*. Others, more difficult, must be picked out of the air. One of these, to my mind, is the French Revolution. It is incorporeal, as is the Word to the Hindu; it has no one base; it invests the very air of Paris but cannot, simply cannot, be rooted.

We know, of course, where the momentous events occurred, but I would defy even the most vivid imagination to whisk Hittorf's "improvements" out of the Place de la Concorde, or the showcases out of the Versailles Jeu de Paume, or the moldering medal shops out of the Palais Royal, and to reinstall in these affable sites the specter of the Revolution. We are all its heirs, nonetheless—all of us, that is to say, who have a painter's liking for that best of flags, the Tricolore, a suspicion of paper money, or a fondness for the most civilized of all forms of address: the appellation "Monsieur."

The Revolution of 1789 was in many respects a street revolution; a matter of colloquies at the double, pamphlets passed from hand to hand, inflammable groups at street corners, and combats glimpsed at a distance or inferred from cannon shot. Paris has never quite lost its revolutionary habits. The profusion of its newspapers, for instance, was for generations a souvenir of those times, and the public meeting, as a political instrument, is still vastly effective there. Anyone who has lain awake in Paris at a time of crisis and heard the conversations beneath his window will know that the temper of 1789 can be revived at any moment.

All these are intangible things, matters of instinct and experience. It is by them that we learn to judge the effects of 1789, for the Revolution added no one great monument to Paris. The structures to which it gave rise were grandiose, but ephemeral; of its fêtes, temples, arenas, colossal figures, altars, obelisks, and "Fountains of Regeneration" nothing at all now remains.

It was not that poetic imagination was lacking. The 1780s marked, in fact, a period of luxuriant fancy in French architectural projects. Louis XVI, so far from inspiring this, thought rather of pulling down: in 1787, for instance, he gave orders that the châteaux of La Muette, Madrid, Vincennes, and Blois should be sold or demolished. But in Rome, where the prizewinning students of the Académie de France lived opposite Piranesi and enjoyed, in many cases, the privilege of his friendship, the beginnings of an unbridled romanticism and an uninhibited taste for the colossal gave rise to projects that, if fulfilled, would have transformed Paris in a decade. In Russia and in Sweden, the innovations of Charles-Louis Clérisseau and J.-L. Desprez were noted with excited interest by Catherine II and Gustave III; but at home the Gothic Dairies, Castles in the Middle of the Sea, Egyptian villas, circuses to seat three hundred thousand people, globular police stations, and Temples of all the Virtues did not get further than the drawing board. Nor did the Revolution bring a new liberty of thought in such matters; the great historian Louis Hautecoeur lists some forty distinguished names and concludes, "whether in exile, in prison or in hiding; whether ruined, or merely under suspicion, all these architects stopped work and could do nothing to embellish France with their talents." Pierre-Adrien Paris, the personal favorite of Louis, built little after 1786, when his castellated windmill (a water pump in disguise) went up in the Jardin Beaujon; he retired to his house in the Doubs and became a pioneer of central heating. Of the architects who hurried to fly the new colors, none perhaps was more successful than François-Joseph Bélanger, who already in April 1789 had become *premier électeur* of the district of Saint-Joseph and moved for the demolition of the Bastille.

The Bastille! The name speaks, as does none other, for the summer of 1789. Sympathizers who make their way to the site today do not, of course, see anything of the fortress. (Part of one of its eight towers was dug up in 1899, during the construction of the Métro, and reerected in the Square Henri-Galli, next to the Pont Sully.) They will have to go to old prints for an idea of its somber bulk, and to the painting by Hubert Robert in the Musée Carnavalet for a whiff at second hand of the moment in July 1789 when the fires were lit at the foot of the cumbrous, demoded, and (to us) altogether unfrightening Bastille.

If Jacques Necker had had his way when he was Director-General of the French finances, the Bastille would have been razed several years earlier, and in its stead the incendiaries of 1789 would have found a decorative mound of broken locks, bolts, bars, chains, and portcullises, and on top of this a statue of Louis XVI the Liberator. The fortress, as it stood in 1789, had a small and largely ornamental garrison and served mainly as a depository for arms. Prisoners were traditionally few, but distinguished: Montgomery, Captain of the Scottish Guards, had been put there in 1559, after he had killed Henri II by accident; Bernard Palissy, potter and ceramist, had taken up residence in his eighty-first year; in the seventeenth century, Bassompierre, the rival of Richelieu, and Fouquet the financier had been followed by the Man in the Iron Mask (velvet, not iron, according to the journal of the prison commandant), who eventually died there in 1703. In the prerevolutionary era, men of letters were consigned there in considerable numbers. Voltaire and Marmontel figure beside Cagliostro and Cardinal Louis de Rohan in the register, and it was only by chance that the mob did not liberate one of the most revolutionary of all writers: the Marquis de Sade. It was from the Bastille, in the 1780s, that this great scalawag wrote some of the letters to his wife that are among the most magnificent in the history of invective. In his appeals for clean linen and fresh fruit we glimpse the relative liberty that was accorded to well-born and affluent prisoners: "air and fruit," he wrote in September 1784, "are the two things I live by and, especially in this season, I would as soon have my throat cut as forgo them. If you saw the abominable, debased, and stinking vittles that are served to us here, you would understand that anyone who is used to a more delicate diet must needs supplement it with purchases of his own . . . so please take note of this list

A basket of fruit, made up of
Peaches	12
Nectarines	12
Poires de beurre	12
Bunches of grapes	12

(half of these to be ripe, and the rest ready to eat in 3 or 4 days)
Two pots of jam.
A dozen cakes from the Palais Royal (six of them orange-flavored) and two pounds of sugar.
Three packets of candles for the night.

It was not from sympathy with these fastidious requirements that an enraged mob penetrated the outer courtyard of the Bastille on the morning of 14 July 1789. Many, as Michelet tells us, regarded the fortress as "the dungeon of the free mind"; "nobody proposed," he goes on, "but all believed, and all acted." For those who did not particularly care about the free mind but were in need of something on which to fix their imaginations, the Bastille and its glowering cannons became a symbol of the Enemy. (Even in distant Moscow people wept for joy in the streets at the news of its fall.) And there were doubtless many among the crowd who, in the words of one skilled observer of the Revolution, "were there, and yet did not know it, so little apparent was the danger and singularity of their position."

The story of the taking of the Bastille must be read at the length it deserves, in Michelet, or in Lavisse; none should hurry through the glorious day. Our concern here is not so much with individuals—though it is difficult to forget either Hullin, the enormous Genevese clockmaker, who led the attack in his Hungarian chasseur's costume, or the crazed prisoner who greeted his liberators with the words, "Gentlemen, I am the Major of Immensity"—as with the quarter of Paris that adjoined the Bastille and provided many of its besiegers: the Faubourg Saint-Antoine.

East of the Place de la Bastille, the foreign visitor is rare. Michelin has little to say about the Faubourg Saint-Antoine; the Métro station Reuilly inspired one of Utrillo's best pictures but could not be called a stronghold of tourism; and few are the *flâneurs* who seek out the Quai de la Rapée, where the long boats unload the wood that keeps much of the Faubourg alive. For this is the cabinetmakers' quarter of Paris, and has been so for many generations. (They have even their own official school, the Ecole Boulle, 57, Rue de Reuilly.) The craftsmen concerned are, in general, individualists, high-mettled and, for all that they are dispersed throughout the quarter, quick to band together in time of need. (Popular risings have been recorded in the Faubourg Saint-Antoine since 1357.) Already in April 1789 there were five hundred casualties in a premature rising in the Faubourg; in October of that year it was the Faubourg that drove Lafayette to seek out the King at Versailles; in 1793 the Faubourg marched against the Girondins; in 1832, and again in 1848, summer saw the quarter in arms. Victor Hugo in *Les Misérables* describes the barricade that, in 1848, barred the entrance to the Faubourg Saint-Antoine from the west; three stories high and seven hundred feet long, it stretched across three streets, and nineteen smaller barricades branched off from it. It was made, he tells us, of "paving stones, scrap-iron, rubble, floorboards, bundles of old rags, cabbage stalks, broken chairs. . . . It was big, and it was small. It was the Acropolis of the barefoot. Up-ended carts stood on its slopes and on the very top was an omnibus which had been dragged up, hand over hand, by a laughing crowd. It was the sweepings of a whole people, a lumberyard of bronze and wood and iron and stone, and you would have thought that one huge broom

The Fall of the Bastille. Anonymous, late 18th century (above)

had swept it into place. . . . Senseless it was; but heroic too, for this old Faubourg is a hero."

The Archbishop of Paris, Monseigneur Affre, was killed on one of those barricades; and after the insurrection of 1871, many of the best craftsmen in the Faubourg went into exile or were deported. In 1944, when the cabinetmaker's trade had perforce slumbered for four years, the Faubourg did a good deal more than its share in the Resistance; those who prowl among its ancient courtyards will find on every hand the gray marble plaque that bears a hero's name. It is not by visiting the over-restored dungeons of the Conciergerie, nor even—admirably as it is arranged—the Carnavalet itself, that the visitor will come nearest to the true flavor of the French Revolution, but by patrolling the Cour du Nom-de-Jésus, the Cour de l'Etoile d'Or, and the other evocative alleys of the Faubourg Saint-Antoine. Supersensitive it remains, from a political point of view; and the great cortèges of May 1 and July 14 have their private counterpart in that fever of discussion which is part of the heritage of the French Revolution. The idea that every citizen may actually have a share, however minute, in the government of his country has never palled in the Faubourg, and as there are few large factories the movement of thought remains largely individual and unorganized. Saturday afternoon in the Rue du Faubourg-Saint-Antoine displays if not Revolution, a revolutionary potential which should be seen and experienced by every visitor who cares for France. This is an area in which opinions are

The Oath of the Tennis Court. After Jacques-Louis David

On 20 June 1789, there occurred in Versailles one of the decisive events in French history. Finding themselves shut out by royal decree from the hall in which they normally met, the members of the National Assembly adjourned to a nearby indoor tennis court, or Jeu de Paume, where they swore not to separate until they had established a constitution for France under which they would form the national legislature.

The Fête de l'Unité. Pierre-Antoine Demachy

The French Revolution was famous for the scale, the splendor, and the imaginative ardor of its festivities. In the Place de la Concorde on 10 August 1793, the emblems of monarchy were set ablaze in the selfsame square that had witnessed the execution of Louis XVI and Marie-Antoinette.

Quick Way for the People to Strip a Nobleman's House, 13 November 1790

not simply held. They are acted upon—to the death, if need be. As recently as 1962 people were killed outside the Métro station of Charonne for manifesting against the war in Algeria.

The Revolution, as I have said, was made in the streets. Today the crowds might huddle in silence before the television set, but in 1789 they went out into the streets to listen for the gunshot or horn call that would bring them, downwind, ambiguous tidings. The posters, the street markets, the orators spouting like Icelandic geysers at some small traditional provocation, the ambulant orchestras, the pamphlets passed from hand to hand, the souvenir pots and plates—all can be found near the Bastille, even today, and the great *place* itself has still a gamy, proletarian savor. Picture to yourself a large shelving open space—marine on one side (barge and sluice have edged well inside its perimeter), metropolitan on the others. Its Métro station is one of those, prized by connoisseurs, at which the trains come to the surface and the layout bespeaks the limited expectations of eighty years ago. To the west, the dome of Mansart's Temple de Sainte-Marie adds a note of high art to the uproarious scene; to the north is the never-quite-dismantled fair; and, in the *place* itself, a quietly delirious commercial activity that is cut off, as if by a guillotine, when we turn into the Marais. The Bastille is to the Marais as Marseilles is to Aix-en-Provence, raw meat to rillettes, blowlamp to vesta.

Things do tend, all the same, to fall off in quality. The visitor to the souvenirs of the Revolution in the Musée Carnavalet comes away thinking that every printer in those days was a Firmin Didot, every potter a Bernard Leach, every wallpaper designer a Paule Marrot. And, just as these things have gone steeply down, so has the standard of street entertainment. Perhaps the exploitation of a handful of ephemeral favorites has in some way drained their rivals of the personality that, in other ages, was theirs by right. Certainly (and although there existed till lately, near the Bastille, the last of the cafés-concerts, the Concert Pacra) the visitor will look in vain for the equivalent of Bordier, the peerless Harlequin of revolutionary times, who excelled, the Goncourts tell us, as "Arlequin Hulla, Arlequin odalisque, Arlequin ainsi-soit-il, Arlequin sentinelle, Arlequin tout seul, Arlequin Doge de Venise, Arlequin incombustible, Arlequin journaliste, decorateur, bon fils, beau-fils, tailleur, afficheur, joker, perruquier, receveur de loterie, etc. . . ." Bordier took to politics and ended badly; but perhaps, in the wake of some great catastrophe of the future, performers of genius will spring up by the dozen and distract their fellow survivors where now the traffic swirls, erratic but determined, across the windy spaces of the Place de la Bastille.

The Faubourg Saint-Antoine is not exclusively somber in its associations. It is, on the contrary, the traditional headquarters of all that is most spirited, elegant, and accomplished in French decoration. It is here that, from the time of Colbert onward, wood, bronze, velvet, tin, cotton, paper, and china clay were metamorphosed into objects of lasting beauty. Though, here again, aesthetics and politics go hand in hand: visitors to

Workshops, from Diderot's *Encyclopédie,* 1762–77. Furniture-maker (upper left); Wood-gilder (upper right); Cabinetmaker (lower left); Mirror manufactory (lower right)

Memorable Journey of 6 October 1789

In October 1789 the people of Paris marched to Versailles and demanded that Louis XVI and his family should leave Versailles and come to live in Paris. When this was agreed, the joy of the Parisian expedition knew no bounds. It soon became the stuff of legend—not least for the boisterous high humor with which the women of Paris fraternized with the royal guards.

the Forney Library at 1, Rue du Figuier, which has probably the finest collection of wallpapers in Europe, should remember as they pore over the *papiers peints* that it was over fair wages at the Réveillon wallpaper manufactory that, on 28 April 1789, the first troops—dandies to a man, in their waisted topcoats—fired on the first victims of the Revolution.

That particular engagement took place at the corner of the Rue de Montreuil and the Rue du Faubourg-Saint-Antoine. It was a savage affair, in which nearly two hundred people were killed and some three hundred wounded. Réveillon made very good wall-paper—so much so, in fact, that Louis XVI named him wallpaper maker to the king in 1784—and he also had a vein of fancy and audacity. But in social matters his touch was less sure. When the government promised to reduce the price of bread in 1789 he said that he would reduce his workers' wages in proportion. There were four hundred of them, and they didn't like it at all. People from all over the Faubourg took their side. The army was brought in to suppress the rising, and Réveillon ran to the Bastille and asked for safekeeping.

Réveillon's craftsmen were perfectionists. Like all such people they worked slowly and steadily but in a state of high nervous tension. They were artists, not bureaucrats, and they had the artist's temperament in full measure. All over the Faubourg Saint-Antoine there were craftsmen who worked to the highest possible standard for customers who knew the best and would not be content with less. In the 1770s alone, some six hundred grand town houses were built in Paris. They were impressive enough outside, but it was when it came to the inside that the householder had to dig deepest into his pocket. To furnish and decorate a town house cost three or four times as much as to build it. This was not a matter of "buying antiques." It was a matter of having everything made to order, at no matter what cost.

To have an idea of the diversity, the ingenuity, and the originality of what was made

The Place de la Bastille.
Alain Perceval
photograph

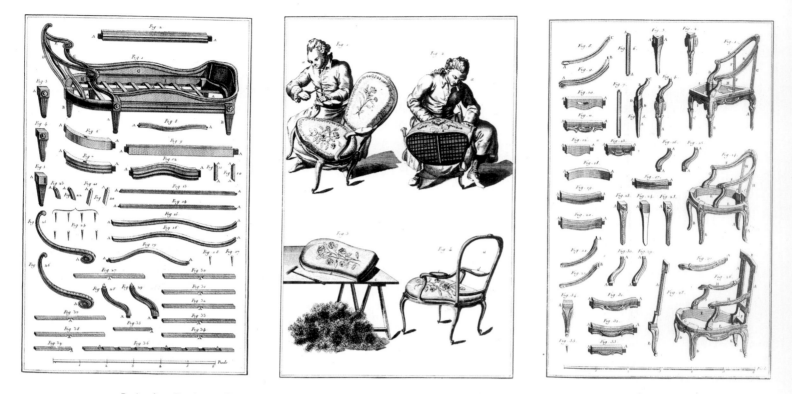

Design for a Duchesse, *Upholstering an Armchair in Tapestry,* and *Designs for Armchairs,* from Diderot's *Encyclopédie,* 1762–77

in the Faubourg Saint-Antoine just before the French Revolution, we should remember what F. J. B. Watson says in his introduction to the catalogue of the Wrightsman Collection: "Chairs and sofas perhaps reflect the prevalent love of comfort and social life even more than contemporary ebenisterie. . . . The *duchesse,* for instance, could hardly be improved upon for complete relaxation. Chairs were produced in an extraordinary variety to meet every need, ranging from the *voyeuse* with which the onlooker could watch others gaming, the low *chauffeuse* to facilitate the undressing of children at the fireside, or the *coiffeuse* for having the hair dressed, to the elaborate push-button chairs for reading such as Mercklein fitted up for Louis XV or those *fauteuils d'invalides* with mechanically adjustable backs and leg rests. Such conveniences are sufficiently familiar today to awake little surprise, but in the eighteenth century they reflected a totally new attitude toward furniture. Even the names of other specialized types, the *confidant,* the *tête-à-tête,* or the *chaise en confessionnel,* suggest the importance that the French attached to private social intercourse, just as the *ottomane* and the *paphose* hint at a striving after an Oriental degree of luxury and the creation of the *chaise volante,* the prototype of the elevator, reveals a quite modern attachment to the contrivances of indolence."

Chairs and sofas were not, of course, the only kinds of furniture that were produced in the Faubourg Saint-Antoine. The *menuisier* made tables, screens, stands for plants, stools, pedestals, picture frames, looking glasses, and kennels for very grand dogs. The *ébéniste* made coffee tables, writing tables, tables to put beside the bed, gaming tables, chests of drawers, desks, corner cupboards, shelves, cabinets, and caskets for jewels. Dexterity and finish were highly prized, but the real function of all this superfine furniture was to make life as agreeable as possible for those who could afford it. It would hardly be too much to say that Parisians in the 1770s and 1780s made love to their houses; and the instruments of their lovemaking came primarily from the Faubourg Saint-Antoine, where many of the greatest names in French furniture had their workshops within a short walk of the Bastille.

As goes without saying, these things were not mass-produced. They were made in ones and twos in aromatic dens all over the Faubourg Saint-Antoine, which for this reason ranks high in the geography of French cultural history. The quarter was also and quite coincidentally a favorite with holy ladies, who assembled there in great numbers; and although many of the convents have disappeared, several of them may still be found in the tranquil Rue de Picpus. At No. 35 in this street is the convent of the Dames du Sacré-Coeur; and at the bottom of its baronial park is the Little Cimetière de Picpus, in which are buried the 1,305 persons who were executed in the summer of 1794 in what is now the Place de la Nation. Many of the greatest names in France—Montmorency, La Rochefoucauld, Noailles, Rohan, Chateaubriand, Gontaut-Biron, Lafayette, Choiseul—figure on the list of victims. Ash and sycamore give these gardens a Pre-Raphaelite quality; and in general it is here that we are nearest to the Faubourg as Hubert Robert knew it when he was commissioned by Madame Geoffrin to record the look of her rooms in the Abbaye de Saint-Antoine-des-Champs, and of the gardens outside.

The Faubourg was remarkable, too, for its great houses. Those who would now live near the Avenue Foch came here for their overhang of trees and built the metropolitan manors of which one or two still survive. These were strongholds of enlightened curiosity: private theatricals were of professional standard, ballooning was encouraged (it was from 31, Rue de Montreuil that, in 1783, Pilâtre de Rozier and the Marquis d'Arlandes made their pioneer ascent), festivity reigned in many a heavy-leaved summer garden, collectors ranged far and discerningly for their treasures, and at the Hôtel de Mortagne, in the Rue de Charonne, there were to be found at varying times an exemplary manufactory of velvet, a colony of state-aided painters, and Vaucanson's celebrated collection of automata. And, like every other fashionable quarter of Paris, it had its indispensable doctor.

No account of the French Revolution would be complete without some mention of Doctor Belhomme. This ingenious individual, at the time of the Terror, made good use of his Bunyanesque surname and all-but-sanctified calling. His private asylum at 157 (today's numbering), Rue de Charonne was turned into a nursing home; the thirty-seven real lunatics were sent elsewhere and their rooms given to affluent make-believers who would otherwise have been in prison. It was not cheap (a thousand livres a month) and the table was one of the worst in Paris; but the security was all but perfect, the company congenial and select (three duchesses, a fashionable deputy, a famous restaurateur, a sociétaire from the Comédie-Française), and the amusement diurnal. By night the gardens were full of beautiful women dressed up as men; but anyone who was amused to the point of overlooking his monthly bill could count on being guillotined in a matter of days. Belhomme himself was apprehended on 27 July 1794, but contrived to get back to the Rue de Charonne: he was eighty-seven years old when he died there in 1824.

It was until recently worth taking the trouble to see the garden at the back of the house. With its high walls, its eighteenth-century pavilion, and its ancient trees, it was a place that Watteau would have loved. But both house and garden are gone, and for a glimpse of what the quarter was once like we have to go to the Hôtel de Mortagne at 53, Rue de Charonne, which was built by Delisle-Mansart around 1650 and became the home in the 1740s of the collection of *automates* that belonged to Jacques de Vaucanson.

The Faubourg Saint-Antoine was just the place for those marvels of fine-fingered ingenuity. Where else but in the headquarters of French craftsmanship should we expect to find automatic figures that played the flute, beat the drum, and carried on a game of chess? Or an automatic duck that quacked and moved its wings? Or an automatic artisan that could produce a chain that never ran out of links? Louis XVI was so amused by all this that not long after Vaucanson died in 1782 he bought the house and everything in it. The *automates* went to the Conservatoire des Arts et Métiers, and Louis XVI went to the scaffold, but the Hôtel de Mortagne kept in step with the Faubourg Saint-Antoine. Under the Empire it was turned into a nest of painters—not all of whom behaved well— and after that it became known as a place where very good velvet was manufactured. After a long period of near-dereliction it has lately been brought back to something approaching its original distinction.

The Revolution, as I said, did nothing to embellish Paris—least of all, perhaps, in the quarter of its origin. Ledoux's pavilions and high Doric columns in the Place de la Nation date from just before the Revolution. The enskied Eros in the Place de la Bastille was put up many years later, in 1840–41. The most characteristic building enterprise of

The Elephant Fountain in the Place de la Bastille. Jean Antoine Alavoine
Napoleon had planned to have a monumental fountain in the form of an elephant where the Colonne de la Bastille stands today. The plaster was never cast in bronze, however, and was eventually removed.

the 1790s is the Cour Betave in the Rue Saint-Denis—an ensemble of shops and apartments designed by Sobre and Happe for a group of Dutch speculators. None of the architectural projects submitted for the competition organized in 1795 by the revolutionary authorities was ever erected: not even Détournelle's mammoth Castello-Sant'Angelesque prison. (Perhaps the jury of "discerning but uneducated citizens" saw through them all.) So extreme was the revolutionaries' failure to adapt themselves architecturally that only with the greatest difficulty was anywhere found for the government to meet. (It took Gisors and Leconte two years to redesign the Palais Bourbon for this purpose.) Altogether, Le Breton was quite justified in saying, in his report of 1808 to Napoleon, that "architecture suffered more from the Revolution than any of the other arts."

And so it is that the Revolution has no décor of its own, but must be looked for in the dis-tented gardens of the Palais Royal, chased out of a solander case filled with engravings after Swebach-Desfontaines, or glimpsed, *mutatis mutandis,* when hands are raised in anger in the streets that lead to the Place de la Bastille.

IX

The Palais Royal

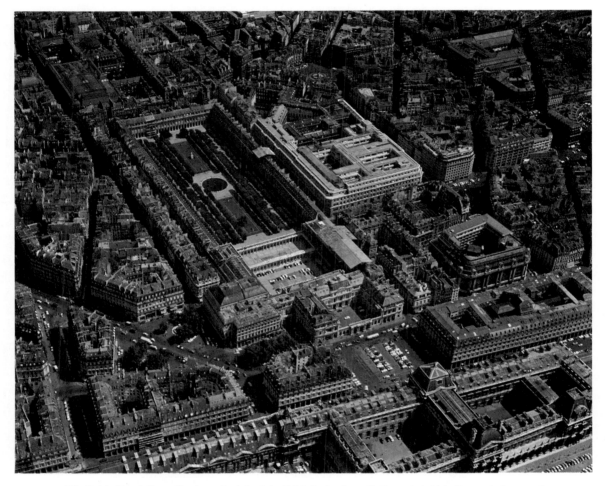

The Palais Royal. Immediately to the left of the Palais is the Comédie-Française. Alain Perceval photograph

All persons of good character like the Palais Royal. Nowhere is Paris more quiet, for one thing. Not Venice itself is more free from wheeled traffic, the windows overlooking the garden are unimpeachably private, and although there are shops in plenty beneath the arcades, the traffic within them is of a secretive and all but soundless character. Out of school hours the garden has an occasional wild animation, but on the whole the atmosphere suggests a rather grand almshouse or home for convalescents of distinction. Spectatorship is the main local activity; and Colette, one of its finest practitioners, once kept a whole book afloat with what she could see from her window above the Palais Royal gardens. The daydreamers, likewise, can remember with pride the famous opening sentences of Diderot's *Le Neveu de Rameau:*

"Fine weather or foul, I go most evenings, around five o'clock, and walk in the Palais Royal gardens. I am the person you will find day-dreaming, alone, on the *banc d'Argenson.*

188

Politics, love, philosophy and taste are the subject I discuss with myself, and as I do so I allow my mind to wanton as it pleases, free to follow the first idea, sound or senseless, that presents itself." An ideal program, and one to which the gardens still lend themselves. And as for the palace itself, it is one of those metropolitan ensembles—like the Piazza San Marco in Venice, the Grand' Place in Brussels, and the Josefplatz in Vienna—that constitute an enclosed world so perfect as to drive out of mind, for a while, all thoughts of the country.

What we enjoy today is not, as it happens, very old, although the importance of the Palais Royal dates from the beginning of the seventeenth century. The original Palais Cardinal, which Richelieu built, was never very stirring. Even those who most admire the architecture of Jacques Lemercier must feel that Corneille was piling it on a bit when he makes Dorante say, in *Le Menteur,* that in the whole wide world there was nothing to equal the exterior of the Palais Cardinal. But "exterior" was the word that counted; doubtless Corneille was thinking of the splendid garden that stretched, then as now, for several hundred yards northward from the second courtyard of the palace itself, ending in a little wood that everyone delighted in. Mathematics and arboriculture combined to put both town and country in their place, whereas the house itself was modest in scale, and has indeed remained so.

What now holds the eye is the great three-sided addition that was made for the Duc de Chartres, in the 1780s, by Victor Louis, the architect of the Grand Théâtre in Bordeaux and of the Comédie-Française. Louis acted on the principle that if you have a good idea it doesn't matter how often you ram it home; and so it is that the ensemble strikes us immediately by its really stunning regularity. The 180 uniform arches of the arcading, the orderly rows of trees, the sumptuous pilastering, and the ash-blond gaslight—all gain by repetition, and in combination they make a commandingly noble effect. The Palais Royal has never been parceled out to its disadvantage; such dilapidations as it has to show are lightly borne and add, if anything, to its air of high breeding.

To get into the original palace is now neither easy nor rewarding; and of the buildings that played in the history of France a role altogether out of proportion to their size nothing really remains, save the Galerie des Proues, with its naval embellishments, on the east side of the inner courtyard. Yet the Cardinal would not, I think, feel at a loss in his own quarter today. There is a good deal of juvenile horseplay at certain times in the Palais Royal gardens, but we must remember that Richelieu himself was not always the unruffled prince of the church whom we see in Philippe de Champaigne's portrait. Often he would tease away his chronic melancholia with crude practical joking: with blowpipe and pea-shooter at the ready, tripping and tweaking in season and out, he would have his ministers set upon by genuine brigands hired for the purpose, throw books at their heads when they entered his study, or challenge them after luncheon to a session of high jumping in the courtyard. And, although he might blanch at some of the plays that are now put on in the Théâtre du Palais Royal, he would certainly have turned a connoisseur's eye upon the pretty little auditorium. As a collector, he set a pace that only a very few of his royal successors were to equal; today he would find many of his books, in their red armorial bindings, in the nearby Bibliothèque Nationale, and in the Louvre, just across the road from the Palais Royal, he would find, among other survivors from his collection, Leonardo's *Virgin and Child with St. Anne,* Veronese's *The Pilgrims at Emmaus,* and the two Poussin *Bacchanals.* So that, in one way or another, he would find things little changed. Nor is it difficult, even now, to reconstitute in one's imagination the out-of-doors life for which the Palais Royal has a great name in Parisian history.

What is irrecoverable in today's terms is the richness and subtlety of the life lived in Richelieu's palace between his death and the end of the Régence. There is simply no way back through the dumpy civil service apartments of today to the court of Monsieur—Philippe de France, brother of Louis XIV—and his mother-in-law, Henrietta Maria, widow of Charles I of England. From the inventory made after the death of Henrietta Maria in 1670 we know of the Tintoretto, and the Titians, and the tapestries—Gobelins, Brussels, and Flanders—that hung on the walls; and from other records we know something of the elaborate table that was kept. (Owl and whale were on the menu.) But what we cannot recapture are the originality and the delicate judgment of Henrietta Maria herself.

Madame was the first and the greatest of those women who, from one generation to the next, set the tone of Parisian life. It is not a question of rank, or of wealth—though both count, of course—but of the superfine judgment that makes people put forward the very best of themselves. "Madame created," Sainte-Beuve wrote, "the loveliest, or at any rate the most graceful of all moments at the court of Louis XIV. That court was later to achieve a greater splendor and, it may be, grandeurs more immediately impressive; but never again did it have so much distinction, so much finesse." And after describing how Madame knew to spur on old and young, veteran and debutant, Corneille and Racine, to equal effect, he concludes by saying: "In those courts which had immediately preceded Madame's, there had been an admixture of taste that was already old and would soon become out of date; with Madame began the truly modern taste, the taste of Louis XIV; and she helped to crystallize it in all its purity."

Well, it's a great thing to be first with what is newest and best. Leadership of this kind no longer comes from the top of society, as that top was then conceived; but the Palais Royal was to house another great exemplar of this kind, in the person of the Régent, Philippe d'Orléans, son of Philippe de France. He too liked all that was new, and was himself a painter and composer of presentable gifts. He was also a chemist, who had his apparatus specially made for him at Sèvres. As a patron of the decorative arts he distinguished himself by commissioning the *grand salon* by Oppenord which did much to launch

The Gallery of the Palais Royal. Abraham Bosse, 17th century

Design for the Salon d'Angle in the Palais Royal. Gilles-Marie Oppenord, 1719–20

the Régence style. As a picture-fancier he was one of the greatest in the history of collecting, and his silver, furniture, jewelery, glass, and porcelain were the topmost class.

Tantalizing as it is to read of houses that no longer exist, I cannot resist describing the great drawing room, devised by Oppenord, which looked on to the Rue de Richelieu; it was demolished at the time of the building of the Comédie-Française. An easy elegance and nonchalant ingenuity were the marks of Oppenord's craft; the boiseries were gilded, the damask crimson, the chandelier of rock crystal, and the tall pier glasses brilliantly clear. Above the four doors were the Veroneses that had belonged to Christina of Sweden; on the walls hung two huge canvases by Rubens, *Thomyris* and *The Continence of Scipio,* six Titians, among them *Venus and Adonis, The Rape of Europa,* and *Perseus and Andromeda,* and nineteen other important works.

It is when we turn to the more disreputable side of the Régent's activities that the Palais Royal begins to assume the shape familiar to us from the novels and prints of a hundred years later. Court life has always been a great strain on people of lively and independent intelligence, and the Régent made no bones about being of their number. Impeccable in his discharge of all formal duties, he knew when to cut himself off from them. But let Saint-Simon speak of this:

"After the council, or at about five o'clock if there had been no council meeting, business was over for the day. Often he would give a supper-party, leaving the palace by the back entrance, or causing his guests to be brought in by the same route. These parties were always very strangely composed. His mistresses, sometimes a dancing-girl from the Opéra, often the Duchesse de Berry, and a dozen or so of the men-friends whom he described simply as his 'roués.' Broglio was there, and Noce, four or five officers, though never the highest in rank, the Duc de Brancas, Biron, Canillac, a few accessible society ladies and some young men born on the wrong side of a noble blanket; and a few people, as yet quite unknown, who stood out by reason of their wit or their debaucheries. The food, always exquisite, was prepared in a kitchen specially built for the purpose next door to the dining room. The service was of silver, and the guests were not above giving the cook a hand on occasion. In the conversation nobody was spared—not even the ministers, not even their own close friends—and the talk was astonishingly, illimitably free. The Duc d'Orléans did his share with the rest, but only very rarely did he take serious note

The Public Promenade. Philibert-Louis
Debucourt, 1792

The Palais Royal in 1810. Carle Vernet

of what was said. All drank unceasingly, waxed hotter and hotter, bellowed indecencies across the table, and swapped impieties as hard as they could; and then, when they had made a tremendous noise and were all as drunk as could be, they went off to bed and began all over again the next day."

Transpose this lower down the social scale, add a restaurateur, an orchestra, and some supernumerary trollops, season with gambling, vaudeville, circus, and freak show, and you will have something very like the scene that later made the Palais Royal famous throughout Europe. The disreputableness of the Palais Royal is by now a thing of the distant past; and in some of its records—in Debucourt's engravings, for instance, or the drawing by Carle Vernet in the Carnavalet—the facts are so well lavendered that we can hardly guess what all the fuss was about. And sometimes, as in Restif de La Bretonne's book on the subject, the tale has the monotony not easily avoided in pornography. But Balzac, for one, knew how to sew the facts of the Palais Royal into the whole fabric of Parisian life: it was there that Rastignac gambled with Delphine's money, Joseph Bridau lost his last *écu*, and Bixiou and Blondin dined at Véry's. And for the feel of the gaming rooms nothing will ever better the opening of *Le Peau de Chagrin*.

Life keeps well up with the novelists, all the same, in the pages of the Galignani *Paris Guide* of 1822. In the Palais Royal, we read, the ingenuous visitor will be pillaged by "Greeks of all nations"; "*Chevaliers d'industrie*, and Ladies equally industrious" abound in the underground cafés, and "in truth, to make our language appropriate to those we are describing, the *ladies* of these grottoes are no better than decoy ducks, and the *gentlemen* generally unprincipled bullies, billiard sharks, and cheats, with overpowering mustachios and cigars in their mouths."

But these strictures related mainly to the *bas-fonds* of the Palais. Even Galignani admitted that "in the brilliant shops of the stone galleries round the garden may be found . . . crowded together merchandise of every kind, the richest stuffs, the most precious trinkets, masterpieces of clockwork, and all the most modern productions of the arts. Here fashion has established her empire: here she reigns over the metropolis and over all France. By the side of magnificent coffee-houses are magazines of every exquisite viand an epicure can desire. . . . Tailors exhibit clothes ready-made, of which the cloth, the cut and the color are quite à la mode. Money-changers, portrait-painters, engravers, and sellers of china invite everyone to gratify their whims."

Of the restaurants and the coffeehouses Galignani had much that was good to say; but the gaming rooms brought out the stern moralist in our guide, and no words were too strong for the people who ran them. "When they pour out their rich libations of Champaign and Burgundy, do they ever think of the widows' tears with which they were purchased? When they repose their bloated forms on beds of down, do they dream of the miseries their vile and tempting traffic has made? No!"

"No!" was doubtless the right answer. (The profits of the gaming rooms ranged, during the period 1828–32, from six to ten million francs a year.) But today it would be difficult to get a partner even for tiddlywinks, and the Palais has the severe, sedate, rather crumbly appearance of a great building in retirement. Gone is the café where Fragonard is said to have died of an ice cream in August 1806. Gone the sixteen portrait painters, the seventeen billiard saloons, the eleven usurers, and the eighteen gaming houses that occur in the directory for 1804. Gone the waxwork man whose niece came to London as Madame Tussaud. Gone, above all, the temporary wooden buildings in which much of all this went on; for these were pulled down in 1828, and on 31 December 1836 the gaming rooms were closed by law, and the Palais Royal began to look rather as it looks today.

The Palais Royal quarter was, at the turn of the nineteenth century, the prototype of certain forms of Parisian enjoyment. (Michelet had a marvelous phrase for what it offered: "le plaisir rapide, grossier, violent, le plaisir exterminateur"—"pleasure—but pleasure that is instantaneous, coarse, and violent: pleasure that kills.") These amusements may still be found in Paris, but not in such concentration, and not, certainly, in surroundings of such magnificence. Some way to the east you will find *bars à filles*, but the atmosphere there is on the whole tranquil and domesticated; Montmartre and Montparnasse are unaffectedly crapulous; in the *beaux quartiers* many an hotel is not quite what

Interior of the Galerie and Rotonde Colbert. Levilly, after J. Billaud, 1828

Following pages:
The Galleries of the Palais Royal. Louis-Leopold Boilly, 1809

it seems, and many a restaurant has things to offer that are not marked on the menu. But these have not, either singly or in combination, the style of the Palais Royal in its heyday.

Many of the more reputable amenities of that quadrilateral may still be found near at hand. Not everyone has my fondness for the surviving shops in the Palais Royal, with their strange jumble of old stamps, colonial campaign medals, and Art Nouveau exercise books. But the ices and sorbets of the old Café de Foy can still be got round the corner; the toy-soldier shop hard by Molière's statue is one of the most delightful in Paris; foreign newspapers (the specialty of the Café de Corrazza in 1806) are on sale in all weathers in the Place du Théâtre-Français; and although the underground cafés have all been cleaned out of the Palais Royal itself, there is a restaurant in the Rue de Montpensier which still keeps something of their look and scale. Gaslight and old stone wreak marvels by night; a footfall is still the unit of movement; and when the railings cast their arrowy shadows on the gravel it is easy to remember that here, when the wet summer of 1789 drove everyone into the cafés, Republican France began.

The Palais Royal extensions, quite new at that time, had been run up by the Duc de Chartres as a piece of speculative building. The duke was a natural gambler (in early youth he had bet the Comte de Genlis that he would make five hundred thousand dots on a large sheet of paper more quickly than Genlis could ride from the Palais Royal to Fontainebleau and back); but he was also a man of sure taste. The patron of Gluck and Mozart had a flair for the best; and when, at the age of twenty-nine, he went to Bordeaux and saw the Grand Théâtre, he decided that Victor Louis was the man to enlarge the Palais Royal. Financially erratic (the duke borrowed five and a half million francs from a

Camille Desmoulins Makes a Proposal in the Palais Royal, 12 July 1789

Reading the Regulations in Le Moniteur *in the Garden of the Palais Royal, 16 July 1830.* After Hippolyte Bellange

private company, sold the Régent's engraved stones to Catherine the Great, had a windfall legacy that brought him in three million a year, and even so was in constant difficulties), the venture proved the greatest possible outward success; to the very best shops were soon added the attractions of circus, balloon ascent, and orchestra, and by the fatal summer of 1789 the Palais Royal was famous all over Europe.

It was at half-past two on the afternoon of Sunday, 12 July 1789, that Camille Desmoulins got up on one of the tables in the Café de Foy. In his own words:

"Hardly was I up there when I realized that an immense crowd had gathered around me. This is what I said to them, and never shall I forget it: 'Citizens, there is not a moment to be lost. I have come from Versailles. Monsieur Necker has been dismissed. His dismissal gives the alarm for a patriot's Eve of St. Bartholomew. Tonight the Swiss and German battalions will come out in force from the Champs-de-Mars and cut our throats to a man. There is only one thing for us to do: take up arms and choose a cockade, so that we can recognize one another.'

"I had tears in my eyes and my gestures were such as I can neither remember nor describe. My suggestion was received with tremendous applause, and I went on:

" 'What color will you choose? The green, color of hope, or the blue of Cincinnatus, the color of American liberty and democracy?'

" 'The green, color of hope!' "

And so it was that the green leaves of the Palais Royal garden became the color of revolution. Chamfort, the master of the maxim, who lived at 18, Arcades du Palais Royal, has a wonderful description of how later in July the gardens became the forum of all Paris. "In six minutes," he says, "you could suppose yourself in a smoking-room, a dance-hall, a fair-ground, a harem, and an armed camp. The disorder led to a general stupefaction, and the confusion of ideas made me think at once of Athens and Constantinople, Sybaris and Algiers. Suddenly a new sound was heard: the drum! The drum calling for silence. Two torches, waved high in the air, drew all eyes towards them. And what we saw! A severed, bleeding head, held full in the ghastly torchlight, with a man walking in front and crying out in a dismal voice, 'Make way for the people's justice!' and everyone watching without a word! And not many yards away the evening patrol, in uniform, took notice of all what was going on and marched in silence among the astonished multitude."

Much has happened since in the Palais Royal—not least in May 1871, when much of the Palais itself was burned by the Communards—but its effect has usually been that of a decline in fortunes. The Duc de Chartres—or the Duc d'Orléans, as he then was—sold his pictures in 1790 to two syndicates of enterprising bidders from England. The gardens lost, as we have seen, the character—that of a *foire aux idées*—which they had had for an inspiring moment in the 1780s. The new Avenue de l'Opéra drained off the smart shops. The Pavillon de la Rotonde was pulled down and its fragments rebuilt in a private garden at Versailles. By 1864 the Goncourts, when they went to what had once been the Café des Aveugles, treated the underground rooms as we now treat the ruins of Pompeii or Troy.

Today there is a great deal of private life in the tapering cabins to which Colette and Jean Cocteau gave a renewed celebrity, but of the old public life of the Palais Royal the last traces are probably to be found in the Restaurant du Grand Véfour, whose tattered lettering (SHERRY GOBLER for decades lacked its G) and modest exterior are no guide at all to the proceedings within. It's not a place to drop into for a sandwich, but if you should happen to be invited there you can reflect between mouthfuls of *Toast aux crevettes Rothschild* and *Lamproie Bordelaise* that Lamartine, Thiers, Sainte-Beuve, MacMahon, Duc d'Aumale, Cocteau, and Colette may each and all, at one time or another, have sat where you sit.

Perhaps it is above all of Colette that we should think when ambling around the Palais Royal. The latter part of her long and immensely fertile life was lived in an upstairs apartment at 6, Rue de Beaujolais. Even when bedridden, toward the end, she exerted an almost palpable presence. Though by any standard a great lady of letters—the equal in recklessness of George Sand, in brilliance and mischief of Madame de Sévigné, and in stoicism of Madame du Deffand in her sightless days—she was to the day of her death a working writer, and one who refused the status of historic monument.

It is she who best brings back to life the Palais Royal as it was in the middle of this century. She was as attentive to the successive pregnancies of her downstairs neighbor as she was to the visits of this great person or that. Even when she could no longer get to the Grand Véfour she wanted a detailed rundown on the day's menu and would comment upon it in growly Burgundian tones. And she was particularly eloquent on the subject of the Palais Royal during the German occupation, when men on the run were hidden every night in a different attic and even the politest of German officers got nowhere with the Palais Royal shopkeepers. Colette had one of the great unsubdued French natures, and, even if one of the busiest squares in Paris now bears her name, it is in the half-asleep northwestern corner of the Palais Royal gardens, beneath what was once her window, that we should think of her.

X

The Comédie-Française

Opening Night at the Comédie-Française, Intermission. Edouard-Joseph Dantan, 1886

Just before eight o'clock on a fine evening in October, few places in the world are more dear to me than the peristyle of the Comédie-Française. There is a continual pit-a-pat of hurried footsteps along the colonnade. Within, the great theater is getting ready to open its doors. All around, the gas globes are beginning to glow with an opaline light. Before long, the curtain will go up after the three mandatory thumps that call the audience to order, and the Comédiens Français will begin the evening's work, just as they have done year in and year out for three hundred years, with only minimal interruption.

The Place du Théâtre-Français was for generations, and to a certain extent is still, one of the most agreeable places in Paris in which to pass the time. It has a bookshop in which the novelties of the day lie side by side with sets of the more forbidding classics and senior editions of the *Encyclopédie Larousse.* It has cafés and brasseries, though it has lost the Café de la Régence, sacred to the chess player since the days of Chamfort and

Jean-Jacques Rousseau. It has the hotel from an upper window of which Camille Pissarro painted the Place du Théâtre-Français in 1898.

It has a bus stop that is one of the most promising in Paris for those who value chance encounters. It has a vista—that of the featureless avenue that leads to the emerald rooftop of the Opéra. The cliff that darkens it to the south is that of the Palais du Louvre—the somber, ministerial nineteenth-century wing, but the Louvre nonetheless. In quiet moments, the high voices of children carry through the Palais Royal gardens. The newspaper kiosk signals the news of all the world. In what was once a department store—the Magasins du Louvre—there is an antiques market, and on the corner of the Rue de Richelieu there is an exemplary gunsmith called Faure-Le Page who has been in business since 1718.

A square of this quality banishes boredom. But, of course, the great business of the Place du Théâtre-Français is the Comédie-Française. For close on two hundred years, the skyline of the southwestern corner of the Palais Royal has had that semicylindrical hump that is the mark of a theater the world over; and this particular hump is that of the headquarters of the French theater: the Théâtre Français, in fact. Fig-brown and purple are the discreet colors of its playbills; anything more insistent would be unworthy of this theater and these actors. Only at the approach of curtain time does the colonnade become distinctively theatrical in tone; at other times it is hardly more animated than that of the neighboring Cour d'Honneur. The cafés, too, come to life only when the mummers, buskin and cothurnus laid aside, hurry in for a restorative or mount the stairs, after midnight, to an upper room.

The Comédie-Française is, as we are often told, "not an ordinary theater." It is an association of actors and actresses that has been formally adopted by the French state, enjoys a large subsidy, and has the use, rent-free, both of the Théâtre Français and the Théâtre de l'Odéon. Members of the Comédie are largely exempt from the unemployment that torments nearly every actor in the world. Their work is, in fact, highly bureaucratized, and what was originally a victory over the natural precariousness of theatrical life has become, in the eyes of many, stuffy and archaic. The history of the Comédiens Français might, indeed, be said to have come full cycle; just as, between 1645 and 1658, Molière and his troupe were forced to bumble round provincial France for lack of a theater in Paris, so after World War II much of the creative work of the French theater was owed to the Théâtre National Populaire (TNP), which took Corneille, Kleist, and Molière himself to garages and cinemas and communal centers that had never before witnessed a stage performance.

But the position of the Comédie-Française is a great deal more complicated than that. In one prime respect, after all, it has overcome the natural instability of theatrical life: it is always there. And not only is it always there, but it always has been there. Ever since 1658, when Molière played for Louis XIV in the Salle des Gardes of the Vieux Louvre, and 1660, when his company used the Salle du Petit Bourbon, just west of Saint-Germain-l'Auxerrois, this part of Paris has been the preserve of the Comédiens Français. In one respect only has it lost all resemblance to the association founded by Molière in 1643—it no longer makes its own plays.

In many ways, however, the Comédie of today is recognizably the descendant of the Comédiens du Roi to whom Louis XIV gave his protection in 1680. Its members have not, of course, the monopoly of playacting "within the city and suburbs of Paris," which that troupe enjoyed. Nor are they empowered, as were the Comédiens in the eighteenth century, to act as arbiters in all theatrical disputes. Nor, for that matter, do they run the risk of being thrown, one and all, into prison (as the Comédiens were in 1765, although they were let out each evening in time for the performance). They have traded power for security; and what was, under Louis XIV and again under Napoleon, the private troupe of an autocratic ruler is now a branch of the civil service. These are not the conditions in which an "art theater" can exist. But in matters of organization the Comédiens have much of their old autonomy. The system of *dixièmes* (by which the actor's share in the receipts varies according to his seniority), the system of *feux* (by which the actor receives a small sum, nominally for coal and candles for his dressing room, every time he appears)—these date from the 1680s. The guest appearances date from the engagement of la

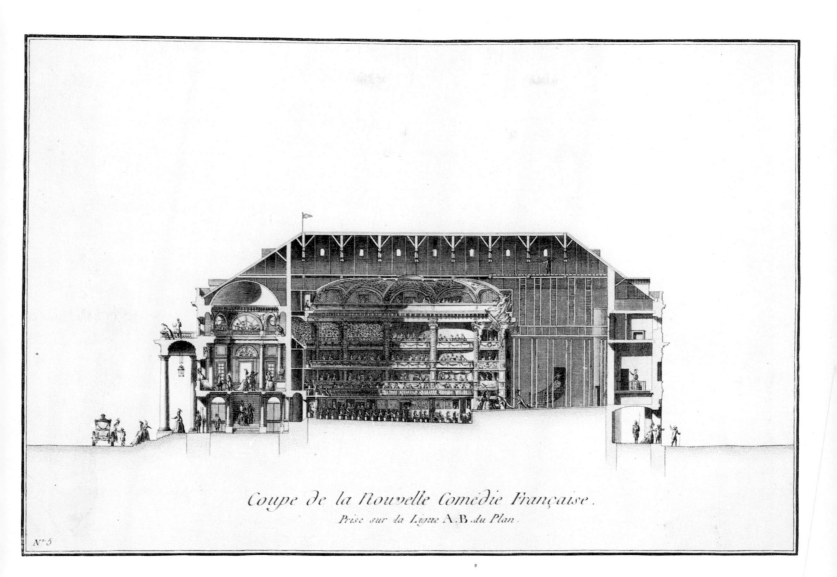

Coupe de la Nouvelle Comédie Française.
Prise sur la Ligne A.B. du Plan.

N°5

Champmeslé in 1679. Hallowed, too, are the truancies by which Rachel, Sarah Bernhardt, Lucien Guitry, and more recently Pierre Fresnay, Jean-Louis Barrault, and others have broken away from the great theater. (Members of the Comédie have the strangest fancies: Coquelin *cadet* wanted to stand for Parliament, and was convinced that he could always get along to vote after curtain-fall.)

But it is in its choice of plays that the Comédie-Française shows itself the guardian not merely of the French theater but of the French language. The basis of this repertory is what it always was: the classics of the seventeenth century. (In this respect the Comédie had, until lately, held even closer to tradition: not only had it at any one time an average of at least twenty plays by Molière, Racine, and Corneille in its repertory, but the proportion of plays written before 1850 to later plays had markedly increased.) Louis XIV said once to Molière that it was better "to write for laughter than for tears," and the Comédie long bore him out—to the extent, for instance, that the classical tragedies were often followed by a one-act farce. But the Comédie exists to instruct, and to enlighten, as much as to amuse. Valéry's "Honneur des Hommes, Saint Langage" is no idle phrase in France, where the idea of civilization is verbalized, brought into the open, defined, and made explicit.

There are many historical examples of this. Take, for example, Lord Chesterfield's *Letters to His Son*: "I recommend," he wrote in 1750, "theatrical representations to you, which are excellent at Paris. The tragedies of Corneille and Racine and the comedies of Molière, well attended to, are admirable lessons, both for the heart and the head. There is not, nor ever was, any theatre comparable to the French." *Lessons* is the word that

matters here. Some thirty years later, the Marquis de Tilly, most delicate of libertines, broke the flow of his memoirs to say that: "Our theaters are, for Europe and for ourselves, a school of politeness, reason, and good behavior, an exhibition of all those incidents of nature, be they gay or distressing, which work directly on the hearts and minds of mankind." A *school*, we note. And, a century later, Sainte-Beuve could say that, "Despite all its vicissitudes, the Théâtre Français is a school of taste and fine language, a living monument in which tradition and novelty are reconciled to one another. Its role is, after all, just that: to be the opposite of all that is easy and commonplace." A *school*, again.

A theater of this kind could easily become a museum. If it has not done so, the credit must go in large part to the actors and actresses concerned. They it is who reanimate, for each generation, the style and timbre of the great classical repertory; and they who, from the recesses of their natures, create that mysterious momentum that can make the most familiar text seem new and surprising. The portrait gallery of the Comédiens Français is so rich and varied that, if I take Edmond Got as my example, it is because the rough-tongued and parsimonious *doyen* exemplifies an aspect of the Comédie to which I should like to draw attention. There are greater actors on the roster, and more spectacular characters, but Got is one of those whose somber persistence keeps the great theater in being.

He had begun life as a soldier, and in the 1870s, when the Comédie was in desperate straits after the Franco-Prussian War and the Commune, his martial qualities kept it together. Danger brought out the best in him: in normal times he could be a pedestrian performer, and as surly as a bear offstage. No martyr to art, he detested having to take a cab to his house in Passy and would put on an extra turn of speed onstage if it seemed

Jean-Paul Roussillon directing a rehearsal of *La Dame de chez Maxim's* by Georges Feydeau in the Salle Mounet Sully. Photographs of the Comédie-Française by Robert Doisneau

likely that the last omnibus would leave before the end of his performance. No martyr to "gracious living," he could be found at home in a workman's jersey and blue linen trousers. He was what is called *un acteur de composition*, whose performances were based upon continual shrewd observation. "Like all those," the Goncourts wrote, "whose talents are modern and alive, he keeps his ears pricked in the street, and on the top deck of the omnibus." In preparing a part, he always tried to harmonize the text with a face, or a gait, or a gesture that he had picked up in life.

The settled existence of the Comédiens is nowhere better reflected than in their *loges:* dressing rooms, we would say, if the word did not stand for something altogether more garish and ephemeral than these evocative parlors. Even Got, the least fanciful of men, had (so the Goncourts tell us) "a divan running round the walls of the room and covered with a huge carpet on the floor, three étagères, and a fine show of swords and sabers." In other *loges,* extremes of fantasy take over: one would think oneself in the home of a servant, it might be, or a *grande cocotte,* or a sea captain, or a demented armorer. Not merely do they reflect a personality, but that personality is at full stretch, enhanced and, it may be, deformed by a lifetime of cultivation. Some of these rooms retain a delectable flimsiness and an air of inspired caprice, but more often the note is that of a paradoxical solidity. Heavy country-house wardrobes, upholstered chimney pieces, marble busts, and ceremonial velvet—such is the tradition of which some trace may still be found.

Anyone who has passed through the iron door that leads backstage at the Comédie-Française will know how strikingly these rearward areas contrast with those of an ordinary theater. The space, for one thing: the staircases with room for three people to pass, the landings that seem to invite the lavish gestures of swordplay, and the enormous pieces of country-house furniture, which so magically do not encumber the view . . . And nowhere, surely—unless it be in Westminster Abbey—are vanished seniors so piously bodied forth in marble, and plaster, and stone. As for canvas, there is enough to rig out an East Indiaman. Offices at the Comédie really are offices, and not holes in the wall. Even the *guignol*—the little room near the stage that is used for rapid changes of costumes—even the *guignol* has style.

Annie Ducaux in her dressing room

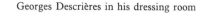

Georges Descrières in his dressing room

Claude Winter in her dressing room

All this bespeaks a certain settled amplitude of outlook, a continuity of approach. The juices that flow through the great theater are analyzably the same as those that animated it three hundred years ago. The actor or actress who goes to hear a new play read before the *comité de lecture* can glance, on his way in, at Laissement's painting of an identical scene. Laissement did it in 1886, when the author in question was Dumas *fils*, and the committee included Got, Worms, Mounet-Sully, Coquelin *cadet*, and Jules Claretie. *Autres temps*, certainly: but when he goes into the committee room he will find the same oval table, the same green cloth, the same carafe, the same glasses, and the same crystal sugar bowl. Pajou's bust of a great Harlequin from the Comédie-Italienne has given place to Guillaume's Emile Perrin on the chimney piece; but in other respects the room is the same: the dusky, atrocious paintings tilt down from the wall, the figurines gesture behind glass, and around the table the worked, familiar faces of his colleagues wait for the reading to begin. It is the scene which has repeated itself since 1688, when Article One of the regulations was drawn up: "In the case of a new play, the troupe shall meet together and hear it read aloud. The author will then leave the room and the Company will reach its decision, either by a majority in open debate, or by a ballot with black balls and white."

Other customs, too, date from the earliest times. In 1712, for instance, Louis XIV sent a memorandum to say that he had heard with displeasure that: "Whenever there is any kind of general meeting, the members of the Company spend their time wrangling, and saying to one another things which are always hurtful and sometimes outrageous." No great changes there; actors are disputatious people, and the headline "Crise chez Molière" is one that no Parisian editor can set aside for long.

That same year, 1712, saw the establishment of a regulation that gives the key to the Comédie's repertory: tragedy and comedy were to alternate, it was said, on pain of a substantial fine. This regulation is not, of course, followed literally; but the oscillation between the high tragedy of Racine (the finest thing of its kind since the Greeks) and the comedies of Molière is still the essence of the Théâtre Français. The one is marble: the other a vegetable growth, rare yet simple, matured in the warm and various earth of

France, and retaining an indefinable element from the southerly provinces through which Molière and his company vagabonded—the countryside near Bordeaux, Toulouse, Albi, Carcassonne, Agen.

Molière himself was all comedy. As one of his contemporaries wrote: "He was a comedian from head to foot. He seemed to have many voices, and with a smile, a wink, a nod of the head or a movement of his foot, he could say more than the most eloquent of talkers can say in an hour." These are not the instruments of catastrophe, and although he did, at one time, make a conscientious attempt to play in tragedy, another observer reported that "the words poured out so quickly that he lost control over them, and, in trying to speak more slowly, developed a permanent hiccup." He was a pure comic actor: and one who, though he loved to improvise, took care to see that all his actors had parts that suited them and that the risks or unpleasantnesses fell to himself.

The unselfish and dependable quality of Molière's direction is something that does not often recur, and it would be pointless to deny that when André Malraux took office most of the more imaginative work in the French theater had for many years been done outside the Comédie. There are several reasons for this. One is that, since the time of Antoine's Théâtre Libre, it is to the *chef de troupe,* and not to the theater, that prestige attaches. Great solitaries—Jean Vilar, Jacques Copeau, Louis Jouvet, Charles Dullin—had been the heroes of the previous thirty years; Jean-Louis Barrault and Madeleine Renaud founded their company with their own small savings; even the state-subsidized TNP was primarily Vilar's creation and, subsidy apart, owed everything to him. Secondly, the Comédie's terms of contract, once so attractive, had become a hindrance. Actors who can live off the cinema like to be free to do what they please on the stage. And, finally, there had been a failure of nerve within the Comédie itself. No one knew quite what to do with it. Theater people who could make it on their own did not, on the whole, want to sign themselves away for a lifetime. Politicians and amateurs lacked the knowledge and the stamina to do more than peck at the problem. Even the continuity was in danger: many of the actors who had been in the Comédie before 1939 were dropping out, or being forced out. From all this there resulted a general crisis of confidence: authors would not

Dominique Costanza and Béatrice Agenin in the Foyer des Artistes

The Foyer des Artistes before a
performance of *La Dame de chez Maxim's*

give their plays, actors would not be recruited, and the Comédie itself tried to broaden the base of its appeal by presenting spectacles more elaborate than distinguished: dressed up, rather than thought out. The amateur of *le bien parler et le penser fin* went elsewhere, and the old, grand, strict function of the Comédie was gradually dying out.

Or was it? Some took a less somber view. The decline in the Comédie's great name was in part, of course, the result of a decline in quality—even though that too was relative; ours is a spoiled, inattentive, half-educated age. But there was at the same time a general loss of interest in the kind of thing for which the Comédie stands. People were more interested in personalities than in plays. The old delight in exact and vigorous speech was going out, and more store was set by the television screen than by direct contact with the seventeenth-century lords of language. The Comédie was still a school, and people thought themselves too grand and too clever to go back to school. Indifference to the Comédie sometimes implied great sensibility—unwillingness to put up with the second-rate, fidelity to the remembered image of Louis Jouvet as Tartuffe or Madeleine Renaud as Araminte— but it was more likely to signify a failure of intellectual curiosity.

The Comédie is not an institution that can be judged by a single visit. Anyone who is interested in the theater should haunt the peristyle; find out what seat suits him; somehow manage to drop in; not mind a few rebuffs; and get his ear and eye into trim before passing judgment. The feel of the house, too, is very important. (Charles Laughton, appearing as Sganarelle in *Le Médecin Malgré Lui* at a midnight matinee before World War II, was appalled to find that his great speech went off without so much as a chuckle from the silent house; but at the end they applauded for four minutes.) Molière still works on his audiences: much of what he has to say is like a grenade that his hearers must hurl back before it explodes. And the classical theater is, after all, a dictionary of possible attitudes in the face of triumph, uncertainty, and misfortune; there exists no better lexicon. Anyone who has nothing to learn from *Bérénice*, or from *Le Bourgeois Gentilhomme,* or from *Cinna* is as immune from the hazards as he is from the delights of ordinary life.

The seventeenth-century French drama is unique, too, in that it has never fallen into disuse, never been deformed, and never lost its power to surprise. And, although the Comédie has played an immense amount of tosh in its time, its French repertory has been greatly enriched in the last two hundred years. In England a play by any Elizabethan or Jacobean dramatist other than Shakespeare has very little chance of being seen in London, but the Comédie-Française ranges with almost suicidal impartiality among the entire gamut of French drama. It is still, in its field, the greatest educational force in the world; and although in the past it performed some of the worst plays ever committed to paper, it has latterly been altogether more exacting.

There have also, of course, been radical changes at the Comédie-Française. (Had there not, it would long ago have withered on the branch.) As in every other great theater, the director has tended to replace the player as the magnetic attraction. Until after World War II, the Comédie-Française was dominated by the Comédiens Français. People went there to see this or that actor or actress, just as they had done for two hundred and more years. Then the great players died off or went elsewhere, and it was for the visiting director to act as a regenerative force. Not only did he bring new ideas, but he made us see the company in a new way. In Paris, as in London, Berlin, Vienna, and Milan, the director was the galvanic element.

With this, there came a renewal of the repertory. In the nineteenth century the Comédie-Française put on a prodigious number of new plays, but very few of them lasted more than a few performances and most of them were by the now-vanished race of professional Parisian dramatists who could turn out play after play and count on seeing every one of them on the stage. Since 1945 quite another policy has been pursued, and the subscriber to the Comédie-Française can expect to see world theater, rather than Parisian theater, even if the great French classical holdings in both comedy and tragedy are still the capstone of the repertory. People today go to see the play, not the player, and before they go at all they like to be sure that the play is worth the effort. This makes for a Comédie-Française that is very different from the Comédie of a hundred years ago, when people went to see their favorite players in any old rubbish and did not think the evening wasted. When we remember how Maurice Baring said that Sarah Bernhardt "enlarged,

Jeannine Morice, Wardrobe Mistress

rather than interpreted" the masterpieces of the past, we realize how much has changed. In our own day that enlargement is likely to be a collective effort under the guidance of a great director.

In this matter, as in all others, a certain French lucidity and practicality can be relied upon. A new equilibrium now reigns between *anciens* and *modernes*, stability and innovation, risk and continuity. The Comédie-Française is still the repository of standards long vanished elsewhere—in what other theater can an actor in eighteenth-century costume count on having custom-made eighteenth-century underwear to wear beneath it?—and it still plays an ambassadorial role on its visits abroad. But it takes its chances, too.

I should add that one recent change turns out to work against the foreign visitor. Once upon a time we could walk into the Comédie-Française almost at will. We could stroll in on a Thursday afternoon and come out at the violet hour when the great "All change!" begins to sound and day gives place to night. Equally well, we could drop by after a brief and early dinner and take our pick of whatever was going on.

But no longer. Since World War II two things have happened. One is that the number of subscribers has increased enormously, with the result that relatively few seats are available for casual sale. The other is that the theater itself, which was never large in relation to its importance, has got steadily smaller. Initially it was a bastion of the box— that instrument of collective torture in which nobody was comfortable and hardly anyone saw well. By packing people into those boxes, the Comédie could sell 1,900 tickets and

Catherine Samie (left) and the cast in a performance of *La Dame de chez Maxim's*

get away with it. But the Parisians are a highly combustible people, and there came a time when they simply wouldn't put up with it. (Many of the other seats in the house offered only a partial view, and some of them to this day are far from ideal.)

So boxes went. Columns went. Sightlines were adjusted to the limits of human tolerance. The Comédie reopened, to general approval. But when the seats were counted, exactly 892 remained. One set of annoyances gave way to another. But when that is said, what a joy it is to be in a great theater where every whisper tells, where the word "microphone" is never heard, and there is that sense of community that no huge impersonal theater can hope for. Not every production at the Comédie-Française is one to remember forever, but when great expectations are greatly fulfilled, the result is a duet for actors and audience, rather than an act of one-sided aggression.

On occasions of that sort it is worth all the trouble and all the ingenuity that it takes to get into the Comédie-Française. And when you get out, somewhere between eleven and twelve in the evening, the tin clocks will strike all around you, the kiosks will have folded up like fruit bats, the cafés will be stacking their chairs, and in a little while the Comédiens Français, muffled in all seasons against a treacherous turn of the weather, will dart out of their seignorial stagedoor and make for home.

XI

The Case of Haussmann

The Place de l'Etoile and the Arc de Triomphe. Alain Perceval photograph

There is a point in every visitor's experience of Paris at which he has to come to terms with Haussmann. He may delay it for as long as possible, by setting up as the hermit of the Marais, or hurrying with averted head from the Invalides to the Jardin des Plantes, or lingering till closing time in the Luxembourg Gardens; but sooner or later he will have to set foot on the great blank-faced indistinguishable boulevards and reckon with one of the most unpopular men in French history.

But sentiment is one thing, and fact another. And the fact is that Paris as we know it is very largely the creation of Haussmann. We cannot turn on a tap, or light a gas stove, or take an omnibus without falling in with his plans. Nor is there anywhere in Paris, from the Bois de Boulogne to Vincennes, and from the Buttes-Chaumont to the Parc de Montsouris, that does not bear the print of his heavy Alsatian thumb. When he came to power in 1853, the Paris of the Middle Ages, and of Henri IV, and Louis XIII, and Louis XIV, and Louis XV, and Louis XVI, and Napoleon, and Louis-Philippe—the Paris of all these

epochs was still reasonably intact. By 1870 it was unrecognizable, and in its place was an impersonal nineteenth-century capital. Such, at any rate, is the accepted account of the long commotion that ended with the rejection and disgrace of the Préfet de la Seine.

In examining Haussmann's career we must never forget that he was one of the most obnoxious of recorded beings. The only person who ever spoke wholeheartedly in his favor was George Sand. In her memoirs she writes of the efficiency and dispatch with which he once rendered her a delicate service. More: he so far exceeded the letter of his Prefectoral duties as to offer her two days' hospitality. "Two days of rest," she remarks, "of peaceful outings on the pretty stream of the Beise, and along the banks which, so tradition has it, witnessed the youthful romance of Florette and Henri IV." The Sous-Préfet was, she concludes, "an earnest young man, with a passion for general ideas; but one who was prevented, by an exquisite *savoir-vivre*, from raising any question that might have proved delicate."

We must savor these words, for we shall not meet their like again. Even such friends as he had were forced to admit that Haussmann was a brute—heavy of eye and tread, stiff, coarse, demanding, humorless, and vain. He was, on the other hand, an incomparable administrator, and there are in his biography the elements of an agreeable and original human being. What became of these elements? Was Haussmann alone responsible for their disappearance, or should we rather blame the society that he served?

Haussmann was born in Paris in 1809, at 55, Rue du Faubourg-du-Roule (now Rue du Faubourg-Saint-Honoré). It was a house of the kind that he was later to sweep away: the small *hôtel*, that is to say, with its own garden and courtyard. His family were what we would call textile manufacturers, and their factory was near Colmar. Like nearly every Frenchman of his generation, he was a lifelong Imperial daydreamer. He had, of course, particular links with the regime: he was the godson of Eugène de Beauharnais, and there is on record an occasion, unprofitable even as such occasions go, on which the infant Haussmann was presented to Napoleon I in the gardens of the Trianons. He was also a fellow pupil of the Duc de Chartres at the Lycée Henri IV. At that time he seems to have had no fixed ideas as to how his life should be spent. He might, indeed, have ended up as first cello in the Conservatoire orchestra; as an eminent chemist; as a fencing master; or as the successor of Gay-Lussac as France's leading physicist. All these possibilities emerge from the confused history of his later schooldays. It is certain that he knew Berlioz and Ambroise Thomas, took private lessons in composition from Cherubini, went to Gay-Lussac's lectures, was a keen shot, rode, swam, and skated, was an enthusiast for the acting of Mademoiselle Mars, and had been known to sing the romances of Casimir Delavigne in the drawing rooms of Poitiers. (His thirty-two attendances at performances of Auber's *La Muette de Portici* may be ascribable to an intrigue of which we know nothing.)

In the Revolution of 1830 he cannot be said to have played a heroic part, since he was in bed with fever during nearly the whole of it; but he commended himself at that moment to an eminent politician, by whose good offices he entered the civil service in 1831. For the next twenty-two years he remained in the provinces. He made his name as a tough negotiator who had broken the back of socialism in the Var and of republicanism in the region around Auxerre. Even the working-class center of Ancy-le-Franc bowed to his will, and at Bordeaux he displayed the gift for well-calculated hospitality that was to reach its climax when it fell to him to entertain Queen Victoria in Paris. Perhaps, too, he was inspired by the example of the remodeling of Bordeaux, which had been carried out with such signal success in the eighteenth century. He may well have thought that, one day, a greater city than Bordeaux could be rescued from its near-medieval slumber. Be that as it may, his history merges with that of the Empire itself from the day, in 1853, when Napoleon III made him Préfet de la Seine.

"In less than ten years," Voltaire had written, "Paris could become the marvel of the world." All that was needed, he said, was an administrator with the zeal, the strength of character, the enlightened vision, and the necessary credits. Haussmann took more than ten years to effect his changes; but, when they were completed, they were as extensive as any that Voltaire could have imagined. Before considering whether they were for the better, or entirely for the worse, we must realize what sort of a city he butchered.

For butchery it was. Haussmann destroyed not merely a great many irreplaceable buildings but—what is more important—a whole way of life. We should all have liked, of course, to penetrate the Paris of the Romantic movement and find it intact. That approachable, rusticated, unemphatic Paris is one that many of us would prefer to the Paris of Haussmann. Yet there are many parts of the city in which it can be recaptured. The Cour de Rohan is only a yard or two from the Boulevard Saint-Germain; part of Balzac's own street, the Rue Berton, is much as it was when he lived in it; and the quarter near the Gobelins factory, the alleys of Bercy, and even the slopes of Montmartre have plenty to yield to an unhurrying observer. What cannot be replaced is something that was evoked in Jules Ferry's pamphlet *Les Comptes Fantastiques d'Haussmann*—"the old Paris, the historical, thinking Paris which is now at its last gasp; the Paris of art and philosophy, where people could live a modest life on three thousand francs a year and devote themselves to intellectual pursuits; where there were such things as groups, and neighborhoods, and quarters, and local traditions; where the oldest of relationships and the most precious of habits were not threatened at every moment by the fear of expropriation; where the artisan, who is now being expelled without mercy from the center of Paris, lived side by side with the man of affairs; where intellect was prized above wealth; and where the tone of life was not yet set by the brutal, spendthrift foreigner. . . ."

This too might seem no more than sentimentality: but in fact this division of the classes created precisely the situation that Haussmann and his master had set out to avoid. Their policy was dictated to a considerable degree by the fear of popular risings; straight lines and commanding *carrefours* were their answer to the revolutionaries who counted on the inaccessible barracks and Daedalian roadways of 1830. But, in removing the means of revolt, they provided something more dangerous: the motive which has again and again brought bloodshed to the streets of Paris. They created the double world of Third Republican Paris, in which the eastern half of the capital foundered in penury, while the west shivered with apprehension behind its glass front doors. With the opening of the Boulevard de Strasbourg in 1853, a new frontier was marked out in Paris; and rarely, for more than a century, did anyone live to the east of it who could afford not to do so.

Haussmann did more, therefore, than ruin the 1,253 registered water carriers who were still in business in 1860. He did more than put out the oil lanterns which many preferred to the toxic novelty, gas. And he did more than substitute a uniform municipal omnibus for the many independent lines—the Swallow, for instance, the Gazelle, and the Assembled Ladies—to which we might still have been giving our custom. He killed off not only the Paris of Restif de La Bretonne but the Paris of Diderot and Voltaire, in which one street was as good as another. The old integrity was gone. The traveler gave place to the tourist, the grand to the grandiose, and the individualism of the private *hôtel* to the long uniformity of the Boulevard Malesherbes.

Much of this was inevitable. Paris was growing too fast. (Its population nearly doubled in the first thirteen years of Haussmann's Prefecture.) The problem of the railway had to be solved in a hurry—though here Haussmann was less radical than might have been expected: his only contribution was the delightful and unpretending Ceinture line; in other respects the network remained as it was under Louis-Philippe. There was a great deal of money about, and it was all being put to work. Life was losing the quality of improvisation which had marked the streets of Paris even in the 1830s. Scribes and marionettes were common on the boulevards when Haussmann entered the public service; convicted criminals were displayed in chains before the Palais de Justice; and it was still quite legal to spend every evening at the gaming table. Those who saw that most Balzacian of films, *Les Enfants du Paradis,* will remember how beautifully the sense of that period was caught—the sense, that is to say, of life lived at random. Haussmann gave Paris the apparatus of pleasure, but pleasure itself often stayed away. The Goncourts, for instance, remarked in their diaries on the difference between the generation of 1860 and that of thirty years earlier. "It's amazing," they wrote, "how that generation amused itself with next to nothing, and kept alive that ingenuity of first youth, which has no need to be whipped up with the promise of an orgy before it consents to enjoy itself. . . ."

Changes of this kind are little more than atmospheric, and Haussmann would certainly have been indifferent to them had they been brought to his notice. What did sting

Following pages: *The Pré Catelan.* Henri Gervex, 1909

A restaurant in the Bois de Boulogne

him—as emerges from his charmless memoirs—was the activity of a lot of piffling anti-quarians who persisted in alleging that he had cared nothing for the historical graces of Paris. Such persons, he replied, were bookworms, armchair aesthetes, patrons of the unreal. How many of them had ever set foot in the immense cloacas that he, Haussmann, had had the courage to clear? "Much they care," he continued, "if those narrow and tortuous streets were filthy, reeking, impenetrable, and dangerous to health. One might expect them to be pleased that our 'so-called improvements' have endowed these districts with air, and space, and light, and flowers, and the green of grass and trees—but not a bit of it! All that does not concern them."

It was a spirited defense, and it relates to a good deal that we now take for granted. Sewers and gas pipes and artesian wells are not what one wants to hear about when on holiday, and our appreciation of Haussmann's pioneering in these grim departments is mainly negative. We know, that is to say, that we no longer risk cholera by drinking from a Parisian tap, that we are rarely forced into the gutter in a Parisian street, and that even in the satyr-haunted Bois de Boulogne we can walk the night through without having to grope our way. These things were novelties in 1860, and it was Haussmann who brought them about.

The "green of grass and trees" is a more controversial issue. It was originally from Anglomania that Haussmann and the Emperor decided to lighten and aerate the remodeled capital not only with parks but with squares of English design. (It was also, perhaps, to some extent from remorse at the great number of private gardens that were destroyed in the course of their operations.) At their worst, as in the Place Louvois, opposite the Bibliothèque Nationale, or in the Place Sainte-Clotilde, they are pathetic, stunted affairs. French genius inclines to the open *place*, not to the square, and most of the twenty-four squares of the Second Empire have an uneasy air about them. As one of Haussmann's bitterest adversaries once said, they look "like dubious bandages on an open wound." In the case, however, of the larger open spaces for which Haussmann and his assistant Alphand were responsible, such strictures would be absurd. The Champs-Elysées, the Bois de Boulogne, the Bois de Vincennes, the Buttes-Chaumont, the Parc Monceau, and the Parc de Montsouris are six of the most delightful things in Paris. Admittedly, several

Morning in the Avenue du Bois. 1889

Parc Monceau

of them were in existence long before Haussmann's term of office; but it was he and Alphand who took them in hand, knew exactly what could best be done with them, and presented Paris with examples of urban landscape gardening that could not be bettered.

In the case of the Bois de Boulogne—which I cite because it is the best known of these transformations—the changes went far beyond considerations of aesthetics. The Bois had been accessible only by the post road. Encircled by high walls and traversed by unvarying *allées*, it had the appearance of a broken-down woodland with occasional comfortless clearings. Vistas were unknown, and its only distinguishable "feature" was the Mare d'Auteuil, a stagnant, viscous, frog-loud lake. To go there was a day's expedition, and it was reputed to be the resort of kidnappers and thugs. One memorialist assures us that the Bois, "inaccessible alike to the more energetic of the *petite bourgeoisie* and to the artisan, belonged exclusively to the aristocracy—but to an aristocracy that was sick, and old, and sad, and brought nothing but its own griefs and distresses to this pitiful desert."

"But now," she went on, "all is changed. The Bois has drawn nearer to Paris and has opened out on every side into a series of delightful vistas. Its gray walls have been razed to the ground, its grilles newly gilded, and its keepers housed in pavilions that charm the eye. Its horizons are wider and deeper; the Mont Valérien, the Muette, the hills of Meudon, the bend of the Seine, cascades, lakes, immense lawns studded with flower beds, villas, and chalets diversify the view from moment to moment. There are gondolas on the lakes, cafés in the chalets, horse races on the turf, parades on the lawns, and concerts and sporting events to catch the fancy of the leisured throng. The *allées* have been widened, and properly sanded and watered; and along the lakeside, at the hour decreed by fashion, you can see the carriages, four and five abreast—phaetons, victorias, ponies-and-traps, and *huit-ressorts*. The 'high-life' ladies, as they are called, and the other, more venal ladies with whom it amuses them to mingle, dismount from time to time and sweep the ground with their trailing froufrous. In the side-*allées* there is a rapid to-and-fro of horsemen, each with his cigar in his mouth, and of those Amazones whose echoing laughter and cosmopolitan tones of voice amaze the listening trees."

The metamorphosis of the Buttes-Chaumont was not less remarkable. In his handling of landscape, the Préfet was as supple and imaginative as he was stiff and coarse in his handling of architecture. For there, after all, is the final charge against him: that he substituted for the reserve of French classical architecture habits of building, and of thought, that were shallow and demonstrative. Consider, for example, the Rue Saint-Antoine, which runs from the end of the Rue de Rivoli to the Place de la Bastille. This is a street that has gone down in the world; and although it contains, among other things, a domed chapel by François Mansart, the best Renaissance *hôtel* in Paris (the Hôtel de Sully), and the Italianate church of Saint-Paul-Saint-Louis, it is rarely visited for itself. Booths and roundabouts and acrobats may be found in abundance on Sunday afternoons, for the street is both fairground and highway, and has been so since Roman times, when it was raised above the marshes on blocks of stone and served as the first part of the route from Paris to Melun. It has an extraordinary natural majesty. In fact, I think that it is the most beautiful street in Paris. Haussmann never got anywhere near it. It is curved, for one thing, and the Emperor's famous red and blue pencils always ran straight. There is an inspired strangeness in its proportions. The right angle has no place in the Rue Saint-Antoine, and its *hôtels* are of the kind that can be added to, and painted over, and put to the most inappropriate uses, and yet retain something of their original dignity. Of which of Haussmann's creations could this be said?

It could, of course, be argued that the failing there was the failing of the period, and not of the Préfet himself; 1860 was not a great moment for architecture anywhere. It was, however, possible to find architects whose work had a personal flavor which could conceivably endear itself to those who lived near it. Such architects were, in fact, on the Préfet's registers: Hittorf, for one. No one could say that Hittorf was a man of delicate fancy. He was something of a pig, like his employer, and his Germanic appearance and heavy Rhineland accent caused him to be nicknamed—not, I must say, with characteristic

The Alley of Acacias.
Roger de la Fresnaye,
1908
An avenue in the Bois de Boulogne

Parc des Buttes-
Chaumont

French logic—"the Prussian." Hittorf was a man of learning who had published, in 1851,
a monograph on the Temple of Empedocles at Selinunte. His touch was not always
happy—the Mairie of the 1st *arrondissement*, for instance, is one of the most comical
buildings in Paris—but in the Gare du Nord, which he rebuilt in 1864, he produced
something with a vigor of its own. Hittorf's work has a rough male power quite lacking
from the anonymous architecture of Haussmann's boulevards. In fact, these have a quality
that makes it difficult to imagine that they ever took shape in any individual human mind.
They are committee work, one feels.

Even the Préfet's pastiches did not come off. The Second Empire, like other basically
uncreative periods, had a learned and reverent approach to the past. In private hands, this
attitude sometimes produced remarkable results. The work of Viollet-le-Duc, for example,
is full of curiosities of this sort. And few houses of the period can have been so interesting
as the Pompeian palace that was erected in the Avenue Montaigne by the prince Napoleon.
It is one thing, however, to indulge such learned fancies on the scale of a royal pleasance
in the leafy make-believe of the Champs-Elysées, and quite another to put them forward
as the grave culminations of the capital of the world. Haussmann's repertory of pastiches
included German Gothic (Sainte-Clotilde), Romanesque (Saint-Ambroise), the French thirteenth century (Saint-Jean-Baptiste-de-Belleville), and the Renaissance (Saint-François-
Xavier). There is even a Romanesque synagogue in the Marais. These buildings please
nobody.

This failure to endear is typical, not only of Haussmann's creations, but of the man
himself. He was, in many ways, a host of genius. Already at Bordeaux he had made history
by the ingenious luxury of his official receptions; and hardly was he installed in Paris

before he organized a superb divertissement in which the Champs-Elysées were turned into a kind of Alhambra and the night was made dazzling by half a million jets of gas. As for the Bals de l'Hôtel de Ville, they had a gross opulence that imposed itself on all but the most skeptical. Banked myosotis and verbena left the guests giddy from the very beginning. The artificial lakes with their grassy islets, the indoor fountains, the *tableaux vivants* of scenes from Egypt and ancient Greece—these charmed nearly everyone.

The Goncourts, admittedly, were not taken in. "It's rich and poor at once," they wrote in April 1858. "Gold everywhere, and the rooms and galleries at their most magnificent; damask everywhere, hardly any velvet, tapestry wherever you look, but art *nowhere*. And some of the walls covered with insipid allegories, painted by some Vasari or other whose name I'd hate to know. . . . But the twelve thousand guests are not exacting, and their eyes shine. What impressed me, and are really worth seeing, are the inkwells of the Conseil Municipal. You can see them—they're shown to the public on great days such as this. They're monumental. Earnest, preoccupied, opulent, imposing, formidable, and square, they reminded me at once of the Pyramids of Egypt and of M. Prud'homme's paunch."

And so it was, even with guests less difficult than Edmond and Jules de Goncourt. They came, and ate the quails, and listened to the band, and goggled at the tableaux, and then they went away and made fun of Haussmann's inkwells. For he was a man of very little tact. His memoirs are full of avoidable quarrels, and of occasions on which he disappointed others, or was himself disappointed, by some predictable failure of human understanding. Typical of these was his obstinacy in pushing the idea of a cemetery at Méry-sur-Oise, to which coffins were to be whisked by special trains on a line built for the purpose. The idea was hardly launched before the householders whose gardens would face onto the line joined forces with the horde of thwarted mourners and made the Préfet's life unendurable. Scouts were sent even to England to discredit the plan; and discredit it

Eglise de Saint-Philippe du Roule. Jean Béraud, c. 1880
Though prized by architectural historians for its hefty Doric columns and its echoes of the basilicas of ancient Rome, the Eglise de Saint-Philippe du Roule, just south of the Boulevard Haussmann, has also its place in social history. It attracted in Jean Béraud's day a fashionable congregation that has never since deserted it.

they did—by reporting on the inconvenience and low social prestige of a similar experiment on the outskirts of London. "No gentleman," they reported, "was ever buried in Woking." But Haussmann was unpersuadable; and it was his obstinacy over points such as these that made him detested even by those who were making great fortunes as a result of his activities.

Haussmann never shared in these fortunes. Whatever else may be urged against him, he was not corrupt; and when he came to resign, in 1870, he was left with nothing but his pension of six thousand francs a year, his barony, and his Orders from Italy, Russia, Mexico, Persia, and Guadeloupe. This probity in matters of finance has not, it seems to me, been sufficiently stressed. The Second Empire was remarkable, even by French standards, for its lack of scruple in such matters, and Haussmann was in charge of operations in which thousands of millions of francs had changed hands. Others, less delicate than he, habitually bought up houses that were due for demolition and soon afterward received indemnities amounting to five and ten times what they had paid. Construction work was also peculiarly fruitful; it was not unknown for there to be a difference of over two hundred million francs between the real and the estimated cost of one of the Préfet's larger operations. There is something admirable in Haussmann's almost Roman refusal to benefit by any of this, and in the twenty years of unregarded office work with which he eked out the last part of his life.

It was, in fact, at the age of sixty-three that he went to his private St. Helena: the bureaux of the Compagnie d'Entrepôts et Magasins Généraux. He had doubtless made

The Gare de l'Est. Designed by F.-A. Duquesney, 1847–52, renovated and enlarged in the 1890s and again in the 1920s. Alain Perceval photograph

errors of judgment that are as blatant, a century later, as his errors of taste. But overconfidence was the malady of his age. Haussmann, like most of his contemporaries, expected not only to get his way, but to be confirmed in his belief that his way was the only right one. History was on his side, he felt, as he indited his unreadable memoirs and summoned the gardens of Sesostris and the aqueducts of Appius Claudius to fill in the background to his own parks and canals. He never doubted that his Paris was greater than those which had gone before it; and at the climax of his reign—the Exhibition of 1867, that is to say—there were very few who echoed Ernest Renan and dared to say that such exhibitions were "dazzling to the eye, and instructive to those whose work is concerned with technical advancement, but more or less null, where thought is concerned." The rare voice of the discontented intellectual was drowned by other and louder assertions—those, for instance, of Victor Hugo.

Hugo was an old man in 1867, but he had lost none of his rhetorical power. Perhaps he did not regret the Paris of 1825; certainly he was the first to acclaim the Paris of Haussmann: "The city that lives by, and for, the whole of the human race, the city that is privileged to act for Europe." "And those who are coming to this Exhibition," he went on, "are not coming from Europe alone. Our old civilized world—England with its gilded pyramid, sixty feet high, symbolizing the yield of the Australian gold mines, Prussia with its temple of Peace and its grotto of rock salt, Russia with its Byzantine goldsmith's shop, the Crimea with its wool, Finland with its linen, Sweden with its iron, Norway with its furs, Belgium with its lace, Canada with its rare woods, New York with its 8000-pound block of anthracite, and Brazil with the rare birds and insects that flourish in its sunshine—these are not all. With them, making haste towards Paris, are ancient fantastic Tibet, and Kolkar, and Travancore, and Bhopal, and Drangudra, and Attipor, and Gundul, and Ristlom; and the Jam of Norvanaghur, and the Nizam of Hyderabad, and the Kao of Rusk and the Thakore of Morwee. . . ."

These transports may seem to us absurd, but they reflect a real generosity and a

L'AVENUE DE L'OPERA

genuine internationalism which have vanished from the world. The cosmopolitanism of Haussmann had its triumphs—but nothing now remains of these triumphs but a few crumbling catalogues, a few lines of simple-hearted rhetoric, and a picture by Manet. The three volumes of Haussmann's memoirs sank without trace, and the voice that has endured is that of cantankerous Renan: "Our century is heading neither for good nor for evil. It is heading for mediocrity. What succeeds today, in every sphere of life, is just that: mediocrity."

That sounds like a definitive judgment. But "After me, mediocrity" is a form of words into which older people fall easily. And today, after more than a hundred years, the achievement of Haussmann does not look so mediocre, either in itself or by contrast with the work of his successors.

Nor did Renan realize that the energies set in motion by Haussmann would dominate the development of Paris for quite some time to come, and not to its disadvantage. The Avenue de l'Opéra, for instance, was not finished till 1879. Alphand, who had been a colleague of Haussmann's, was still at his post in the 1870s, and in one way or another the grand design of Haussmann went forward. It is to this day the decisive factor in central Paris, and every visitor—whether he knows it or not—is the guest of Haussmann, as much as of any other one man or woman, during his sojourn in central Paris.

The Avenue de l'Opéra, the Boulevard Saint-Germain, the Rue Etienne-Marcel, the Rue de Rennes, and many another long straight street did not take their final form until long after his death. But he presides over them, just as until lately his well-founded fear of unscrupulous development set a maximum height for all new buildings in the center of Paris. Heat, light, and water were concerns of his. We cannot doubt that he would have clapped his hands to see electric street lighting, the spread of the telephone, and the sage prescriptions of Poubelle, the Prefect of Paris who gave his name to the Parisian trash bin.

It should also be said that the new quarters for which Haussmann was ultimately responsible often took on a personality that was the stronger for not having been foreseen. This is true architecturally—the swing of taste in such matters has taught us to see the period from 1871 to 1914 as one of almost headlong evolution—and it is also true socially. Who would have thought, for instance, that the Boulevard Malesherbes, completed in 1863, would have overtones to this day of art, theater, music, and literature? It could have been just one more dull upper-bourgeois street, even if a new network of streets nearby was named after Rembrandt, Van Dyck, Murillo, Ruysdael, and Velázquez. But in no time at all it was the home of one of the best actors of the day (Coquelin *cadet*), of composers (Gabriel Fauré and André Messager), of writers (Dumas *père*, Pierre Louÿs, and Catulle Mendès), and of painters (Edouard Detaille, Henri Gervex, and Meissonier).

In fact it would have had a Meissonier museum if Meissonier had had his way. He lived in grand style in one of the more eccentric of the houses along the Boulevard Malesherbes. Visitors would find him dressed in flowing robes of brown or blue velvet. Costume balls were his preferred way of entertaining. Even to see him light a cigar was as good as going to the Comédie-Française. He never doubted that his work and his house should be preserved for posterity, conjointly. But the day after he died his children had the house pulled down so that they could put up a five-story apartment building and live forever on the proceeds.

It was the same, and it is the same, all over the city. If the Avenue Montaigne has overtones of exalted enjoyment it is in part because of developments for which Haussmann can take no credit—the existence, for example, of Auguste Perret's Théâtre des Champs-Elysées, which has heard as much good music as any auditorium in Paris, and of the little Comédie des Champs-Elysées, right next door, in which the bar was decorated by Edouard Vuillard in 1912. No other bar in the world has decorations of such quality.

But already in Haussmann's day the quarter had something of this histrionic quality. In February 1860, to be precise, the prince Napoleon, nephew of Napoleon I, inaugurated the Pompeian palace that he had had built at what is now 18, Avenue Montaigne. The alliance of Pompeian idiom, correct in its every detail, with modern technology made problems for the architect, but the prince Napoleon was almost as exacting in such matters as his uncle had been, and he got his way.

Rehearsal of "The Flute Player." Gustave-Clarence-Rodolphe Boulanger, 1860

Luckily we have a painting by Gustave Boulanger that shows us not only what the inside of the house looked like but the extent to which more than one eminent figure of the day was pressed into its service. For the inaugural evening Théophile Gautier wrote a prologue in verse and Emile Augier, the Neil Simon of the day, wrote an imitation of the kind of play that might have whiled away a long wet evening in Pompeii. Got himself was asked over from the Comédie-Française to lead for the professionals, and both Gautier and Augier were prevailed upon to appear on the stage in Roman dress. It might have been great fun, but conceivably it wasn't. In any case, the prince Napoleon gave up the house in 1866, and in 1891 it was pulled down after a rather degrading period in which its scholarly *impluvium* was rented for some performing seals.

Haussmann had of course had some horrible ideas. He would have allowed the Rue de Rennes to be continued all the way to the Seine, thereby cutting a wide swath through the historic heart of the 6th *arrondissement*. Happily Alphand dismissed this idea in 1878. As against that, Haussmann set the style all over Paris for broad straight tree-lined avenues that once looked stiff and impersonal but have turned out to adapt themselves rather well to changes in fashion, in mores, and in function. Of how many of the urbanists of our own age will as much be said? With every year that passes, Haussmann on balance looks more and more like a true friend of Paris.

XII

The River and the Islands

The Ile de la Cité Seen from the Port Saint-Nicolas. Alexandre-Jean Noël, c. 1780

Opposite: The Ile de la Cité. Alain Perceval photograph

It is not easy for a city to come to terms with its river. Moving water is a symbol of impermanence, and as such unwelcome to the city fathers. Rivers have bad habits, too; they overflow, on the one hand, and on the other they dry up at inconvenient moments. Architecturally speaking, they set difficult problems; few buildings look their best across a ditch up to a hundred yards wide. Socially, too, a river may soon become unmanageable; the water's edge lends itself too well to low amusement. Trade drives away the private resident, as in the City of London; and it is a mistake, as in Budapest, to have too sharp a class division between one bank and another. Small wonder that the Liffey in Dublin is half causeway, half gutter, that Vienna keeps the Danube in its backyard, and that in Berlin the Spree is kept as nearly as possible out of sight.

Paris is the only city in which a great river has been used for mile after mile, on right bank and left, as the natural center of a work of art. Between the Pont d'Austerlitz

The Pont Saint-Michel.
French school (possibly
Perelle), 17th century

*The Port Saint-Paul in
1782* (detail). Louis-
Nicolas de Lespinasse

in the east and the Pont d'Iéna in the west it was difficult until quite lately to stand on either bank and point to anything ignoble. It is not simply that Paris has "got everything," on this long semicircular reach, but that it has got the right amount of everything. Parks are all very well, for instance, but in a venture of this magnitude they must know their place; and this the Cours-La-Reine and the Jardin des Tuileries unquestionably do. It is good for a waterfront to have centers of administration somewhere along it; but Authority, too, must know its place, and in Paris neither the Affaires Etrangères nor the Chambre des Députés nor the Préfecture de Police nor even the Palais de Justice is objectionably out of scale with its neighbors. And it is clear from paintings by Van der Meulen, Bouhot, Noël, Canella, and Girtin that good manners have always prevailed beside the Seine. It has, for instance, one of the world's great palaces—the Louvre; but the Louvre does not dominate the houses opposite it. It has a cathedral, Notre-Dame; but Notre-Dame likewise is not at all domineering.

There is enough of a harbor along its central five miles for there to be a continual commotion of yachts and barges and tugboats; but the real harbor is far enough distant for all these to seem merely ornamental. It is hard to find an ugly bridge in Paris. A waterfront without shops is dull, in the end; and the Paris waterfront has not only its bookstalls—now much diminished, alas!, in quality—but also a bird-and-animal market, antique shops of the first order, an all-purpose music shop, and a department store named after the Woman of Samaria. Its hotels are few, but august; in one André Breton lived, in another Baudelaire, Rilke, Walter Sickert, and Wagner. Restaurants of many kinds may also be found by the Seine. Not all of them, be it noted, in the same area: variety plays

The Quai des Tuileries, 1855. Adolphe Braun photograph

The Flower Market.
Giuseppe Canella, 1832

its part. It is one thing to sit outside behind a fence of evergreens on the Quai de Mon-tebello and quite another to battle for a seat among the international civil servants on the Avenue de New-York or the Quai d'Orsay. There are also, one must own, a number of deceitful duds: "recent recommendations only" should be our motto when hunger strikes on the quays.

So much for the elements of the scene. We should add, perhaps, the note of frenzy which has been struck these last few years by ever faster and more voluminous traffic along the banks of the Seine. Nor should the Eiffel Tower be left out; and of course I have left to the last the classic Parisian variant of the metropolitan river scene, the point so marvelously taken by the creators of Paris ever since Fouquet embellished Etienne Chevalier's *Livre d'Heures:* the two islands, la Cité and Saint-Louis. Of these, the Ile de la Cité has been handled at its western end with all possible assurance; there is nothing finicky about the Pont-Neuf, the narrow entrance to the Place Dauphine, the Square du Vert-Galant, the trees at one level and another, and the relation between these nearer elements and the towers and domes beyond. The island moves into view like a ship, certainly, but a ship with a strong beak to it. The Ile Saint-Louis is, by contrast, a pleasure cruiser: slimmer, more delicately built and boned, untouched by great affairs or the rough traffic of the law, and marked along the whole length of its inner street by a certain slumbrous distinction.

Stone and water do not come into, or go out of, fashion; the quays have, for almost the whole of their length, a timeless nobility. Their special characteristics were decided a very long time ago, and nothing has happened to change them. In this they differ from

The Quai du Louvre.
Claude Monet, 1867

certain other famous Parisian sights which have changed subtly in character while remaining physically much the same. The Champs-Elysées, for instance, are in outline much
as they looked twenty years ago; but now they are becoming more and more the preserve
of the airline and automobile industries, and it is not much fun to sit out on the great
Avenue. Nothing like this will happen to the quays. It is, in any case, not easy to sit out
on them, unless you squat on the bare stones. For the *flâneur,* on the other hand, they
are ideal, and it is at a stroller's pace that they are best seen in detail. For a first rapid
swoop a taxi—or, better, an open car of ancient design—will do very well. The view from
a bus also may be recommended, though you will need a virtuoso's command of the route
map; and perfectionists claim that there is nothing so good as sailing one's own boat up
river from Le Havre.

As one whose first sight of the quays was obtained from the afterdeck of a *bateau-
mouche,* I can testify to the intense pleasure that was given by these amiable veterans.
Sixty-tonners they were, with a length of just over a hundred feet and a best speed of
eight or nine knots. When abolished in 1934, they were working a round trip from
Suresnes to Maisons-Alfort; for just a few pennies, you could embark on the far side of
the Bois de Boulogne, skirt the Parc de Saint-Cloud and the laundries and factories of
Boulogne-Billancourt, and enter Paris itself near the Porte de Saint-Cloud. Eventually,
after traversing the whole of the city, the sturdy craft would push out into more or less
open country and put down its passengers at Maisons-Alfort, having kept to the mainstream at the junction of Seine and Marne. The service ran from six till nine in the
morning, lay up during the forenoon, and resumed after an early luncheon till nightfall.

The *bateaux-mouches* have to a limited extent come back into service, but with the difference that they are now tourist boats pure and simple and make merely a fixed nonstop circuit from the Pont de Solférino. Their customers are nearly all foreign visitors, and although the run has still its unique beauties it no longer offers an introduction at close quarters to Parisian and Parisienne. Nor does it take us around the great loop of the Seine that bears within it the Bois de Boulogne. The boats are sprucer, certainly, but in the cicada click of cameras and the bellowing of the guide there is no trace of the atmosphere (how Maupassant would have portrayed it!) that dated originally from the Exposition Universelle of 1867.

So there is still only one way of getting to know the river and the islands—on foot. A word of warning, in this context: the distances are greater than they seem. The Eiffel Tower, for instance, throws everything out of scale. Things look near, but are not: and because the river "composes" well at almost any point it is not easy to bear in mind that it does not by any means pursue a straight course. Léon-Paul Fargue claimed in his *Piéton de Paris* to have walked "a hundred times" along the Seine from Charenton to the limits of Auteuil; but I notice that when he counts up the names of his favorite quays they all lie within that small central section that contains, as it were, the quintessence of Paris. "As far as History and Geography are concerned, the names of Orsay, Mégisserie, Voltaire, Malaquais, Gesvres, aux Fleurs, Conti, Grands-Augustins, Horloge, Orfèvres, Béthune, and Place Mazas are quite enough for me."

On a fine Sunday, this stretch of the Seine is used as Venetians use the Piazza San Marco: as a general rendezvous and place of gentle recreation. Plane trees and old stone go well together; fishing of a kind can be had below; and on the ancient parapets the zinc-topped boxes lie open and the *bouquinistes* await your pleasure. These boxes may be found from the Quai d'Orsay to the Pont de la Tournelle on the left bank, and from the Samaritaine to the Place du Châtelet on the right bank. The normal frontage is of eight yards, and in principle the tenants are mutilated ex-servicemen or fathers of large families; but these regulations, like much else in Paris, are subject to violation. Any experienced bookman will soon discern the special flavor that attaches to each frontage: he will learn,

The Pont Alexandre III.
Pierre Jahan photograph

A La Tête Noire. Gabriel de Saint-Aubin, 1767
A shop on the Quai de la Mégisserie

for instance, to look for music on the Quai des Grands-Augustins, postcards and English pornography not far from the Hôtel de Ville, coins and the surrealists just below the Pont-Neuf, and so on.

The quays have lost much of their character in recent years. Many *bouquinistes* have given in to the mass market and now offer only prints, maps and trumpery reproductions. But the ancient fascination still holds, even if we can no longer hope to see what Fargue saw: Maurice Barrès, Edmond Rostand, Jean-Paul Forain, Paul Bourget, and Anatole France bent over the book boxes, and beside these august persons a number of others—"elderly Parisians of no particular importance, dressed to the nines; gray trousers and spats, moustaches carefully combed, impeccable top hat, walking stick under the arm, imposing collar and conspicuous necktie, smile and buttonhole always in place. . . . They were well-cared-for old gentlemen; each had his private income; and while waiting to go off to their *rendezvous galants* they would hover in a trance of pleasure above astronomical maps, and postage stamps, and erotic prints, and first editions."

Other cities have *bouquinistes,* of course, but the point about their Parisian counterparts is that they ply their trade in surroundings of extreme beauty. They render, what is more, a public service in preserving an asylum of idleness in the very middle of the restless city. Elsewhere it requires real strength of will to stand motionless on the pavement against a stream of irritable Parisians; but here, if your eye is caught by the Institut de France, or you notice in the Hôtel de la Monnaie the beginnings of the *style Louis XVI,* you may ponder these matters for as long as you like; nobody will think it odd. The automobile is here an intruder, and you will not be alone in wishing to put it in its place.

The mention of the Institut de France reminds me that everyone who loves France must sooner or later make up his mind about the Académie Française, whose headquarters in the Institut so nobly ornament the left bank of the Seine. It is, to my mind, irrelevant that the Académie does not always welcome those writers whom posterity will most admire. The fact that Baudelaire, Flaubert, and Proust were never elected would be damaging if the Académie had ever claimed to assemble the best creative writers, as such, beneath its dome. But this was not Richelieu's idea when he founded the Académie in 1635. What he had in mind was to give official patronage to a group of intelligent people who would meet once a week for literary discussion. Richelieu had a profound belief in the French language as the ideal instrument of international diplomacy, and he felt that the establishment of an Académie Française would be in the interests of the language, as much as in those of the Académie's individual members. (It was also, of course, in his own interest to have his private talking-shop.)

Bouquiniste on the Quai de Montebello. Robert Doisneau photograph

The Pont des Arts. Pierre-Auguste Renoir, c. 1868

The Institut de France. Alain Perceval photograph

The charter members of the Académie were not, and did not claim to be, the best writers or the greatest men of their day. Just how obscure they were we may guess from a passage in *Cyrano de Bergerac,* where Rostand makes fun of the first Immortals:

> Bardin, Boissart et Cureau de la Chambre
> Porchères, Colomby, Bourzeys, Bourdon, Arbaud,
> Tous ces noms dont pas un ne mourra, que c'est beau!

"All these names, and every one of them immortal . . ." Well, Descartes and Corneille were alive at that time, but the Académie preferred to call upon Manet, Malleville, Giry, and Colletet. As time went on, the Académie slowly became what it is today: a club for distinguished senior citizens of many kinds, to which one or two writers are admitted. (In London, one or two writers are members of White's, but no one would call White's a literary club.) Louis XIV enjoyed the company of writers and insisted that the Académie should be housed in the Louvre. On occasion he would remain at table with his Academicians for as many as six hours, and he had a genuine personal liking for Molière, Racine, Boileau, and Bossuet. Not all his Academicians quite shared his enthusiasm. Bussy-Rabutin, for one, wrote that "the Académie consists very largely of people of high breeding. But we have to allow for a certain number of men of letters—if only to get on with the Dictionary, for they show an assiduity in that respect which could not be expected of people like ourselves." And the writers knew that their King's interest in them was not that of a detached aesthete. Racine once said in one of his academic discourses that: "If we set a high value on every word and every syllable of our language it is because they are so many instruments that must sing out in praise of our glorious Protector."

The Académie is beautifully housed. Upstairs there are rooms with a view on the river (some have a second window on the Rue de Seine) which would make the best of all bachelor apartments; the inner courtyards are as near to Oxford (Corpus Christi, perhaps, or Jesus College) as we can get on the mainland of Europe; and Le Vau judged as nicely as possible the relation between the two arms of his forecourt and the Palais du Louvre across the river.

Not many visitors can hope to witness the ceremonial reception of a new member of the Académie; for although, in an average year, two Immortals considerately die off and make way for others, there is a tremendous demand for the very uncomfortable seats that are allotted to the public. It is an engaging feature of the Académie that no one can be admitted to membership until he has composed and delivered a eulogy of his predecessor. In this we see once again the reverence for language which should make the Académie respected by all who live by the pen. The speech in question may, of course, be sad and thin stuff; but just occasionally—as in Paul Valéry's tribute to Pétain, the hero of World War I—one hears something that would have drawn a "Bravo!" from Richelieu himself.

Valéry saw the Académie as a kind of ideal magistracy which, without exercising effective powers of any kind, would watch over all that was best in human activity and bring it "subtly, indefinably, and constantly" to the notice of the rest of the world. It is more commonly seen, of course, as a collection of oddly assorted old people who wear bottle-green uniforms and spend every Thursday afternoon squabbling about how to define words like "crayfish," "golf," and "appendicitis." And it is true that dictionaries quite as good are produced by other means; but the point is that the Académie gives prestige not to the writers or thinkers who are members of it, but to all writers and thinkers, and through them to language and thought as two of the noblest of human concepts. It is not by accident that a member of the Académie ranks with a *Duc et Pair* in the French hierarchy. So we should not laugh when we see Monsieur Un Tel tottering into the Institut; we shall have revenge enough if we cross to the quayside and note that his last book has been marked down to a dollar. Perhaps, in any case, the Académie was best summed up not by Valéry but by the derelict who said to Léon-Paul Fargue that he always slept out, if he could, at the water's edge below the Quai Conti. "We feel more at home there," he said, "and our dreams have more distinction."

The Pont-Neuf Seen from the Rue Dauphine. Nicolas Guérard, late 17th century

View of the Pont-Neuf, the Tower, and the Old Porte de Nesle. Jacques Callot, 1630

The buildings in the Place Dauphine can be seen in the distance as they originally looked.

Sooner or later the temptation to turn left at the Pont-Neuf and embark on the Ile de la Cité will be too much for even the most sedulous bibliophile. Sébastien Mercier said in the 1780s that the Pont-Neuf was to Paris what the heart is to the human body— "the center of all movement and the source of circulation"—and we know from paintings by Adam Frans van der Meulen that it was once one of the busiest places in all Paris. (An eighteenth-century globe-trotter once said that the three finest sights in the world were the Golden Horn, the port of Goa, and the Pont-Neuf.) The Pont-Neuf was not just a beautiful bridge; it was fairground, department store, employment exchange, picture gallery, and poor man's medical center. You could have a tooth pulled out, go through the "Help Wanted," watch the tightrope dancers, buy a Lancret or a Fragonard, join the army, pick up the new book by Marivaux or a first edition of *Manon Lescaut*, arrange to go up in a balloon, watch a bullfight, take fencing lessons, and attend a surgical demonstration. Gradually, of course, these amenities dropped away, and the Pont-Neuf became a thoroughfare like any other; but we can still stand in the hooped embrasures that were once bookstalls, pharmacies, swimming masters' agencies, and *cabinets d'aisance inodores*. The last toyshop closed in 1847, but we still have the sensation when we head north from the Rue Dauphine that we are crossing from one world to another.

Henri IV still bestrides the center of the Pont-Neuf and, quite rightly, he faces toward the mysterious entrance to the Place Dauphine. André Breton has an anatomical explanation, too gross to be set down here, for the fascination of this inlet; let us say merely that few things in Paris are prettier than the play of old brickwork against old stone that was devised in 1607 by Achille de Harlay. The Place Dauphine lost much of its secret quality when Haussmann destroyed its eastern wall in 1874, and if it were not for the restaurant much favored by English-speaking visitors, few of us would have any business there. But the little triangle has seen great days: the entrée of Louis XIV and Marie-Thérèse, for instance, in 1660, when there was built a gateway of solid sugar and a merry-go-round revolved in the square. And in the history of French art the Place Dauphine has a place of honor: for it was there, in the open-air exhibition on Corpus Christi Day, 1728, that Chardin first showed his *La Raie*, which now hangs in the Louvre.

But there is no doubt that Haussmann ruined the Place Dauphine. The enormous quasi-classical west front of the Palais de Justice will forever cast a gloom upon the

Dufyesque proportions of the square—and a gloom that is not merely aesthetic. For the Law has laid a damp hand on the Ile de la Cité: what with the Préfecture de Police, the Palais de Justice, the Quai des Orfèvres, and the hardly less penitential Hôtel-Dieu, the whole island is now *triste* beyond redemption. The streets that Haussmann pulled down might by now have gone anyway, so extreme was their decomposition. The reader of Balzac, or of Eugène Sue, will not need to be reminded of what they were like: ". . . so narrow were the roads that the mud-gray houses, with their worm-eaten window frames, almost touched at the top. Dark and foul alleys led to even darker, even fouler staircases so steep that you had to haul yourself up with the help of a rope. On the ground floors of these houses coal-merchants, fruiterers, and bad-meat butchers lived side by side, and although their wares were next-to-worthless the shop-fronts were solidly barred with iron, such was the audacity of the thieves who abounded there."

This was what people really meant when they twaddled on about Héloise and Abelard and the cradle of France. And yet there is little to be said for a solution that turns the very beginnings of Paris into a flavorless city center with overtones of informer, executioner, and attorney's clerk. There are few places in the Ile de la Cité where one can walk, and still fewer where one can sit, with pleasure. Haussmann was proud of the way in which the Boulevard Saint-Michel gives on to the spire of the Sainte-Chapelle, but the truth is that although he touched not a stone of the Chapelle he robbed it of all its significance in the Parisian landscape. We should laugh at anyone who used a Cellini saltcellar as a doorstop, but that is how Haussmann treated the Sainte-Chapelle, and I know of few beautiful buildings so oddly abused.

The Sainte-Chapelle was completed a little over seven hundred years ago. Not much of what we see today can be said to go back to those times, however, for spire, doors, sculpture, stained glass, gilded timberwork, and paintings are almost all either of the nineteenth century or very thoroughly restored. But even if much of it is no more venerable than, let us say, the Cathedral of Saint John the Divine in New York, the proportions remain of a marvelous delicacy, there are still some pieces of thirteenth-century glass, and the visitor to the Musée de Cluny can see four of the statues of Apostles which once stood

Above: *Playing-Card Factory in a House on the Place Dauphine.* Anonymous, c. 1680

Opposite: The Sainte-Chapelle. A. F. Kersting photograph

in the upper chapel. The building, though destined by Saint Louis to house the Crown of Thorns, was eventually put to humbler uses: it served, for instance, as a grain store, a revolutionary club, and an auxiliary Archives. As late as 1837 it bore the notice "National Property: For Sale." Today all is done that can be done to treat the inspired veteran as it should be treated; but, like a stuffed okapi at town council meeting, it is as incongruous as it is elegant.

Certain phrases stick in the throat, even if they offer nothing that is analytically improbable. "A dashing Swiss officer" is one such. Another is "the beautiful Law Courts": and it would be difficult to call to mind a court of law, designed as such, that gives much pleasure to the eye. If the Palais de Justice—the side on the Quai de l'Horloge at any rate—has nothing ignoble about it, the credit goes back to Philippe le Bel who built, in the first half of the fourteenth century, the four towers that give the waterfront such character as it now possesses. The Cité was, after all, the headquarters of the Kings of France till the reign of Charles V, and even Haussmann could not quite do away with their traces. Justice, too, has been dealt out of this corner of the island since Saint Louis sat out in his garden in fine weather and settled case after case where now the Cour de Cassation is to be found. He did not need ten thousand tons of masonry to tell right from wrong (at Vincennes he sat out under an oak, in the summer, when he wanted to dispense justice); and it is a curious thing that society has so often put its faith, or lack of faith, in buildings that seem designed to crush the ideas of individual liberty and unprejudiced judgment before even we get inside the door.

The Palais de Justice has one great difference from its equivalents in London and elsewhere; it is not a creation of the late nineteenth century. The site is colored, even if the stones are not, by a tradition that goes back to the Capétiens. French justice has embraced many a strange compact. As late as 1653 it was possible for a husband to rebut a charge of impotence by public demonstration in the presence of fifteen medical witnesses, and in the early eighteenth century a jeweler took God into formal partnership, with full legal honors. Lawyers prospered greatly under the patronage of Saint Nicholas, and their Basoche, or subordinates' trade union, was a delightfully lively and inventive affair. (It is in honor of their traditional May tree celebration that the main entrance to the Palais is still called the Cour du Mai.)

The Palais has a tradition of violence: Armagnacs massacred by Burgundians, the future Cardinal de Retz all but throttled by the future author of the *Maximes de La Rochefoucauld*, and the activities of Fouquier-Tinville, most implacable of prosecutors, during the period of the Tribunal Révolutionnaire. And it was from the Tour de l'Horloge that the alarm was given for the massacre of Saint Bartholomew's Day. Its procedures are more orderly now; but if we think of the three round towers and the single square one as illustrations to an unwritten novel of Walter Scott, we should remind ourselves that even quite lately they were fulfilling their ancient function. Ravaillac, the assassin of Henry IV, may not trouble us as we walk past the Tour César, but in the Tour d'Argent the young Duc d'Orléans was imprisoned as recently as 1890.

So the visitor to the Conciergerie and the Palais has much to think about. If he ventures into a courtroom, he may be lucky enough to hear one of those rare great pleaders who are the glory of the bar—a Berryer, perhaps, such as Sainte-Beuve described him: "If ever an orator was born and not made, he is that man. When he speaks, his whole being is brought into action: the magnificent set of the head, the eye alive with fire and light, the noble line of the nose, the profile made for a Roman coin, a Ciceronian lawyer with full-modelled mouth, broad chest and ample voice. . . . A man who goes to the stand as others go to a holiday." A Berryer doesn't come in every generation, but there are many worse schools of life than a French courtroom, and it is well worthwhile to seek out an interesting case and follow it through.

The Ile de la Cité was once, of course, the headquarters of France. It had the Monarch, the Church, and the Law: all within a very few acres. It still has the Law, as we have seen, and indeed the Law has made further encroachments even within the last hundred years. I cannot recommend a visit to the Préfecture de Police on any grounds other than those of necessity; but those who have business with the Préfet himself will find that his chamberlain wears full evening dress and has across his chest a chain of more-than-mayorial proportions. In details such as these, and in the studied comforts of the Préfet's own sanctum, there is much to reward an observant visitor.

Nor should the crime-fancier who finds himself at liberty between two and five o'clock on a Wednesday or Thursday afternoon neglect to go to the Musée de la Préfecture de Police, now located at 1 bis, Rue des Carmes in the 5th *arrondissement*. To go in costs nothing, and you are likely to find yourself alone with the exhibits. There are few more disquieting sights in Paris than the enormous collection of weapons, with every one of which a murder was committed. The evolution of the policeman's uniform may be said to yield light relief, and we must raise our hats to the statue of Lépine, the Préfet who first gave the gendarme his white baton. But the souvenirs of our own time give the museum a chill particular savor. This comes not from isolated episodes like the assassination in 1932 of President Doumer (you will be shown the novel by Claude Farrère that he had just bought, and find it still stained with his blood) but from the vast consistent inhumanity of the Occupation of 1940–44. Many would gladly forget this—but no one who has visited the museum is likely to do so.

Between the Church and the Law it would be possible to find a distant cousinage. But cousins don't always get on together, and in the Ile de la Cité the Law and Authority between them have done a great deal of damage. The Law did not always have the upper hand: medievalists delight to run over the list of the eighteen saints who once had churches named after them there, and there are still traces of the time when the eastern end of the island was a little universe all its own. At 19, Rue des Ursins, for instance, we can see the last vestiges of the Chapelle Saint-Aignan, sole and fragmentary survivor of the island's medieval churches. In the Rue Chanoinesse there is a house, No. 12, which has the unassuming distinction of the Grand Siècle, another, No. 17, from which the great preacher Lacordaire used to walk over to the cathedral, and a third, No. 16, in the inner courtyard of which Racine is said to have lodged.

But these are mere fragments: for the general color of the Cité during its great period

Lawyer Pleading. Honoré Daumier, c. 1845

Following pages: Windows in the Sainte-Chapelle

we must go to the Musée Carnavalet and look at Hoffbauer's scale model. There we see the canons' houses (thirty-seven in all), and the canons' gardens by the Seine, and the proportions of the Parvis. We see how the cathedral once dominated the island, with the little toy houses huddled like piglets beneath a great sow. All this is now changed, of course; the view from the west door of Notre-Dame is one of the ugliest in Paris, and Notre-Dame itself is no longer the center of a vast miscellaneous activity.

And yet one cannot but feel that the Parvis de Notre-Dame is still, in some real sense, the center of France. The geographers, at any rate, acknowledge this to be so: in 1768 it was announced that all distances were to be calculated as from the Parvis, and all milestone markings were to be based upon this fact. Nor is it only a geographical matter: it arose because the Parvis was for so many generations the center of gravitation for events great and small. The Church played the prime role in this, of course, and it is worth remembering that the Chapter of Notre-Dame has included to date six Popes, forty Cardinals, and more than two hundred Bishops. But Notre-Dame was more than a church, and more than a distinguished collection of churchmen: it was a world in itself, with a cycle of fairs, a whole company of tradesmen and craftsmen who lived under its protection, and a full complement of scallywags. (Musically it has been to the fore since Jean Charlier de Gerson redrafted the choristers' conditions of life in the early fifteenth century; and when Cavaillé-Coll had finished restoring the organ in 1863, César Franck, Camille Saint-Saëns, Charles-Marie Widor, Alexandre Guilmant, and, ten days later, Anton Bruckner hastened to play in the great building where Pérotin le Grand had been the first organist.)

Notre-Dame has been the scene of tremendous pomps. It would take a Milton or a Thomas Browne to describe the funerals of Philip V of Spain, or Louis XV, or the Grand Condé; and even as late as 1842 the Duc d'Orléans was given a catafalque many feet high with an understructure covered in black velvet and silver tears. David's *Consecration of Napoleon I* gives us an idea of how the Cathedral could be dressed on happier occasions, but there is no doubt that the people most admired in their particular line were the great funeral-architects—men like Berain, who produced the famous Camp de la Douleur in 1687, or the brothers Slodtz, who devised the *pomps funèbres* for the wonderfully named Polixène de Hesse-Rinfels, Queen of Sardinia, in 1735. It was of one of these two brothers that C. N. Cochin said, "Funerals had hitherto been in two dimensions: the Slodtzes made them in three. They were reproached for introducing a certain frivolity of taste and a generally rather festive and unsuitable atmosphere into the grave ceremonial; but they were trying, after all, to please a Court which never took kindly to seriousness if it could possibly avoid it, and they succeeded rather well." If we add to all these the Te Deums that abounded in the Grand Siècle, and the sumptuous processions (in one of which the faithful were encouraged to drop their offerings into the mouth of a wickerwork dragon), and the wedding of Napoleon III and Eugénie de Montijo, it may come as a surprise that the interior of the cathedral as we know it is somber and disgarnished and the exterior curiously lacking in distinction of detail.

The reason is, of course, that Notre-Dame was pillaged at the time of the Revolution and minutiously restored by Lassus and Viollet-le-Duc after the alarm had been raised in the 1830s and 1840s by Victor Hugo, Ingres, Alfred de Vigny, Montalembert, and others. Little remains of the furnishings that once gave Notre-Dame a high place, if also a rather odd one, among European cathedrals. The captured standards, for instance: so many of these were brought in during the reign of Louis XIV that even the most loyal of his subjects thought that it was being overdone. As for the tapestries—those, at any rate, that were given to ornament the choir in the 1650s by Michel Le Masle, and a more beautiful set it would be hard to find—they were sold to Strasbourg in 1739.

Another misfortune for the Cathedral and for the history of French art occurred when the "Mays des Orfèvres" were dispersed in the eighteenth and nineteenth centuries. These *mays* were a revised version of the gifts traditionally offered to Notre-Dame on the first of May in each year by the goldsmiths of Paris. These gifts had been, successively, a tree in leaf, an altar of foliage, a tabernacle of architectural design with sonnets attached to it, and *petits mays*—paintings of modest dimensions on themes from the Old and New Testaments. All these had been withdrawn at the end of the year of their donation. But from 1630 onward it became the custom to give a large painting that would remain

The Cathedral of Notre-Dame. J. Feuillie photograph

Cathedral property. Seventy-six such gifts are recorded, and many of them can be found in churches and museums all over France. They were hung not only in the side chapels but high up along the sides of the nave and would have looked, to modern eyes, decidedly bizarre.

The Gothic rood screen and twelfth-century windows were removed when Louis XIV honored his father's promise that France should be dedicated anew to the Virgin. The treasure was looted in the Revolution of 1789; further harm was done in 1830 and again in 1831. Many of the best sculptures have vanished altogether or must be sought out in the Musée de Cluny. (No visitor should miss the twenty-one heads from the Galerie des Rois that were found in 1977 not a mile from Notre-Dame and now rank high among the treasures of the Musée de Cluny.) The amateur of the *dix-huitième* is well rewarded, certainly, by the sculptures of Coustou and Coysevox in the choir, and the marvelously beautiful choir stalls that were designed by Robert de Cotte. But this is, after all, the cathedral of Saint Louis and Philippe le Bel, and one can sympathize with the medievalists who feel little but dejection as they prowl from one restoration to the next.

And yet Notre-Dame remains tremendously moving. Nothing can take away the fact that it is essentially a family church, with all France for its family. Its bells, for instance: the *bourdon* of Notre-Dame is *the* voice of France, and the individual bells speak for a great nation as much in their names (Gabriel, Guillaume, Pasquier, Thibault . . .) as in their ability to survive (Emmanuèle has been there, in the south tower, since the 1680s). "Notre-Dame," as Jacques Hillairet put it, "has always been the Maison Commune of the French people. The people of Paris have always made it their meeting-place: serfs were set free there, mysteries played, and banquets given. The hunted and the poor could always find asylum. Anyone who went on a long journey could leave his valuables in safekeeping in Notre-Dame; contracts were drawn up there, and oddities put on exhibition: elephants' tusks, ostrich eggs, the carcass of a whale. . . ." It is the church where Saint Louis walked in barefoot and Philippe le Bel rode in on horseback; where Henry VI of England was crowned king of France in 1431, and Henri de Navarre and La Reine Margot

Below: The Pont de l'Archevêché and the Quai de la Tournelle, with Notre-Dame. Samuel Chamberlain photograph

Opposite: *Notre-Dame in the Late Afternoon.* Henri Matisse, 1902

Following pages: Flying buttresses, Notre-Dame. Marc Lavrillier photograph

were married a week before the massacre of Saint Bartholomew's Day; where Napoleon I was crowned, Monseigneur Sibour was murdered, Foch and Joffre were given a hero's funeral, and Charles de Gaulle made haste to worship on his return to Paris in August 1944.

Notre-Dame has always had a mysterious power over human destiny. It persuaded Gandhi that "the men who made such things must have had the love of God in their hearts." In 1886 it brought Paul Claudel back to the Roman Catholic faith, in what was surely the most dramatic and best-described rediscovery of the last hundred years. And even Saint-Simon, most worldly of diarists, felt constrained to write down the story of Chardon, the great lawyer, and his wife, who were convinced Huguenots until they were kept waiting in their carriage one morning on the Parvis de Notre-Dame. "Madame Chardon was looking idly about her," Saint-Simon tells us, "when her eyes happened to fall on the west door of Notre-Dame. Little by little she fell into a deep reverie—or perhaps it would be more accurate to say 'a profound meditation.' Finally her husband noticed this, asked her what was the matter, and nudged her with his elbow to make her answer. And she said that as the statues of the saints had been on the west door of Notre-Dame for centuries before Luther and Calvin were born, this showed that people had been praying to those saints for many centuries, and that the reformers' ideas were comparatively new. This novelty in itself made their ideas suspect, when one compared them with the ancient traditions of Catholicism; and although she had never thought of this before it was causing her grave disquiet. She would feel bound, she said, to review the whole problem." And, sure enough, both Chardons retired from the world and returned to it as convinced Catholics.

From Notre-Dame, toward Saint-Julien-le-Pauvre. Pierre Jahan photograph

Statues, Notre-Dame.
Pierre Jahan photograph

Following pages: Interior
of Notre-Dame. Marc
Lavrillier photograph

One does not need to be a Catholic, or indeed a believer of any sort, to accept the proposition that Notre-Dame has a magic all its own. "France began here" is what it says to us; and it is not surprising that, like the Institut de France, it has its devotees among the quayside tramps. From the south, Notre-Dame dominates the water landscape as it did three hundred years ago. More so, indeed, for the Archbishop's Palace has long been destroyed by the mob and there are now no houses on the Pont Saint-Michel to block the view. And when the bell called Emmanuèle gives forth her flawless F sharp we can believe the story of how, when she was recast in 1686, the women of Paris, high and low alike, gave their jewels to gladden and perfect her timbre.

The rear, or east, end of Notre-Dame is imposing from any angle and at any distance, so great is the effect of the flying buttresses erected by John Ravy in the fourteenth century. But, to my eye, it is best of all when seen from afar: from the Pont d'Austerlitz, for instance, or when driving westward along the Quai Saint-Bernard and the Quai de la Tournelle. The Quai de Béthune is also advantageous: from its eastward extremity you have the remains of what Tallemant des Réaux called "the most beautiful view in the world, save only that from the Seraglio, at the confluence of the Bosphorus and the Golden Horn."

More than a hundred years after Tallemant des Réaux set down his opinion, a young English artist, Thomas Girtin, spent the winter and spring of 1801–2 in Paris. It was the twenty-seventh and last winter of his life; and to those who know this, there seems to be a suggestion of farewell in the vast and tranquil panoramas that were later aquatinted

The rear of Notre-Dame.
Samuel Chamberlain
photograph

by F. C. Lewis. An especially fine example is one of just this view, drawn, I fancy, from the now-vanished Pont de Constantine, with Notre-Dame athwart the middle distance and the Quai de Béthune conspicuous to the right of the picture.

What Girtin could not give in monochrome was the beauty and subtlety of color that distinguishes the Ile Saint-Louis and combines with the elegance of the facades to make this one of the most aristocratic of townscapes. To arrive in Paris on a fine summer evening after a long day's journey from the south, turn out of the Gare de Lyon, drive westward along the quays and watch the relations of tone on the inhabited cliffs of the Ile Saint-Louis, the gradations of silver-gray and palest yellow—all this is one of the greatest rewards of European travel. Nor is it simply a subject such as Bellotto would have delighted in: it suggests that somewhere among the tall-faced houses, behind the balconies that Le Vau made obligatory, the enlightened life is going forward. At such moments the Ile Saint-Louis is like some phantom city to which none but the good and the clever and the beautiful may seek admission. Is there, we wonder, a side door where we ourselves might sneak in?

Closer acquaintance does not, I'm afraid, quite bear out this first impression. The Ile Saint-Louis is what it always was—a piece of unified town planning that happened to get built at one of the noblest moments in the evolution of French architecture; and as it has been relatively little altered, it still presents, on every hand, a look of grand and simple amenity. If much of it is a little shabby, we are reminded of how Baudelaire, one of its admirer-citizens, used to rub his suits with emery paper in order to remove that look of newness "so dear to the philistine," as Gautier says, "and so repugnant to the true gentleman."

Even twenty years ago, life on the Ile Saint-Louis had still a note of discretion and

Henri Le Secq at Notre-Dame, 1851. Le Secq was a friend of Charles Nègre, who took this photograph.

retirement. The telephone alone seemed to link the island to the city proper: omnibus and Métro were excluded, dogs went to sleep in the middle of the main street, and if you chose to dream the day away by the water's edge nothing and nobody would disturb you. Today this is not quite the case. The island has been "discovered." Tenants of long standing dread the day when easy money will outwit the law and send them packing from their apartments. The insides are being ripped out of old houses for the sake of an "amusing" interior. Nightclubs are opening up, and you may be surprised by the bill for your simple luncheon.

Of course there is another side to the matter: the newcomers may bring new marvels, as Antoine Bibesco did when he got Vuillard to decorate the rooms that overhang the Seine at the sharp northwestern point of the island. Landlords cannot be blamed if they want to get something more than a peppercorn rent for some of the most delectable properties in Europe. Much of the Ile Saint-Louis was in very bad condition, and new money may prevent it from becoming to Paris what Chioggia is to Venice. And the island will in any case resist any attempt to jazz it up: certain places simply cannot be vulgarized, and one of them is the Ile Saint-Louis.

One of the misfortunes of Parisian history is that Henri IV did not live long enough to realize the project that would surely have put the Ile de la Cité beyond Haussmann's reach: that of treating the two islands as a single coherent unit. Not Saint Petersburg itself would have been more beautiful, as an ensemble. But, as it happened, it was left to Louis XIII and Marie de Médicis to take over half the project. Although its realization took considerably longer than the king's initial instructions allowed for—fifty years (1614–64) instead of ten—the result was almost ideally happy. What had been the preserve of bow-man, laundress, and canoeist became a metropolitan paradise, with a long thin straight street down the middle and, facing outward to the Seine, house after house of the finest and simplest distinction. People developed the strong local loyalties that still operate in the island. Philippe de Champaigne, for instance, was one of the founder-tenants of the Quai de Bourbon, and his nephew Jean-Baptiste was responsible for much of the decoration of the island's one church, Saint-Louis-en-l'Ile. The Hôtel Lambert belonged to the Czartoryskis for nearly one hundred and fifty years. Once aboard the island, people loved to ornament their houses: at 51, Rue Saint-Louis-en-l'Ile, for instance, you will find the rococo, or more exactly the *rocaille* embellishments added by François de Chenizot in the 1760s; at 20, Quai de Béthune there is a ceiling by Mignard, at No. 28 the façade bears mythological reliefs, and at No. 30 music takes over, where ornament is concerned, from mythology.

Something of this affection has persisted; but there are also instances in which the island has been betrayed by its inhabitants. At 24, Quai de Béthune, for example, you will find one of the most magnificent doorways in Paris, with rams' heads by Le Hongre, who gave that erratic animal a look of priestly wisdom; but if you ring the bell you will not find behind those doors the elegant courtyard and still more elegant elevation of the Hôtel Hasselin. That house, built by Le Vau in 1642 for Denys Hasselin, *intendant des plaisirs* to Louis XIII, was pulled down in 1955, with the agreement of the Beaux-Arts and on the instructions of a manufacturer of "beauty products."

The Hôtel Hasselin was one of the three noblest of the island's houses, the other two being the Hôtel Lambert, 2, Rue Saint-Louis-en-l'Ile, and the Hôtel de Lauzun, 17, Quai d'Anjou, both of which still exist. Quite apart from their physical beauty, those houses harbored at one time or another some of the most rewarding people of their day. They in every case were highly individualized. Of how many householders can it be said, as it was said of Denys Hasselin, that he died after swallowing the kernels of 294 nuts for a bet?

The Hôtel de Lauzun has not an exterior to stun us. Le Vau's design has, in fact, an almost Arab disinclination to reveal what lies behind the sober exterior; the very beautiful iron balcony, at most, would suggest that he was working at full pressure. Inside, however, the work not only of Le Vau himself, but of Le Brun, Lesueur, Lepautre,

Notre-Dame and the Ile Saint-Louis. Alain Perceval photograph

Anguier, and Sebastien Bourdon combines to create an ensemble of extraordinary splendor. The initial thrust in all this came from Gruÿn des Bordes, the caterer son of Gruÿn the cabaret-keeper whose establishment, the Pomme du Pin in the Ile de la Cité, enjoyed the patronage of Molière, Racine, Boileau, Lully, Mignard, and La Fontaine. But Gruÿn died in prison in 1672, and ten years later his house was sold to the prestigious Gascon whose name it now bears. Lauzun only lived in it for three years, and it has had other tenants—Baudelaire, above all—who perhaps have a stronger claim upon our admiration. But Lauzun deserves, for at least two reasons, to have his name commemorated. First, for having inspired one of the strangest and most deeply felt of Saint-Simon's prose-portraits; and second, because his manner of life so nicely corresponds to the magnificent but never inhuman grandeurs of the house.

Lauzun was Saint-Simon's brother-in-law, and they saw one another constantly. Saint-Simon never lost, however, his initial wonderment at Lauzun's bizarre and resourceful nature. "He was a character so extraordinary, so unique in every way," he writes, "that La Bruyère was quite right to say of him that 'Other men cannot so much as dream of living as Lauzun lived.'" And Saint-Simon goes on to build up, as only he can, the portrait of Lauzun as someone who was forever discontented, rarely read a book, kept much to himself, was basically sly and ill-natured, and yet had a fine pair of legs, a tall thin intelligent cast of features, and a commanding nobility in all his ways. By the time he has finished, we seem almost to see the moody and ingenious master of the Hôtel de Lauzun peer down at us from one of Le Vau's windows.

When Saint-Simon tells how Lauzun hid under the bed on which Louis XIV and Madame de Montespan were making love, and later confronted her, word for word, with all that had been said between the sheets, we too are lost in admiration at his daring; and when Saint-Simon looks back over his long experience of life with Lauzun we seem, once again, to see him walking in through Le Vau's doorway, there to feign deafness and half-blindness, the better to surprise what he was not meant to see or hear. Lauzun "dined and supped on the grand scale every day, kept a table as sumptuous as it was delicate, invited good company both morning and evening, and ate everything, fat and lean alike, that pleased him. He took chocolate in the morning and there were always, on a side-table, such fruits as were in season and, at other times, a cooked dish of some sort. Beer, cider, lemonade, and other drinks were kept ready on ice; and Lauzun would eat and drink as he pleased, between meals, and encourage his guests to do the same; in the evening he left the table after the fruit had been served and immediately went to bed. Once, I remember, when he was in his eighties and had lately been seriously ill, he ate so heavily in our house—fish, vegetables, and all sorts of other things—that I sent round to him in the evening to see if he was all right. He was at table again, and eating with a capital appetite."

Lauzun's appetites were exceptional in other fields also. His secret marriage to la Grande Mademoiselle, the daughter of the Duc d'Orléans and granddaughter of Henri IV, was not altogether a success: ". . . at Eu, I heard, M. de Lauzun could not resist running after light women when he came to visit Mademoiselle. Mademoiselle found this out, flew into a great rage, scratched him in the face, and turned him out of the room. A reconciliation was arranged: Mademoiselle appeared at one end of a long gallery and there, at the other end, was Lauzun, and he traversed the whole length of the room on his knees before falling at her feet. There were many such scenes. In the end he wearied of being beaten and, in his turn, he gave Mademoiselle a royal thrashing. After this had happened several times they got thoroughly tired of each other, quarrelled once and for all, and never saw one another again. But he had several portraits of her in the house and never spoke of her except with the greatest respect."

No student of the great world will fail to recognize in Lauzun certain traits that, in Paris as elsewhere, may still be noted in those who rank success above all things. "His manners," Saint-Simon tells us, "were measured, reserved, sweet-seeming, respectful even, and his voice was soft and honeyed. But what he said, and said in two or three words and, as it seemed, naively or absent-mindedly, could pulverize by its acuity and penetration. And so it was that everyone without exception was frightened of him and he had many acquaintances and few or no friends." Such people are still with us in Paris; but

few of them will live, as Lauzun did, to break in young horses in their ninetieth year.

Saint-Simon was afraid he had gone on too long about Lauzun, and I daresay I have done the same. But the recital may have helped to place the Hôtel de Lauzun in the history of Paris. After Lauzun's brief tenure, the house began that slow withdrawal from influence and power which, in Paris as much as in London, has been the fate of many a great seventeenth-century mansion: from grandee to great official, from great official to successful lawyer, and from lawyer to antiquarian, connoisseur, and man of letters. But when the men of letters are Baudelaire and Gautier, we may regard affairs of state as well lost.

It was in the 1840s that Gautier and Baudelaire lived in the Hôtel de Lauzun. Their apartments were connected, Gautier says, "by a secret staircase hidden in the thickness of the wall, a staircase haunted by the shades of the beautiful ladies whom Lauzun had once loved." But, as a matter of fact, the two young writers had beautiful ladies of their own, and did not need to bother themselves with ghosts. Baudelaire at the time was in the full éclat of his beauty and singularity. His close-cut black hair came down over his dazzlingly white brow like a Saracen helmet; his eyes were the color of Spanish tobacco; the delicate enquiring nose, the closely shaven, rice-powdered cheeks, the narrow, checked cravat of *madras des Indes,* the black formal coat and nut-brown trousers, the white stockings and the varnished pumps—all made the vividest impression on Gautier. There was nothing casual or bohemian about Baudelaire's looks and bearing; his manners were almost excessively polite and "correct," his utterance measured and fastidious, his gestures "few, sober, and slow, for he had a horror of the gesticulations of the South." And he spoke tellingly but not at length, "since an English coldness seemed to him the height of good taste."

Such was the arresting figure who dominated the meetings of the Hashish-Eaters' Club in the big second-story saloon of the Hôtel de Lauzun. The club was the creation of Fernand Boissard, a painter and dilettante who wore himself out, so Gautier says, with one enthusiasm after another, and so never quite fulfilled his friends' first expectations. ("He was too much carried away by others' achievements to give thought to his own.") Boissard was, at any rate, a delightful host, and one whose conversation was "charming, full of gaiety and unexpectedness, for he had a rare gift of phrase, and all sorts of pleasantly bizarre expressions, Italian *concetti* and *aguedezzas* from the Spanish, would pass before your eyes as he talked, like fantastic figures from Callot, twisting and contorting themselves for your delight."

The saloon itself was carrying its two hundred years in just the right way. "It was in the purest Louis XIV style, with boiseries ornamented with gold that had faded just as it should. The ceiling had been decorated by some pupil of Lesueur or Poussin with satyrs hotfoot through reeds in pursuit of nymphs. On the enormous chimney piece of Sarrancolin marble, flecked with white and red, there stood, by way of a clock, a gilded elephant, harnessed like Porus' elephant in Lebrun's battle picture, and bearing on its back a military lookout tower on which was an enamel clockface with blue figures. Armchairs and sofas were old and covered with faded tapestries of hunting scenes by Oudry or Desportes."

The beautiful women who came to Boissard's apartment were not the sparkling choplogicians who later dominated the intellectual *tout Paris.* Their claims to notice were of a different kind. Maryx, for instance, would half sit, half lie on the sofa, with one elbow propped up on a cushion. Her gift of stillness had been perfected by long practice as a sculptor's model. In her white dress, so strangely spotted with red marks "like tiny drops of blood," she listened with one ear to Baudelaire's paradoxes; never a hint of surprise crossed her masklike features; as she slipped her rings from the fingers of one hand to the fingers of the other, it was seen that her hands were as beautiful as her body. No boisterous playmate, it will be clear: perhaps a more positive contribution was made by Madame Clésinger, likewise preserved for us by the sculptor's art, who would arrive in a flurry of green silk, black lace, and white muslin, her abundant brown hair still damp from the swimming pool and, indeed, her entire person, so Gautier tells us, a-steam with the delicious freshness of the bath. "With a look here, and a smile there, she would urge us on in our verbal tourney. Should we flag, a word from her, whether in mischief or approval,

The *chambre de parade* of the Hôtel de Lauzun, 17, Quai d'Anjou. Louis Le Vau, 1656, with many subsequent alterations. The gallery is a 20th century addition, replacing an alcove. J. Fronval photograph

would be enough to set the argument ablaze." What Gautier sets before us is the prototype of one of the most delicious of all societies. Paris has still such things to offer to young people who are clever, or beautiful, or both, and it is not from nostalgia that we treasure Gautier's account.

The Quai d'Anjou has enormous style, and we can well understand that after the Marquis de Marigny, who loved beautiful things as much as anyone in Parisian history, both Honoré Daumier and the seraphic Charles-François Daubigny should have chosen to live there. The island is irresistible. And when we turn the sloping corner, and are almost at the Pont Sully, a high wall topped with evergreens must arouse our curiosity. And no wonder: for behind it is the terrace-garden of the Hôtel Lambert, and the Hôtel Lambert is one of the most enviable town houses in the world. Our curiosity will, however, have to stop short at the door, or at best in Le Vau's noble courtyard, for this is private property, and the gaper is soon sent about his business. It is possible, even so, to get a first impression of the courtyard, the huge double stone staircase that leads up to left and to right of the front door, and the great spread of window on the first floor, where Ionic pilasters support a triangular pediment with escutcheon. Of the garden front, likewise, we can glimpse the Ionic order that runs up to the top of the tall, thin first-floor windows and admire the rounded half-tower that stands out above the quayside.

The interior is not, in point of fact, complete. Much was taken out between 1809, when Montalivet, then Minister of the Interior, took it over and 1842, when Princess Czartoryska bought it and did her best to put it back into good order. (Delacroix, for one,

Courtyard of the Hôtel Lambert. Louis Le Vau, 1640–44. R. Landin photograph

The Galerie d'Hercule, with frescoes by Charles Le Brun

was called in to restore the decorations executed in the 1640s by Le Brun and Lesueur.) Le Brun's Galerie d'Hercule is still one of the greatest rooms in France; and the house as a whole has been redone with a discerning affection.

The Hôtel Lambert, like the Hôtel de Lauzun, has had tenants worthy of itself. And, once again, we can see in them the prototypes of enduring Parisian figures: the great lady with her man of letters in tow, and the foreigners, by exile or caprice domiciled in Paris, who give the city its distinctive note of all-welcoming high perception. Of the first of these, Voltaire and Madame du Châtelet are prize instances; for the second, the Czartoryskis, and in particular Princess Marcelline Czartoryska, for whom Chopin delighted to play and of whom Delacroix has much to say in his diaries.

Thomas Carlyle is not altogether reliable where Madame du Châtelet is concerned. (A much fairer portrait of her is to be found in Nancy Mitford's *Voltaire in Love*.) But as to the general character of her relationship with Voltaire, he has a marvelous phrase or two to offer. "This literary amour," he says, "wears but a mixed aspect: short sungleams with tropical showers, touches of guitar music soon followed by Lisbon earthquakes. . . ."

These words could serve as an epigraph for many later attachments; but nowhere, we may be sure, has love-play been more nobly housed than in the Hôtel Lambert, where even the pettiest tantrum must take on the resonance of the Grand Siècle. Musically, too, Chopin's association with the house must have set a standard not now to be surpassed, given the quality of his playing, with its element of creative improvisation, and the near-conspiratorial character of his visits. Princess Czartoryska, née Radziwill, was herself a very capable pianist who had studied with Czerny in Vienna, and she may well have been the last person (she died in 1894) to give an authentic impression of how Chopin himself played. The depth of their friendship was such that she was one of the three people who were with Chopin when he died at dawn on 17 October 1849.

To one who revered Chopin as Delacroix did, Marcelline Czartoryska must have had an intense fascination. *Le tout Paris* was, then as now, totally unmusical. For Delacroix, to be able to talk seriously of music with a beautiful woman and, still better, to hear her play the music that he treasured—all this was a blessing beyond words. (It is surely significant that his apparition-like *Amoureuse au Piano* dates from 1843, the year after Princess Czartoryska bought the Hôtel Lambert.) It was in her drawing room that Delacroix had some of his profoundest musical experiences. In June 1853, he said of Mozart's Fantasia in C Minor, K. 475, that it was "a serious work, verging on the terrible, with a title too light for its character." And of Chopin, as played by the mistress of the house: "nothing commonplace, perfect composition. He is nearer to Mozart than anyone and, as with Mozart, his melodies run so smoothly as to seem almost inevitable." Nothing in the world is, of course, quite perfect; in April 1854 we find Delacroix saying, "Concert at the Princess's. It was intolerably hot and there was an equally intolerable smell of dead rat. The concert was very long, too." But in general the Hôtel Lambert was a source of unflawed happiness to both Chopin and Delacroix; and for this, as much as for its own splendors, it has a claim upon our affection.

For such private moments the Ile Saint-Louis is ideally designed; for them, and for the old-fashioned craftsmen, the one-man shops, and the secret gardens with which it is still well supplied. A house like 18, Quai de Béthune, for instance, keeps its own counsel,

Eugène Delacroix at a Musical Evening, with Alfred de Musset, Prosper Merimée, Daniel Auber, and Charles Gounod. Eugène Lami, c. 1850

The house in which this gathering took place is not recorded.

with nothing much to show at street level. But, once inside, majesty reigns everywhere; even the garden walls are arcaded, and an underground passage leads through to the private dock at which, in former times, pleasure craft could deposit guests and, in due time, fetch them away.

In the main street, the Rue Saint-Louis-en-l'Ile, the emphasis has always lain on commerce, but commerce of a humane and leisurely sort, with every opportunity, from 1629 onward, for a game of *boules* to take the taste of trade out of one's mouth. And at No. 82 there lived the original Colline of Mürger's *Vie de Bohème;* one could, in effect, imagine Act I of *La Bohème* set not in Montmartre but at the top of one of the high-faced houses of the Ile Saint-Louis. The island has been for three centuries one of the strongholds of a working democracy, in which people great and small can live amicably side by side in houses as well adapted to the one as to the other.

Quite apart from that, the river at this point in its course "composes" in ways that are a continual astonishment to us. Moving water and old stone combine with unhurrying barges to make one of the world's great metropolitan backdrops. If you have to drown— as Charles Méryon pointed out in one of the most remarkable of his Parisian etchings— there is no better place than this to do it. And if you just sit on the bank and watch the boats go by on a fine morning in October you will see, as Elizabeth Bishop saw, how

> Each barge on the river easily tows
>   a mighty wake,
> A giant oak-leaf of gray lights
>   on duller gray;
> And behind it real leaves are floating by,
>   down to the sea.

The Seine and the Quai des Orfèvres. Camille Corot, 1835

The Canal Saint-Martin
and the Quai de Valmy.
Robert Doisneau
photograph

The Front de Seine.
Robert Doisneau
photograph

But although the two islands belong to the river Seine and would make no sense without it the river Seine does not belong to them. It is an independent and self-governing force. By turns reticent and peremptory, panoramic and all but invisible, it is never the same for ten minutes together. And the Parisians have always been drawn to it, in fascination. Now this stretch, and now that one, has been in particular favor. Even auxiliary Parisian waterways have come to have their turn; and the Canal Saint-Martin, once thought of primarily in the context of *Hôtel du Nord,* one of the greatest and most fatalistic of all French movies, has come to be regarded as an agreeable stretch of water by which to live.

But it is of course the mainstream of the Seine that gives the city so much of its character. As of quite a long time ago, there has been an unspoken agreement that the historic center of Paris, and in particular the waterfront from the upstream end of the Ile Saint-Louis to the Pont de la Concorde, should stay much as it is. That agreement has been challenged here and there for this reason or that, but in general it has been kept to. Nor is it likely that anyone will try to improve on the look of either the right or the left bank as we move downstream past the Chambre des Députés, the Esplanade des Invalides, and the Cours-la-Reine. But from there onward, all can change, and all *has* changed, once, twice, and thrice in the last hundred and some years.

This was bound to be. The banks of the Seine are just too tempting to leave alone. Sometimes a great exhibition, sometimes the dilapidation of a whole quarter, sometimes an industrial upheaval, sometimes social changes on a very large scale have been responsible for alterations so radical that a returning visitor would hardly know where he was. There were those who grieved for what was lost, and there were those who gasped aloud at what had taken its place. But that broad open stretch of moving water and that gigantic sky were too good to leave alone.

That was how Paris got the Trocadéro (now gone), the Eiffel Tower (now loved by all), and the exhibition buildings on the Colline de Chaillot, which date from the Exposition of 1937. No one has ever managed to love the Palais de Chaillot. Even at the time of its conception it had a totalitarian look, and its component parts have in many cases aged badly. Today it often seems as if the liveliest thing about the Colline de Chaillot is the Saturday morning market which brings meat, fish, fruit, and vegetables in superabundance to the middle of the Avenue du Président-Wilson. But the commotions that the Palais de Chaillot caused now seem mild and remote when compared with what has happened on the left bank of the Seine, downstream from the Eiffel Tower.

The changes in question relate to a whole series of socio-aesthetic convulsions. Upward, downward, and sideways, they have altered not only the look of Paris but the character of Paris as a place in which to live (or not to live, as the case may be). On the one hand, we have in the Front de Seine—the waterfront of the 15th *arrondissement,* starting a little way downstream from the Eiffel Tower—a coordinated panorama which in its way is a considerable success. The tall buildings are huge by Parisian standards—thirty stories, in all just under three hundred feet high—but they are not at all demeaning. They have a very fine site, and they are almost worthy of it. Those who can afford to live in them are well pleased. They suit the Eiffel Tower, and the Eiffel Tower suits them. What people call *le nouveau Paris* is here on its best behavior.

On the other hand, the Front de Seine involved the elimination of a quarter that had served a great many people very well. Whether they liked it or not, they had to pack up and go. With them went the kind of one-person culture that high buildings are there to abolish. Doubtless the slow-moving, villagey kind of life that had been lived there offered a very low return for an era that could be changed overnight into prime quality real estate. Those tumbledown one- and two-story houses with their midget gardens were survivors— almost, if not quite—from the days when hare and partridge could be hunted not half a mile away. They and their inhabitants were an anachronism—one of many in Paris that

Gas Tanks at Clichy.
Paul Signac, 1886

had lain low and escaped notice—but they helped to nurture the irreducible individualism that is fundamental to our notion of Paris. Without them, Paris does not seem bigger and grander and more streamlined. It just seems a little more like everywhere else.

Among the casualties of the development of the Front de Seine was the Vélodrome d'Hiver, a covered stadium that from 1910 to 1959 played a large part in the emotional life of many thousands of Parisians. Like Madison Square Garden in New York, and like Olympia in London, it was the locus of those deep collective feelings that are discharged by a race, a fight, or a great speech on some urgent matter of the day. In particular, the Six Day Bicycle Races of 1929–30 at the Vélodrome d'Hiver constituted a historic ordeal for those who took part. Among those who sat and watched, they aroused feelings that can still be made vivid to us. (A wonderful example of this occurs in Ernest Hemingway's *A Moveable Feast.*)

The Vélodrome d'Hiver has also its place in literary history. By his own account, Hemingway sat in a box at the finishing line for one of the six day races and worked on the proofs of the ending of *A Farewell to Arms*—thirty times in all, he told one of his biographers—while sustaining himself with "good inexpensive champagne" and *crabe mexicaine* sent across the river from Prunier's. As a place of popular assembly, the stadium will never have its equal. If we do not wish that it was still there, it is because we remember too well how thousands upon thousands of French Jews were collected there in 1942 and "processed" before being sent to camps in Germany from which few or none of them would return. After that, the savor went out of the Vélodrome d'Hiver.

Rare is the visitor in our day who goes downstream from the Front de Seine otherwise than by road. Short of sailing one's own felucca, it is difficult to get a ride by water. Such is the configuration of the Seine, moreover, that it would take a very long time to negotiate the huge loops with which it winds itself through one suburb after another. Some of those suburbs—Meudon, Sèvres, Saint-Cloud—have august overtones from the past. Others are primarily industrial in tone, with harbors (Gennevilliers, above all) as active as many a seaport. What they have in common is that almost all of them have been transformed in the last twenty-five years.

In this, they follow a pattern that few French towns, large or small, have escaped. France in 1939 was still pretty much of a piece. During World War II and for some years afterward it stagnated, in architectural terms. And then quite suddenly—and, as it seemed,

Tondeur-Baigneur—grooming dogs by the Seine, 1898–1900. Eugène Atget photograph

in no time at all—almost every old town was twinned with a new town, back to back. The tall building took over. Industry was modernized. Public transport, likewise. The French interior, theretofore remarkable for its stability, took a running (sometimes a stumbling) jump forward. Patterns of behavior unchanged for centuries were cast aside. People had new ambitions, new desires, new standards of comparison.

If I advance these notions here, it is because they can be checked out by anyone who follows the Seine on its serpentine course between Boulogne-Billancourt and Gennevilliers. For the last hundred years and more this area has had a manifold identity. It had, and has still, vestiges of a royal past. Anyone who has a sense of that past will be touched by the park at Saint-Cloud and the Château de Malmaison. It was at Saint-Cloud, after all, that a delegation from the Sénat came to offer Napoleon the imperial crown in 1804, and it was at Malmaison that Joséphine, the former empress, lived out her last days.

The area was also a great one for painting. Contrary to what is often supposed, Paris has never been a prime subject for painters. Many of the greatest French painters—from Poussin through Fragonard, Ingres, and Delacroix right to Cézanne—touched it barely or not at all. We treasure the rare David, the rare Corot, the rare Degas, the rare Matisse that touches even incidentally on the center of Paris. But when it comes to the banks of the Seine, just a mile or two from the center of Paris, we have fine painting in abundance.

Where was it that Courbet set down the archetypal Parisian woman, once and for all? By the Seine. Where was it that Impressionism prospered most? By the Seine. Where did Seurat paint one of the few French figure paintings that can stand with Poussin? By the Seine. Where did Cézanne come momentarily to terms with the Parisian scene? By the Seine. Where did van Gogh feel most at home when he got to Paris? By the Seine.

This was not an aesthetic choice: the Seine as against the Yonne, let us say. Courbet, Monet, Sisley, Seurat, van Gogh, and the others chose the Seine—and that particular stretch of the Seine—because it was the point at which ancient and modern, permanent and ephemeral were most nicely matched. It was there that the steam train was revolutionizing the conditions of everyday life. It was there that the industrial revolution was sinking its teeth deep into the soft flesh of the countryside.

We got used to the idea that painting had given us a decisive idea of that countryside. To this day we think of Seurat and Sisley and Monet along that stretch of the Seine. There is a specific tension in their paintings between the thing seen and the thing done. Having once experienced that tension, we somehow think that it must be there always—as, indeed, to a certain extent it is. What they saw we still see. Even if there is a great deal about the Seine in our day that those painters did not see and could not imagine, the relationships of wind and water, factory and lunch break, tall poplar and dawdling white sail are much the same. As to the ways in which a great city can meet and mate with the countryside, those few miles of the Seine still set the standard.

This notwithstanding, their very essence has changed. They look quite different. The pace of life is quite different. Their role in French society is quite different. At the time of Courbet and the Impressionists, those reaches of the Seine were as far from Paris as most people could comfortably go in a day. Everything was done for them when they got there. This was the last metropolitan frontier, and it offered a happiness that was the more intense for being momentary. Impermanence was taken for granted, and when the sun went down people began to worry about the time of the last train home. From all this there came a rare poignancy. What was said by the Seine, what was pledged by the Seine, what was done by the Seine was never forgotten.

Everyone knows this. Stories by Maupassant bear it out. So does Jean Renoir's classic movie *La Partie de Campagne*. So do the paintings of Gustave Caillebotte and others. We know from Seurat's painting *La Grande Jatte* that within just a mile or two of the Arc de Triomphe there was in the middle of the Seine in the 1880s a playground of a vivacious and unaffected sort to which people of every kind were attracted. Ferries kept up a shuttle service. Riverside restaurants did a terrific trade. Hardly a city in the world was so well served by its river.

But since World War II those leisured loops of the Seine have lost out to the second residences, the garden cities built somewhere in the remaining forest, the shopping centers, the tall apartment houses with a view on the river, the throughways and expressways.

At the bridge, 1855.
Adolphe Braun
photograph

Noise and busyness have crept in almost everywhere. Ever since 1955 or so, the French have been pressured to think that their lives will be a shame and a sham if they do not fulfill the dream of a little place in the country. To us it may seem that by fulfilling that dream they destroy it. But, be that as it may, those first loops of the Seine have become somewhere to pass through—or, alternatively, somewhere in which to seek new kinds of satisfaction.

So there it is. Each generation has its own idea of a blissful weekend. It also has its own idea of the best way to travel. We may daydream of riding the paddle steamer on which Frédéric Moreau traveled from Paris to Nogent-sur-Seine in Flaubert's *Education Sentimentale.* But what Flaubert actually tells us about that boat is that you had to be there before six in the morning. Once aboard and under way, you did indeed from time to time see a delicious little house with a terraced garden leading down to the river. "More than one passenger envied the owner of that house," Flaubert tells us, "and dreamed of living there to the end of his days, with a decent billiard table, a little sailboat, and a wife at his side."

None of that has changed. But Flaubert also tells us that the boat was crowded with dreary and disreputable people, that the deck was covered with "nutshells, cigar butts, pear skins, and ends of sausage," that a blind and ragged harpist twanged all pleasant thoughts away, and that before long a universal boredom seemed to permeate the entire ship, until even the paddle wheels could hardly be bothered to keep turning.

So maybe it *is* more fun to sit in a sneaky little automobile beside the person you like most in the world and watch the kilometers slip by on your way to open spaces that are still open, village squares that have yet to get their supermarket, and houses that still slumber silently behind high walls. But if you turn aside, there are still secret places to be found near the river, and near the islands. Turn aside toward Ville d'Avray, and you will find the house where Balzac did his best to acclimatize the pineapple. (He failed.) Turn aside at Courbevoie, and you will find the house where the Duc de Guisnes pored over the concerto for flute and harp that Mozart had written for him and his daughter. (Mozart had great trouble getting paid, by the way.) Turn aside at the Pont de Saint-Cloud, in Boulogne, and you will find the Jardins Albert-Kahn, which were devised from 1893 onward as a selective dictionary of the ways in which Nature can be brought to heel. The visitor will find successively an English garden (not a straight line in sight), a geometrical French garden, a Japanese garden (fixed with the help of the emperor of the day), a cedar forest planted with azalea and rhododendron, and a patch of forest in the style for which the Vosges are well known (even the stones are authentic).

So our last word on the river and the minor islands is that, though much manhandled and sometimes greatly misused, they are not at all dull.

XIII

The Seventh Arrondissement

Entrance portal of the Hôtel Gouffier de Thoix. Early 18th century. Viard photograph

The 7th *arrondissement* is the last sanctuary of style in Parisian architecture. It was not, of course, the last quarter to be developed; but it was the last that could pretend to classical distinction. And, more than any other part of Paris, it has kept its original dignity. Only by a feat of historical imagination can we restore the pristine graces of the Place des Victoires or the Hôtel de Chalons-Luxembourg; but those who live in the Faubourg Saint-Germain have kept it remarkably intact. Here and there in its great houses, life is carried on in a manner not too remote from that which prevailed under the Régence, and those which have gone out of private hands have done it in such a way that the essential tone of the district has never been destroyed.

This tone, in general, is one of dignified withdrawal. In contrast to the narrow-fronted town houses of London, with their coffin-shaped plans and high thin faces, the *hôtels* of the Faubourg Saint-Germain have a noble wastefulness of design. From the street, little may be seen but a flaking stucco wall, a stout wooden door, and a heraldic knocker. Sometimes—as at the Hôtel Noirmoutier, 138, Rue de Grenelle—a triumphal arch may set the scale for the courtyard within; elsewhere—the great example is the Hôtel Gouffier de Thoix, 56, Rue de Varenne—there may be no such boastful break in the line of the street, but in its place is a shell-headed doorway of superabundant fancy. The courtyard may well be as large as the house itself. Irregularly set with cobbles, it has often a rusticated air. The stables may no longer be used, but one can sense that these were once country houses that happen to be in Paris. A glance at the original plans will show the truth of this. No. 78, Rue de Varenne, for instance, is now the Ministry of Agriculture. It has suffered gross indelicacies at the hands of the State, and only the garden front retains the elegance with which it was invested, in 1724, by François Debias-Aubry. (This architect can be judged more fairly by the Ministry of Defense, 14–16, Rue Saint-Dominique.) What emerges from Aubry's original plans is that the house itself occupied only about a seventh of the site. What with the *basse-cour* (itself larger than the house), the stables (Aubry traced out stalls for fifty horses), the elaborate service quarters, the lime alley, the exemplary quincunx plantation (Euclid himself could not have drawn it more nicely), the two long pencil-shaped parterres of flowers, the half-moon recess with its vases and statues, and the shrubberies (Salle Verte and Cabinet de Verdure are their stylish names)—what with all these, the house itself becomes not a solitary urban monument, like 20 Berkeley Square in London, but a part of an estate. There is no attempt at domination in the Faubourg Saint-Germain: no vistas, no eye-catchers, not even an imposing symmetry—nothing but the perfection of discreet good living.

Entrance portal of the Hôtel Neufchâtel, 5, Rue Saint-Dominique. 1713

Even the ivy in the 7th *arrondissement* has more class than in other parts of Paris. "English ivy, we call it," says Eleanor Pereny in her book *Green Thoughts,* "but no city has more of it than Paris. It is everywhere, clambering over walls, substituting for grass in the parks and private gardens. In the Faubourg St. Germain it mounts to the tops of forest trees, where little owls nest in the branches. I have always admired Paris ivy, but never examined it closely until a recent visit, when I had occasion to walk daily past the wall that guards the Italian Embassy on the side of the cul-de-sac called the Cité de Varenne. High as a fortress, the wall was dense with ivy that I noticed had an unfamiliar leaf: glossy as black onyx and sharply pointed. . . ."

The history of the quarter is well known. At the beginning of the seventeenth century the scene was one of watery dereliction. Rude woodmen toiled in ramshackle workshops. Market gardens tottered into bankruptcy. The wasteland was the preserve of bad characters and duelists. But when the Jardin de la Reine Margot was parceled out in the reign of Louis XIII, a new and brilliant phase began. The Church, the Army, and the world of fashion turned to the empty acres beside the Seine. The woodmen and the deleterious loungers were turned adrift, and the Dominicans, the Recollects, the Théatines, the Ladies of the Visitation, the Daughters of Sainte Valère, and the Sisters of the Word Incarnate took their place. The Canonesses of the Holy Sepulcher usurped the game reserve of Bellechasse, and the Gray Musketeers took over the market buildings of the Pré aux Clercs. In 1670 Libéral Bruant began building the Hôtel des Invalides which, then as now, marked the southwestern frontier of the Faubourg. The new Pont-Royal, completed

Entrance portal of the Hôtel de Brienne, now the Ministry of War. François Debias-Aubry, 1724, with many subsequent additions

in 1690 at Louis XIV's expense, was for more than a century the only bridge west of the Pont-Neuf, and led directly into the new quarter.

Most important of all, however, was the activity of the great architects of the period. It is to their skill and sharp business sense that we owe the Faubourg Saint-Germain as it stands today. It was in 1686 that Jules Hardouin-Mansart built a house (78, Rue de l'Université) and let it out to the sculptor Noël Jouvenet. He was later joined in speculation by Lassurance, Robert de Cotte, Aubry, Jacques Gabriel, Courtonne, Bruant *fils,* Mazin, and Boffrand. The practice continued right up to the Revolution. As late as the 1780s Brongniart bought several building sites in the Rue Monsieur and erected, at Nos. 12 and 20, two of the most beautiful of all Parisian town houses. Among earlier speculations of this sort, the two houses built by Boffrand at 78 and 80, Rue de Lille are noble examples of a practice which, though displeasing to the champions of a planned society, often proved a delight to the eye.

The Faubourg Saint-Germain has always been a favorite with foreign residents in Paris. In Brice's *Description de Paris,* published in 1752, we read that "in one winter there could be counted twelve princes from the most famous German dynasties, more than three hundred counts and barons, and a much greater number of ordinary gentlefolk." And even today a glance at the Bottin will show, side by side with Radziwills and Esterhazys, the royal families of the once-private bank, the Bolivian tin mine, the convertible roadster, and the suave Italian vermouth. There are fewer convents; the musketeers have backed into the pages of Dumas; the Bouchardon fountain in the Rue de Grenelle spouts for civil servants, not for under-footmen; and where once a domesticated Abbé read aloud from Richardson to his languishing employer, a sweet-mannered American student now teaches business English at ten dollars an hour. But as we walk along between the high garden walls, and the wind sounds like a distant sea in the invisible foliage, we realize that the Faubourg is still quite unlike any other part of Paris. Passy has its gardens, but they are

Above: Louis XIV Inaugurating the Church of the Hôtel des Invalides, 28 August 1706. Pierre-Denis Martin called Le Jeune

Opposite above: Cour d'Honneur of the Hôtel de Bourbon-Condé, 12, Rue Monsieur. A. T. Brongniart, 1781

Opposite: Ground floor plans for two *hôtels,* by Jules Hardouin Mansart (right) and Germain Boffrand (left). In each house, the portal opens into a *grande cour,* and there is a *cour des écuries* (or a *basse cour*) off to the side. The main rooms are in the back of the house, facing the garden.

sooty, upstart affairs; the Plaine Monceau has grand houses, but they show their ambitions too clearly; the Faubourg Saint-Honoré has gone into trade.

The Faubourg Saint-Germain has avoided these errors. It is so private that till lately a good restaurant and a cruising taxi were rarely to be found within its boundaries. Omnibus and Métro pass by. Its cinemas are those of a country township. Theater and multiple store are unknown. Shops have a dust-thick villagey air, and bars a way of retreating into the innards of apartment houses. The great mansions are still cushioned from the street by gatehouses—desirable turrets in which desirable bachelors play out the comedy of early manhood. Yard upon yard of fresh-raked gravel separates the visitor from the front door of the house itself. In the front hall, large dogs pace the Savonnerie carpet. On the garden side of the house, the interconnecting salons slumber beneath dust sheets for three hundred and sixty days in the year; only once or twice each winter, and once or twice each summer, will a dinner of forty covers be laid and the whole grandiose façade come alive with light, like an ocean liner aground in a forest. At other times these great houses, as much as any in the Sologne or the Berry, evoke the deserted and rustic dreamland of Alain-Fournier's novel *Le Grand Meaulnes;* and everything—the cobbled courtyards, the unvisited gardens, the green shadows on the fading gold of the boiseries, the dry fountains and the stone chargers that prance above the stable doorway—reminds us that these are not really town houses at all, but country houses besieged by the town. That they may make ideal offices and flatter the vanity of some ephemeral minister does not affect their essential nature, any more than in England Blenheim and Wilton were diminished by adaptation to the necessities of World War II.

It is for these informal glimpses of a vanishing formality that a walk through the 7th *arrondissement* is irreplaceable. Here for instance is one that Rilke recorded in one of his letters. "The musty old mansions of the Faubourg St. Germain," he wrote in October 1907, "with their gray-white shutters, their unobtrusive gardens and their courtyards

Left: *Rocaille.* C.-A. Duflos after François Boucher
An example of the quintessential 18th century rococo decorative motif. Such motifs—asymetrical shell and plant forms—were used to ornament *boiseries,* textiles, sconces, candlesticks, bronzes for furniture, and so forth.

Below: Two designs for Sèvres porcelain: a tureen and cover, and a tray. c. 1760

behind the bars of their tight-fastened grilles and cumbersome, well-closing entrance gates. Some of them were very disdainful and inaccessible. They must have belonged to the Talleyrands, the La Rochefoucaulds, unapproachable lords. Next there came an equally silent street with houses not quite so large, but as distinguished in manner, and very reserved. A gate was being closed, and a valet in his morning jacket turned and looked at me, attentively and thoughtfully. Had a tiny little thing happened differently in the past, he would have recognized me and held the gate open deferentially for me. And, upstairs, an old lady, a grandmother, would have welcomed her grandson, even at such an early hour."

The Faubourg is, in fact, one of the inmost refuges of the daydreamer. In many ways the least private of cities, Paris for many generations lodged nine-tenths of its population in reeking, ill-lit, poky, papier-mâché-walled apartments, offensive alike to eye, ear, and nose. So it is hardly surprising if the palaces, manors, and exemplary villas of the 7th *arrondissement* should have captured for a lifetime the hearts of those happy enough to inhabit them. Madame de Staël, for instance, was not a particularly metropolitan woman; but when she looked around the very comfortable property on which she spent the period of her exile in Switzerland, she declared that she would exchange the whole thing—the well-ordered country house, the mountain prospects, and the peachy brick-work—for "the gutter of the Rue du Bac."

Now, the Rue du Bac was never the most imposing of the streets in the Faubourg Saint-Germain. The Rue de Varenne and the Rue de Grenelle were manifestly its supe-riors, and they have more than maintained their supremacy in recent years. The Rue du Bac has not kept the serenity, the sense of high walls and overhanging trees, that dignifies many less interesting streets. It has lost a good deal of the frontage that it possessed in the Plan Turgot of 1734–39, and has gained little in exchange. It has not even had a large share in those developments of the last fifty years that have turned the 7th *arrondissement* into "a capital within a capital" (the phrase is Jules Romains's), "the French equivalent of a condensed Washington." The Rue du Bac has, in fact, gone down since Baron de Staël-Holstein came to it as Swedish Ambassador in 1785.

Yet there is much to see in this street, which was founded in 1564 to mark the location of a ferry by which materials could be sent across the river for use in the con-struction of the Tuileries. To the reader of Saint-Simon, the Rue du Bac has the honor of having lodged many of the minor characters in the *Mémoires*—notably the Marquise d'Alluye, who stayed up till four every morning of her life and died, fresh and plump after innumerable well-chosen *galanteries*, at the age of eighty-two. The Marquis de Nan-

Rue de Varenne, from the *Plan Turgot*, 1738

At the center is the Hôtel Matignon, 57, Rue de Varenne, designed by Jean Courtonne in 1722, now the official residence of the Prime Minister of France.

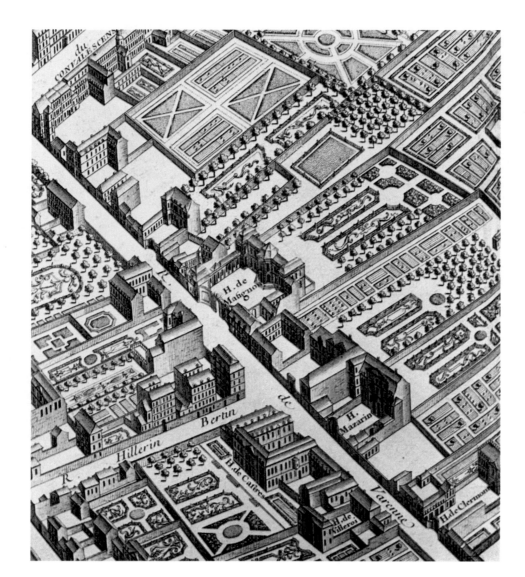

A room from the Hôtel de Varengeville, 217, Boulevard Saint-Germain, with paneling designed by Nicolas Pineau, c. 1735 with later additions. In the 1880s, the woodwork was installed in a house in the Rue du Faubourg Saint-Honoré, where it remained until 1963. It is now in the Metropolitan Museum of Art in New York. The room is arranged in the Louis XV style. The writing table, by Gilles Joubert, was delivered to the King at Versailles in 1759 for the study in his private apartments.

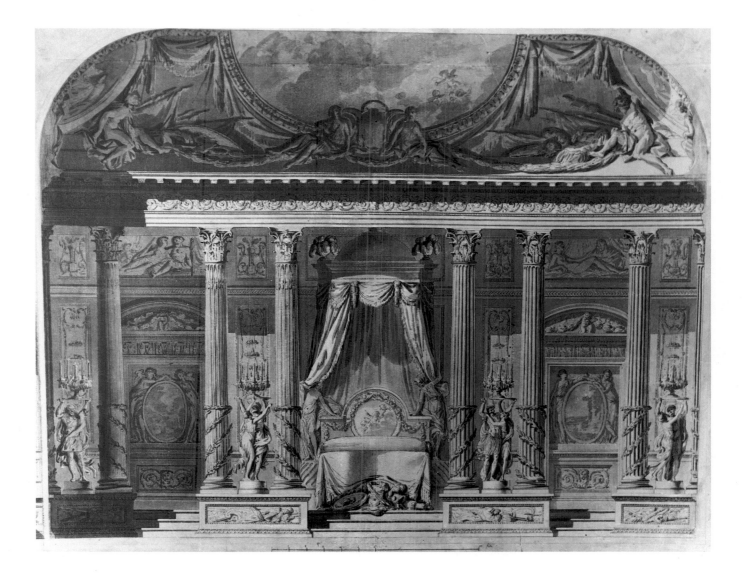

Design for a bedroom in the Hôtel de Mailly-Nesle. Gille-Paul Cauvet, 1770s

gis, Marshal of France, the Duc de Coislin, the Marquis de Brancas, hapless Ticquet, and the Prince de Robecq were other residents of the Rue du Bac who caught the great diarist's eye. Passing over such persons as Marmontel, Badget the anatomist, and the indecipherable Comte Serft-Pilsah, we find that both Montalembert and Chateaubriand died in the Rue du Bac, that Corot was born there, that it witnessed, during the 1850s, the inauguration of a new and original kind of shop, the Bon Marché, and that it counted for much in the lives of at least three great names in the French theater: Adrienne Lecouvreur, Mademoiselle Clairon, and Madame Saint-Huberty.

Even those who are disposed to lump all actresses together as poor mindless parrots must allow that the great ladies of the French stage have often been people of exceptional distinction. They deserve, in fact, some part of the credit that is due to the French classical theater for offering us what Henry James called "a double vision—the strongest dose of life that art could give, and the strongest dose of art that life can give." Mademoiselle Clairon's association with the Rue du Bac was not altogether happy, for it was there, in 1773, in her fiftieth year, that she had to sell nearly all her effects in the hope—vain, it need hardly be said—of stanching the extravagances of her lover, Valbelle. She had been in the habit of removing each afternoon from her house in the Rue du Bac to the Hôtel Valbelle, taking with her her books, her needlework, and her visitors; and from time to time she would pace the formal gardens that lay behind the house. When the day of the sale came, she was revealed as the most personal of collectors. That she should have wonderful jewelry surprised no one: even the German earpick was of solid gold. But the Egyptian mummy in her sycamore box, the manuscript written on palm leaves, the well-chosen Rembrandt etchings, the Japanese masks, the ostrich-feather parasol, the calf-bound illustrated books, and the silk stockings torn from the leg of a noble dwarf—these pointed to a diversity of taste which baffled even the auctioneer.

Madame Saint-Huberty's connection with the Rue du Bac was also amorous in its

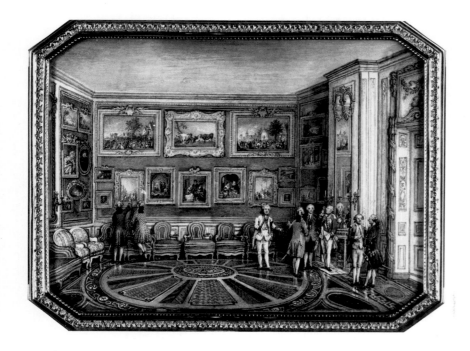

Four panels from a gold snuffbox with miniatures by Louis-Nicolas van Blarenberghe set beneath crystal glass, c. 1770

The miniatures depict scenes from the life of the Duc de Choiseul. The house is the Hôtel Crozat de Chatel, later called the Hôtel de Choiseul, which was in the Rue Richelieu, in the 2nd *arrondissement*, but the interiors preserve the flavor of a great house in the Faubourg Saint-Germain. Except for the Duc's famous collection of paintings, carefully rendered in these miniatures, all is as it would have been in houses across the Faubourg.

In his bedchamber (above left), the Duc has risen from his writing-table to take a letter from a lady, probably his mistress the Comtesse de Brionne, while his entourage looks on. In the *Premier Cabinet* (center left), Choiseul's brother-in-law, the Duc de Gontaut, and a friend are examining a painting by Wouwerman hanging on the far wall. In his study (below left), the Duc, Louis XV's Minister of War, is working at his desk, a famous piece of furniture that passed upon his death to Tallyrand and then to Metternich. The *Cabinet à La Lanterne* (below right) was designed for the display of the Duc's favorite paintings, with a glass dome to give natural light.

origin. She was the mistress, and later the wife, of Comte Louis d'Antraigues, whose house was at what is now No. 27. Geographer, balloonist, philosopher, and democrat, d'Antraigues had a southern exuberance which served him very well when he began, in 1783, to pay court to Madame Saint-Huberty. This great performer was at the farthest remove from the discreet, ingrown gentlewomen who make up so much of the history of the Faubourg. A consummate but never emphatic worldliness has been the mark of these *maîtresses de maison* for two hundred and fifty years. They have never been the heroines of aquatic fêtes at Marseilles, as was the Saint-Huberty in 1785; Louis XVI did not alter the time of his cabinet meetings for them, as he did when she first sang Didon. *Tout se paie,* however, and when Madame Saint-Huberty and d'Antraigues were murdered in Barnes Terrace by their Piedmontese valet, there were doubtless many in the Faubourg who shivered with satisfaction.

Yet it is the inspired scallywags who set off the correctness of the others: the unhistoried many draw color from the reproachable few. The Quai Malaquais, for instance, is dignified at Nos. 15–17 by the Hôtel de la Bazinière, built by Mansart in 1640. Once the home of the widowed Henrietta Maria, and later decorated by Le Brun and adorned with a garden by Le Nôtre, it has for us the added charm of grandiose ill-doing: for Mazarin's niece, the Duchesse de Bouillon, who lived in it from 1676 to 1714, was implicated in the *affaire des poisons.* And No. 9 on the same quay: that the façade and several rooms are *classés* (officially protected, that is to say, as being of artistic importance) may not stir the blood, but no lover of Prévost, Massenet, or Puccini can grudge a grateful glance at the house that was the original of the gambling rooms in *Manon Lescaut.* For it was there that the Prince of Transylvania installed in 1714 his "Académie de Jeu," and there that des Grieux tried in vain to recoup his fortunes.

But of course the quays, though geographically a part of the Faubourg, have long detached themselves from its traditional quietism. They have given in to modern life. The real Faubourg is still so far from having accepted the twentieth century that it is hardly more accessible to the visitor now than it was in the golden age of protocol. In fact there is at any rate one house of the first interest which even the hardiest will not easily penetrate. This is the Hôtel d'Estrées, 79, Rue de Grenelle. From photographs we may judge this to be one of the best works of Robert de Cotte—flawlessly severe in both façades, with a first-floor salon spanned by three semicircular arches and an adjoining room in which the triglyphs and metopes are in the purest Régence style. Even in the first decade of the eighteenth century Robert de Cotte was faithful to the older traditions of French domestic architecture, and particularly to that of sacrificing external decoration to the internal arrangement of the house. His houses were meant to be lived in first and looked at afterward. The Hôtel d'Estrées has been heightened by a whole story since the eighteenth century, so that it has lost something of its pristine proportions, but it has gained, in return, a rich deposit of associations—not merely with the Marshal of France whose name it bears, but with a style of hospitality that has now rather gone out.

"At the Russian Embassy," as a survivor of pre-Revolutionary days once put it, "oriental luxury prevailed. At the gateway in the Rue de Grenelle, two enormous giants from the Urals stood on guard, wearing tasseled cocked hats and white greatcoats braided with gold. As each carriage drove up, they brought their halberds to the salute. The servants' livery was of white and gold, with powdered wigs, siguillettes, breeches, silk stockings, and pumps. Dinner was served on gold plate, and the table was covered with rare orchids and purple lilies that had been sent by diplomatic bag from the Imperial hothouses at Livadia in the Crimea. A special train, moreover, had brought the caviar from Archangelsk, the fish from the Baltic, and the hazel-grouse from Norway." Perhaps it is only fair to warn intending pilgrims that the Soviet Embassy does not encourage those who hope to relive this inspiriting scene.

At the opposite end of the scale from the Soviet Embassy are those rare great houses that are open to everyone—which are, in fact, museums. The finest of these is the Hôtel Biron, now the Rodin Museum. This is a great favorite with visitors to Paris, who find an understandable fascination in the gutted house and its remodeled gardens. The gamut of Rodin's work is on view, as are also a number of objects from his own collections. But public ownership is no substitute for individual fancy. The gardens, though conscien-

A commode by Jean-Henri Riesener, 1783–87. This piece, in the Louis XVI style, stood in Marie-Antoinette's private apartments at the Château de Saint-Cloud. Riesener was the greatest cabinetmaker of his day, and his refined design and exquisite craftsmanship epitomize the taste of the Faubourg Saint-Germain in the 18th century.

tiously restored in 1927, have a municipal flavor. And unluckily the house, which had survived intact until 1820, was turned in that year into a convent school. No doubt this institution was governed according to high principles; but respect for beauty was not one of them, and the Mother Superior allowed the interior to be stripped of nearly all its fittings; these she then sold. Majestic, therefore, as the Hôtel Biron still is, it gives only a very rough idea of what a house of its class can be—just as the trim gardens and their patrolling guardians are very different from those, abandoned beyond the dreams of melancholia, that abound to the east of the Hôtel Biron.

In general, however, the casual visitor will not get inside the houses, whether great or small, of the Faubourg. The forms of life in this quarter are still pre-Revolutionary. The Church has gone, very largely, and has left behind it only such fragments as the Temple de Pentémont, 106, Rue de Grenelle. The Army likewise has gone, very largely, and the civil servants who have crept into the Faubourg are grim little persons who endow whole streets with a pursy, un-Parisian air. It is only the *beaux esprits* of the French Foreign Service who restore to the Faubourg something of its traditional dexterity of tongue. But, there too, the stranger can do no more than amble through the characterless courtyards of the Foreign Ministry itself, just as he is likely to gaze in frustration at that noblest of houses, the Hôtel de Beauharnais, 78, Rue de Lille, which has been restored to perfection by the Federal Republic of Germany.

In fact the only way for the visitor to get his teeth into the Faubourg is to take a house there and live in it. Those fortunate enough to be able to do this will have a wide range of distinguished exiles on whom to model themselves. My own favorite is William

The bedroom of Queen Hortense in the Hôtel de Beauharnais, 78, Rue de Lille. Built in 1713 by Germain Boffrand, the Hôtel de Beauharnais was rebuilt and redecorated in 1803–4 for Eugène de Beauharnais, the Emperor's stepson.

Hope, who lived at 57, Rue Saint-Dominique from 1838 to 1855. Hope took over one of the most cosmopolitan houses in the Faubourg and wrecked it. Turks, Hungarians, and Monégasques had been quite content with Brongniart's original design, but Hope was hardly inside the door before he set to work—raising the house by one story, gutting the staircase, pulling down the adjoining convent, rebuilding the stables, and installing no fewer than three dining rooms in the house itself.

Dinner was of great importance in Hope's life, for it was only at that point in the day—here I quote from the British *Dictionary of National Biography*—that he began seeing his friends. The three dining rooms were of varying sizes. Indifferent to masculine society, the householder habitually supported some eighteen young ladies—chosen, the *Dictionary* tells us, for outstanding proficiency in music or the fine arts—and it was from their ranks that his preferred guests were drawn. Perhaps, indeed, we should consider him as an educationalist with a curriculum all his own. Be that as it may, he could hardly have done more costly damage to the house. Eight million francs were spent on the reconstructions, and the diarists of the time bear witness to the amazement of all those who were invited to examine the results. Hope was eccentric, even for an Englishman, and the oddest rumors about him went around: when he had sent out an invitation nothing, it appeared, could persuade him to open the reply, so sensitive was he to the possibility of a rebuff. If one of his horses displeased him, there was no nonsense about the coper or the knacker's yard: Hope would draw a revolver and dispatch the animal forthwith, in his own stables. After the Revolution of 1848, he again astonished Society by having all his silver melted down in his own furnace.

The nineteenth century added little of consequence to the Faubourg Saint-Germain; but within the walls of this great secret park the enclosed society moved into its silver age. Changes of regime affected the life of the Faubourg as little as was possible, and the memoirs and novels of the period describe the settled elegance of its manners.

"On a night in February 183–, . . . the wind whistled and drove the rain against the windows of an apartment in the Rue de Varenne. The boudoir of this apartment was shaped like a tent; rose-pink and pale gray in color, it was as warm, as softly padded, and as sweetly scented as the inside of a muff.

"It was the home of a woman who had never protested very much against the change of regime, and who now did not protest at all: the old Marquise de Flers.

"A little table of Chinese lacquer was laden with Chinese porcelain and stood behind a big fire that was bravely blazing its last.

"The teapot, with lid raised, stood waiting for the scented draft. The silver kettle kept up a dreamy murmuring—a sound of which Wordsworth, the Lake poet, has sung.

"On either side of the fireplace, in their large blue-velvet armchairs, two women, both elderly, with square foreheads outlined in perfectly kept gray hair and a general air of aristocracy—a bearing that grows daily rarer—were talking. They might have been talking for hours. They had no work to do; were perfectly idle, in fact, but with that idleness that is so becoming to dignified old age."

Thus runs the opening of Barbey d'Aurevilly's *Une Vieille Maîtresse*, which lays before us the shuttered life of the aristocracy in the years that followed the coup d'état of 1830. In later years this severity was partly relaxed: but at the time of which d'Aurevilly was writing, the simple perfection of manners and conversation was such as to make other diversions superfluous. These were the relics, after all, of the tradition which had grown up in the worldly convent of Saint-Joseph (at the corner of the Rue Saint-Dominique and the Rue de Bellechasse) where Madame du Deffand had held her salon for half a century. Her apartment, hung with watered silk and flame-red curtains, was known to rival Voltaire's house at Ferney as the home of good talk; and something of this survived the Revolution and lingered in the age which Madame d'Agoult describes in her memoirs.

Her world acknowledged no social change. "Its habits," she says, "were regularity itself, and it recognized no others. Six months in the country, and six in Paris; dancing at carnival time, concerts and sermons during Lent, marriages from Easter onward; the theater, very rarely; traveling, not at all; cards at every season—such was the invariable order of our pleasures and occupations. 'Everyone,' as we said then, when speaking of ourselves and our friends, did exactly the same as everyone else. But the manners of

The Eiffel Tower Being Painted. Late 19th century

'everyone' were as simple as they were noble." In that society, she tells us, "everyone" knew everyone else from the cradle ("from before they were born, one might almost say"); wealth, rank, titles, and worldly position were taken for granted; old and young alike were animated by identical principles: "equality among themselves, proud obedience to their rulers, an abundant charity toward the poor, and confidence in God and the fortunes of France."

From all this there came "a perfected ease of manner, a feeling of security, an openness of face and nature, and a cordiality of welcome such as I have never encountered anywhere else. . . . Coquetry and gallantry marked the relations between the sexes at every age; in love, as in friendship, ties were light and easy; once formed, however, they were rarely broken; and when old age came, they were usually strengthened, rather than enfeebled, by the action of time and habit. . . . Time and habit gave, in fact, to good society a perfection of intimacy, and with it a strength of opinion, such as our newer, more variable society can never hope to attain."

There will never again be a book of memoirs that can speak of the Faubourg Saint-Germain as the property of a single society. It has become something different: a secretive corner of Paris in which seven or eight societies live side by side, each feigning to ignore the other. To the diplomatists, for example, the civil servants, and the embattled descendants of those who first peopled the great houses of the Faubourg—to these there have recently been added some of the more successful French men of letters. These have not, on the whole, clung to the ancient traditions of the quarter. Severity of decoration—classical purity of taste, in other words—is rare among writers.

Let us therefore take refuge in an earlier interior—that of Edouard Pailleron, who lived at 1, Quai d'Orsay during the last decades of the nineteenth century. This particular house bears—or bore then—a rich deposit of the authentic history of the Faubourg. Built by Robert de Cotte during the high summer of French classical architecture, it was the scene of Adrienne Lecouvreur's visits to d'Argental; it was the home of the painter Robert Lefèvre, who was so fanatical a monarchist that he went off his head after the Revolution of 1830; and Pailleron himself—one of the most well-liked, though not one of the most enduring, of French playwrights—amply maintained the theatrical traditions of the quarter. His idiosyncratic interior was enlivened by visits from nearly every player of any standing; though padded against the din with the heaviest of Gobelins tapestries, his rooms rang night and day with the conversation of those who had little to say but said it consummately well. The house, we are told, reflected in all its details the taste of "un artiste doublé d'un gentleman"—gilded boiseries, wrenched from a Chinese pagoda, disputed with a Dutch chandelier for the visitor's attention; Pailleron himself had looted the monumental keys of an Italian church and added some charred fragments of an earlier establishment of his own which had been destroyed by fire. A billiard room and a portrait of the entire family by John Singer Sargent paid homage to the Anglomania of the time.

There is of course one monument of the Pailleron era in the 7th *arrondissement* which even the blindest visitor cannot ignore: the Eiffel Tower. This remarkable construction has nothing in common with the area to which it is bound for reasons of postal convenience; but for many visitors to Paris it is the great sentimental symbol of the city; none, certainly, would wish it away. But this was not always the case—as we may judge from a letter that appeared in *Le Temps* of 14 February 1887. The tower was not yet in being and the signatories—"impassioned lovers of beauty"—protested to Alphand, the director of the 1889 Exhibition, against the erection of a "useless and monstrous" architectural caprice: a project, they added, which even America, though crazed by its passion for commerce, had had the sense to reject. What if it lasted for twenty years? they asked. Even its shadow would contaminate the city, foreshortening the triumphs of earlier ages and lying like a smear of ink across the pages on which Mansart and Gabriel had left their mark.

Were these signatories perhaps interested persons? Professional reactionaries? Or cranks?

Not at all: they included Maupassant, Gounod, François Coppée, Sardou (the most popular playwright of his day), Garnier (the architect of the Opéra), Sully Prudhomme, and Leconte de Lisle. But time has encouraged us to take a very different view of the

Statue on the Pont Alexandre III. Pierre Jahan photograph

View of the Seine, 1894. Alfred Stieglitz photograph

Tower; and although it is true that the Avenue Bosquet and the streets that run into it seem almost to sink into the earth if we force them into perspective with the Tower, I have never noticed among natives of this quarter that sense of humiliation which was foreseen in the columns of *Le Temps*. For ourselves, the Tower and all its fittings are a delightful anachronism—so much so that we may even regret the Big Wheel that formerly stood beside it: "like the mystic O," one enthusiast wrote, "beside the sacred I." The "sacred I" is, moreover, an appropriate phrase on which to take leave of a quarter that breathes in its every stone a serene, a justified, an anachronistic egotism.

XIV

The Sixth Arrondissement

The Luxembourg Gardens. Robert Morton photograph

Not many places in the world were absolutely and uniquely agreeable in the late 1940s and early 1950s; but one of them was the Café des Deux-Magots, which still stands at the corner of the Place Saint-Germain-des-Prés and the Boulevard Saint-Germain.

The fact requires investigation, for nothing outwardly marked out this café from a hundred others of its sort and size. The two oriental figures from which it takes its name were "skied," in exhibition terms, and not, in any case, of much quality. The drinks and the food were what you got anywhere. Newspapers and writing materials were not to be had for the asking, as once they would have been. The amenities—telephone, wash basin, lavatory—were something to remember with laughter and tears.

Yet this was for people of my generation the true center of Paris. No matter what the time or the season, and irrespective of one's circumstances or state of mind, the Deux-Magots was the quintessentially Parisian place. It was incomparable as a listening post;

if you wanted to know "who's in, who's out," you could find out more from an hour at the Deux-Magots than from any other source.

The Deux-Magots was not only an ideal acclimatizer. It was a place that notoriety had not spoiled. It was neither so big that all feeling of community was lost, nor so small that the great men felt conspicuous and went elsewhere. Unlike its neighbor, the Flore, it had (and has still) a noble outlook to the east: the tower of the abbey church of Saint-Germain-des-Prés, with its adjacent few inches of hard-won turf, and—until very lately—the sign, yellow on blue, of Le Divan, where for many years Henri Martineau worked on his editions of Stendhal. ("Peut-on avoir," I once asked, as a timid undergraduate, "la *Correspondance de Stendhal?*" "Non, Monsieur," said Martineau, without looking up from his desk, "ça ne se trouve pas"; yet six separate sets of the treasured collection stood on the shelf behind him.)

There was much to be learned through the windows of the Deux-Magots. Even Dorothy Wordsworth might have found it a good place to see the seasons round; the umbrella stand, the rear platform of a passing omnibus, the trees on the Boulevard, and the incidence of grog—each had its message for the experienced observer. And, although a great deal of nonsense was talked and lived at the Deux-Magots, it was one of the last places where an idea—*any* idea—was judged without prejudice, and on its merits, in what foreigners still regarded as the classical French style.

All this was still of quite recent origin. Montparnasse in the 1920s had had a preeminence all its own. And it still has merits of a sort. But as a place to live in it cannot compare with the 6th *arrondissement*. The Boulevard Montparnasse is featureless and gross; Notre-Dame-des-Champs is no rival to the ancient Abbaye de Saint-Germain-des-Prés; the famous cafés seem cavernous and impersonal to the habitué of the Deux-Magots or the Flore; and the nightlife is peculiarly blatant and commercialized. Montparnasse is at its pleasantest where it has gone back to grass—where village life has reasserted itself

Henri Martineau at Le Divan. Robert Doisneau photograph

against all the odds and there can still be found, in a drowsing side street, something of the rustication that Sainte-Beuve must have known during his long residence there, and details such as Apollinaire picked out in his poem about Montparnasse:

> O porte de l'hotel avec deux plantes vertes
> Vertes qui jamais
> Ne porteront des fleurs

Just when Montparnasse began to lose its status in the world of art and literature it is not easy to say. But there must have come a time when everyone decided that it was really too dismal, as a landscape, and too far from the effective center of Paris. Gradually it must have got about that in the 6th there were the best publisher in Paris, an hotel of *palace* quality, the pick of the younger art dealers, and a landscape cut to the human scale.

There were also, of course, more urgent reasons for making a change. And as the name of Jean-Paul Sartre is often linked with that of Saint-Germain-des-Prés, readers may like to know how he, for one, moved northward:

"From 1930 to 1939," he once said, "I went regularly to the 'Dôme' in Montparnasse. As I was a teacher and hadn't much money I lived in a hotel; and like all people who live in hotels I spent most of the day in cafés. In 1940 the 'regulars' of the Dôme began to go elsewhere, for two reasons: the Métro station 'Vavin' was closed, and we had to make our way to the Dôme in the evenings, in complete darkness and on foot from the Gare de Montparnasse. Besides, the Dôme was overrun with Germans, and these Germans were tactless enough to bring their own tea and coffee, and to have these prepared and served in front of us Frenchmen, who were already reduced to drinking some anonymous and ghastly substitute.

"The fortunes of the Café de Flore at that time were made by the fact that it was

An existentialist interior.
Robert Doisneau
photograph

just across the road from the Métro station of Saint-Germain-des-Prés. It had previously been merely an annex of the Deux-Magots, but in 1939 or thereabouts Picasso, Léon-Paul Fargue, and André Breton began to go to the Flore. A lot of cinema people followed their example, and a lot of successful painters and celebrities of one sort or another. I was only a shabby little teacher at that time and I was too shy to go in.

"But in 1940 the clientele became quite different, for the reasons I've just given, and Simone de Beauvoir and I more or less set up house in the Flore. We worked from 9 A.M. till noon, when we went out to lunch. At 2 we came back and talked with our friends till four, when we got down to work again till eight. And after dinner people came to see us by appointment. It may seem strange, all this, but the Flore was like home to us: even when the air raid alarm went we would merely feign to leave and then climb up to the first floor and go on working."

The urgent and semiclandestine conditions of wartime vanished in time, of course, but fundamentally the two cafés had still the same character in the 1950s. They were at once office, anteroom, sun trap in high summer, High Court of Justice (summary and informal) in all matters of art and literature, place of rendezvous, casting bureau, observatory. . . . If you grew roots in one or the other you could command Paris, or an important section of it, in the way that a submariner commands the ocean when the periscope gets clear of the waves.

"Rendezvous of the Intellectual Elite" is the device that you will find stamped on your bill at the Deux-Magots; and intellectuals, elite or otherwise, still play a part in the prestige of the quarter. But there is more to Saint-Germain-des-Prés than the whirr of the intellectual bacon-slicer and the thud of the intellectual guillotine. There is the look of the place, for instance. It is, from a painter's point of view, one of the less familiar parts of Paris. Delacroix lived here (Rue Visconti and Place Furstemberg) but he never painted it. The Impressionists preferred the Rue de Rivoli, the Tuileries, and the Grands Boulevards. Thomas Girtin liked the waterfront best, and even John Crome chose the Boulevard des Italiens when he wanted to work something up. Much was lost when Walter Sickert failed to note the moment when, as we walk up the southern half of the Rue Bonaparte, the north side of the Place Saint-Germain-des-Prés is suddenly hoisted above the intervening ground and seems to hang in the air, a dream of white and cream and elephant-gray, like a harbor town glimpsed from the poop of an approaching packet boat.

Picasso's studio in the Rue des Grands-Augustins. Robert Doisneau photograph

The Street. Balthus, 1933

We are dealing, in short, with beauty that has never been given a name: Pissarro did not pass here.

There is, as it happens, a painter of our own time who caught both the look and the life of the 6th *arrondissement* to perfection. Balthus in 1933, and again in 1952–54, produced the kind of paintings that could serve as a record of what Paris was like at that time even if no other evidence could be found. As his later painting is set into the wall of an apartment in Paris, while the earlier one is in the Museum of Modern Art in New York City, I propose to stick here with the one that we can all get to see.

It is called simply *The Street,* but if we go to the Carrefour de Buci and find our way into the narrow sliver of the Passage du Commerce Saint-André we can easily reconstitute the elements on which Balthus built his painting. We shall find the irregular cut of the streets, the look of a market town, the profusion of wordless signs and emblems, and the heterogeneous housefronts that are given over almost without exception to trade of a handmade and individualistic sort. Striped awnings and lamps of a kind long gone out of style complete the furnishing of the scene, which Balthus did not render literally but treated as a small universe of signs that we must learn to read in our own way.

There is no wheeled traffic. The large and forward child in the foreground can play without fear of interruption. So can the young people on the left, whose games are of a more lascivious kind. As so often in the 6th, a carpenter is on his way to work. (As he shoulders his plank, he may remind us of one of the figures in a painting by Piero della Francesca. We may be sure that the reference is intentional.) Next to him on the right is one of the ubiquitous adolescents, neither boy nor man, on whom so much of Parisian life depends. With his huge moonlike face, his unwinking gaze, and the Napoleonic aplomb with which his right hand lies across his diaphragm, he could have stepped straight from the pages of a paper-cutout book, and yet we recognize him as a small monster of resource who will return safe and successful from no matter what errand.

As Balthus enjoys moving from emblem to reality and back again, we are not quite sure whether the very young chef in the background on the left is or is not one of the two-dimensional figures that used to stand outside small restaurants in the 6th with the menu of the day pinned up on their chests. And Balthus completes his cast of characters with two women whose backs speak to us more directly than most people's fronts. They are, first, the classic Parisienne, who brings a needed normality to what might otherwise seem a too arbitrary collection of eccentrics, and, second, the no less classic figure of the aproned woman-of-all-work whose duties include the shepherding of small boys who might otherwise fall into bad company.

The Street is an alphabet of Parisian attitudes as they presented themselves to a major painter who lived for many years in that part of the 6th. It is in every way personal to Balthus. But once we have looked at it in the right way we shall forever after see the side streets around the Carrefour de Buci through his eyes.

The 6th should be novelist's country, in a way—so abrupt are the changes of tone, and so entirely human the scale. But no one in our own time has ever quite brought it off, and there are advantages to the fact that we still experience it entirely through our own eyes, with no memories of some vaster, more conclusive comprehension to give a flavor of foreknowledge to the scene. We are dealing with something that has never been decisively put down, either on paper or on canvas. What it is like to live in one of the coveted round rooms in the Hôtel Louisiane, or to sit in the little garden of the Ukrainian church, or to pause in awed speculation before the prodigious array of surgical instruments at No. 176 on the Boulevard—all this remains to be seized. The Montmartre of *Louise* and the Montparnasse of the 1920s are dead beyond revival; if the 6th is holding out very well it is because there is not much in it for the casual visitor: it needs to be lived, not seen.

The 6th has, apart from anything else, a rich and largely inviolate local life. Until a generation ago, the ancient Cour du Dragon, which ran from the Rue de Rennes to the Rue du Dragon, was especially rich in this respect. Families of ironworkers had lived there, as it seemed, "forever." Gates and grilles and stoves were open to view in the narrow alley, where a central gutter never ran dry and trade signs hung out at first-floor level. Upper windows were garnished with flowers and potted plants, and on August 15 candles were lit in the niche where a statue of the Virgin surveyed the amiable scene.

The Cour du Dragon, 2, Rue de Rennes, 1899–1900. Eugène Atget photograph

All that has been done away with: but you can still eat in the dairy on the Place Saint-Sulpice and fancy yourself in Nevers or Caen; provincial, too, is the solemn fatuity of the souvenir shops in the same holy square. The Rue des Canettes is known to many English-speaking visitors for a long-running Italian restaurant, and to a few for the Hôtel d'Alsace et Lorraine, which was owned by Proust's servant, Céleste Albaret. But the 6th was once known for much that the holiday-maker was likely to pass by: hotels below Michelin's Plimsoll line, like the bird-haunted one in the Rue des Ciseaux and others, of an almost Gorkyesque grimness, in the Rue Guisarde; drinking shops like Ma Cave in the Rue des Canettes or the Sauvignon de Quincy at the corner of the Rue des Saints-Pères and the Rue de Sèvres; and survivors of an earlier, handmade civilization, like Monsieur Soliltage, who would sell you twelve dozen brooms if you were bent on spring cleaning, or Monsieur Roussel in the Rue Gozlin, who had sold Matisse palette knives for more than half a century, or Monsieur Gaucher the bookbinder in the Rue Jacob. Every quarter of Paris had once such characters, but in the 6th they had not been overwhelmed: it was still they who set the tone, and rare was the intellectual who had their ripeness of response. Monsieur Folantin, in Huysmans's *A Vau l'Eau*, is not one of the more engaging characters in French fiction, but we can all agree with him when he singles out (or did single out, in the early 1880s) the 6th as one of the sanctuaries of the idler in Paris.

"Once," Huysmans tells us, "he had liked to amble about in forgotten side streets, humble provincial alleys where the secrets of simple homes were suddenly revealed at ground-floor windows. But now all that was finished; and where there had been fresh leaves and groups of fine trees there were only unending garrison buildings, one after the other. M. Folantin was seized, in this new Paris, with feelings of uneasiness and disquiet. He was a man who loathed luxury shops. Not for anything in the world would he have set foot in a smart hairdresser's or in one of those modern gas-lit grocers'; what he liked were those ancient and simple shops where you were received openly and honestly, and

294

The Rue de Seine, 22 July 1914. Auguste Léon autochrome

The Petit Saint-Benoît. Robert Doisneau photograph

Interior of Lemercier's Lithography Shop.
c. 1845
The shop was at 7, Rue de Seine.

the owner did not try to throw dust in your eyes or overawe you by the luxury of his installation."

It was for an element of "benevolent intimacy" that Huysmans's old codger prized the 6ᵗʰ, and it still has much of this quality. The Petit Saint-Benoit has the classical cut of the small eighteenth-century restaurant, the Temple of Friendship in the garden of 20, Rue Jacob seems to spread its influence over the whole quarter, and most of the shops and galleries have the look of one-man concerns, even if they are sometimes much grander than they at first sight appear. Monsieur Loliée in the Rue des Saints-Pères is a bookseller of international standing; and you will be lucky if you pick up a bargain in the elegant *antiquaires* of the Rue Bonaparte. But in each of these cases it's the stock, not the showcase, that counts, just as the great print shops in the Rue de Seine waste no time on window display and Monsieur Chéramy and his colleagues in the autograph-and-manuscript department are discreet about what they have in reserve.

Learning likewise has its place in the 6ᵗʰ. University presses in France do not go in for elegance of presentation; French works of learning often look, indeed, as if they had been printed on flannel and sewn up with tape. But if geography or anthropology or agriculture or medicine or the sciences are among your subjects you can profitably bog down in the strange charmless *librairies universitaires* of the 6ᵗʰ.

The 6ᵗʰ, moreover, has a long-standing academic resource, which has lately become more accessible than ever before to the visitor. This is the Ecole des Beaux-Arts, which has its postal address on the Quai Malaquais and its main entrance at 14, Rue Bonaparte. Until quite recently the Ecole des Beaux-Arts was forbidden ground to the stranger. You could peek through the grille on the Rue Bonaparte, and if you were ready of speech and had a bank note in your hand you could sometimes get into the chapel. In the nineteenth century, this chapel was the place where Georges Seurat and many another aspirant artist got a crash course—through copies and casts—in the great painting and sculpture of the Italian Renaissance. It was here, and not in Arezzo or Borgo San Sepolcro, that Seurat learned to revere Piero della Francesca; and he was by no means the only student to take

The *cour vitrée* of the Ecole des Beaux-Arts in 1929. Felix-Jacques Duban and Ernest-Georges Coquart, designed 1863, built 1871–74

fire from the curious and almost hallucinatory jumble that we can still see inside the chapel.

Apart from that, the school was forbidden ground. It had been moved across the river at the beginning of the nineteenth century to rehouse the students of art and architecture who had for many years been given studio space in the Louvre. In 1807 they were told to go elsewhere, and in 1816 the school was allotted the buildings that had previously been occupied first by the Couvent des Petits-Augustins, a seventeenth-century foundation, and more recently by the post-Revolutionary Musée des Monuments Français. In the course of the nineteenth century, the school buildings were enlarged in a way that ideally combined reverence for the past with an appreciation of what could be done with metal and glass. These new buildings were primarily the work of Félix Duban, an architect who at the time of his death in 1871 had been connected with the school for more than half a century.

In 1892 the school acquired a great town house, 17, Quai Malaquais, which had been built in 1640 by François Mansart. If we consider that in our own century some additions to the school were designed by Auguste Perret, the pioneer poet of concrete, it will be clear that the Ecole des Beaux-Arts as it exists today is a veritable echo chamber of French architecture in almost all of its phases. This character is owed in part to the anthology of architectural fragments that it took over from the Musée des Monuments Français. These include a part of the façade of the Château d'Anet, which was designed by Philibert de l'Orme, a part of the façade of the sixteenth-century Château de Gaillon

(Eure), and as a souvenir of an even remoter past some capitals from the twelfth-century church of Sainte-Geneviève in Paris. The ensemble makes up in variety and high quality for what it may lack in reason, logic, and homogeneity.

Less than ten years ago it began to be mooted that so far from being an architectural dead end, the Ecole des Beaux-Arts had in point of fact stood sponsor to nineteenth-century buildings in Paris and elsewhere that were remarkable for serene ambition, majesty of statement, perfection of craftsmanship, and finesse of detail. The "Beaux-Arts style," as apotheosized in a famous exhibition at the Museum of Modern Art in New York, is precisely the style that had been execrated throughout the heyday of the International Style in architecture. As lately as 1968, at the time of the student uprisings in Paris, the Ecole des Beaux-Arts was high on the hit list of institutions that stood for a despicable past. But times change, and tastes change with them, and one consequence of this was the decision to relieve one of Duban's more spectacular spaces of its academic function and turn it into an exhibition gallery on a very grand scale.

Not only would this add a great deal to the amenities of the 6th, but it would allow the Ecole des Beaux-Arts to put on view for the first time some of its enormous archive of paintings and drawings by former students. The list of alumni goes back for two centuries, more or less, and it includes many of the greatest names in French art. To have access to that archive, and to examine it in one of the noblest public buildings of its date, would clearly be a major experience. The idea was not popular with the students of the Beaux-Arts, since they would have found themselves turned out of studio space within five minutes' walk of the Louvre, but to the rest of us it seemed a very good idea.

The 6th meanwhile is what it always was: a very curious mixture. Napoleonic in its taste (you will never have seen so many bronze eagles), fetishist in religion, improvisatory in the theater, secretive, almost, in the cinema, afflicted in places by the brutal high spirits of the medical student but in general of a rather melancholy, meditative turn of mind, unostentatious where money is concerned but ten times as expensive, in terms of real money, as it was before fashion seized it. It is a place where a great many nearly young people have suddenly begun to make money; for this reason, a gloss of high or easy living has come over the apartments in many an ancient and beautiful town house. But the Japanese video recorders, the Scotch whiskey, and the brand-name furniture are all part of today's variant of the "amusing interior." Externally, the 6th is not smartening up at all, I'm glad to say, and attempts to launch a really expensive restaurant or bar do not often come off.

The Brasserie Lipp, for instance, is the great permanent success among the restaurants of the 6th, but Lipp is not very comfortable, and the decorations in mosaic and faience by the father and uncle of Léon-Paul Fargue have certainly never brought customers in from the street. The food, too, could be called plain and unvarying; beer is the staple drink, and the bills are not small. But people line up to get into Lipp because it has what counts in the 6th: style. I'm not sure, in fact, that it is not one of the last sanctuaries of Parisian dandyism. Everything at Lipp's "is what it is," as the philosophers say, "and not another thing." The cuts of meat have an almost English simplicity, the great sheets of looking glass are there to inform, not to insinuate, and although there are frauds among the clients, as there are everywhere else, the general note is one of candor and forthrightness.

Intellectual pleasures are taken seriously in the 6th—so much so, in fact, that it is one of the few places, either in Paris or anywhere else, where the professional entertainer has almost no foothold. People would really rather talk, in the 6th, than pay somebody else to amuse them. If you are a jazz musician you can make a living there; but if you are an actor, or a lieder singer, or a chamber musician, you will soon learn to go elsewhere. Talk comes first; and after talk, reading. Publishing is big business in Paris, as much as anywhere else, and the money is made from best sellers which only occasionally overlap with the preferences of the 6th. A group of friends such as that which founded *La Nouvelle Revue Française* in 1908 would find it difficult to keep going today on the scale on which the prestige of the *NRF* was founded. No longer is a book expected to wait its turn, selling fifty or a hundred copies a year, until suddenly the public gets around to it. And yet it was in the 6th that writers like Beckett, Butor, Ionesco, and Barthes found a little

Project for a Pulpit in Saint-Sulpice. Charles de Wailly, 1764

Though best known today for its mural paintings by Eugène Delacroix, the Eglise de Saint-Sulpice is remarkable for its enormous size (it is broader than the Cathedral of Notre-Dame, and hardly less long), for the perfection of its proportions, and for the astonishing pulpit by Charles de Wailly, built in 1789, that seems to hoist the preacher high above our terrestrial concerns on a flying carpet of marble.

corps of adherents which was denied to them elsewhere. The "work of pure literature" is not in favor today, among French publishers, as it was when *Monsieur Teste* by Paul Valéry and *Les Nourritures Terrestres* by André Gide first came out; but even if the book-club reissue, the illustrated volume of travel, and the enormous novelette marked *traduit de l'américain* have been the saving of the balance sheet the opinion of the 6th still counts for much.

A publisher's office is nothing much to look at (a publisher's cocktail party, on the other hand, is a very different matter, as you will find if you are invited to one of Monsieur Gallimard's), but there is one building in the 6th that till lately could be visited with pleasure both for itself and for its associations with the great early days of *La Nouvelle Revue Française*—and that is the Théâtre du Vieux Colombier.

The "intellectual's theater" is one of those concepts that can never quite lose their original grandeur, no matter how much they may have been abused. And when Jacques Copeau opened the Vieux Colombier in October 1913 with his own translation of Thomas Heywood's *A Woman Killed with Kindness*, Rodin, Debussy, Bergson, Péguy, and Granville Barker were among those who hurried to support him. It is easy enough for us to see, at nearly half a century's distance, an element of comedy in the extreme purity and severity of Copeau's intentions. The willful sobriety of the auditorium, the unvarying scene structure, the refusal to take on any actor "corrupted by success," the ban on tips to program sellers, the Wagnerian bolting of the doors as soon as the houselights went down—all this added up to "les Folies-Calvin" in the eyes of some of Copeau's contemporaries.

But we must remember what the theater was like before Copeau began; we must remember, for that matter, what most of it is like now. This passage, for instance, from Copeau's inaugural lecture is as true today as it was when he wrote it: "Our stage, ever more subject to a process of cynical industrialization, has lost the support of the cultivated public. Most of our theaters have been taken over by a handful of 'entertainers' who do the bidding of a shameless commercial cartel. Everywhere we see squalid motives, bluff, inflated reputations, the craze for quick returns. Exhibitionism and speculation have grown fat upon an 'art' which is dying and, indeed, no longer deserves the name. Disorder, indiscipline, stupidity, contempt for the creative artist and hatred of beauty reign everywhere; 'production' run wild, critics who say 'Yes' to everything, and a public whose taste grows ever more debased—these are the things which enrage us, and those the things we stand against."

Copeau was lucky, of course, in finding from the very first two men of genius, Charles Dullin and Louis Jouvet, for his troupe. (Other men of genius took humbler roles: Roger Martin du Gard, later to win the Nobel Prize for Literature, once acted as cloakroom attendant.) But there was nothing accidental about the choice of plays, or the high principle that animated the whole enterprise, or the methods of teaching, which were later to be taken up in many other parts of the world. The Vieux Colombier was a holy place for those who believed that the best writers ought, if the world were properly arranged, to produce the best theater.

There are still theaters that try to do something of what Copeau did: to give the audience (the words are Paul Léautaud's, and they date from December 1913) "what you don't see anywhere else: auditorium, plays, production, public—all are different." But

On the Pont des Arts.
Robert Doisneau
photograph

these little theaters are not in the 6th; and to reach the grand official playhouse of the quarter, the Théâtre de l'Odéon, we have to walk a little way to the east. The walk takes us into what is perceptibly a more august, less free-and-easy townscape. Even the Marché Saint-Germain (a mere third, by the way, of the compendious erection designed between 1813 and 1818 by Blondel and Lusson) had dignity till what remained of it was torn down; and the streets themselves bear the names of some of those Benedictine savants (Clément, Félibien, Montfaucon, Mabillon) to whom the quarter first owed its lofty intellectual standing. When we get to the Carrefour de l'Odéon it becomes clear that, although in our own day acting and production have often been at their best in a poky little den, there was a time when it was unthinkable that they should not be fittingly housed. The Odéon is one of the handsomest and best-sited theaters in Europe; and its immediate surroundings are sacred ground for those who prize *Saint Langage,* whether written or spoken, as one of the highest of human achievements.

The beginnings of the quarter as we know it can be traced to the year 1773, when Louis XVI bought the gardens of the Hôtel de Condé and gave them to the city of Paris with the proviso that they should erect upon the site a new home for the Comédie-Française. This theater, our Odéon, was designed by Poyré and Wailly and built between 1779 and 1782. Set on top of a little hill, it offered the opportunity of a noble vista; and this was well taken in the Rue de l'Odéon, which runs up from the Carrefour. Such was the status of the new theater that in 1779 the Rue de l'Odéon was awarded two features as yet untried in Paris: pavements, and gutters at the side, rather than in the middle, of the street.

The Rue de l'Odéon forms, with its contemporaries the rues Rotrou, Casimir-Delavigne, Crébillon, and Corneille, a nucleus of systematic elegance that has never lost its power to surprise and delight. The heart of the quarter is of course the semicircular Place de l'Odéon; creamy-white housefronts and the smell of good food make this, for a sensitive visitor, one of the most treasured of all Parisian *places,* while the proportions of it, the sense of *mesure,* the glimmer of distant foliage, and the echo of a rapid footfall along the arcades—all combine to create the atmosphere of classical French comedy. And that atmosphere is here by right: for at 2, Rue de Condé, in 1776, Beaumarchais wrote *Le Barbier de Séville,* and at 1, Rue de Corneille lived Louise Contat, the first of all Suzannes in this most exhilarating of comedies. Rossini's version of the *Barber* has of course given it an extra dimension of Italianate high spirits, and it is difficult for anyone who has been carried away by the irresistible momentum of a good performance of the opera to cut back to Beaumarchais's original. But the effort will be rewarded: we may even end by agreeing with Edmond de Goncourt, who wrote in 1895 that "for all their light and bantering tone, there is as much philosophy in Beaumarchais's conversational exchanges as in any of Ibsen's bookish harangues."

Ideally, all plays put on at the Odéon would be as good as *Le Barbier de Séville,* and all conversations in the *place* would have the easy, nimble, and pertinent character that Beaumarchais knew how to impart to even the simplest exchange. But these ideals, like most others, go by default. The Odéon has had many ups and downs in recent years, one at least of the restaurants has got a little above itself, and we have said our goodbyes to the old Café Voltaire, where the Encyclopedists were followed, at a century's distance, by Verlaine and Mallarmé. The bookstalls that stood till 1952 in the arcades on either side of the theater, and the tradition by which you could do practically anything you liked with the books, short of actually putting them in your pocket and walking away—both are gone. And yet, doubtful as it may seem from the evidence of the playbills, the theater in Paris is a part of literature. Not that there are any specifically theatrical bookshops in the Odéon quarter (Rue Bonaparte and Rue Marivaux are the places for those), but there will be enough plays on offer for you to notice that the theater has tempted one after another of the greatest names in French literature.

Coming down toward the Carrefour you will see, at 7, Rue de l'Odéon, an art gallery; and, almost opposite it, at No. 12, a shop that was once a bookstore called Shakespeare & Co. and now sells surgical instruments. These are historic places: in the one, Paul Valéry was launched on his career at a reading organized by Adrienne Monnier, and the other was once the rendezvous of James Joyce, Hemingway, Scott Fitzgerald, and many

It was in 1615 that Marie de Médicis asked Salomon de Brosse to build her the palace that still stands in the Luxembourg Gardens. Those gardens were also brought into being at her request. They have always been, and they are today, one of the great amenities of Paris. Parisians of every age, station, and turn of mind take pleasure in them. Now the home of the French Senate (above), the Palais du Luxembourg was radically transformed in the 19th century. It has been endowed through the years with a large and heterogeneous collection of decorative sculptures—some of them distinguished, some of them not. Pierre Jahan photograph

other English and American writers. Sylvia Beach long ago gave up Shakespeare & Co., and both she and Mademoiselle Monnier have been called to a place where readers even more distinguished than Valéry are doubtless heard from time to time. So there is not a great deal to be gained by mooning about in front of these two shops as if Les Amis du Livre were still a bookshop and you could warm yourself in winter at the stove before which Mademoiselle Monnier would stand, like a secular abbess, in long Puvis-gray robes. But it is worthwhile to pause there, all the same, because these shops marked the very last stage in a process that can be followed in the 6th from its beginnings among the Benedictines of the eighth century. When *Ulysses* was first issued, over the imprint of Shakespeare & Co., the printed word was still the surest and most direct way by which a man of genius could communicate with the world. Today this primacy is in dispute, and it may be that by the year 2000 men of genius will address themselves to their public in some quite other way. If this is so, the little shops of the 6th will have a purely antiquarian interest; but there may remain one or two old fogies to recall the intense excitement with which a new book was snatched up in the Rue de l'Odéon, opened on the way home, and raced through in a hotel bedroom.

Fear of the future is a sure sign of failing vitality; and it may well be that people will always prize the relationship of writer to individual reader. But what may be lost, even so, is the quality of indifference to conventional success which has always been the mark of the 6th. This quality comes in part from a Stendhalian refusal to be duped and in part from a determination to take each writer, and each book by that writer, on their own merits and without regard for what the book clubs or the regular reviewers or the television spokesmen may have to say. Reading remains an original experience in the 6th; with love, travel, politics, music, and the fine arts, it is one of the grand objects of human existence.

The Luxembourg
Gardens. Alain Perceval
photograph

It is because of this emphasis on firsthand experience that the 6th makes so little of its associations. Original thought is nowhere more highly prized; yet not one person in ten thousand in the 6th can show you the funerary tablets of Descartes in the church of Saint-Germain-des-Prés. Talk, as I have said, rates high; but people prefer to make it for themselves, rather than to hang around the Café Procope in the Rue de l'Ancienne-Comédie, where the resident shades are those of Voltaire, Danton, Musset, and Gambetta. But perhaps the most neglected of all the sights of the 6th is the Rue Visconti, which runs, parallel to the Rue des Beaux-Arts, between the Rue de Seine and the Rue Bonaparte. It's a mere slot, by present-day standards, and those who come upon it by accident are not often tempted to linger between the tall faceless mansions. But here at No. 24, Racine lived out the seven sad years that led up to his death in 1699; in the same house, half a century later, could be found Mademoiselle Clairon, one of the greatest of Phèdres; in No. 17, Balzac set up as a printer, in his late twenties, and wrote the first novel that he was to publish under his own name, *Le Dernier Chouan;* and on the second floor of the same house, a decade later, Delacroix had his studio. It was in the Rue Visconti, in fact, that Delacroix painted the tumultuous *Entry of the Crusaders into Constantinople,* a huge canvas which contrasts almost comically with the confined and seedy surroundings in which it was conceived. The Rue Visconti is more suited to the tête-à-tête of portraiture, and it is not difficult to imagine Delacroix at work on the memorable portrait of Chopin which now hangs in the Louvre. It is a triumph of close knowledge, that painting; and it has the kind of searching affection that is one of the qualities most prized in the 6th. Passivity, whether of the mind or of the heart, is not welcome here; the street market in the Rue de Buci has an almost Neapolitan intensity, and in bar after bar the long sheets of looking glass throw the visitor's reflection back in his face with a tacit, "*That's* who you are, and what are you going to do about it?"

A taxing milieu: but, to many, indispensable.

XV

The Fifth Arrondissement

The Jardin des Plantes. Robert Morton photograph

Many of the *arrondissements* of Paris have a continuity of tone that extends from one boundary to the other. The 1ˢᵗ, the 6ᵗʰ, the 7ᵗʰ, and the 8ᵗʰ all stand for specific activities, specific attitudes of mind; and as for the 16ᵗʰ, it is so distinct that the remark "Ça fait très Seizième" has a universal implication—that of a formality fixed once and for all—and can be applied indifferently to a hat, a sheet of writing paper, an automobile, a way of entertaining, or a tone of voice. The somber 19ᵗʰ and the rude but savorous 20ᵗʰ have also a cohesion of their own.

No such unity marks the 5ᵗʰ *arrondissement*. It includes, of course, the Latin Quarter, but the Latin Quarter is only a part of it. An address in the 5ᵗʰ does not by any means imply participation in *la vie de Bohème*, nor does the view from that address necessarily give on to a row of semirusticated garrets. It may embrace any one of a great variety of

townscapes: a tannery, an arm of the Seine, a laboratory, a seventeenth-century hospital, a Roman arena, a market the size of Smithfield in London, a greenhouse, or a mosque. It is, in fact, one of the richest and most concentrated parts of Paris. Dead ground, in the shape of nineteenth-century residential avenues, is rare. In its place there is a breadth and vitality that carry the visitor in two paces from the intellectual eminence of an Henri Bergson or an Auguste Comte to the daydreams of a transplanted Moroccan or the irreducible prosperity of the sole Parisian agent for Pommard or Pomméry.

The 5th *arrondissement* is the rendezvous of the scholar, the botanist, the cleric, the Sinophile, the tanner, the bowls player, the trade unionist, and the tramp. There are cafés in which you can sit all day over the philosophy of Malebranche, and cafés in which you would be unwise to sit at all. Your neighbor in the restaurants on the Quai de Montebello may be a Tunisian laundryman, a furrier, an all-in wrestler, or a Professor of the Collège de France. The 5th never yields its last surprise. Architecturally, it suffered as any part of Paris from the decrees of Haussmann; yet the persevering visitor will find many surprising things—a seventeenth-century farmhouse at 262, Rue Saint-Jacques, an eighteenth-century pavilion at No. 269 in the same forbidding street, the fastidious ironwork that faces one of the nightclubs in the Rue de la Harpe, the manorial graces of Anne of Austria's wing of the Val-de-Grâce, and the smell of the souks just north of Saint Séverin.

Geographically, the 5th is bounded by the Boulevard Saint-Michel, the Boulevard Port-Royal, the Boulevard Saint-Marcel, and the Seine. Its main features are the Panthéon, the university quarter, the Val-de-Grâce, the lately upgraded medieval hovels between the Boulevard Saint-Germain and the Seine, the Jardin des Plantes, and the reeking, evocative area of the tanneries. In the middle of it is the curving hump of the Montagne Sainte-Geneviève, which has been for some eight hundred and fifty years the sanctuary of French intelligence. There is nothing across the English Channel that corresponds to this quarter: it is as if Eton, Harrow, Oxford, Cambridge, Manchester Grammar School, the London School of Economics, and the Royal Institute of International Affairs were all bundled into an area less than a mile square. Education elsewhere is diffuse, and seems haphazard, when we compare it with the concentration of intellectual power that has marked the 5th since Abelard first broke away from the Ecole de Cloître Notre-Dame. Good schools in England have to flatter themselves that once a Kirke White or a John Dyer graced their classrooms; but in the 5th a school can number Bossuet, Voltaire, Molière, Baudelaire, and Paul Claudel among its former pupils and take it as a matter of course. The French examination system makes most others look undemanding, and even those who feel that

View of Paris from M. Fournel's Turret on the Rue des Boulangers Saint-Victor. Louis-Nicolas de Lespinasse, 1786
Above: Looking north
Opposite: Looking south

it sometimes confuses education with instruction must pause in awe before the intellectual history of this dumpy hillock.

No such reverence need be paid, however, to the buildings that now comprise this intellectual powerhouse. The Sorbonne is ugly beyond belief. Nor do the great schools of the quarter aspire to beauty. There is little to be said either for, or about, the erections that bear many of the greatest names in European education. Their aspect is penitential. The area may be, as the Goncourts remarked, "the wet nurse of learning and the Vatican of letters"; but it has changed very considerably since they tossed off these phrases. Nothing remains but the lay of the land and those vestiges that are the delight of the antiquarian.

The visitor may wish, for example, to pay his respects to the Collège de Dormans-Beauvais, in which Boileau and Cyrano de Bergerac were students and Saint François-Xavier once taught philosophy. But he will find, when he reaches 9 bis, Rue Jean-de-Beauvais, that the college, having served after the Revolution as a town hall, an arsenal, a hospital, a music school, and a garrison, was razed to the ground in 1880. Only by penetrating into what is now the Romanian orthodox church will he discover certain elements of the chapel in which Rollin preached and Saint François meditated.

Frustrations of this kind beset the intellectual tourist at every turn. There is no better example than the Collège Coqueret, whose entrance was in the Impasse Chartière. The Collège Coqueret could claim to be the birthplace of French as a classical language. Of the seven poets who formed the Pléiade in 1549, four were members of this College—Dorat, its principal, Ronsard, Joachim du Bellay, and Antoine de Baif. It was at the Collège Coqueret that Ronsard, stricken with deafness at the age of twenty, remained for six years as a pupil of Dorat. His studies were intensive even by French standards; but, unlike many gladiators of the examination room, he carried his talents intact into life. The history of the Pléiade is not strictly part of the history of Paris; but the eclecticism of Ronsard, the antipuritanism, the passion for novelty—all these (and, with them, his fascination for certain ladies of high fashion) are so much in keeping with the capital that it is tempting to regard Ronsard as the first truly Parisian writer.

When Sainte-Beuve set out, in the 1820s, to write on Ronsard he pointed, among other things, to his effect upon French diction: "There was no such thing in France," he said, "as a really expressive vocabulary. Ronsard needed one, and he set to work to devise it. He created new words and reanimated old ones. Sometimes—though less often than people supposed—he borrowed whole phrases from Latin and Greek. He drew upon the early French romances, upon dialect (Picard, Wallon, Merceau, Lyonnais, Limousin), and upon many arts and trades (hunting, falconry, seamanship, and the craft of the goldsmith); he took, unhesitatingly, whatever seemed useful for his purpose; and he turned, too, to popular speech, used it most deftly . . . until the French language seemed to have recovered its independence, and to stand, in vigor, second to none." When we return to Paris after a few months' absence, there are always new turns of phrase to surprise us; the French language ticks up like a taximeter. For those who value this vitality, the Collège Coqueret is holy ground—holy, but barren, for there remains nothing of the original buildings.

The Sorbonne is not one of those universities to which there is attached a powerful and legendary personality. To say of someone that he has "an Oxford accent" means something. But to say of a Frenchman that he has "a Sorbonne accent" does not. The adjective *normalien* is perfectly comprehensible when applied to the kind of intelligence—dry, nimble, skeptical, and disciplined—that is perfected at the Ecole Normale Supérieure. *Sorbonnard* has not, to my knowledge, any such clear connotation. Taine, Michelet, Baudelaire, Musset, Sainte-Beuve, Bergson have all won prizes at the Sorbonne; none of them has left any determining stamp upon it.

Nor is there a way of life that we can recognize as characteristic of the Sorbonne. "A Sorbonne luncheon party"—no, the phrase will not do at all. There may at one time have been some semblance of an academic circle in the area, with savants toiling up the slopes from one argumentative salon to the next, but the housing shortage has changed all that. People no longer live where they wish to, and the Professors of the Sorbonne are among those least able, in this respect, to defend themselves. No longer have they first claim upon those hilltop rooms within sight of the tinkling mosque; the apartments shaded by tall trees on the west side of the Jardins du Luxembourg have been taken by plausible Bolivians; and an international civil servant has ousted them from the sixth-floor apartments on the Quai aux Fleurs. Taste and convenience now play no part in their choice of a lodging. They are lucky to doss down at the back of a dairy near the Porte de Versailles, or to share with a night watchman the almost windowless aeries of an office building near the Gare du Nord.

The Sorbonne is, in fact, a thinking-shop with no worldly appurtenances. There is no poetry in it: nothing for eye, or ear, or nose: no centenarian lawns, no bells (as Virginia Woolf once said) "like porpoises turning in oil," no breeze of syringa, nothing but intellectual energy in its purest, most absolute form. This energy is not confined to the lecture room, as it often is in England. Paris is the center of France, and although the University is not the center of Paris its reverberations are felt throughout the capital in a way that academics from elsewhere may well envy. From Renan to Sartre and Lévi-Strauss, it is the university lecturer who has knocked everyone sideways. It is he who sets the pace. To men like Taine and Bergson, our approach to literature would seem halfhearted and amateurish. This is a city in which writers feel it their duty to ride their talents right into the ground. As Renan said to a young Oxford graduate, "You Englishmen think of Paris as a great fair, a place of frivolity and amusement. I tell you it is nothing of the sort. It is the hardest working place in the world." Our habits seem to them desultory and slack, for they are still ruled by the spirit of the great Benedictine scholars, and there is something in each of them of the spirit that compelled Ducange, for example, to work for fourteen hours on his wedding day.

All this is not easy for the casual visitor to seize. There is no point in denying that most lectures are dull. Not every generation has its Renan. ("I see him," H. A. L. Fisher wrote in his fragmentary memoirs, "a fat, squat, broad-shouldered old man, looking like a benevolent toad, who rolls into a crowded little lecture-room, seats himself at the end of a table, where he opens an old Hebrew Bible, and then with a look round his audience of professors, students, and ladies of fashion, pours out a stream of vivid, malicious, melodious French, to the accompaniment of intermittent chuckles of delight from his enthralled audience.") But there are still, very occasionally, lecturers of this order, and it is for the curious visitor to smell them out.

The Sorbonne buildings were entirely rebuilt between 1885 and 1901. Inauspicious numerals! The myth of French good taste has never been more thoroughly exploded than in this lugubrious congeries. The historian of *l'art pompier* may take a perverse pleasure in the wall paintings of Flameng, Weerts, Merson, Clairin, Brouillet, Chartran, Dewambez, Lerolle, Aubertin, Soitoux, Craux, Toudouze, Saulo, and Allouard; but it is doubtful that tourists normally constituted will do so. This vast scheme of patronage could not have fallen at a more unhappy moment in the history of French art. Even allowing for the universal blindness of academic persons in matters of art, it would surely be difficult to pick a worse team; the names of Eugène Carrière and Puvis de Chavannes merely set off the obscurity of their companions. Neither to the buildings nor to the decoration of the Sorbonne will the visitor turn in grateful reminiscence.

Only in the Eglise de la Sorbonne does there linger some part of the dignity that Richelieu bestowed upon the University. This church, like much else that gives pleasure in Paris, was built by Jacques Lemercier. It differs from most churches in having two ceremonial façades—one facing, though not at all involved in, the democratic bustle of the Boulevard Saint-Michel, and the other giving on to the solemn quiet of the main courtyard of the Sorbonne. In other respects it is not an original building. Anthony Blunt in his classic study of French architecture caught Lemercier out in what is almost an exact copy of Rosato Rosati's plan for the church of San Carlo di Catinari in Rome. Not only does the ground plan, with its central dome, its nave and choir of equal size, its shallow transepts, and four rectangular side chapels almost entirely correspond to it, but the dome itself has features that occur nowhere else but in San Carlo. All but the most censorious will condone this, for it has endowed Paris with a design of Roman amenity. The façade on the courtyard, with its free-standing classical portico, its urns and statues, and the elaborate cartouche that encloses the arms of Richelieu, has a suavity flawed only by that ever-disturbing feature: the French nineteenth-century municipal clockface.

The dome is the first in date of those that now embellish the Parisian skyline. With the four octagonal lanterns at its base, the winged figures that ornament the top of each pilaster (these, unlike the statues on the north façade, were not replaced in the nineteenth century), the slate-roofed cupola, and the elegant lantern above, Lemercier's dome should have been to the Sorbonne what the dome of the Radcliffe Camera is to Oxford: an aristocrat among equals. In fact, of course, it is nothing of the kind. Even the church beneath it is little more than the carcass of the church that Richelieu knew. The Eglise de la Sorbonne is a distinguished victim of the Revolution, and one that has never recovered from it. Lists drawn up in 1793 allow us to glimpse what the interior must then have been like.

From the beginning there must have been a premonitory gloom in the dark, damp, and lofty building. Marble, bronze, and a forest of white statues cannot altogether have relieved it. The great altar with its Corinthian columns, its white marble crucifix, and the golden sun that cost Richelieu twenty thousand livres—none of these could quite lighten an atmosphere that in the view of Lemercier's contemporaries evoked a foretaste of the grave. Painters were called in, among them Richelieu's favorite, Philippe de Champaigne, whose frescoes may still be glimpsed. The church was looted during the Revolution, and nothing remains but the tomb of Richelieu. This masterwork of Girardon was designed to stand in the middle of the choir, on the north axis of the church. Girardon was an eminently professional artist, and a good deal of his intention has been lost by the transference of the tomb to the transept. There remains, however, a haunting magnificence in this funereal group, which now seems to have been thrust aside in the course of some vast general process of desolation.

Intellectual passion is all very well, but there are times when even the gravest among us may weary of paying homage to Robert de Sorbon. Humanity strives beneath a noble star in the 5th, but it is a star that casts little light for the casual visitor. The Law School, the Chemical Institution, the Pedagogical Museum, the Deaf-Mute Institution, the Faculty of Science (Annexe), and the Institute of Agronomy make dusty walking. At these moments of weakness, the Mosque, the Arènes de Lutèce, and the Jardin des Plantes put forth an irresistible charm.

The Mosque is not, in point of fact, a convincing addition to the monuments of Paris. It brings an element of the Colonial Exhibition which strikes unhappily in a quarter where the plight of the North Africans has been anything but picturesque; but on a fine

The west façade of the
Eglise de la Sorbonne.
Jacques Lemercier,
begun 1635

*The Tomb of Cardinal
Richelieu.* François
Girardon, 1675–94

Marc and Constantine.
After Jean-Baptiste Huet
"Lions brought from
Africa and tamed by
their keeper, Felix
Cassal, with their little
ones, born at the
Museum of Natural
History, 18 Brumaire,
year 9." The date is our
8 November 1801.

afternoon there is pleasure to be had from the enclosed garden, with its Hispano-Maur-esque decoration and long-shadowed minaret. The second- or third-century Roman arena, not five minutes away, is another incongruity, but one that has weathered into the daily life of Paris. Its sandy floor serves admirably for *boules;* shrubs and grasses are not dis-couraged; the general feeling is friendly and provincial. The Arènes are of local interest only; and the Parisian, with his great gift of disparagement, is not the man to rank them higher than they deserve.

The Jardin des Plantes is not much visited by foreigners. The Gare d'Austerlitz, most secretive of stations, is at its gates, but in general its surroundings are somber and inaccessible. (Taxi drivers, on hearing the name, have been known to demand a double fare.) Its *fidèles*—and they are many—live near to it, and its aspect on a summer afternoon is that of a public garden in some dilapidated spa. It is mercifully un-up-to-date. Its scale, and to a large extent its appearance, are the same as they were when Buffon was in charge of it. Menagerie, aquarium, and botanical gardens are man-sized and unpretentious. Buf-fon's labyrinth would not deceive a child of two. But the Jardin is what it always was: a monument to disinterested curiosity.

It was founded in the 1630s. The original idea was provided by Jean Héroard, who was Louis XIII's doctor from childhood onward and the author of a journal that at times makes Boswell's seem circumspect. The first Director, Guy de la Brosse, made the Jardin not a park but a place of serious study; and during the next two hundred and fifty years Buffon, Bernardin de Saint-Pierre, Geoffroy Saint-Hilaire, Lamarck, Cuvier, Gay-Lussac, and others made it one of the finest things of its kind in the world.

As a promenade, it has known many vicissitudes. It was always a little out of the way, at the unfashionable extremity of Paris. The quarter was one of the poorest and most low-spirited in the city. Respectable dejection was its keynote, and the Jardin des Plantes

310

had its share of it. But in the 1820s it enjoyed one of those bursts of celebrity that are especially Parisian. This it owed to its menagerie.

The menagerie had been established some thirty years earlier. The author of *Paul et Virginie* had argued its case with his usual lofty straight-faced eloquence. He invoked the ancient authors; he argued that tourists would come in their thousands to see a hyena; he reminisced among his own experiences of the tropics; and he conjured, for his readers' delight, the image of an ideal republic in which pelican would play with bulldog and tiger lie down with seal. Duty had led him to inspect the remains of the royal menagerie at Versailles. There he had examined the rhinoceros. A most curious monster! And one that offered a new combination of forms: notably "le membre génital tourné en arrière, par lequel nous lui vîmes lancer au loin son urine, comme un jet d'eau."

These considerations proved decisive, and before long the Jardin des Plantes rated twenty-two pages in Galignani's *Paris Guide*. It was, however, the affair of the giraffe that made it, in 1825, the most sought after of Parisian recreations. The giraffe in question was a present to Charles X from Mehemet Ali. Its journey from Egypt was long and painful but, thanks to a diet of fresh milk, it arrived in splendid trim. So great was its success with the Parisians that even politics were forgotten when the animal was served lunch from a first-floor window. Dressmakers, chansonniers, potters, and poets combined to praise the giraffe; spotted materials, long thin necks, and an air of timorous surprise were sported by all who could muster them. Other animals shared in the overflow of warm feeling, and poets were even found to praise

le grave bison au regard sérieux

and

l'onagre du désert, fils de la Palestine.

Opposite: *The Giraffe in the Jardin des Plantes*
"This giraffe, two and a half years old, thirteen feet high, was sent by the Egyptian Pasha to the King of France. The first live giraffe in Europe, it was presented to the King on 9 July 1827 at Saint-Cloud."

Below: *Jardin des Plantes*. Gustave Doré, 1850s

LA GIRAFE,

Agée de 2 ans et demi, haute de 13 pieds, envoyée au Roi de France par le Pacha d'Egypte.
Elle est la première amenée vivante en Europe; elle a été présentée au Roi le 9 Juillet 1827,
à Saint-Cloud.

LA GIRAFE A LA MODE. -- Air: *A la façon de Barbari.*

On parle souvent aujourd'hui
De nouvelle méthode;
A la Girafe, chacun dit:
Faut se mettre à la mode;
Tout le monde prend le bon ton,
La faridondaine, la faridondon,
On s'met à la Girafe ici, biribi,
A la façon de Barbari, mon ami.
On n'est jamais bien habillé
Dans le siècle où nous sommes,
Si l'on n'est pas bien costumé
Au genre qu'on renomme.

A la Jazo n'est plus de saison,
La faridondaine, la faridondon,
A la Girafe on habille ici, biribi,
A la façon, etc.
Des tètes de toute façon
On imprime au plus vîte;
Robin des bois n'est plus d'saison,
Tout un chacun le quitte;
Grand falbala, et grands frisons,
La faridondaine, la faridondon,
Ajoutez la Girafe aussi, biribi,
A la façon, etc.

Filles et femmes d'aujourd'hui
Ont très-belle tournure,
Tout un chacun en est séduit
Voyant leur chevelure:
On peigne beaucoup de frisons,
La faridondaine, la faridondon,
Tout est à la Girafe ici, biribi,
A la façon, etc.
Chapeau de paille surmonté
De rubans, de panaches,
Colerette, corset moncé
Qui souvent rien ne cache.

On croit quelquefois qu'c'est du bon ton,
La faridondaine, la faridondon,
Tout s'fait à la Girafe ici, biribi,
A la façon, etc.
Pour les modes en vérité
On ne sait plus que faire;
On a toujours beau rechercher,
L'on ne sait comment plaire:
Café, musique et chanson,
La faridondaine, la faridondon,
Enseigne à la Girafe aussi, biribi,
A la façon de Barbari, etc.

MONTBÉLIARD, de l'Imprimerie de DECKHER; et à LYON, au dépôt, chez P. RUNZ, Libraire, rue Lafuerie p.° 12.

Course in Comparative Anatomy in the Jardin des Plantes. Gustave Doré, 1850s

Children in the Jardin des Plantes, c. 1910. Seeberger Frères photograph

But such things pass, and nowhere quicker than in Paris; before long the Jardin des Plantes was once again the preserve of locals and lovers—and also of painters and sculptors like Delacroix and Barye, who found in its captive lions a bodily magnificence and an innate pride that are all too rare among human beings.

The Hôpital de la Salpêtrière is not strictly in the 5th, but in the adjacent 13th. It belongs, however, to pathology rather than to proletarian busyness, and I make no apology for hauling it across the border. Except for the Hôpital Saint-Louis, it is the grandest of seventeenth-century hospitals; but there hangs about it a stench of violence, madness, and decay, which many visitors find forbidding. Its buildings, designed originally by Libéral Bruant and later extended by Le Vau, are at once majestic and lugubrious. The majesty is implicit in the seignorial layout—the massive chapel with its octagonal dome and eight-fold nave, the three-story façade, the somber inner courtyards, and the valiant little *jardins à la française*. But the Salpêtrière was a prison, as much as a hospital. Beggars and vagabonds were admitted to it, and put to labor as hard as they seemed fit for. Prostitutes and deportees were collected there (Manon Lescaut among them). At one time, no fewer than eight thousand persons were imprisoned in the Salpêtrière, and taxes on theaters, wine, and salt were levied to help keep up the cumbrous establishment. The quarters reserved for madwomen would have surfeited Géricault himself; the prisoners were kept in chains, often with water up to their ankles and a hardy company of rats. The Salpêtrière is not a building that can be looked at for its architecture alone. Its past has marked it; and its secret museum is reputed to be more horrific even than that of Scotland Yard.

The waterfront of the 5th is as varied as the *arrondissement* itself. Returning from the Jardin des Plantes, the visitor comes upon a stretch that is at once distinguished, pictorial, and decrepit. The Quai de la Tournelle and the Quai de Montebello have something of everything: a garage, a Public Assistance Museum (less dull than it sounds), the last of the zinc-topped bookstalls, a celestial view of Notre-Dame, the Tour d'Argent, and until lately the most heterogeneous animal shop in Paris. (Next the first-edition shop there was

Corner of the Rue Valette and Panthéon, March, 1925. Eugène Atget photograph

Interior of the Panthéon.
Jacques-Germain
Soufflot, 1755–92. A. F.
Kersting photograph

a guinea pig in a cage, with ferret, hedgehog, civet, and raccoon for its neighbors.) Prize-fighters and Algerians know this stretch of the waterfront; the privet hedges and the young white wines remember the Canal de la Loire, and on the cobbled walk along the river's edge the bracken lies thick and spiky—not so spiky, however, as to prevent one or two veterans of the open air from taking their ease upon it with a bottle of some unnameable *pinard* at hand. Great individualists, these, who may at times be seen locked in violent combat, only to fall and lie, as if dead, face downward on the cobbles; in brighter moments they exchange with the crew of each passing barge a series of alembicated greetings.

Above, the bookstalls string out beneath the tall trees and the traffic, delivered from the narrows of the Quai des Grands-Augustins, instantly doubles its pace. The good restaurants move upstairs, and the streets that run back from the Seine become mere slots in the old side of the city. It is from here, rather than from the shelving Rue Soufflot, that one can appreciate the virtues of the Panthéon.

The Panthéon is the most prominent building in the 5th, and it can be seen from a great distance. It has a splendid aridity; nobody has ever admired it, few people care much about the august ashes or moldering bones that lie beneath it, and it doesn't seem like a church, or like a pagan temple, or indeed like anything in particular except a half-baked and timidly rebaked general idea. The concept of a Pantheon, in which the great and the

Laying the First Stone of Sainte-Geneviève. Pierre-Antoine Demachy

What is now called the Panthéon was originally the Eglise Sainte-Geneviève, designed by Jacques-Germain Soufflot at the request of Louis XV. The first stone of the new church was laid by the King himself in 1764. To add luster to the occasion, the painter Pierre-Antoine Demachy and one of his colleagues painted a full-scale replica of the projected façade, complete with *trompe l'œil* effects.

good are brought together after death, is attractive to many ardent natures; but in practice it rarely works very well. The visitor to San Croce in Florence sees the names of Dante, Machiavelli, and Rossini; but the tablets do not persuade us that all that is best and rarest in human nature has been gathered within four walls. If this is the case with Dante, how much more firmly can it be said of the strange rabble in the Panthéon! Soufflot's building is arresting, but inhuman; the wall paintings (Puvis excepted) are disastrous; and the selection of *grands inhumés* reflects the chaos and diversity of French life in the last hundred and fifty years. Voltaire and Rousseau, Hugo and Zola, Gambetta and Jaurès are strangely assorted; and stranger still is the collection of "public men" who have been stowed away beneath the vast, dull-echoing, unfurnished nave. Lazare, Sadi Carnot, Doumer, Painlevé, Langevin . . . the building that can shelter them all does not stand for anything, except the will to house, somehow and somewhere, public figures for whom a state funeral seemed necessary at the time.

But for all this, the Panthéon can provide an unwary walker with more than one magniloquent surprise. Where most of the Montagne Sainte-Geneviève has an air, at best, of learned poverty, the colossal dome and encircling columns of the Panthéon introduce an element of cold-hearted majesty that I, for one, never fail to relish. And the faceless brick walls that tower at the end of the little streets running to north and south of the Panthéon—these, too, have their impressive side. There are greater fiascos than the Panthéon.

Its colossal bulk now tends, of course, to assimilate everything around it to its own scale. The ceremonial approach along the Rue Soufflot plays up to this; and so, in their way, do the Mairie of the 5th *arrondissement* and the Bibliothèque Sainte-Geneviève, which date from the 1840s but continue the monumental tradition of Soufflot. In all these buildings there is an element of display that is quite foreign to the real traditions of the quarter. Not only is there a desire to impress, but there is even, in the Bibliothèque Sainte-Geneviève, a desire to make things pleasant and comfortable. The wide corridors, the learned and agreeable staff, the abundance of works of art—all this would have seemed unbelievable to those who, like Calvin, Erasmus, and Ignatius Loyola, had once lived on

that very site. Aquinas, Leibnitz, Jean-Jacques Rousseau, Watteau, and no doubt many another former resident in the quarter would not recognize our Place du Panthéon as representative of the 5th that they knew. For that particular flavor we must press out and downward from the monumental summit of the Montagne.

The Rue Valette, due north from the Panthéon, has existed under one name or another since the end of the eleventh century. At No. 4 there stands the Collège Sainte-Barbe, the only survivor of the *collèges* of the Montagne Sainte-Geneviève and the oldest public school in France. At No. 21 is the Collège de Fortet, which still has its Gothic cellars and the hexagonal tower that is named after Calvin. At No. 19 there are medieval cellars in which Huguenots took refuge on Saint Bartholomew's Day; and the street as a whole, though ennobled at No. 7 by a seventeenth-century hotel of unusual magnificence, contrives to be decrepit without being forlorn. The quintessence of the quarter is, however, to be found in the church of Saint-Etienne-du-Mont.

This building has now the air of an appendage or dower house to the great bulk of the Panthéon, but for several hundred years it stood free on the hilltop, with the abbey church of Sainte-Geneviève beside it and trees to cast their shadows on the square. There was a view across to open country, horsemen passed at a trot, and the general feeling was nearer to that of an English cathedral close than would today seem possible. Saint-Etienne-du-Mont is not one of those churches that delight us by their harmony of form. It is built in several styles, and the west façade does not even accord with the axis of the nave. The stone varies in color and texture from the salutary darkness of charcoal to the flat gray of pumice and the high polish of silver. Essentially a flamboyant Gothic church, Saint-Etienne-du-Mont was refaced by Claude Guérin in the seventeenth century, and its medieval rose window stands above a monumental four-columned portico and beneath a curved pediment of belated Renaissance design. The clock-and-bell tower dates from the sixteenth century, and inside the church the large and sumptuous rood screen of the same century suggests the hand of Philibert de l'Orme. There is some fine seventeenth-century glass and, most precious of all for the enthusiast of the seventeenth century, there are the tombs of Pascal and Racine, who contributed as much as any two Frenchmen in history to our knowledge of human nature. Here, and not across the way, is the true Panthéon of Paris.

It is a long pull up the Rue Saint-Jacques, and the visitor who climbs up to No. 269 will find little but the shell of the Chapelle du Couvent des Bénédictins Anglais, in which James II and his elder daughter were buried. He will find, in fact, that the chapel was converted, after many previous manipulations, into the concert hall of the Schola Cantorum. The reputation of this school has dimmed a little with time; so close was its association with the disciples of César Franck (most particularly with Vincent d'Indy, who took a leading part in its activities from its foundation in 1896 until his death in 1931) that it has shared in the general disregard that now surrounds that ponderous group of men. D'Indy himself—with his militarism, his anti-Semitism, his anti-Dreyfusism, his vile temper, and the obstinate dullness of his own compositions—is not an attractive figure. The Schola Cantorum is, nonetheless, important in the history of French taste; for it was there, and at d'Indy's instigation, that there was revealed to the French public the threefold riches of Palestrina, Gregorian chant, and the music of the French seventeenth and eighteenth centuries. The true stature of Rameau, Lalande, and Marc-Antoine Charpentier was recognized there; and d'Indy was also responsible for the resuscitation of one of the greatest of all operas: Monteverdi's *Orfeo*.

This is reason, therefore, for some friendly attention as we pass No. 269.

It is on its southern boundary that the 5th hides its noblest ornament: the church and hospital of the Val-de-Grâce. Whereas the Panthéon stands on high ground and can be glimpsed from a great distance, the Val-de-Grâce—in every way the more distinguished of the two—is seen only by those who seek it out. It stands in a part of Paris that was for a long time little more than a vast lazar-house; but when it was begun (by François Mansart in 1645) it stood in open fields, and as late as the 1760s it was the center of a large area of countrified Church properties. Life had a brisk and healthy complexion in this all-but-Alpine region. Affluence and holy living for once went together, and the Val-de-Grâce, itself an abbey of the grandest proportions, had for neighbors the Capucins, the Bénédic-

Studio of a Ceramicist, Rue Saint-Jacques, 1910–11. Eugène Atget photograph

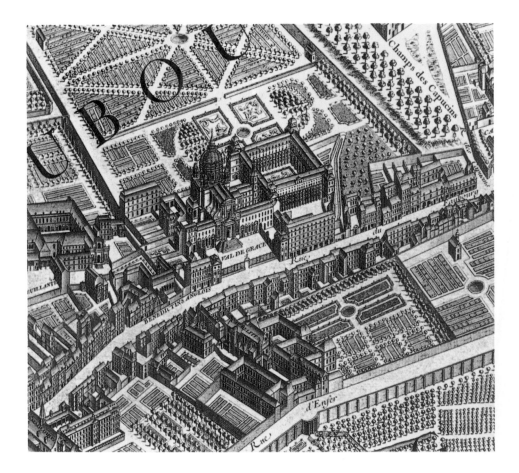

The Val-de-Grâce, from
the *Plan Turgot*, 1738

tins Anglais, the Feuillantines, the Carmelites, and the Visitandines. The maps of the
time give some idea of the scale of these properties: the ample courtyards, the parklands
of ten, twenty, and thirty acres, the imposing chapels, and, at a respectful distance, the
high road into Paris, along which trundled daily importations of wine, sugar, salt fish,
spices, wool, and hemp.

It is in this context that the Val-de-Grâce should be examined. Its tone today is as
much military as holy. David d'Angers's statue of Baron Larrey, a renowned military
surgeon in the time of Napoleon, sets the general note. The Abbey buildings were taken
over by the Army Medical service in 1793, the benevolent wraiths of the seventeenth
century were drummed out of the precincts, and the occupation still continues today. We
have to force ourselves to remember that the Visitandines were founded by Saint François
de Sales, and that Madame de Sévigné often used to visit her daughter there; that in the
garden of the Feuillantines, immediately to the north of the Val-de-Grâce, Victor Hugo
played as a child. (Long afterward he wrote:

> Je te raconte aussi comment aux Feuillantines
> Jadis tintaient pour moi les cloches argentines.
> Puis tu me vois du pied pressant l'escarpolette
> Qui d'un vieux marronier fait crier la squelette . . .
>
> Le jardin était grand, profond, mystérieux,
> Fermé par de hauts murs aux regards curieux.)

Within a few yards of the Val-de-Grâce there lived, at one time or another, Pasteur,
Lamennais, George Sand, La Fontaine, and the part-author of *Le Roman de la Rose*. Louise
de la Vallière retired to the Carmelite convent in 1674 when she was supplanted by the
Marquise de Montespan as mistress of Louis XIV; and there, some months later, Bossuet
preached one of his most marmoreal sermons. The funeral service for François I was held
in the Chapelle de Notre-Dame-des-Champs. The Hôtel de Clagny, once the property of
the architect Pierre Lescot, was bought in 1625 for the Abbaye de Port-Royal-des-Champs.

There was, in fact, hardly a pole or a perch in this region of Paris that had not,

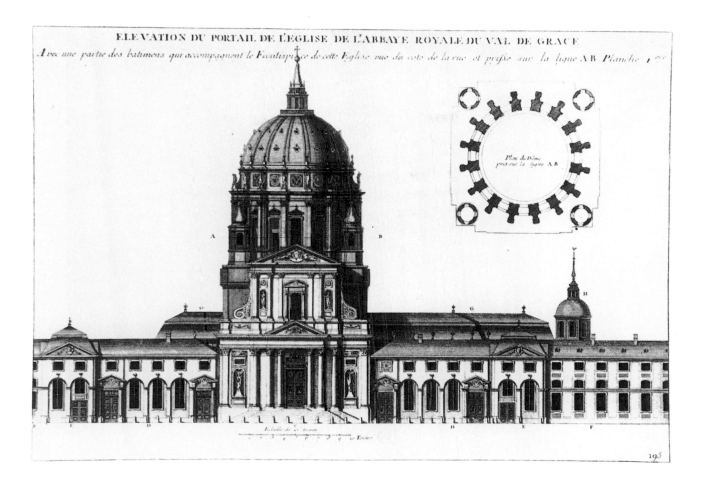

ELEVATION DU PORTAIL DE L'EGLISE DE L'ABBAYE ROYALE DU VAL DE GRACE

Avec une partie des batimens qui accompagnent le Frontispice de cette Eglise vue du coté de la rue et prise sur la ligne A B Planche 1.er

Eglise du Val-de-Grâce.
Jean Marot, 17th
century

somewhere about it, the odors of sanctity, wealth, and high breeding. None of this is much in evidence today. The well-born nuns have moved elsewhere; the Abbaye de Port-Royal has become a maternity hospital; the gardens of maize and lavender have been torn up and tenements built in their place; and our own century has contributed only a museum of wounds in the head.

There remains, however, the arresting beauty of the Val-de-Grâce itself. It alone, among the abbeys of Paris, has kept its seventeenth-century buildings intact; and even today, after three hundred years of gradual dilapidation, it retains its original aristocratic distinction. (Anthony Blunt remarks, of the dominant central domed space, with its three equal apses for choir and transepts, that "this arrangement is quite unlike anything that has been built in France up to this time, and seems to derive from Palladio's Il Redentore in Venice.") The Val-de-Grâce, though completed by Lemercier, Le Muet, and Le Duc, was planned by François Mansart, who was responsible for the layout of the church and for its construction up to the entablatures of the nave and the lower story of the façade.

Lemercier had, of course, only just completed the Eglise de la Sorbonne, whose more delicate façade looks almost feminine when contrasted with the thrustful power of Mansart's heavy double columns and richly plastic modeling. Paris has many fine domes, but that of the Val-de-Grâce has a controlled exuberance that is unique. It was commissioned by Anne of Austria to celebrate the birth, after twenty-two years of marriage, of her first son, the future Louis XIV; and no building could do so more aptly, for it has precisely the unforced grandeur that was to distinguish the monarch himself. The prince was born in 1638; but already since 1621 the Queen had installed a company of Benedictine nuns on the site of the Abbey, and was herself using the property both as a country retreat and as an accommodation address for her secret correspondence.

The Abbey bears many emblems of its first beginnings: the two founders of the Benedictine Order, Saint Benoît and his sister Sainte Scholastique, appear on either side of the portico. Anne of Austria herself is seen, in Mignard's mammoth fresco, proffering the model of the church to God; her initials form the motif of the marble pavement in the choir.

There are, of course, other Italianate churches in Paris; but they are confined by later buildings, whereas the Val-de-Grâce has still, on three of its four sides, the environ-

ment for which it was designed. The Abbey buildings have the character of a large country house, with a cloister added, and to the east an immense garden, or small park, with *parterre à la française,* fountain, and kitchen garden. Vineyard and meadows are gone, but in other respects the Abbey is complete—even to the private apartment of Anne of Austria, with its late Renaissance Ionic portico, and the sculptured pelican that symbolizes maternal love. And even at the topmost point of the dome, above the thirteen windows, there are touches of individual fancy.

The Abbey has yet to find, in modern times, the employment that would best befit its particular qualities. It has, in fact, been pursued by elements of the painful and the grotesque, which were manifested most memorably at the time of the Drolling scandal. This affair, like Drolling himself, is generally forgotten, yet it is one of the strangest in the history of art. Martin Drolling was a subject painter whose popularity survived into the reign of Louis XVIII; but this particular incident occurred at the time of the Revolution. One of the chapels behind the high altar in the Val-de-Grâce was known to be used as a repository for the hearts of deceased princes and princesses of France. In 1792 some forty-five such relics were preserved there—among others, the hearts of Henriette d'Angleterre, Marie-Thérèse, the wife of Louis XIV, Philippe I of France, and Queen Marie Leczinska, the wife of Louis XV. The chapel was desecrated by the revolutionaries and the hearts were put up for sale. One was eaten by a Great Dane; another (that of the Grande Mademoiselle) exploded as a result of faulty embalming; but Drolling was able to lay hands on quite a number, and with these august organs he devised some part of the paint that he used for his big decorations in the Louvre and at Versailles.

Drolling is not represented in the little Musée du Service de Santé which forms so incongruous a part of the Abbey buildings; and indeed art, though smuggled in in the form of documentary subject pictures, has no place in this severe museum. The greater part of it—to which the ordinary visitor is not admitted—is taken up with a survey of the medical services in wartime from the year 1791 onward; but the tourist who perseveres will be rewarded with a visit to the private *pavillon,* now most tactfully restored, of the founder of the Abbey.

Once again, meanwhile, we must reckon with human frailty. The charms of the 5th may pall. Even a bison becomes wearisome in time; the visitor may have *pensées* of his own, quite as absorbing as Pascal's, which need to be thought out and thought through in an atmosphere less glacial than that of Saint-Etienne-du-Mont; the names of Curie and

The Eglise de Saint-Medard and the Rue Mouffetard. Robert Doisneau photograph

Au Port Salut, 2, Rue des Fossés-Saint-Jacques, 1903. Eugène Atget photograph

Marché des Patriarches.
André-Marie Chatillon,
c. 1835

Lavoisier may have lost their luster for him. How can he revive himself in the 5th? Not, perhaps, by a visit to the church of Saint-Médard, though that squat building mingles flamboyant Gothic with the *style Soufflot* in a way that will send a shiver of excitement down the spine of any ecclesiologist who may happen to venture inside it. Marxists may care to explore the Place Maubert and its surroundings, for to these there clings a certain savor of left-wing activity. It is, however, the tradition of poverty, rather than poverty itself, that haunts this region. In the same way the little streets between Place Maubert and the Seine have lost the diabolical vitality that they possessed even twenty years ago and become a kind of transplanted suburb of Casablanca.

No, it is probably in the Rue Mouffetard that the visitor will come nearest to reviving himself by contact with unpredictable Everyday. This narrow street has a Maubertian tradition of popular revolt; and it has an irrepressible secret life of its own—a life that has survived every attempt to regularize it. It is not only one of the best markets in Paris; it is the one that has the oddest and oldest concentration of human types. Every shade of propriety and impropriety can be found on its slopes; and the diversity, let us say, of cheese, or the multiplicity of early vegetables is uniformity itself when compared with the variegations of complexion and parlance and gait that will be revealed to the most casual stroller. I doubt if there is any other street in the world in which an eight-ounce croquette of foie gras can be bought with one hand and a *cornet de frites* with the other; or in which your neighbor at the bar may be either the General Secretary of the Académie Française or a starving Tunisian. And the noise of the Rue Mouffetard! It combines the monotony of Fez, the unending repetition of near-oriental cries, with what can be found only in Paris: the chop-chop of tongues that cut like the guillotine. As an introduction to Paris, few streets are more expressive than this companionable inferno.

XVI

The Ile de France

La Grenouillère. Pierre-Auguste Renoir, 1869

Paris ends at the gates of Paris, and is almost as self-contained, in this respect, as Lucca or Avila. But its vibrations may be felt for many miles—well into Burgundy, on one road at least, halfway to Rouen on another, as far as Beauvais, certainly, and some way into the battlefields of the Marne.

Every visitor, in fact, will form his own notion of the point at which Nature says "No" to the great city and reassumes control of the landscape. Unflawed perspectives are not the true criterion, for they can be found within a few miles of the capital. Even at Saint-Cloud, for instance, there are forest walks which have a desertedness—a quality of forlorn silence—that is preeminently non-Parisian. The first smallish town of truly independent character is a better landmark, but which one to choose? Versailles, Chantilly, Rambouillet, Fontainebleau? None will do, for all turn to Paris as a caged bird turns to the window. I myself would choose Meaux—an authentic provincial capital, though no more than twenty-five miles distant.

Open country, too, yields quickly to the contamination of Paris. The first part of any journey on the Fontainebleau road, for instance, is passed in one of the more degraded of European landscapes. The industrial suburbs of Paris—toward Saint-Denis, especially—await their Zola; and if this were a book of grave social intent there would be much to say about the conditions in which people live on the very edge of Paris, within sound of the outer boulevards. But if we press on, talking of other things, we come in time to one part or another of the Ile de France, which encircles Paris and gives it, besides wood, stone, water, butter, chalk, and cheese, a backdrop at once intimate and majestic.

Everyone has his own idea of how best to explore the Ile de France, and it must be said at once that it is not a matter in which improvisation pays off. The motorist can get lost in an industrial *maquis*, the patron of the Ligne de Sceaux get out at the wrong station, and the walker miss, by a hundred yards, the great building that he has set out to see. The Ile de France remains secret country, with forests of from thirty thousand acres upwards, crooked elbows of the Seine valley to destroy all sense of direction, and one or two "attractions" so compulsive that they drain off all but one visitor in a thousand. It is also, of course, commuter country and has not escaped the general standardization of French life. Anyone who proposes to potter northward on the electric train from Paris must remember that it is already a hundred years since Gérard de Nerval wrote: "How I bless the railway! An hour at most, and I am at Saint-Leu-la-Forêt. The route lies along the Oise, so calm and so green among its poplared islets, and I recognise the village names that are called out at every stopping-place, the horizon festooned with hillock and wood-land, the identifiable accent of the peasants who get in at one station and out at the next, and the way the girls do their hair."

We have lost, of course, the holy quiet, the traditional headdress, the distinguishable accent; but we can still savor the decrescendo of which Nerval wrote. The Oise valley, in particular, stands a little apart from modern life. When the express tears through the

A Suburb of Paris, Seen from a Height. Vincent van Gogh, 1887

village station like a panicked housewife, the umbrella-topped fishermen sit on, never stirring, as if waiting for Monet to paint them. It is as true today as it was in 1858 that— Nerval again—"Pontoise is one of those high-lying little towns which delight us with their matriarchal quality, their leafy walks, their 'extensive views,' and the continuance of certain ways of life that are not to be found elsewhere. People still play in the streets, and stop to talk, and sing in the evenings in front of their houses. Restaurateur and pastrycook are one and the same person, and his shop has still something of family life; every street is built like a staircase, and to clamber among them is the greatest fun. Along the promenade, which overlooks the magnificent valley where the Oise flows quietly by, pretty women and nice-looking children walk up and down. The visitor can glimpse, and envy as he passes, the peaceful, separate little world which keeps itself to itself in those old houses, beneath ancient trees, where the air is pure and 'every prospect pleases.' . . . What delights me about these small and ever so slightly derelict towns is that they remind me of the Paris I knew in my youth. The look of the houses, the layout of the shops, certain tricks of behavior, certain costumes. . . ."

There are other such towns. In Saint-Germain-en-Laye, for instance, and even in Versailles, life has an effaced distinction, a savor as of forty-year-old claret, which those who take their own excitement with them will find very agreeable. But there are towns that have given in altogether to the traffic which passes through them, and others where life seems to have been turned off at the tap. Another category must be distinguished: places that a famous restaurant, or a famous host or hostess, has corrupted. Small and ancient towns like Montfort l'Amaury can be made unrecognizable in a year or two if *le tout Paris* thinks well of them; and in many villages there is a house where on Sundays a weekend party cackles through the long forenoon as, one after another, the black limousines swing into the forecourt. It is not in the great houses, on the whole, that such things go on. The châteaux that get into the guidebooks are for the most part shuttered and still.

Street with People Walking and a Horsecar near the Ramparts. Vincent van Gogh, 1887

326

From top: *First-, Second-, and Third-Class Carriage.* Honoré Daumier, 1864

Cottage, mill house, pavilion, octagonal shooting lodge; these are the places where people amuse themselves in the Ile de France, and it is in a garden by Russell Page, not by Le Nôtre, that the handyman from the Veneto tends the English turf.

Altogether, therefore, the Ile de France takes knowing. Time spent with road map, timetable, and standard guide is never wasted. It is also a good plan never to be put off by the seeming difficulty of any particular journey, and almost never to refuse an invitation, for the Ile de France is a place in which the great rewards come by the way. No two people, in any case, see them as the same; and as the area is too large and too rich to allow of detailed study in a single chapter, it may be best to analyze it element by element.

Light, then, first: and air. There is in the atmosphere of the Ile de France a noble transparency which makes it, to a supreme degree, painters' country. Only Provence can rival it in the history of French art, and in Provence nature goes almost too far to meet the painter. Even van Gogh never painted better than at Auvers-sur-Oise; and as for the sky men, Pissarro, Sisley, and Monet, they found in the Ile de France a great dome of light, an impersonal vast that stretched, but did not dispute, their powers. The air is neither vaporous nor overbright: does nothing to force the painter's hand; retains, in fact, a classical moderation of tone. And as the landscape is on the whole reserved and undramatic in its implications, the eye looks instinctively to the immensities of the upper air. It is, after all, Baudelaire, the most Parisian of poets, who conjured for us in his prose poem "L'Etranger" the image of an enigmatic stranger who, loving neither father, mother, sister, brother, friends, country, money, nor idealized Beauty, cared only for "the clouds—

The Hermitage at Pontoise. Camille Pissarro, c. 1867

the clouds on the move . . . up there . . . up there . . . the marvelous clouds!" It is in the Ile de France that one sees such clouds.

Next, water. An island without water would be a strange thing, and the Ile de France is alive with rivers of every kind and size. It would be pointless in a book of this kind to stick too closely to legal or geographical boundaries. It is simpler and more profitable to say that the Ile de France has the shape of an irregular circle, and that the outline of this circle is adumbrated by the Eure, the Epte, the Thérain, the Autonne, the Ourcq, the Grand Morin, the Aubetin, the Voulzie, the Essonne, the Juine, and the Voise. The circle is traversed, meanwhile, by the Esches, the Sausseron, the Mauldre, the Chevreuse, the Yerre, the Bièvre, the Juine, and the Yvette. There is no such thing in France as an insignificant river, and each of these, we may be sure, has a character of its own. Nor have I yet listed the Seine, animator of the whole region, or the festive and plebeian Marne, or the pacific Oise.

To all these we must add the invented waters, if I may so call them, in which the area is so rich: the ponds, lakes, canals, and formal gardens. The great country palaces of the Ile de France owe much of their grandeur to the innumerable *bouches* that, at the touch of a button or the turn of a tap, direct a jet of water high into the air. Few private houses can ever have rivaled Versailles or Sceaux, but there are many which, like Chantilly or Fontainebleau in miniature, are to a certain extent waterborne and rise, in a dream of blue and silver *douves*, above a moat, a pond sluggish with carp, or a geometrical lake. The unwatered mansion is, in fact, an exception; and if we turn to the diminutive bowers of the present day we shall find that the first favorite, in the Ile de France, is a reconditioned mill house within sound of a disemployed river.

Water kept Paris going for centuries. The Essonne paper mills and the flour mills of Corbeil, the squat, heavy-paddled *moulins à bateaux* on the Marne, and the imposing Pont de Charenton, with its inhabited central section and four great turning wheels—all these made economical use of what, elsewhere, was turned to pleasure. (Nor should the hydromane ignore such inventions as the enormous artificial fishpond that victualed the Abbey of Les Vaux-de-Cernay.) But to most people the rivers of the Ile de France are pleasure places, and it is not by accident that in painting and in literature alike the river party has been the subject of many a marvelous evocation. I do not think that I am alone in finding the boating scene in Henry James's *The Ambassadors* one of the most beautiful things in all fiction. As for the freshwater pleasures of La Grenouillière, the most famous of nineteenth-century bathing places, Monet, Renoir, and Guy de Maupassant vied with one another as to who should best perpetuate them. The two painters were there in 1869, and La Grenouillière looks wonderful in their canvases. But perhaps there is lacking from them the element of rowdiness and near-burlesque on which Maupassant seized some fifteen years later. This is how he describes it in *Yvette.*

"They came upon it quite suddenly. The enormous flat-roofed boat was tied up at the bank, and on it was a great crowd of men and women—some sitting drinking at small tables, others standing about hallooing, singing, shouting from sheer excitement, or kicking up their legs to the sound of an out-of-tune piano. Big brown-haired girls, crupper and breasts at the *garde-à-vous!,* made their way among the crowds, catching an eye here, pouting with red lips there, foul-mouthed and well away in drink. Others broke into a wild dance before their half-naked cavaliers, most of whom wore linen trousers, a sleeveless cotton shirt, and a bright-colored cap such as jockeys sport. Over all hung the smell of sweat and rice-powder, perfume and armpits.

"As the drinks—white, red, yellow, and green—went hastily down, the drinkers set up a motiveless shouting and bellowing. What they wanted was noise for its own sake; what they felt was a brutish longing to be 'up to the ears' in it. Every few moments a bather would jump off the roof into the water, drenching the tables nearest to him and drawing a tumult of curses from the people sitting there. Meanwhile, the river itself was alive with boats. Long slender skiffs went skimming by and on the oarsmen's bare brown arms the muscles came and went. Their ladies, dressed in red or blue flannel, with open umbrellas to match, made a dazzling sight in the hot sunshine as they lay back, luxurious and still, in the stern. Other craft were clumsier, and there was one over-excited student who, wishing to show off, rowed with a windmill motion, bumped into every boat that

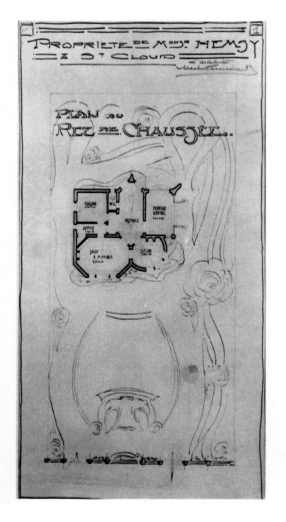

came near, got himself roughly abused for his pains, nearly drowned two swimmers who came within range, and eventually vanished from view amid general execration. . . ."

Bougival and its neighbors are very different now—one of Bougival's restaurants, for one thing, is about the most expensive in France—but there is still boating to be had, and those who make the pilgrimage to Berlioz's house on the Avenue Paul Doumer in Bougival may catch, perhaps, a diminished something of what Maupassant was talking about. The nearness of Paris has spoiled Bougival, but it has not spoiled places every bit as pleasant, and if you have an automobile, or a good head for a railroad map, you will soon find them.

Air, then: light: and water: the combination produced masterpieces like Seurat's *Baignade*. Add wood, and you have a mingling that few painters of the nineteenth century did not attempt at some time or another. And there is wood and to spare in the Ile de France, which was once one huge and inhospitable forest. In the Vexin and the Valois, the Gâtinais and the Brie, this original wildness has been cut away; it survives tamed and ennobled in the parks of Meudon and Saint Cloud, to name two only, and in forests like those of Marly, Carnelle, Halatte, and Fausses-Reposes. Rare is the country house in the Ile de France that has not great trees in attendance, or the auxiliary river that has not poplar and willow to shade it. If you climb, downstream from Paris, above the embanked and serpentine Seine, you will find that it is to the forests that the landscape owes its characteristic tone. They it is that give the simplest manor house its secret, seignorial element, and it is their shade that points up the peach-and-lavender brickwork and makes it a constant delight to the eye. The great forests of the Ile de France—Compiègne, Villers-Cotterets, Chantilly, Rambouillet, Fontainebleau, l'Isle-Adam—are grand enough to speak for themselves; what is less often noted is the skill with which the *Urwald* has been adapted to our own quasi-conversational purposes. Even Versailles, after all, can be seen, and experienced, as a deserted forest in which the big house has got a bit above itself.

Ground-floor plan for a villa at Saint-Cloud (above left), and design for a villa with figures (above right). Both by Hector Guimard, c. 1900–1905

The Road from Chailly to Fontainebleau. Claude Monet, 1864

The fourth great natural resource of the region is stone. It is from the Ile de France that a great part of Paris takes its complexion: the *pierre fine* of Arcueil, Clamart, and Meudon has served Paris much as a pink sandstone of the Vosges has served Strasbourg or Chartres been ennobled by the quarries of Berchères. The contributor quarries can often be identified: Meudon for the colonnade of the Louvre and the façade of the Ecole Militaire, Saillancourt for the Pont de la Concorde, Senlis (limestone, especially) for the Château de Versailles, and Pontoise for that least visited of great monuments, the Abbaye de Saint-Denis. Fontainebleau sandstone made many of the original pavements of Paris, and in the country round Sannois, d'Avron, and Villemomble, the plasterer—or, more exactly, his *fournisseur*—has taken a good deal out of the landscape. The materials of the builder's trade lie everywhere to hand in the Ile de France, and it is natural that the level of custom building should be wonderfully high. Nowhere is the margin between gray and silver more sensitively explored in stone; textures, too, may be vellum smooth in one façade, and in the next as crumbly as a ripe Wensleydale cheese; nowhere are there more beautiful walls. Walls tend to be high in the Ile de France, and gardens sheltered and secret, and farm buildings donjon-girthed, so great is the abundance of stone.

But of course the Ile de France owes most of its character to resources of quite a different sort: human beings. Its distinctive bloom comes, in the last resort, from the energetic and fastidious stamp of the men who have shaped it. Other regions, after all, have great natural resources and yet slumber in near-dereliction. What marks out the Île de France is that it has been, as it were, directed in all its particulars by superior human beings. Lists make bad reading, and as the Ile de France is the garden of Paris it is natural that almost every great Frenchman has had his connections there. At Ville d'Avray, for instance, there is a little house, 14, Rue de Sèvres, which was lived in at one time or another by Balzac, by Corot, and by Gambetta. An extreme example, certainly, but one typical of an area in which the association-hunter will sooner or later come across almost anyone, from Calvin to Caran d'Ache, who takes his fancy. A countryside that has Racine for its poet, Delacroix for its painter, Dumas *fils* for its romancer, and Jacques Lemercier for its architect cannot complain of its sons. Intellectually, too, the Ile de France has a tradition that goes back to the twelfth century, with Suger, the great Abbot of Saint-Denis, and reached a point of particular heroism at the Abbaye de Port-Royal. Its adopted children—Jean-Jacques Rousseau, Chateaubriand, Monet, Gérard de Nerval, Corot, Ravel, Derain, and Vlaminck—have endowed it with a private magic to which the nearness of Paris gives a redoubled resonance, a heightened intensity. All is possible, we feel, beneath these immigrant skies. And we come to believe that this is a region in which life is ordered by discernment and good sense: *directed,* as I said earlier, rather than just lived.

Many of the great things in the Ile de France are so well known that I do not think it necessary here to go into them at all closely. Versailles above all, Fontainebleau hardly less, and to most people Chantilly, Compiègne, Rambouillet, and Saint-Germain-en-Laye are part of the very idea of a visit to Paris. (To them should now be added the rehabilitated house and garden of Claude Monet at Giverny, so evocative of the environment that the great painter built for himself over many years.) Certain noble towns, such as Meaux, Provins, and Senlis, have a sturdy independence which makes one hesitate to tag them as Parisian auxiliaries. And more than one of the great forests is, in many of its aspects, so sadly suburbanized that there is no point in rehearsing the disappointments in store for a casual visitor.

But this still leaves an immense deal of country untouched—and many wonderful sights, moreover, which, themselves almost unknown, relate closely to others more famous. The Ile de France includes, for instance, many of the world's best-known buildings, but it would be hard to name one finer than the little Château de Chamarande, near Etampes, which was built by François Mansart in 1654. The visitor who seeks this out can also find, not far away, the feudal fortress of Farcheville, which was built around 1300 by Hugues II de Bouville. (Such machicolations! A strange sight in the peaceable Hurepoix of today.) The enthusiast for Compiègne (and nowhere is there, after all, a better First Empire ensemble) and for Malmaison (now in very good order, by the way) should not miss the Château de Grosbois, where the same style is seen at one step down. (It was there, for instance, that in December 1809 Joséphine made her last appearance as empress, and the company included the kings of Saxony, Westphalia, Wurtemberg, and Bavaria and the queens of Naples, Holland, and Spain.) Not every house has been kept as carefully as Grosbois, and there are times when the amateur of the grotesque will find a rare satisfaction in the Ile de France. An example of this is the Château de Coubert, twenty-four miles from Paris on the Provins road. It is still possible to see from the classic orangerie, the two *pavillons de garde,* and the exemplary avenues that this was once an almost flawless ensemble of the early eighteenth century. But the house itself, rebuilt, the *Guide Bleu* tells us, "in the Normandy-villa style," is ridiculous.

Roses play a great part in the Ile de France, and have even given their name to more than one of its townships. (The crimson roses of Provins are said to have been brought back from the Holy Land at the time of the Crusades.) The visitor to Coubert will find, only a mile or so away, the very centers and origin of the rose industry: the commune of Grisy-Suisnes, where Bougainville, the great explorer, and Cochet, his gardener, introduced the practice of rose-growing toward the end of the eighteenth century. Roses do well in the region of Brie—and so, of course, does the famous cheese of that name. (Bernard Champigneulle in his book on the area distinguishes three kinds of Brie: the dry, strong-flavored Melun, the white-fleshed Coulommiers, and the familiar Meaux, which should be eaten just as it is starting to decompose.)

Roses, a great cheese, and the high waists of the Empire all reinforce the idea of the Ile de France as one vast national park of fine living. And of course it has, in great numbers, country houses as beautiful as anyone could wish. It has the proto-Versailles, Vaux-le-Vicomte; it has, at Courances, the apotheosis of the *cascatelle*—a water garden so pretty that it would in itself repay a long journey; and it has, at Raray and Jossigny, houses in which the idea of country life and country pleasures is delightfully made mock of. There is nowhere quite like Raray, where in the arcaded *cour d'honneur* a frieze of sporting dogs surmounts the grave Immortals in their niches; nor is there anywhere quite like Jossigny, where the little house, inside and out, has kept intact the amenities of the age of Louis XV.

From all these, the visitor may well emerge in a relaxed and well-contented frame of mind. The Ile de France, he may say to himself, is a place where people have always taken things easily. Eclecticism in architecture and decoration is an unfailing mark of this; it is only when life is settled and sure that people can send a thousand miles for a chimney piece or reerect in the Ile de France a cloister from Saint-Genis-des-Fontaines in the Pyrénées-Orientales. This is what was done at Les Mesnuls, and it is by no means the only respect in which the plain-spoken original of 1530 has since been reembellished. The paneling came from England, the fountain from Lombardy, and the Renaissance staircase from a château in the Sarthe. These procedures were, in Bernard Champigneulle's view, "d'un Elginisme assez provocant," and it is not for one of Elgin's fellow countrymen to contradict him.

But it would be a mistake to think of the Ile de France entirely as a pleasure ground. The golden age that Ingres frescoed at the Château de Dampierre may well have had its counterpart in life, there and elsewhere, but the original or initial monuments of the Ile de France are quite different in character. "Bare ruined choirs" it has in profusion, and both Châalis and Longpont (Aisne, by the way, not Seine-et-Oise) are of exceptional interest in this respect. And the tourist who motors to Provins will find, within a few miles of that splendid town, much that points to a disregarded element in the Ile de France: its military history.

That history was brief. It was only for a few years in the 1420s and 1430s that the Ile de France was the scene of struggles vital to the whole nation: and Charles VII, once reconciled with Philippe le Bon, did not take long to clear the Brie Française. But, between the occupying English forces and the Ecorcheurs (mercenaries drawn from all over Europe), the countryside paid heavily. Not far from Provins, for instance, Rampillon was once a place of importance: the Templars' church alone remains to show something of its dignity, but that something is, where sculpture is concerned, one of the most remarkable of all the monuments in the Ile de France. "Burnt by the English in 1432" says the guidebook, but among the things that resisted the fire were the Templars' tower, the great

Early Snow at Louveciennes. Alfred Sisley, 1870

A Carriage at the Races. Edgar Degas, c. 1870–73

west door, and an ensemble of thirteenth-century sculpture that would stand out even in a cathedral city. The proportions of this great church would provoke wonder anywhere: at Rampillon, and in its present state of near abandonment, the half-military, half-religious building brings a ring of iron into the domesticated bell-note of the Brie.

The year 1432 was a bad one also for the monastery of Saint-Loup-de-Naud, five miles southwest from Provins. Of this nothing remains but the refectory and a tall tower, for what the English spared in 1432 the Protestants finished off in 1567. But, once again, a great church survives and may be seen from a long distance up the valley; and, once again, the main door, iron-faced on ancient wood, is surrounded with sculpture of a magnificence equaled only, perhaps, at Chartres. And the church presents, in its interior, an anthology of vaulting that seems to stand on the very edge of Gothic and yet never quite to take leave of the Romanesque. For every ten thousand visitors to Fontainebleau, perhaps one or two—not more—go to Saint-Loup-de-Naud.

The same is true of Champeaux, which is four miles at most from the great château of Vaux-le-Vicomte. A visit to Vaux is, after all, obligatory for anyone who has any sense at all of the history of France. But Champeaux, in its way hardly less remarkable, has no public. Like its neighbor, Blandy, it is half-military, half-ecclesiastical in tone; but where Blandy lies all in ruins, Champeaux preserves intact a great church more than two hundred feet in length. Although it goes back to Abelard's master, Guillaume de Champeaux, who died in 1121, it also has to show one of the masterworks of French Renaissance art: the stalls sculptured in 1522 by Richard Falaise.

Such are the surprising conjunctions of the Ile de France. I doubt, indeed, if there is anywhere in France a greater abundance of unexplored marvels. But the charm of the area does not reside only, or even mainly, in places of evident beauty or historical interest. The tone is set rather by anonymous things: manor houses that no one has bothered to classify, slumbering market squares, or the far glint of cornfields at the edge of a great

The House and Factory of M. Henry. Camille Corot, 1833

forest. It is worth remembering that when Manet summered at Bellevue he would make any old bramblered wall his subject; and Vuillard, sojourning at Les Clayes, never bothered to look for a "beautiful view" but took the country as he found it, undressed and abounding in gravel, 1880ish villas, and the apparatus of bourgeois life. These are good models. It is possible, moreover, to nourish too idyllic a view of the Ile de France, and probably I myself have erred in this direction. Aviation, crime, and the turf play, after all, a considerable role in the life of the area. Truck drivers bulk large, in every sense. There are many places in which it would be disagreeable to spend more than an hour. (Names are deceivers, in this context: Deuil is not as sad, nor Plaisir and Corps Nuds as amusing, as one might suppose.)

The Ile de France is a part of the world where everyone, sooner or later, finds what he wants. It is difficult, nonetheless, to end on a reliable note. What will please the visitor who fancies a *vieille France* stillness, a plume of wood smoke, and a meal that has been prepared by hand will not please another; for many there are who feel lost without a Parisian turn of voice at the next table and a black Mercedes, by way of escape, in the yard. My own advice would always be to choose as your base a market town—Provins, Senlis, Beaumont-sur-Oise, Dourdan; to take a room with tall windows and a prospect of silvered stone; and there, near Paris but yet not in it, to linger for several days until the look, the touch, the dimensions, and the smell of the Ile de France are with you for a lifetime.

Index

Théâtre de la Porte-Saint-Martin

Théâtre de
l'Ambigu-Comique

Rue de Lancry

Paris boulevards in 1853

BOULEVARD SAINT-MARTIN (north side)

Porte Saint-Denis et Rue du Faubourg-Saint-Denis

Porte Saint-Martin et Rue du Faubourg-Saint-Martin

BOULEVARD SAINT-DENIS (north side)

Café de Paris   Rue Taitbout   Tortoni   Maison-Dorée   Rue Laffitte   Café Riche   Rue Lepelletier

BOULEVARD DES ITALIENS (north side)

Passage de l'Opéra   Café Mulhouse   Opéra   Rue Drouot   Jockey-Club   Cercle Montmartre

BOULEVARD DES ITALIENS (north side)   BOULEVARD MONTMARTRE (north side)

Rue du Faubourg-Montmartre

BOULEVARD MONTMARTRE (north side)

BOULEVARD POISSONNIÈRE (north side)

342

Rue Vivienne   Maison Frascati Rue Richelieu Café Cardinal

BOULEVARD MONTMARTRE (south side)   BOULEVARD DES ITALIENS (south side)

Rue Favart   Opéra-Comique   Rue Marivaux   Café Anglais   Rue de Grammont   Bazar

BOULEVARD DES ITALIENS (south side)

Rue de Choiseul   Bains Chinois   Rue de la Michodière   Pavillon de Hanovre   Rue Louis-le-Grand

BOULEVARD DES ITALIENS (south side)   BOULEVARD DES CAPUCINES (south side)

345

Rue de la Paix, Place et Colonne Vendôme

BOULEVARD DES CAPUCINES (south side)

Rue Saint-Denis   Rue de Cléry

BOULEVARD SAINT-DENIS (south side)   BOULEVARD BONNE-NOUVELLE (south side)

Gaieté   Funambules   Délassements   Maison construite sur   Rue d'Angoulême
                        -Comiques   l'emplacement de la maison Fieschi   au Marais

BOULEVARD DU TEMPLE (north side)

Sources of Illustrations

The author and publisher would like to thank the following libraries, museums, and private collectors for permitting the reproduction of works in their collections. The pages on which the works appear are indicated by *italic* type.

Albright-Knox Art Gallery, Buffalo, New York. Gift of Seymour H. Knox *247*; Art Institute of Chicago. Charles H. and Mary F. S. Worcester Collection *19*; Bibliothèque Nationale, Paris *42, 45, 56 left, 74 top, 82, 93, 97, 112, 113, 199, 212, 213, 224, 293, 317, 321 bottom*; Burrell Collection, Glasgow Museums and Art Galleries *111, 120 top*; Christ, Yvan, Paris *268*; Chrysler Museum, Norfolk, Virginia. Gift of Walter P. Chrysler, Jr. and Grandy Fund, Landmark Communications Fund, and "An Affair to Remember," 1982 *223*; Collection Albert Kahn, Département des Hauts-de-Seine, Boulogne *22 all, 118, 123, 294 top*; Cooper-Hewitt Museum, New York. The Smithsonian Institution's National Museum of Design *190, 276 right, 279, 298, 329 both*; Corcoran Gallery of Art. William A. Clark Collection *110*; Daniel J. Terra Collection. Terra Museum of American Art, Evanston, Illinois *94 bottom*; George Eastman House, Rochester, New York *4-5, 114*; Haags Gemeentemuseum, The Hague *231*; Leonard, Harriet, New York *115*; Louvre, Paris *53, 55, 69, 83*; Margaret Woodbury Strong Museum of Fascination, Pittsford, New York *138*; Metropolitan Museum of Art, New York. Bequest of Eda K. Loeb, 1951 *16*; Metropolitan Museum of Art, New York. Bequest of James Alexander Scrymser, 1926 *167*; Metropolitan Museum of Art, New York. Bequest of Mrs. H. O. Havemeyer, 1929. The H. O. Havemeyer Collection *61*; Metropolitan Museum of Art, New York. Bequest of Stephen C. Clark, 1960 *122*; Metropolitan Museum of Art, New York. Bequest of William K. Vanderbilt, 1920 *282*; Metropolitan Museum of Art, New York. David H. McAlpin Fund, 1947 *34, 124, 128, 229, 270*; Metropolitan Museum of Art, New York. Gift of E. Weyhe, 1923 *295*; Metropolitan Museum of Art, New York. Gift of Harry G. Friedman, 1963 *201, 228 top*; Metropolitan Museum of Art, New York. Gift of Mr. and Mrs. William B. Jaffe, 1955 *220*; Metropolitan Museum of Art, New York. Gift of Theodore de Witt, 1923 *237*; Metropolitan Museum of Art, New York. Harris Brisbane Dick Fund *44 all, 91, 170, 171, 276 left*; Metropolitan Museum of Art, New York. Purchase, Mr. and Mrs. Charles Wrightsman Gift, 1963 *278*; Metropolitan Museum of Art, New York. Rogers Fund, 1962 *255*; Metropolitan Museum of Art, New York. The Elisha Wittelsey Collection, The Elisha Wittelsey Fund *41 right, 90, 191 top, 192, 233 top, 284*; Minneapolis Institute of Arts *26*; Musée Carnavalet, Paris *6, 17, 35, 36, 39, 47, 48, 49 top, 59 both, 63 both, 79, 87, 89 bottom, 94 top, 98, 100-101, 104, 106, 107, 127, 139, 151, 175, 178, 179 both, 180, 182 both, 186, 191 bottom, 194-195, 196, 197, 218, 227, 228 bottom, 230, 235, 236, 238, 263, 274, 304, 305, 309, 311, 315, 316, 319, 320, 322*; Musée Condé, Chantilly *148*; Musée de l'Affiche, Paris *119 both*; Musée des Beaux-Arts, Rouen *131, 222*; Musée

Photograph Credits

Bildarchiv Preussischer Kulturbesitz, West Berlin *18*; Caisse Nationale des Monuments Historiques et des Sites/© Arch. Phot. Paris/S. P. A. D. E. M. *245, 262, 275 top, 308 top, 312 bottom*; Direction Générale du Tourisme, Paris *169*; Ets. J. Richard, Paris *130*; Felgar, J., Los Angeles *29, 117*; Giraudon, Paris *10, 17, 47, 89 bottom, 100-101, 104, 127, 131, 145, 148, 151, 186, 189, 191 bottom, 194-195, 218, 225, 228 bottom, 235, 238, 261, 263, 274, 296, 304, 305, 308 bottom, 322*; Hachette Photothèque, Paris *147, 260, 271*; Hutin, M., Compiègne *51*; © Interphotothèque *85, 143*; Landshoff, Herman, New York *138*; Lapi Viollet, Paris *31*; Lavrillier, Marc, Paris *2-3, 6, 35, 36, 39, 48, 49 top, 59 both, 63 both, 79, 87, 94 top, 98, 106, 107, 139, 175, 178, 179 both, 180, 182 both, 196, 197, 227, 230, 236, 242, 243, 309, 311, 315, 316, 319, 320*; Musée Bricard, Paris *157*; Museum of Modern Art, New York. Film Stills Archives *121 both*; Pocock, Philip, New York *23 left, 32, 41 left, 76-77, 80, 81, 84, 89 top, 105, 116, 133, 216, 310, 312 top, 338-350*; Publications Filmées d'Art et d'Histoire *174*; Roger-Viollet, Paris *27 top, 30, 31, 49 bottom, 129, 141, 156, 217, 219, 272, 273*; S. R. D., Bagneux *258, 283*; Service de Documentation Photographique de la Réunion des Musées Nationaux, Paris *53, 55, 69, 83*; Studio Lourmel, Paris *56-57, 70-71, 214-215*; Top, Paris *95, 134, 146*; Union Centrale des Arts Décoratifs, Paris *119 both*; © Vu du Ciel par Alain Perceval *154, 163, 183, 187, 211, 221, 226, 234 bottom, 256, 302*; Webb, John, London *54*.